John J. Robinette

John J. Robinette

Peerless Mentor: An Appreciation

George D. Finlayson

THE DUNDURN GROUP
TORONTO · OXFORD

Editor: Don Bastian
Copy-Editor: Jennifer Bergeron
Design: Jennifer Scott
Printer: Transcontinental

National Library of Canada Cataloguing in Publication Data

Finlayson, George D.
    John J. Robinette : peerless mentor : an appreciation / George D. Finlayson.

Includes index.
Co-published by Osgoode Society for Canadian Legal History.
ISBN 1-55002-463-9

1. Robinette, J. J. (John Josiah), 1906-1996. 2. Lawyers--Canada--Biography. I. Osgoode Society for Canadian Legal History. II. Title.

KE416.R62F55 2003   340'.092   C2003-902956-5   KF345.29.R62F55 2003

1 2 3 4 5   07 06 05 04 03

We acknowledge the support of the **Canada Council for the Arts** and the **Ontario Arts Council** for our publishing program. We also acknowledge the financial support of the **Government of Canada** through the **Book Publishing Industry Development Program** and **The Association for the Export of Canadian Books**, and the **Government of Ontario** through the **Ontario Book Publishers Tax Credit** program, and the **Ontario Media Development Corporation's Ontario Book Initiative.**

Care has been taken to trace the ownership of copyright material used in this book. The author and the publisher welcome any information enabling them to rectify any references or credit in subsequent editions.

J. Kirk Howard, President

Printed and bound in Canada.⊕
Printed on recycled paper.
www.dundurn.com

Dundurn Press	Dundurn Press	Dundurn Press
8 Market Street	73 Lime Walk	2250 Military Road
Suite 200	Headington, Oxford,	Tonawanda NY
Toronto, Ontario, Canada	England	U.S.A. 14150
M5E 1M6	OX3 7AD	

TO JOAN

with gratitude and love
for our years together

Contents

Foreword

GEORGE FINLAYSON IS A DISTINGUISHED Ontario lawyer and judge. As a partner in McCarthy and McCarthy, he worked closely for many years with John Robinette. He was successively Robinette's student, junior, and partner. At the request of the Osgoode Society he agreed to provide us with his intimate recollections of the man who is generally acknowledged to have been Canada's foremost counsel of his era. Justice Finlayson writes with grace and charm and with an unerring eye for the legal skills that made Robinette such a great counsel.

Comfortable before any court or tribunal at any level and regardless of issue, Robinette combined all the technical skills of the finest courtroom tactician with a superb judgment that kept him cerebrally above the fray while at the same time allowing him to participate with relish in the forensic battle on the hearing room floor. A formidable verbal gladiator to his adversaries, he is as well remembered for his unfailing courtesy to court and counsel alike. He never took unfair advantage of an opponent and outside the courtroom he was revered for his kindness and generosity to younger counsel whom he treated, unpretentiously, as equals.

In these pages, Robinette emerges once again as a simply marvellous counsel quite without equal in his day. *John J. Robinette, Peerless Mentor: An Appreciation* is an intensely personal and engrossing account of the professional life of a great advocate told against the changing background of his time.

The purpose of the Osgoode Society for Canadian Legal History is to encourage research and writing in the history of Canadian law. The society, which was incorporated in 1979 and is registered as a charity, was founded at the initiative of the Honourable R. Roy McMurtry, a former attorney general for Ontario, now chief justice of Ontario, and officials of the Law Society of Upper Canada. Its efforts to stimulate the study of legal history in Canada include a research-support program, a graduate student research-assistance program, and work in the fields of oral history and legal archives. The society publishes volumes of interest to its members that contribute to legal historical scholarship in Canada, including studies of the courts, the judiciary, and the legal profession; biographies; collections of documents; studies in criminology and penology; accounts of significant trials; and work in the social and economic history of the law.

Current directors of the Osgoode Society for Canadian Legal History are: Robert Armstrong, Jane Banfield, Kenneth Binks, Patrick Brode, Brian Bucknall, Archie Campbell, Kirby Chown, J. Douglas Ewart, Martin Friedland, Elizabeth Goldberg, John Honsberger, Horace Krever, Vern Krishna, Virginia MacLean, Wendy Matheson, Roy McMurtry, Brendan O'Brien, Peter Oliver, Paul Reinhardt, Joel Richler, James Spence, Norm Sterling, Richard Tinsley.

The annual report and information about membership may be obtained by writing: The Osgoode Society for Canadian Legal History, Osgoode Hall, 130 Queen Street West, Toronto, Ontario. M5H 2N6. Telephone: 416-947-3321. E-mail: mmacfarl@lsuc.on.ca. Website: Osgoodesociety.ca.

R. Roy McMurtry
President

Peter N. Oliver
Editor-in-Chief

Acknowledgements

I N THE WRITING OF THIS memoir, I have received encouragement and helpful advice from many sources. I cannot thank each and every one of them, but I would be remiss if I did not single out the following persons for special thanks.

First and foremost is Alison Warner, a fine lawyer who was once my law clerk. I took advantage of her unique editing skill and her knowledge of my writing style and persuaded her to act as an editor and advisor for my rough drafts, chapter by chapter. Her revisions and suggestions were invaluable to me. Next to Alison in order of importance was my secretary, Michele LeBlanc, who acted as my production quarterback throughout. She typed out my recorded interviews and portions of old trial transcripts, remedied the mistakes I made on my not altogether user-friendly computer, and saw to the printing and binding of the last drafts of the manuscript.

I wish to express a special thanks to Muriel Reid, the personal secretary to John Robinette for many years and a person whose friendship I hold in the highest regard. She went through all the files that McCarthy Tétrault had retained and produced the very few that were helpful to me. In this she received the help and encouragement of the library staff at McCarthys, headed by Mary Percival and her assistants Diane Balatoni and Paula Bokis.

Last and by no means least, I recognize the contribution of my law clerks, whose computer skills and resourcefulness in research were invaluable while they were seconded to me at the Court of Appeal. They were Doug Nathanson, Gabriel Fahel, Chris Tortorice, and Eric Reither. While they were available to me individually and sequentially, their cumulative efforts made provided me with a research team without equal. Thank you, lads.

Introduction

ONE BEAUTIFUL FALL DAY A few years ago, I left Osgoode Hall with my friend and colleague, Archie Campbell of the Ontario Superior Court of Justice. We were on our way to our usual Saturday luncheon to meet several friends and colleagues or former colleagues. I was not surprised to find that Osgoode had been turned into a temporary movie set that day. The courthouse is a popular film location in Toronto. In the eyes of the moviegoer, the grounds and building can readily be converted into a number of exotic sites. This time, it appeared to be the perhaps not so exotic site of Hamilton, judging from the insignia on the police cruisers positioned in the driveway. The actors were in clothing that reflected the more formal dress of about fifty years ago. Archie and I were looking around curiously when a middle-aged man whose name card identified him as a "liaison" told me, "This is a film that should interest you. It is called *Torso* and is about Evelyn Dick."

My mind raced back to my university days at Holwood House, a men's residence at the University of Toronto, and to the press coverage of a famous murder trial and the following retrial. At the centre of what turned out to be three trials was Evelyn Dick, who stood accused in separate indictments of the double murder of her husband and her infant son. I looked at the cast in period dress and pointed immediately to an attractive brunette. Standing there wearing a pillbox hat, she was the recreation of the photogenic woman whose picture had become instantly recognizable from the extensive newspaper coverage of her murder trials. "That is Evelyn Dick," I said.

I looked also for an actor who was tall, handsome, and who asserted a significant presence despite his considerable weight, wearing a navy blue overcoat and a grey felt hat. That was how, in my mind's eye, I pictured Evelyn Dick's defence counsel, John J. Robinette, because that is how I saw him for the first time in the same newspaper coverage. If the actor was in that scene on the steps of Osgoode Hall, I missed him.

About six months later, I was invited by the Treasurer of the Law Society of Upper Canada, Robert Armstrong, Q.C. (now Justice Armstrong of the Ontario Court of Appeal), to a luncheon to determine who the Osgoode Society for Canadian Legal History should approach to write a biography of John Robinette. Present were R. Roy McMurtry, the Chief Justice of Ontario; Peter Oliver, editor-in-chief of the Osgoode Society; Neils Ortved, Q.C., managing partner of Robinette's former firm and mine, McCarthy & McCarthy (now McCarthy Tétrault); and Justice John W. Brooke, my old friend and colleague at the Court of Appeal and before that at McCarthys. It rapidly developed that I had been deceived as to the purpose of the meeting. It had already been decided that I should write the biography, and it was only necessary to get me to agree to make the decision unanimous.

I was reluctant at first, but on reflection I realized that, as a former student, associate, partner, and friend of his over a forty-five-year period, I probably had more access to Robinette in his professional life than any person still living. However, what I have undertaken here is not a biography in the accepted sense of an impersonal third-party history of a prominent man. It is a memoir. Although I have researched his early years, in the main it is John Robinette as I saw him from our first meeting in June of 1951 when I articled as a law student at McCarthy & McCarthy until shortly before his death in 1996.

When I met him he was in his early forties and very much established as a leading counsel in the fields of civil and criminal law. Accordingly, I am obliged to rely on secondary sources for his earlier history. But, by and large, I am trusting my own memory and insights to attempt to explain this remarkable advocate and his tremendous impact on the legal profession and indeed on the Canadian community.

This project seemed straightforward enough until I received a series of shocks. I had been assured that I would have access to an abundance of material in the Law Society's Archives, notably an extensive oral history that had been obtained relatively recently. I was also assured that Robinette's old files at McCarthy Tétrault would be available to me. Family records were also to be at my disposal. Regrettably, a close examination of what had been offered in good faith proved to be of limited value. The fact is that Robinette was a man who left no footprints except the cases that he tried. There is no personal diary, no personal letters commenting on his professional life, his family, or his hopes or plans for the future or his regrets for the past. The files at McCarthys contain factums and isolated pieces of paper, some opinions on matters of significance only to the clients to whom they were directed. I went through them all with the assistance of Robinette's secretary, Muriel Reid, and found very little that was helpful.

The oral history was the biggest disappointment of all. It was recorded beginning June 18, 1987, and I can only conclude that Robinette was already suffering from the symptoms of the disease, Alzheimer's, that was to ravage him later. Muriel Reid said that he hated the experience and was sorry he agreed to it. "They couldn't get him to sit still for it," she told me. Robinette was supposed to edit the transcript (and it does require editing), but on March 12, 1990, he wrote to Mrs. Christine J.N. Kates at the Osgoode Society, stating, "I have attempted to edit my interview but have found that I do not have the time or the energy to do it." For my part, I have made some use of the transcript, which I have edited where I thought it was required to complete a thought, but I have found it replete with errors and have not relied upon it where it conflicts with other data or, for that matter, my own memory.

I did receive some valuable help from members of Robinette's family covering John's early life and have acknowledged it where I have put it to use. But Robinette, like many men who focused their brilliance narrowly, was not interested in history's view of him. If he had been asked to write an autobiography or a memoir he would have said he was too busy and, as we have seen from the oral history, uninterested. Accordingly, I have concentrated my memoir on the man as I knew him, his work as I perceived it, and the legal, social, and political setting in which he performed.

Chapter One
Origins

JOHN ROBINETTE'S FOREBEARS WERE HUGUENOTS who lived on the west coast of France near the Île de Rhé. The Huguenots were followers of John Calvin, the sixteenth-century French Protestant reformer and theologian. This affiliation put them in immediate conflict with the Roman Catholic majority. The Huguenots were one of the nation's most industrious and advanced people. They were skilled artisans, experts in the wool trade as well as craftsmen and designers skilled in the working of gold and silver to make jewellery. They were involved in trade, investment banking, and commerce generally. Some became very wealthy.

The Huguenots vigorously resisted discrimination by the established church in France. They fought an extended war with the Catholics, initially emerging victorious in 1598 when the Edict of Nantes accorded recognition to their religion and some degree of political freedom. The victory was short-lived. The Catholics under Cardinal Richelieu seized the Huguenot strongholds and by the Peace of Alais in 1629 stripped them of their political power. Louis XIV repealed the Edict of Nantes in 1685 and the persecution of the Huguenots began in all its horror. The wisest of the Huguenots fled the country before 1685 and were joined by a flood thereafter. Some settled in the Netherlands, Belgium, and Switzerland, but most went to England, where they lived for a short period of time before sailing for America, lured by the promise of religious freedom and cheap land. Robinette's ancestors probably went to England and settled in the neighbourhood of a small town a few miles from Cambridge called Saffron Walden.

In an address delivered to the Huguenot Society at its Tercentenary Commemorative Dinner in the Great Hall of Hart House on October 26, 1985, Robinette described how he and his wife, Lois, also a direct descendant of the Huguenots, visited the parish church at Saffron Walden. They had taken a detour during their last trip to attend the Cambridge Lectures, sponsored by the Canadian Institute for Advanced Legal Studies. At the church grounds of Saffron Walden, they were shown a marble plaque showing the deceased as "Dorothy Robinet." This was the original spelling of the family name. A second "t" was added so that no one would think they were French Catholics. Some time later, an "e" was added for aesthetic reasons. From this plaque, Robinette deduced that his forebears, like many Huguenots, were engaged in the wool trade: Saffron Walden was one of the most important centres of that trade in England.

These Robinettes stayed in Saffron Walden for a generation, perhaps two generations, before Allen Robinette and his family sailed to North America in about 1687. From his reading, John Robinette learned that while England benefited from the skills of the fleeing Huguenot artisans and the smuggled gold of the richer merchants, these Calvinist refugees were not entirely welcomed by the Church of England. Their skills, though admired, represented unwelcome competition to the local craftsmen. All this probably accounted for the substantial second migration of the Huguenots from England to North America, where they could enjoy complete religious freedom and an opportunity to make their way in a new society through hard work.

Allen Robinette entered America at Charleston, North Carolina, the major point of entry for the Huguenots. He settled soon after in Chester County, Pennsylvania. Some of his branch later moved into Ohio. He died around 1696, but his progeny settled across the United States. It has been estimated that 250,000 of his descendants lived in the United States in the succeeding three centuries. According to John Robinette, many of his kin live in Cleveland.

Robinette's son-in-law, Richard Sadleir, in an unpublished memoir entitled "The Canadian Robinette," dated December 1997, says it appears that a second Allen Robinette, known in the family as "Canada Allen," moved north to Canada from Pennsylvania in about 1812 and settled on farming land on the old Dundas Trail in the Downsview area outside Toronto.¹ This settlement founded the Canadian branch of the Robinette family. Allen's third son, Samuel, and his wife, Mary Taylor, had nine children. The fifth of their children, James, is the direct ancestor of John Robinette's family in Canada: he was the great-great-grandfather of Thomas Cowper Robinette, the father of John Robinette.

Robinette did not have an extended personal memory of his father, who died when John was fourteen. T.C. Robinette had lost his father, Josiah Robinette, when he was only ten. T.C. was raised by his grandfather, Thomas Robinette, who lived in Caradock Township in Middlesex County just outside London, Ontario. John Robinette did recall his father talking about his upbringing in Caradock Township and of his great respect for his grandfather.

John's father went to school in Caradock and put himself through University College at the University of Toronto by working for the summer in the mail cars on the Toronto, Hamilton, and Buffalo Railway. He also taught high school in Strathroy, near London, for one year. Teaching was a common way to finance a university education in those days. But T.C. appears to have had a flair for teaching and remembered the experience with some fondness. When he was older and had become successful, he donated a medal to the school in Strathroy where he had taught as a prize for the best student in public speaking.

At University College, T.C. took courses in modern languages, English, French, and Italian. He became president of the U.C. Literary Society and graduated with the Gold Medal in his class. He then went to Osgoode Hall Law School, where he graduated in 1887, again as the Gold Medallist. He was thirty-six years of age. In 1888, he married Jennie Blacklock Carruthers. The marriage was childless and lasted seven years until her death. Four years later, in 1899, he married Edith May Lindsay, a woman fourteen years his junior.

Sadleir reports that by this time T.C. was a staunch Methodist, perhaps because of the influence of his second wife. The couple became pillars of the Trinity Methodist Church, which was considered a fashionable congregation at the time. It was located on Bloor Street just west of Spadina Road and not far from the Robinette home on Spadina Avenue where the first of the five Robinette children, Thomas Lindsay, was born on April 27, 1900. The Robinettes moved a number of times thereafter but always stayed in the vicinity of Trinity Methodist and consistently, it would appear, on Spadina Road. Four children were to follow: John Josiah (November 20, 1906), Esther Minerva (Counsell) (1909), George William (June 18, 1911), who were all born at 18 Spadina Road, and Allan Edward (January 6, 1915), born at 60 Spadina Road. Sadleir comments that it was ironic that John Robinette would spend the final five years of his life at Central Park Lodge, just across the road from the house in which he was born. It was indeed ironic, and I can attest that the irony was not lost on Robinette. He made the point to me on one of the first of many visits I paid to my former mentor at Central Park Lodge. He spoke with nostalgia of his earlier homes and of his family, including his mother and father. My recollections of these conversations, of which unforgivably I have no contemporary record, have helped me to flesh out his early history.

T.C. Robinette became a prominent Torontonian. He was a distinguished lawyer and was equally at home in civil and criminal cases. He was an active member of the Liberal Party and played a considerable part in the party's organization in Ontario. He had been chairman of the Young Liberal Association in 1885 and vice-president of the Toronto Reform Association in 1903. His influence with the party was considerable. In 1904, he ran unsuccessfully as a Laurier Liberal in the riding of Centre Toronto, which extended from the lakefront north to and including Rosedale. His familiarity with Italian served him well with the Italian community below College Street. The Liberals were also much favoured in the same area by the members of the Jewish community. But Wasp Rosedale remained solidly Conservative, and T.C. was defeated. His wife did not share his disappointment in this result. She had been and remained solidly opposed to her husband's engaging in politics. According to her son, John, it took too much out of him. However, T.C. had the political bug and in 1908 he ran again in Centre North, again without success. The margin of his defeat was only one hundred votes. His final attempt at becoming a member of Parliament was in North York in 1911. He could not have picked a worse time. He was decisively defeated, along with most of his fellow Liberals, on the issue of reciprocity with the United States.

T.C.'s career in politics may have been unsuccessful, but his law practice flourished. He started out practising alone, but in time became partners with men whose names are still familiar in the Toronto legal community. The first of these was John Godfrey, whose son became Senator John Godfrey and whose grandson, also John, is a Liberal member of the House of Commons. The two joined with Thomas C. Phelan, a lawyer who quickly attained a reputation at the negligence bar and who was later to form his own firm, Phelan and Richardson, which survives to this day in the merged firm Aylesworth Thompson Phelan O'Brien. Tom Phelan's son, Roderick, was also a prominent counsel and was later appointed to the bench as a trial judge. The last to join them was Earl Lawson to form the firm Robinette, Godfrey, Phelan and Lawson. Earl Lawson was a very successful solicitor, with substantial clients in the motion picture industry, including Arthur Rank and his company, J. Arthur Rank Company. He was later appointed lieutenant-governor of Ontario. He was to play a significant role in the career of the young John Robinette. T.C. remained the senior member of this firm until his death. His achievements were recognized by his appointment as a King's Counsel in 1902 and his election as a bencher of the Law Society of Upper Canada in 1911 and 1916.

The Robinette family lived very well while T.C. was alive. They had a live-in maid, a gardener, and a chauffeur-driven car. In addition to their various homes on Spadina Road, there was a large summer house that T.C. purchased in 1912 or 1913 on Toronto Island. It was at 266 Lakeshore Road and was formerly owned by one of the Gooderham family of Gooderham and Worts fame. T.C. was a member of the Royal Canadian Yacht Club, and on working days he would walk from the summer house to the yacht club dock and take the club yacht across the harbour, where he was met by his chauffeur and car. Robinette spoke fondly to me of his childhood summers on the island. He had no responsibilities and engaged himself effortlessly in what would now be described for curriculum vitae purposes as unstructured community activities. He watched the Toronto Maple Leafs of the International Baseball League, played cricket, bicycled all over the island, walked the boardwalk, watched the ships (there were a lot of steamers in those days carrying ore and wheat), and attended the amusement park.

Robinette's description of Toronto on a Sunday in the late teens and early twenties intrigued me because it differed very little from my recollection of the city when I arrived here from Winnipeg in the fall of 1946 to attend the University of Toronto. According to him, there wasn't anything to do: there were no motion pictures, there were no sports. "Compared to today," he said, "Toronto was just unbelievable. Toronto was dead on a Sunday. Literally dead." He recalled that at one time in the history of Toronto, some action was taken against the Toronto Street Railway for operating the streetcars on Sunday. It failed, but that obstructionism was reflective of the attitude of churchgoing Torontonians. "This was a city of churches. You can see today the number of churches that are around, that are now obsolete, and are used for some other purposes, but the place was full of churches. And the fear of God was a very important element in Toronto of that era."

Central to Robinette's life was the Annex, so named because it was the area annexed by the City of Toronto from the Township of North York. It was bounded by Dupont Street to the north, Bathurst Street to the west, Bloor Street to the south, and Avenue Road to the east. It of course embraced Spadina Road and was described by Robinette as a distinct community within Toronto. Robinette's knowledge of this area stood him in good stead when he acted for the Annex Ratepayers Association in their opposition to the Spadina Expressway in the early 1960s. He spoke with obvious pride of the community where his roots in Toronto lay:

> Socially, I would describe it as middle class and upper middle class. Let me just tell you about our street and maybe that will give you some idea. Next door to us was Professor Hume who was the head of the department of philosophy at University College. Farther up on the east side, at Bernard Avenue, was Professor Alexander, the head of the English department. Across the road, there was a house, it is still there, where a former mayor of Toronto, whose name was Bosworth, I think, lived. Then the Tudhope family lived nearby at Lowther; they were a family from Orillia. Mr. Tudhope was the president of A. E. Ames & Company, the stockbrokers and investment counsellors. They have gone now, taken over by Dominion Securities, I think. But next to us on

the north was a gentleman by the name of Mr. Irving, the owner of the Irving Umbrella Company. Oh, there was another lawyer across the street, Norman Gash, there was my father, and then, of course, on the north-west corner of Lowther and Spadina, was the Timothy Eaton house. And later Sir John Eaton lived there for a short time until they moved up. So the particular street was very much like St. George Street, which was the deluxe street of the city. It didn't have the Sir Edmund Walkers, or the Mr. Justice Riddells, or Mr. Justice Middletons, but it was getting close.

In contrast to Dick Sadleir's memoir, Robinette recalled that the involvement of his parents at Trinity Methodist, now Trinity United Church, was more social than religious.[2] He said that he never heard his father discuss religion on any occasion. His attachment to Trinity Church was because of his close personal friendship with the Rev. Dr. Wilson who was at one time the minister there.

Wilson was a well-known minister who earned the nickname "Move on Wilson" because of his involvement in a public demonstration, the point of which has been lost to everyone's memory. When a policeman who did not know who he was told him to "move on, move on," Wilson refused to do so. He was arrested and charged with creating a public disturbance. T.C. Robinette was retained to represent the Methodist minister, and the trial generated a good deal of public interest, most of it derisive. Wilson was acquitted but was known thereafter as "Move on Wilson." Out of this encounter, the minister and his counsel became great friends and the two families saw a good deal of each other, but not in church.

About his mother, Robinette said that she went to church and, consistent with Methodist teaching, was intractably opposed to alcohol. But her son did not feel that she was much involved in the life of the church. To my surprise, Robinette said that he was the member of the family who took the most active part in the church. However, his active involvement was limited to a few years when he was in his early teens. Nevertheless, for those few years, his involvement was impressive. Every

Sunday he went to Mission Band at ten o'clock in the morning. The band, incidentally, had nothing to do with music. It was a group organized by some devout ladies in the church to stimulate interest in foreign missions, in China, in the case of Trinity Church. He also went to the eleven o'clock service and returned around two o'clock for Sunday school. During the evening he went with other young people to what was called Fireside Hour. Robinette said his father was so impressed with the constancy of his attendance that he called him "Pope John." However, the principal draw of the church functions for Robinette seems to have been social. The Fireside Hour attracted young people, some of university age. Among them were friends of Robinette, including Lois Bridgland Walker, who was later to become his wife.

One person who exercised an influence over him during his religious years was a very fine young man he remembered only by his last name, Kilgore, a student in divinity at Victoria College, University of Toronto. Kilgore was in Robinette's estimation "a very sensible man that I liked, in fact all the young persons liked him. He wasn't trying to sell religion; he was a man of common sense." Robinette recounts one day when "an awfully stupid Sunday school superintendent, whom I didn't like, got up and asked sanctimoniously that everyone pledge, for their lifetime, not to drink, smoke, or swear." Robinette thought this was preposterous. "After all, we were just kids. You just can't imagine. And you know, that was the first moment I turned a little bit. And that shook me." Robinette did not sign a pledge and thinks that he may have simply absented himself. But "one chap in the class openly said he would not sign it, and he was rather regarded by some of those present as a renegade. I have never forgotten that fellow, he was a good man, did well, and he was right. And Kilgore told us, 'Don't you criticize him, he has made up his own mind, he is not going to sign, so there is no ostracizing him.'"

So far as Sunday observances outside of church attendance were concerned, Robinette regarded his home life as typical of the community. "We didn't dance. I don't think there were any restrictions on card games; I can't recall any. On Sundays in the old days, and this was in most homes, it was a day of rest with a big huge roast beef dinner at noon, so most of the older people would fall asleep. They were great dinners."

What religious fervour Robinette had did not last very long. The end was precipitated by the death of his father when he was fourteen. "It is a childish thing to say, but when my father died, I was mad, I thought that God had let me down, and from then on I gave it up. It was a combination of circumstances." Robinette remained a member of Trinity United Church all his life but did not attend it regularly. He made donations to Trinity and continued to have a great respect for the church "principally because I was associated with it when I was younger and because I met my wife there when she was a young girl."

When T.C. died of a stroke at the age of fifty-nine on March 14, 1920, he left his widow with the very heavy responsibility of rearing their five children, the youngest of whom was only five years of age. The summer place on Toronto Island was sold, and Edith May Robinette was forced to tighten the family's purse strings. Fortunately, her late husband had purchased real estate in his lifetime and some of it had turned out well. She was able to get by reasonably well, educating all five of the children, with the help of scholarships in the case of John, at least.

The results were impressive. The four Robinette boys, Thomas, John, George, and Allan, all attended the University of Toronto Schools that opened in 1910, two blocks away from home at the corner of Bloor and Spadina. Subsequently, each boy graduated from the University of Toronto and Osgoode Hall Law School. Their sister, known to them only as Minnie, attended Havergal College, first at its preparatory school at 186 St. George Street and later on Jarvis Street in buildings that would eventually house the Canadian Broadcasting Corporation. She married James Counsel, the owner of a successful construction company, and became a mother and homemaker, just like her mother. Thomas, George, and Allan were in the private practice of law for a short period of time or not at all. Thomas went to work for the Burton family and became a vice-president of and general counsel to the Burton-controlled Robert Simpson Company. George worked for the legal department of Imperial Oil. Allan moved around in his early years. He first went to the legal department of Odeon Theatres Limited and was associated with Earl Lawson. Later he went with Leonard Brockington and Frank Fisher before moving over to the legal department of the Goodyear Tire and Rubber Company. Robinette remembers with regret that his mother did not enjoy life after the last of her children, Allan, left home to get married. She had worked hard to make them self-sufficient, and when that job was done she felt she had nothing to do. She went "right downhill" and ended her days in a nursing home.

Robinette missed his father very much and resented having to grow up without him. He loved his mother, and his affection for his sister and brothers was boundless. It was clearly a tightly knit family. Robinette provides an insight into the household in which he grew up in his warm reminiscence of 60 Spadina Road following the death of cancer in 1970 of his youngest brother, Allan.[3] Recalling this house where Allan was born, he remembered that Timothy Eaton had built it for his daughter, a Mrs. Burden. T.C. Robinette bought it from the Burdens a few years before Allan's birth. It was a large, Edwardian, red brick house with a covered front veranda, not particularly attractive on the outside by modern standards, but with high-ceilinged, comfortable rooms inside. Typical of the Annex area, there was a large backyard bounded by a high, unpainted wooden fence. The Burden boys had kept pigeons, and there was a shed at the back of the garden where the Robinette children had played imaginative childhood games.

The drawing room in the downstairs of the house was to the left of the vestibule. According to Robinette, it was rather a dull room decorated in browns or beige. Behind the drawing room was the dining room, a much warmer room, or at least the children thought it more comfortable and warmer — possibly, in Robinette's opinion, because of his mother's generous cooking. At the back of the house on one side was a glassed-in veranda. On the other side was a kitchen and large pantry. As one entered the vestibule, to the right was a den called the telephone room. Robinette recalled, "It was there that Dad in the evening during the Sessions would meet with his clients, discuss their cases, collect the fees in cash, and hand them over to Mother. She looked after the banking and deposited the cash in the Dominion Bank at the southeast corner of College Street and Spadina Avenue where the manager was a man with the distinguished name of Mr. Caruso."

On the second floor, there were three bedrooms and a cozy living room at the front of the house. As Robinette put it, "It was the upstairs living room that we really lived in. It was there that the family congregated after dinner, and on a cold night we enjoyed the additional warmth from the gas fireplace." On the third floor there were four bedrooms, one of which was converted into a study "for the boys."

There were always lots of books, magazines, and newspapers at 60 Spadina Road. In those days there were four morning newspapers in Toronto: *The Globe*, *The Mail*, *The Empire*, and *The World*. In the evening, there were *The News*, *The Evening Telegram*, and *The Toronto Star*. T.C. subscribed to them all, plus "out of respect for Sir Wilfrid Laurier," the Montreal paper, *La Presse*.

It is not surprising, given this strong and supportive family, that John Robinette would be a solid performer at school and thereafter at university and law school, but he was much more than that: He emerged as an extraordinary talent.

Chapter Two
Education and Early Years

JOHN ROBINETTE WAS EFFORTLESSLY BRILLIANT. He does not appear to have come in second at any time during his illustrious academic years. In 1929, he received the Gold Medal in his final exams leading to his call to the bar. To be awarded that medal a student must have achieved honours in the two preceding years and headed his or her class in the final year. Robinette had headed the class in all three of his years at Osgoode Hall Law School and so had no problem.[4]

I learned the extent of Robinette's academic prowess at a dinner given by the Advocates' Society in honour of Robinette in 1979. Mayer Lerner, a prominent counsel in his own right and then a judge of the High Court of Justice, was one of the principal speakers. He was a classmate of Robinette's and had obtained a transcript of his marks while attending the three-year course at Osgoode Hall Law School. They were remarkable. Robinette passed with honours and stood first in every year. In his first year, 1926–27, he received 98 percent in jurisprudence, 89 in torts I, 85 in contracts I, 94 in the history of English law, 89 in torts II, 93 in contracts II, 92 in practice, and 93 in property law. His marks in second year were comparable, and in his third and final year his lowest mark was 90 in mortgage law. He stood first in a class of 115. Besides the Gold Medal, he also received the Chancellor Van Koughnet Scholarship, which was worth $400. To measure the significance of this sum, consider that Robinette won scholarships of $100 in his first and second years, and these were enough to pay his tuition for the ensuing years.[5]

All of this was no surprise to Robinette's friends who had watched his spectacular progress through the lower schools and university. He was always at the top of his class. He first attended University of Toronto Schools at the age of seven. UTS was a private school established by the University of Toronto for the best and the brightest of boys. Located at the corner of Bloor Street and Spadina Avenue, it was an easy walk for the young Robinette. It required an entrance examination, but for this young student that was no more of an effort than the walk. Despite the competition, he topped his classes with ease. He made the honours list each year and won prizes in Latin and Greek. He was accelerated one year and graduated at age fifteen, too young to be admitted to university. He spent an additional year at UTS taking Latin and Greek and won the Mary Mulock Scholarship in those two languages.

University College at the University of Toronto saw more of the same. He entered at age sixteen and enrolled in politics and law under the aegis of the department of political economy. He was first in the courses' third and fourth years, won two scholarships, and graduated with the Gold Medal.

Those who reminisce about him now express no surprise that he was such a brilliant scholar; they also warmly remember his qualities as a gentleman first and an advocate second. But I was left with the impression from my informal discussions with him and his wife, Lois, that university in particular was not a great deal of fun for this pudgy prodigy who endured the sobriquet "fat Robinette." He met a lot of people, but I think they became his friends later in life when he demonstrated that he was first among them even as a lawyer. This isolation is touched upon in *Robinette: The Dean of Canadian Lawyers* by Jack Batten,[6] who attributes Robinette's lack of social activity to his youthfulness relative to the other students. But he was only one year younger than most of his classmates, and I believe that he was rather a loner then, as he continued to be in his later years.[7]

Robinette was quite blunt about his social life at law school and stated that even at the post-graduate level he belonged to few if any social organizations.[8] (I am not sure from his description if there were any.) Between working as an articling student and attending classes, Robinette found no time to go out during the week. If not for his courtship of Lois Bridgland Walker, later Mrs. Robinette, he would have had no social life at all.

As for his being a gentleman, he *was* a gentleman by intuition, upbringing, and schooling, and he projected an easy warmth and modesty that endeared him to everyone who came to know him. But while he was genuinely self-effacing about his academic credentials, he was an elitist at heart.

When Robinette received his call to the bar in 1929, "the leaves were falling," to use his memorable phrase. Canada was in a depression and jobs were hard to come by even for a Gold Medallist. He had articled at a very good law firm, Donald, Mason, White and Foulds (now Weir & Foulds), and had been offered a position there. He did not accept it, however, because he would have been restricted to work that he did not particularly care for: taxations of costs and other minor chambers work before the Masters of the Supreme Court. But money was important to Robinette. He had gone through university and law school on scholarships and was anxious to get settled in a secure job so that he could marry Lois Walker.

He was very lucky. Sidney Smith had been one of his lecturers at Osgoode Hall Law School, and he was leaving to become the dean of the Dalhousie Law School. The Dean of Osgoode, John D. Falconbridge, asked Robinette to be interviewed for the vacant post. Robinette met with Dean Falconbridge, C.A. "Caesar" Wright, and Donald MacRae. The three, who constituted the entire teaching staff, were unanimous that he should be accepted for the vacated permanent teaching post. His subjects were those that Smith had taught and consisted of real property, trusts, equity, and mortgages. Equity was a subject that dealt with relief in a variety of circumstances not available to the common law, such as unjust enrichment. These are subjects that remain at the heart of the civil legal process.

His salary was set in May of 1929 at $2,500 per year and was increased to $3,500 the next year.[9] This is more than he could have expected at any law firm in Toronto at that time. I might add that starting salaries for the big legal firms were never much of an attraction for graduate lawyers. Almost twenty-five years later when I was taken on as an associate at McCarthy & McCarthy, in 1953, I was paid $3,000 per year. But $3,500 was a living wage in the Depression, and on June 21, 1930, John Robinette married Lois Walker, the only woman he ever dated.

Lois Walker was born on July 15, 1906. She, too, was of Huguenot background and attended Trinity Methodist Church. She was educated at Huron Public Street School and then the old Havergal College on Jarvis Street in Toronto, where she won a general proficiency award for Upper Fifth Form with honours in French and mathematics. She was to become fluent in French, a matter that her husband spoke of with pride on numerous occasions. Unfortunately, a university education was not available to her. However, she was a woman of artistic talent and enrolled in art classes at Central Technical School. At the time of her marriage, she was drawing fashion illustrations for the Eaton Store.

At a reception following Lois's death on September 13, 2001, in her ninety-sixth year, Lois's eldest daughter, Joan, told a revealing story about her mother and father. After their wedding, John and Lois were honeymooning at the Walker cottage at Southampton, Ontario, the cottage that Lois was later to inherit and which would provide a refuge and haven to John Robinette. This is Joan's account of what happened:

> The care and protection of my father by my mother began in a concrete way on their honeymoon when a wayward bat flew into their bedroom at Southampton, and Dad paid my mother five dollars to kill it, which, of course, she did. And collected the five dollars. She took care of all practical matters after that, and the family tool box was a fundamental part of my mother's kitchen equipment. My father never knew where it was or for that matter probably what it was.

Lois Walker was an inspired choice for Robinette. He needed the love and support of a woman with a good mind, a formal education that complemented his own, and the willingness to be a life companion to a man who was dominated by his profession. She was the centrepiece of the limited social life he did enjoy. I cannot think of a holiday he took without her. He, for his part, returned her love with his own, which was constant and enduring to the end of his days. He always spoke of Lois with warmth and pride. This from a man who rarely revealed himself to anyone.

Robinette was a full-time lecturer at Osgoode Hall until 1932, when he was asked by the Treasurer of the Law Society of Upper Canada to become the editor of the Ontario Law Reports. The Law Society was and is the governing body of the legal profession in Ontario and consists of benchers, lawyers elected by the members of the profession to administer its affairs. These responsibilities included the operation of the Osgoode Hall Law School and the publication of the law reports. The treasurer was elected by the benchers to be the head of the society. In 1932, the treasurer was William Norman Tilley, K.C., a legend among this nation's advocates.

Robinette recalled how he came to the attention of Tilley through Cyril Carson, who had been one of the students that Robinette taught and became the junior to Tilley.[10] Robinette impressed Tilley. In Robinette's words, "Tilley knew all about me and frankly, I think he liked me. Tilley might not have liked many people but I just happened to take his fancy."

With this type of backing, Robinette had no difficulty arranging that he would continue as a part-time lecturer at the law school and spend the rest of his time as editor of the reports of the trial division of the Supreme Court of Ontario, called the High Court of Justice, and the appellate division, called the Court of Appeal. Robinette estimated that the combined salaries from the law school and the Law Society amounted to $6,000 or $7,000 a year, more than double his starting salary in 1929.

Robinette told me that he found the combination of lecturing and editing the law reports to be the best possible training for him as a counsel. He was shy, and the experience of having to stand and address a classroom full of students allowed him to make full use of the magnificent baritone voice with which he was blessed. He developed a presence and the confidence that goes with it. He became by all accounts an outstanding lecturer. John D. Arnup, a distinguished counsel and latterly a justice of the Ontario Court of Appeal until his retirement, attended the law school from 1932 to 1935.

> I soon found out that in my second year of law school I was going to have lectures from John Robinette on the subject of real property, and that took place. I have said many times that John was the best lecturer that I ever

had, either at law school or at university. In my third year, he taught mortgages and, again, he was a superb lecturer. His teaching style had the same hallmark of his advocacy in court, namely clarity and understandability, if there is such a word. There was nothing ambiguous about any part of his lectures, and I used to go home at night and expand the notes I had taken during the day. My notes on real property and mortgages I kept for fifteen years after I was called to the bar as being better source material than any of the textbooks on the shelves of anybody's library. It was a pleasure to take lectures from John Robinette, an observation which could not have been made about some of the other lecturers at Osgoode Hall.

Robinette's classroom experience was complemented by the hard work he put in as editor of the law reports. The discipline of having to write the headnotes for the written judgments that were submitted to him was invaluable, helping him establish an ability to synthesize and compress issues of fact and law to concise summary form. Since the workload was limited so far as the volume of cases was concerned, he attended most of the appeals in the Court of Appeal, listening to and reporting on the arguments of counsel. This permitted him to observe and critique the effectiveness of their arguments, an invaluable learning opportunity not permitted today by the money-driven demands of the practice of law. It also gave him access to prominent counsel, whom he was able later to approach for advice about going into private practice.

Although Robinette was the recipient of a respectable salary for the middle of the Depression and enjoyed both teaching and editing, his heart was always in the courtroom. In 1936 he took advantage of his newfound connections and asked Tilley for advice as to how he could become involved in the practice of law as a counsel. Tilley suggested that he speak to Donald Rowan, an older lawyer with an established solicitor's practice who had his offices in the Canada Permanent Building on Bay Street. They met, and Rowan offered Robinette office space with him on a reasonable cost-sharing basis. Robinette moved in as counsel and began what was to be an astonishingly long and varied career as Canada's greatest advocate.

He gave up lecturing in 1937 but continued on as editor of the law reports until the end of 1941. Later, in the forties, he was approached by Earl Lawson, T.C. Robinette's former junior, and now the senior partner in the firm Lawson, Trebilcock & Stratton (later Lawson, Stratton, Green & Longley), and persuaded to leave Rowan and move to the Sterling Tower on Richmond Street to act as counsel to the Lawson firm.

I was a stranger to Robinette's early career, and I did not learn a great deal about it from talking to him. With typical modesty he said he received some referrals from former students and did a good deal of work as a prosecutor on behalf of the attorney general of Canada during the Second World War for war-related offences such as draft dodging and violations of regulations administered by the Wartime Prices and Trade Board. However, a review of reported cases reveals that his work was much more significant than his offhand summary revealed. Following are just two examples.

In *Greenlees v. Attorney General for Canada*,[11] Robinette represented the Crown in a matter involving the application of the *National Selective Service Mobilization Regulations, 1944* to a member of the Jehovah's Witnesses who claimed to be a minister of that religion. Robinette's reputation as a counsel was then such as to merit being appointed a King's Counsel, and this honour entitled him to attach the suffix "K.C." to his name. And it was an honour in those days. There were very few counsel who were entitled to be described as "One of His Majesty's Counsel, learned in the law," as the appointment by His Majesty certified. Robinette received his K.C. on November 24, 1944, long before the honour had been diluted to the point of meaning nothing at all by attorneys-general who made a practice of conferring it on lawyers who rarely, if ever, appeared in court. Robinette's K.C. was automatically converted to a Q.C. in 1952 when George VI died and Elizabeth II ascended the throne.

The facts of *Greenlees* are a product of wartime. In May 1943, Greenlees was notified, in accordance with the National Service Regulations, that he was to present himself for medical examination before an examining physician. If he was found fit he was to report for military training. Subsequently, he was notified that he was to present himself before the Mobilization Board. He did not and was then given notice that unless he presented himself before the board, action would be taken against him under the regulations. At this juncture, Greenlees brought an action in the Ontario High Court. His action claimed a declaration that he was a minister of a religious denomination within the meaning of the regulations, which therefore did not apply to him; the notices served on him, therefore, were invalid. Greenlees's lawyer was W. Glen How, himself a Jehovah's Witness, and a counsel of considerable ability who had fought and continues to fight vigorously for religious freedom, particularly on behalf of his own religion.

How has expressed bitterness against Robinette for his actions as counsel for the Crown in this case. He maintains that Robinette went beyond arguing points of law and acted as an agent of the Liberal Government in Ottawa to continue its policy of "trying to rub us out," to use How's phrase as quoted by Batten.[12] As is now known, it was the Quebec government's policy at that time to harass the Jehovah's Witnesses in support of the Roman Catholic Church, which objected to what it perceived to be attacks by the Witnesss' literature on the "Mother Church."[13] Batten refers to some evidence that the federal government supported their liberal confreres in that endeavour. However, and with deference to How, who was on the scene, apart from any considerations of Robinette's character, I find it difficult to believe that Robinette with his Huguenot background would have had the slightest interest in assisting the Roman Catholic Church in any attempt to harass a minority religion. Restricting myself to the arguments as recorded in the *Greenlees* case, I can find no support for such a charge.

The historical context is significant to an understanding of *Greenlees*. In 1943, this country was at war and was desperately short of manpower to support its armed forces, which had been expanded far beyond any capability that it achieved before or since. The *National Selective Service Mobilization Regulations* were passed under the joint authority of the *War Measures Act* and the *National Resources Mobilization Act*.[14] These two statutes not only authorized compulsory service for the armed forces, but also provided for the regulation of all industries that were deemed essential to the war effort and all persons employed therein. They were the authority for a far-reaching and, in some quarters, highly controversial conscription program. Exemptions were not to be granted lightly.

Robinette took the position that Greenlees had not satisfied the onus on him of bringing himself within the exemption to the regulations as "a regular clergyman or a minister of a religious denomination."[15] There was no organization known as "Jehovah's Witnesses" that qualified in Canada as a religious denomination, and Greenlees was merely an adherent and devoted himself to the purposes of a Pennsylvania corporation, the Watch Tower Bible and Tract Society. The evidence before the Court, Robinette continued, showed that he and his fellow adherents had no creed, no constitution, and no basic system of organization. Moreover, the American corporation appointed the so-called ministers, and their policies were prescribed by it. The governing body of Jehovah's Witnesses was merely the executive committee of the directors of the corporation. The evidence, Robinette declared, showed that it was the Watch Tower Bible and Tract Society that, in fact, had appointed Greenlees a "minister."

All this seems pretty strong stuff in our era of human rights codes and the Charter of Rights and Freedoms when judges listen sympathetically to claims for special privilege for groups describing themselves as witches and warlocks. But the trial judge, Justice Hogg, while inclined to the view that there was a religious denomination known as Jehovah's Witnesses, held that Greenlees was not a "minister" of that denomination and dismissed his request for an exemption.

In the Court of Appeal, Chief Justice Robertson, speaking for a court consisting also of Justices Henderson and Greene, dismissed the appeal. He set out in full reasons the evidence disclosed as to the origins of the Jehovah's Witnesses and held, "Whatever view is taken, I am far from satisfied that the evidence warrants a finding that the people calling themselves Jehovah's Witnesses constitute a 'religious denomination' within the meaning of the regulations. As the burden of establishing this is upon the appellant, and as such a finding is essential to his success in this action, I would, upon that ground alone, dismiss it." He ended by agreeing with the trial judge that the appellant Greenlees was not a minister within the meaning of the regulations.

In the years following the ruling, Glen How remained bitter. For his part, Robinette shrugged off his criticism. He acknowledged that How's position was a firm one, but as he put it, "this was wartime," and the government was concerned about a flood of applications for exemptions. It was an important case and public opinion was with him at the time.[16]

Robinette argued another, better-known case in his early years in private practice that dealt directly with religious discrimination: *Re Noble and Wolf*,[17] a case involving a clause in a 1933 deed for a summer cottage property that prohibited the sale of the property to any person of "the Jewish, Hebrew, Semitic, Negro or coloured race."

The case involved a cottage lot situated in a summer resort developed by Frank S. Salter Co. Ltd. in 1933 on the shores of Lake Huron and known as Beach O'Pines. The developer created a number of cottage lots and by deed conveyed individual cottage lots to the original purchasers. One of the original purchasers was the husband of Anne Maude Noble. She inherited the property upon his death. His deed to the property, like all the other deeds for the resort lots, required him as purchaser and anyone taking title to the property through him to comply with various restrictive clauses in the deed, including clause (f):

> The lands and premises herein described shall never be sold, assigned, transferred, leased, rented or in any manner whatsoever alienated to, and shall never be occupied or used in any manner whatsoever by any person of the Jewish, Hebrew, Semitic, Negro or coloured race or blood, it being the intention to restrict the ownership, use, occupation and enjoyment to persons of the white or Caucasian race not excluded by this clause.

The deed also provided that this restriction was to remain in force until August 1, 1962. The deed further required that the restrictive clauses in it "should run with the lands and … be for the benefit of and enforceable by the grantor [i.e., the developer] and/or any other person seized or possessed of lands included in the Beach O'Pines Development."

It was commonplace to extract mutual covenants from purchasers of lots and from those to whom they might convey the lots in order to permit enhanced enjoyment of all the lots by insisting on such things as appropriate side lots, set-backs, and a minimum standard of construction. The words quoted directly above were important because they were relied on in the subsequent litigation as conferring the right to enforce these restrictions on all of the cottagers within the building scheme. But while restrictions on the construction of buildings were standard fare and benefited all purchasers by ensuring that the construction of cottages was to a uniform standard and quality, the restrictions on selling to Jews and what were then called "Negroes or coloured people" were directed to an entirely different and perverse form of control.

Mrs. Noble was a resident of nearby London. In 1948 she was prepared to give up cottage life. She entered into an agreement of purchase and sale dated April 19, 1948, with Bernard Wolf, a respectable London businessman, who had migrated to Canada from Ukraine in 1904. He was a Jew. His lawyer, Ted Richmond, searched the title of the lot in question and became concerned when he discovered the restrictions. Richmond wrote to Donald M. Egener, the solicitor for Mrs. Noble, requiring a release of the restriction imposed in clause (f), "in view of the fact that the purchaser herein might be considered as being of the Jewish race or blood." Mr. Egener responded by letter dated May 6, 1948, stating, "In our opinion, the decision rendered in the case of *Drummond Wren*, 1945 Ontario Reports, p.778 applies to the facts of the present sale, with the result that the clause (f) objected to is invalid and the vendor and the purchaser are not bound to observe it." *Drummond Wren* was a decision of Justice Keiller MacKay of the Ontario High Court striking down as contrary to public policy a similar clause in a deed to a residential lot that stated that the property was not to be sold to "Jews or persons of objectionable nationality."

Egener's reply was not satisfactory to the youthful Richmond, who despite his lack of experience had all the instincts of a veteran lawyer. He insisted on receiving an order of the Court declaring the restrictive covenant "void and of no effect." Accordingly, Mrs. Noble brought a motion through her solicitor under the *Vendors and Purchasers Act* (known colloquially to solicitors as a V&P motion) for "an order declaring that the objection to the restrictive covenant made in writing on behalf of the purchaser dated the 5th day of May 1948, has been fully answered by the vendor and that the same does not constitute a valid objection to the title."

This case is a procedural curiosity in that applications under the *Vendors and Purchasers Act* are intended to resolve disputes as to title between vendor and purchaser. In this case both Noble and Wolf wanted the transaction to close and were in agreement that the clause in issue was offensive and should be declared void as a matter of public policy. This eventuality was anticipated by the drafter of the offending clause in the deed who, as I have already noted, expressly provided that other owners of the cottage lots at Beach O'Pines could enforce the restrictive covenant.

As it turned out, the matter initially came on before Justice MacKay. As he had done in *Drummond Wren*, he directed that the notice of motion and supporting material be served on the Beach O'Pines Protective Association and Frank S. Salter Co. Ltd. The development company was dormant, and its patent was forfeit, but the association showed up in force and in opposition to the motion. Kenneth G. Morden, K.C., a prominent Toronto lawyer and later a member of the Court of Appeal, was retained to represent the dissident cottage owners who were supporting the validity of the restrictive covenant. A bitter legal battle was to ensue that was to engage larger issues than the sale of this one cottage lot.[18]

When Ted Richmond became aware of the intensity of the opposition that Mrs. Noble's V&P motion was attracting, he wisely sought the advice of John Cartwright, K.C., perhaps the pre-eminent civil counsel of his day, who had acted for the purchaser in *Drummond Wren*. It was decided that Wolf would retain Cartwright and be responsible for his fees, but he would appear on the record as representing Mrs. Noble. Richmond himself appeared for Wolf.

Noble and Wolf would be a fascinating study for students of the law of property apart from the significant moral and social issue that it has come to represent. It involved erudite discussions about whether the doctrine of *Tulk v. Moxhay,* decided in 1848,[19] applied to covenants that were personal to the user of the land rather than to the use that was made of it; whether the language of the restriction conveyed the intention of the drafter with sufficient clarity to determine whom it was intended to exclude; and whether the clause was an undue restraint on the freedom of a landowner to alienate his, or in this case her, property. Much to the dismay of Bernard Wolf and the Canadian Jewish Congress, which ultimately was to become very much involved in this matter, the courts had astonishingly little interest in the public policy argument advanced by Wolf and Noble that racial and religious discrimination was anathema to a civilized society. Throughout the proceedings, starting with the judge of first instance, Justice Walter Schroeder of the High Court, all the way to the Supreme Court of Canada, the concept of freedom of association was first and foremost in the minds of the judges. They were responsive to Morden's argument that the cottage owners at Beaches O'Pines were entitled to choose their neighbours and had bought their lots relying on the validity of the impugned restriction. The venerable and highly respected Chief Justice Robertson of the Ontario Court of Appeal put it this way:

> The purpose of clause (f) here in question is obviously to assure, in some degree, that the residents are of a class who will get along well together. To magnify this innocent and modest effort to establish and maintain a place suitable for a pleasant summer residence into an enterprise that offends some public policy requires a stronger imagination than I possess … There is nothing criminal or immoral involved; the public interest is in no way involved.

Justice Schroeder dismissed the motion at first instance, holding that the clause was valid. He distinguished *Drummond Wren* on the basis that the restriction there was not time-limited as in the case before him and it involved an urban residential lot as opposed to a recreational cottage lot. He held that he was not bound by precedent to follow the decision of Justice MacKay and furthermore that the case was wrongly decided. Matters of public policy were best left to the legislature. Cartwright pressed his clients to appeal and they did. The appeal was dismissed. The five-court panel, consisting of Chief Justice Robertson and Justices Henderson, Hope, Hogg, and Ayelsworth, was unanimous in upholding Schroeder's decision.

Robinette does not appear in this matter until later, but I would ask the reader to bear with me. *Noble and Wolf* was an important case and reflected an emerging outrage by minority groups against an established Eurocentric society in which distinct minorities such as Jews and Negroes could be lumped together as undesirables and denied the full protection and enjoyment of the law. There were comparatively few black people in Ontario at the time, so it is difficult for me to say to what extent they were the victims of general discrimination, but they shared something with Jews in that they were not welcomed into the legal profession. For example, my friend and classmate at law school, Lincoln Alexander, the son of a Pullman porter, was able to become a member of Parliament, a minister of the Crown, and the lieutenant-governor of Ontario, but he could not find a job with a Toronto law firm in 1953 after his call to the bar.

Toronto had a large and vibrant Jewish community in those days and some of its members were leaders of the legal profession. But when I received my call along with Lincoln, or Linc as we called him, there were no Jewish judges at the senior level, and Jewish lawyers were not admitted into the Toronto Lawyers' Club. I articled at McCarthy & McCarthy in 1951, and there were no Jewish lawyers there despite the fact that Senator Hayden had a substantial Jewish clientele. Several of the senior lawyers were anti-Semitic. One refused to permit Professor Bora Laskin's seminal work on Canadian constitutional law to be in the firm's library. I could name these men, but I will not. They are dead now, and their attitudes were suited to the temper of their time. They could have been charter members of the Beaches O'Pines Protective Association.

I had need of instruction myself in those days. The class I entered at Osgoode Hall was very large. A new dean had been brought over from Manchester, England, to put together the remnants of the teaching staff after the former dean, Cecil "Caesar" Wright, had left with Bora Laskin and the cream of the teaching staff. Dean Smalley-Baker was a bluff and hearty man who, while not in the same league as Wright, brought a certain esprit de corps to a dispirited student body. He called us "my gallant first legion." One day, in the course of a rambling discourse on I am not sure what, he used the familiar expression, "There is a nigger in the wood pile." A long black arm extended in the air. It belonged to Linc Alexander. When acknowledged, Linc said, "I enjoyed your remarks, Dean, but what did you mean by 'a nigger in the wood pile'?" The dean was flustered, but to his credit he apologized fully and promised to be more careful with his language in the future. The incident did not make much of an impact on me immediately.

However, my lack of sensitivity, like that of many of my classmates, was challenged again in the spring of that academic year when we were discussing as a class the times for writing our final exams. Most people wanted them to be written in the afternoons so they would have more time to study in the morning. When this appeared to be accepted, Harry Wolfe, later our Gold Medallist, raised his hand. After being acknowledged by the dean, he said that Friday afternoons were awkward for him because he had difficulty in getting home before sundown to observe his Sabbath. The class groaned. However, Dean Smalley-Baker, who did not have to be told anything twice, jumped to Harry's defence and made a speech about accommodation and recognition of people of different beliefs. And for the first time in my life I said, "Why not? Why shouldn't we accommodate our Jewish classmates?" I think these two incidents based on race and religion did more to stamp our class with a sense of identity than any other combination of factors. When we came to recognize the diversity in our makeup we developed a sense of unity as a class. These two episodes are invariably referred to at our class reunions.

This is a long way around to getting to the point of Robinette's involvement with *Noble and Wolf*, but its purpose is to provide some social context to that case. After the loss at the Court of Appeal level, the unsuccessful parties were in disarray. Mrs. Noble was an elderly lady, and while she was in sympathy with the aims of the Jewish Congress, she was not a Jew and was concerned that the publicity and the hostility generated by these protracted legal proceedings would jeopardize the sale of her property. Bernard Wolf was also losing heart. He was a wealthy man in his own right, but he had spent thousands of dollars and to no effect. While he had been anxious to fight on behalf of the Jewish community and against the oppressive covenant, his wife did not share his commitment and wanted him to retire from the proceeding. On top of all that, John Cartwright was appointed to the Supreme Court of Canada a few days before Christmas 1949 (where he was to preside as a justice and later as chief justice and set a standard for wisdom and courtliness that has not been surpassed).

However, the Jewish Congress was determined to proceed. It virtually bought out the positions of Noble and Wolf and looked to retain a new counsel. They already had Shirley Dennison, K.C., a former treas-

urer of the Law Society and one of Canada's leading authorities on real
estate law acting for the congress in an intervener capacity. The committee that was representing the congress in pursuing this litigation was
a sophisticated group of lawyers and law professors that included Fred
Catzman, Benjamin Keyfetz, Bora Laskin, Lou Herman, S.M. Harris,
and others. They were looking for a top replacement for Cartwright and
first approached Gershom Mason, K.C., another leading Ontario lawyer
and the then treasurer of the Law Society. He was unable to accept the
retainer because he had previously given an opinion to another client
that conflicted with the position that the congress wanted him to argue.
It was a measure of the integrity of this man that he would regard that
as a disqualifying conflict of interest. Most counsel would have considered his position as overly conscientious.

Their next choice was the much younger John Robinette, who was
forty-three at the time. His selection was an acknowledgement that he
was now one of the leaders of the bar. He took over the brief from
Cartwright along with his junior, Paul Hess. He reviewed the file and
limited his argument to three grounds: the clause was contrary to public
policy; the clause was void and unenforceable because it was uncertain
which groups it was meant to exclude; and it was an invalid restraint on
freedom of alienation of property. It was left to Shirley Dennison to
argue the *Tulk v. Moxhay* point that a restriction such as those targeting
Jews and Negroes was purely a personal one, and as such it did not attach
to the land but exists only between the parties to the original contract, in
this case the developer and Mrs. Noble's late husband.

The various counsel for the appellants encountered stiff questioning
from the members of the panel of the Supreme Court of Canada that
heard the matter, composed of Justices Kerwin, Taschereau, Rand,
Kellock, Estey, Locke, and Fauteux; none more than Dennison. But bless
him, his was the winning argument. Only Justice Locke dissented on
Dennison's issue and restricted his dissent to the fact that Dennison's
point was raised by him before the Court of Appeal for the first time and
not before Justice Schroeder. The majority held that the restrictive
covenant was not one that would run against subsequent purchasers of
the land because it did not "touch or concern" the land within the meaning of *Tulk v. Moxhay*. That doctrine requires that the covenant be direct-

ed to the land or to some mode of its use; it does not permit a prohibition of alienation to particular classes of persons. The majority of the judges also accepted Robinette's argument that the covenant was void for uncertainty, since there was nothing in it to enable a judge to say in all cases whether a proposed purchaser was or was not within the prohibited classes; that is to say, how does the Court determine in the given case if a buyer was "of the Jewish, Hebrew, Semitic, Negro or coloured race or blood"? This restrictive covenant contained no indication of any limits to the lines of race or blood that would disqualify a proposed purchaser.

The Canadian Jewish Congress was understandably disappointed in the narrow focus of the Court in striking down the offending clause on what can only be called sloppy drafting. The burning public policy issue was not even addressed. However, as is often the case, time was to take a different view of the significance of *Noble v. Wolf*. It is now recognized as the principled response of the Supreme Court of Canada to covenants in documents relating to land that discriminate against purchasers on the basis of race, colour, or creed.

In his oral history, Robinette was defensive in response to questions about the broader social aspects of *Noble and Wolf*.[20] He seemed to resent the suggestion that he had not stressed the public policy argument. He clearly took offence at his questioner's implication that there was something discreditable about Ken Morden taking the brief of Beach O'Pines. In the first place, Robinette never encouraged discussion about his opinions even in his younger days and he obviously found the persistence of his interviewer on the social aspects of the case irritating. His usual response to me when I questioned an opinion of his (I thought they were merely clarifying questions) was to close the discussion down by saying, "Well, George, that is my view of the matter," while picking up a letter or other document from his desk and reading it ostentatiously.

However, the underlying irritation he had with the line of questions was the smug assumption that there could not be two sides to the issue. The concept that members of society should be able to choose their own company was and still is strongly ingrained. Robinette realized this, as had Cartwright before him. The art of the advocate in this case was to persuade the Court that the drafters of this particular restrictive covenant had gone too far by stigmatizing Jews and Negroes as unworthy. It was not that Robinette was insensitive to the broader social interests. He was very much aware of his own family history and intensely sympathetic to persecuted minorities. However, the first obligation of counsel is to win the case by making full use of the arguments available. Robinette was not one to martyr his client for a greater cause. Remember, the Canadian Jewish Congress may have been financing the litigation at the later stages, but the client just wanted to sell her cottage.

These two cases illustrate the wide range of civil cases that established Robinette's early prominence in the profession. It was to take only one criminal case to forever identify him in the public eye as the greatest counsel of our time. That case was *The King v. Evelyn Dick.*

Chapter Three
Evelyn Dick on Appeal

MENTION THE NAME JOHN ROBINETTE to any person of my era and a consistent response will be, "He was the lawyer who defended Evelyn Dick." This astonishingly strong name association between Mrs. Dick and Robinette persists despite the passage of more than half a century from her trials for the murders of her husband and infant son. The events leading up to and surrounding the arrest of the captivating widow and mother created a media sensation that attracted in-depth newspaper reporting not only in Hamilton, Ontario, where the trials took place, but extending to Toronto, Montreal, and even Buffalo, New York. The second trial, and John Robinette's part in it, was reported in *Time* and *Newsweek* magazines.

The case became a *cause célèbre* as details emerged surrounding the headless and limbless torso of John Dick, found on Hamilton Mountain by a group of young boys on the Saturday morning of March 16, 1946. This bullet-ridden torso was all that was to be recovered of Evelyn's husband. There followed an even more gruesome discovery, a mummified baby wrapped in a Red Cross nurse's uniform, which turned out to be Evelyn's infant son, rumoured to have been born of an incestuous relationship with her father, Donald MacLean.

Spectacular as were these allegations in the press, they paled in comparison with the prurient interest aroused by Evelyn Dick's apparent complicity in the murders. Mrs. Dick's wide circle of sexual liaisons was said to have reached into Hamilton's highest society. There were rumours of pregnancies and the birth of a daughter whose father was stated in hospital records to have been a navy man named White. Added to this, William Bohozuk, Evelyn's boyfriend, was said to have ties with the underworld. There also was the revelation that her father, a streetcar conductor for the Hamilton Street Railway, systematically embezzled money and car tickets from the coin boxes of his employer. To complete the recipe for intrigue, Evelyn Dick, while not a classic beauty, photographed well and appeared to the reading public as an inscrutable enchantress with a smouldering sexuality. Since she was never to testify in court as to what occurred, neither in her own defence nor as a compellable witness for the Crown at the trial of her father and boyfriend, her image as a woman of mystery entangled in the unsolved murder of her husband has remained to this day.

Evelyn Dick was indicted along with her father and Bohozuk for the murder of her husband, John Dick. She was also named along with Bohozuk in a second indictment for the murder of her baby, Peter David White MacLean. This second charge was to be all but forgotten in the stir over John Dick's murder. That matter came on for trial at the fall sitting of the Hamilton court on October 7, 1946, with Justice Frederick H. Barlow of the High Court presiding. Representing the Crown were Special Prosecutor Timothy J. Rigney, K.C., of Kingston, assisted by Harvey F. McCulloch, Crown attorney for the County of Wentworth. John J. Sullivan and Frank B. Weatherston represented Evelyn Dick while G. Arthur Martin, K.C., a well-known criminal lawyer and later Justice Martin of the Ontario Court of Appeal, represented Bohozuk. Henry Schreiber of Hamilton was to join Martin later. Walter J. Tuchtie and Montalieu McLean appeared for Donald MacLean.

On application of the Crown, the trial judge directed that Evelyn Dick should be tried first. It was evident that the Crown hoped to obtain a plea of guilty from her on a lesser charge in exchange for her testifying against her father and Bohozuk at their subsequent trials. In this the Crown was to be sorely disappointed. At no time was Mrs. Dick prepared to make a deal on any of the charges relating to her husband's death, and she consistently refused to testify on behalf of the Crown.

Accordingly, her trial proceeded, and at the conclusion of the case for the Crown on October 16, Sullivan announced that the defence would call no witnesses. After addresses by counsel and the instructions to the jury by the trial judge, the matter was left with the jury. On that same day, the jury returned a verdict of guilty of murder with a recommendation of mercy. Despite this recommendation, the trial judge, as he was obligated to do by law, sentenced Evelyn Dick to be hanged and fixed the date for the execution as January 7, 1947.

Shortly thereafter, John Robinette received a telephone call from the Barton Street Gaol in Hamilton. It was from Mrs. Dick, who asked him to take her appeal.

A few days later, Robinette went to the jail and saw her. Robinette was fully aware of the nature of the case from the extensive publicity it had generated. He did not discuss with her the facts of the case because, in his words, "I did not want to know too much about them from her."[21] He quite properly understood that he was dealing with a factual record from the trial that very shortly would be reduced to written transcript form. Those were the facts, and no others, that he would have to accept for appellate purposes.

He agreed to take the case. Since her trial counsel, John Sullivan, had recommended him, Robinette asked him to appear as his junior counsel.

However, before the appeal was to be heard, Evelyn Dick had another appointment in court. This time, it was as a Crown witness in the trial of her father and her boyfriend for the murder of her husband. Their trial started on October 17, and she was called to the witness stand on the eighteenth. She refused to take the oath as a witness. In response to the statement by the new trial judge, Justice George A. Urquart — "Do I understand that you refuse to give evidence and refuse to be sworn?" — she said, "That is right. I have not had a chance to speak to my counsel." The trial judge offered her the opportunity to think the matter over, and she accepted and was taken from the courtroom. She was recalled on Saturday the nineteenth and again refused to be sworn or to testify. The matter was put over until Monday the twenty-first, at which time Rigney, on behalf of the Crown, asked that the jury be discharged and the matter put over again until the January sitting of the Court, because "certain evidence is not available at the present time." This lack of candour provided a brief respite for the Crown, which had an obvious dilemma. It did not have a case against Bohozuk and MacLean unless Mrs. Dick testified and incriminated one or both. Rigney soon had to confess that Mrs. Dick was not willing to testify, but that he had not abandoned the hope that she would change her mind.

What the Crown was thinking is puzzling. Mrs. Dick had been sentenced to death and was scheduled to die before the next court sitting commenced. She had appealed her conviction. The Crown was now seeking to compel her to give evidence as to events to which she had declined to testify at her own trial. As Justice Urquart observed, he could not compel her to testify; the most he could do would be to hold her in contempt of court, a sanction with limited consequences to a condemned murderess. In the result, and over the strenuous objections of counsel for both Bohozuk and MacLean, Urquart put the case over to the next court sitting with the comment that the conflict between the new hearing date and the execution date was to be taken up by "other authorities."

Robinette's task was to prepare for the appeal on the basis of the transcripts of the evidence, which he obtained from the trial court reporter.[22] From his briefing by Sullivan, he knew of some matters that were not in this transcript but that he would have to deal with at the later trial of Mrs. Dick for the alleged murder of her son. He learned that Evelyn Dick was born in Beamsville, Ontario, on October 13, 1920, to Donald and Alexandra MacLean. Shortly after her birth, the family moved to 214 Rosslyn Avenue in Hamilton. She grew up as a flirtatious teenager and was socially active as a young woman during a wartime regime, with its hosts of restless young men in uniform offering numerous opportunities for promiscuous behaviour. And this had consequences. She gave birth to a daughter on July 10, 1942, whom she named Heather Maria White. Records at the Hamilton General Hospital listed the father as "Norman White, occupation, Navy." No one, not even her parents, recalls ever meeting him. On June 20, 1943, she gave birth to a second daughter, who was stillborn. On September 5, 1944, she had a son, Peter David White (the Crown added "MacLean" in its indictment), who left the hospital with his mother and was never again seen alive.

A reading of the transcript from Evelyn's first trial revealed to Robinette that she married John Dick on October 4, 1945, when she was twenty-five years of age. John Dick was approximately forty years old. He was born in Russia but had lived in Canada since 1924. At the time of his marriage, and for some time prior to it, he had been employed by the Hamilton Street Railway as a motorman. The marriage was not a happy one. There were frequent quarrels from the beginning. Early in the following February, they separated, and John Dick went to board with a Mrs. Kammerer, with whom he had boarded some years before. Mrs. Dick continued to live in the matrimonial home on 22 Carrick Avenue, which, it is said, she had purchased. Evelyn's mother had separated from her husband, Donald, some months earlier and lived with Evelyn. Donald MacLean, who was also an employee of the Hamilton Street Railway, had had frequent quarrels with John Dick, and there is evidence that he and John were on bad terms in the fall of 1945. William Bohozuk, the third person indicted, was also on bad terms with John Dick, who accused him of paying too much attention to his wife.

The transcript disclosed the following items of circumstantial evidence surrounding John Dick's murder. On the afternoon of March 6, 1946, Dick was to report for duty as a motorman at four o'clock. That morning, he left his boarding house and went to the office of the street railway company, where he left his motorman's cap and some other small equipment. He later collected these things and left in their place a hat he was wearing. He did not, however, report for duty. He had a brief and hurried luncheon at a restaurant where he often ate, and left there between two o'clock and two-thirty. No witness was called who saw him alive after that.

On March 16, some children at play found the torso of a man on the side of what is called the Mountain on the outskirts of Hamilton, and the police were notified. The torso was identified as that of John Dick on March 18. An examination of the torso did not disclose the cause of death. There were two holes at one side of the chest, indicating that a bullet had passed through the flesh on that side. The wound was not of a serious character. No other identifiable remains of John Dick were found. Nor did the forensic evidence establish with any certainty where or by what means John Dick came to his death, or where or by whom his body was dismembered.

The evidence also disclosed that at about two o'clock on the afternoon of March 6, 1946, Mrs. Dick borrowed a Packard motorcar from William Landeg, an acquaintance of hers who kept a garage. According to witnesses, this car was next observed at five o'clock or five-thirty the same afternoon. At that time, Mrs. Dick was seen alone in the car, trying to drive it into a garage at the rear of her residence. It was a large car, and she was not able to get it through the garage door. After several attempts, she drove away. The next reference in the transcript to the motorcar was the evidence that at about eight o'clock in the evening, Mrs. Dick left it outside the door of the garage from which she had borrowed it. Later that evening, when the owner of the car went to drive it into his garage, he discovered blood on the front seat. Still later, he found a sweater in the car that later was identified as the sweater of John Dick. Also found there was a necktie, knotted as it would be when worn, which was identified as belonging to John Dick. Both of these articles were stained with blood. The slipcover of the front seat was missing, as was a rug that had been spread over the front seat.

The owner of the motorcar was not at the garage when Mrs. Dick returned it. She left a note for him expressing regret at being late. The note explained that her little girl had cut her face and she had to take her to the hospital for some stitches, and got blood on the seat cover and cushion, which she would replace later. In fact, the statement was quite untrue. Her little girl, Heather, had not even been in the car.

On the morning of March 7, some men going to work on the Mountain found a striped shirt on the roadway, at a point not far from where the torso was later found. The shirt was identified as that worn by John Dick on March 6. This shirt was completely buttoned up as it would be when worn, and both arms of the shirt were cut off. The shirt was stained with blood.

After the torso was identified, a search warrant was issued for the Carrick Avenue residence of Mrs. Dick and her mother. Among the items found there were a conductor's change-holder and streetcar tickets in a small tin box, such as John Dick used to hold tickets; a bloodstained pair of ladies' rubber boots, identified as a pair worn by both Mrs. Dick and her mother; and a blanket or rug, cleaned and folded, identified as the one that had been on the front seat of the borrowed car. Also found were ashes evidently from the furnace in the Carrick Avenue house. Some were in containers and others spread on the ground near the garage door. Particles of bone from a human head and limbs were found in these ashes. There was evidence that

Mrs. Dick had carried out and spread the ashes on the ground near the garage door.

In the home at 214 Rosslyn Avenue where Donald MacLean still lived were found a pair of bloodstained black oxford shoes, identified as the shoes of John Dick, as well as an axe, a saw, a butcher knife, a revolver and other firearms, and a quantity of ammunition. A Crown expert testified that the revolver was of the same calibre as the bullet that wounded John Dick's side. In the opinion of the expert, this revolver had been recently fired. A spent bullet, which may have come from the same revolver, was found in the basement of MacLean's house. Also found was a haversack containing somewhat more than $4,000 in bills and a great number of apparently used streetcar tickets.

In addition to what may be classed generally as circumstantial evidence, there was evidence that a few days after March 6, and before the discovery of the torso, Mrs. Dick, in answer to a question from her mother, had said, "John Dick is dead, and you keep your mouth shut." There was further evidence that on March 12 Mrs. Dick called the central police station in Hamilton and inquired whether John Dick had been arrested. When asked what the charge would be, she said, "Running away with money and tickets belonging to the company — the Hamilton Street Railway."

The circumstantial evidence against Mrs. Dick was not an insurmountable obstacle to her appeal from conviction for murder. Indeed, the main focus of the appellate argument was on various statements that she made to the police during the period when she was incarcerated before her first trial.

Mrs. Dick was taken into custody by police on March 19, 1946, and was escorted to police headquarters. She remained in custody during the entirety of the ensuing judicial process. While imprisoned she made eleven statements in all, seven of which were introduced by the Crown at her trial and which the trial judge decided were admissible evidence against her. Some of the statements were in writing and signed by Mrs. Dick; some were not. Some were taken after the police gave Mrs. Dick the usual caution then given to a person charged with a criminal offence: you are not obliged to make any statement, but any statement you do make may be used in evidence. Other statements were taken without having cautioned Mrs. Dick. In none of the statements did Mrs. Dick expressly admit her participation in the actual killing of John Dick, but in all of them there were admissions tending, in some degree, to involve her in the crime. The circumstances surrounding the taking of these statements were central to Robinette's argument on appeal.

The first statement was made in answer to questions put to Evelyn by Inspector Wood when she arrived at the police station in his custody. Inspector Wood took notes of the questions and answers. No caution was given to Mrs. Dick, nor had any charges been laid against her at this point even though she was in custody, as Inspector Wood admitted when he gave his testimony. Questions were asked and answered, particularly with reference to the borrowing and use of Mr. Landeg's car on March 6 and the blood that was on the seat when it was returned.

A second statement was taken on the same day at the police station also before charges were laid. A shorthand reporter was present on this occasion, and his notes of what occurred were transcribed and put in evidence. Inspector Wood testified at trial that before he began questioning Mrs. Dick, he cautioned her, "Now, I must tell you that you are being detained in connection with the death of your husband. You are not obliged to make any statement unless you wish to do so, but whatever you do say will be taken down in writing and may be used as evidence. Do you understand that?" To which she answered, "Yes." An examination followed, which lasted about two hours. This statement contains a great deal of information about Mrs. Dick's movements, particularly on March 6. She also spoke of the torso being disposed of by a man who was "a member of a gang from Windsor" and who telephoned her for some assistance. She did not elaborate on this conversation, and we are given no clue as to why the gang member wanted her assistance.

A third statement was taken on March 19, again before any charges were laid. Mrs. Dick was driven in a police car over the route referred to in her second statement, and further questions were asked and answers given during this expedition. No caution was read to her. Before going out in the police car, Mrs. Dick asked Inspector Wood what time she would be going home. He said, "You won't be going home; you will be held in custody." He did not tell her why. On the return from the trip a charge of vagrancy was laid against Mrs. Dick, and she was placed in jail.

Vagrancy had no application in law to Mrs. Dick. This was a device, since ruled unconstitutional, whereby the police held suspects in custody.

Detective-Sergeant Preston had some former acquaintance with Mrs. Dick's family, and she seems to have regarded him as, in some measure, her friend. On the afternoon of March 20, Mrs. Dick said to the detective that there were certain things that she wished to put in the statement she had made the day before, and she asked him if she could see Inspector Wood. As the result of this request, a shorthand reporter was obtained, and Mrs. Dick was brought into the detectives' office, where she was examined. The questioning by Inspector Wood began with, "Now, I understand you have been talking to Detective-Sergeant Preston about some further information you want to give us in connection with the death of John Dick. Now go ahead and tell us so we can get it down here." No caution of any kind was given to Mrs. Dick, and the examination was lengthy. She did not, by any means, introduce all of the subject matters of the examination. This was the first statement made after the charge of vagrancy was laid.

The next statement was taken on March 22. Mrs. Dick was taken from the jail to the central police station for further questioning. Before she was questioned, a caution was given to her: "You are charged with vagrancy. Do you wish to say anything in answer to the charge? You are not obliged to say anything unless you wish to do so, but whatever you say will be taken down in writing and may be given in evidence."

An examination began with the statement taken down in longhand by Detective-Sergeant Preston. Before the statement was completed, Walter Tuchtie, a lawyer who was then acting for the entire MacLean family, including Mrs. Dick, arrived and prevented the examination from continuing.

On March 26, Inspector Wood informed Mrs. Dick that a charge of murder was being laid against her, and a caution in the usual form was given. Inspector Wood said to her, "Now, you have given us three statements, do you remember the contents of them?" to which she answered, "Yes." She said further that she wished to change the first two, but that the last statement taken was true, as far as it went. Presumably, the statements referred to as the first two were the statements that had been taken down by a shorthand reporter. Mrs. Dick declined to continue the statement that had been interrupted by Tuchtie, saying that she was told "to keep her mouth shut."

The last statement, and the one the Crown relied on the most, was made on the afternoon of April 12. The Crown's position at trial was that this was the only statement that was reliable; the rest were false. On that same day, Mrs. Dick had sent a message to Detective-Sergeant Preston that she wanted to see him. Preston went to the jail that morning and asked her what was on her mind. She said, "When are you going to bring the old man in?" to which he replied, "Who do you mean?" She said, "My father." Questions were then asked by Preston and a conversation followed, particularly with regard to the connection of Bohozuk and Donald MacLean with the murder and with matters that led to it. In the course of this conversation, Mrs. Dick said that Bohozuk shot John Dick while the three of them were riding in the borrowed motorcar on a side road on the afternoon of March 6. No caution was given to her on this occasion.

Detective-Sergeant Preston returned to the jail on the afternoon of April 12 with Inspector Wood. Preston's reaction to her statement implicating Bohozuk had been, "Oh, that don't add up." Inspector Wood asked Mrs. Dick if she would take them where she thought they might find certain bottles that she said were thrown out of the car, and that might have Bohozuk's fingerprints on them. Mrs. Dick was willing to go, and the detectives took her over the route that she said they travelled on the afternoon of March 6 when Bohozuk shot John Dick. There was much conversation about the murder during the drive, notes of which were made by one of the officers. Again, no caution of any kind was given, although at the conclusion of the trip she was warned that she need not make a statement, and was told that if she wanted to do so she could put it in writing.

This was the case that Robinette had to meet, and a formidable one it was. While the circumstantial evidence taken by itself was not compelling as to Mrs. Dick's participation in the actual killing of her husband, when it was viewed in the light of her rambling statements, the case for the Crown was more than ample to support the verdict of the jury. The challenge to Robinette was to make the seven statements relied on by the Crown disappear.

A five-man court had been established for this appeal, indicating the importance the Chief Justice of Ontario attached to it. He sat with Justices Henderson, Laidlaw, Hogg, and Aylesworth. It was a very strong panel. Chief Justice Robertson was at the pinnacle of an illustrious career and had one of the finest minds in the legal profession. He was particularly helpful in this case because he was very strong on the facts of an appeal. It became evident early on that he had read the entire record in this case. Justice Henderson was described by Robinette[23] as a most outspoken, rough man: "Basically, he had an awful bark." However, he was also a great judge on the facts where he was astute and experienced. Justice Hogg was not as comfortable on the bench as he had been in private practice, but he was a sound judge nonetheless. Justices Laidlaw and Aylesworth, who were later to dominate the court through the early part of my experience as counsel, were both good advocates in their day. They suffered from a lack of patience in dealing with counsel who took a different view of the case from the one they thought appropriate. They, too, were good in assessing the facts of a case.

This was a Court with which Robinette was comfortable. He knew these judges, and they knew him. His presentation was always to the point, and the members of the court treated his submissions with great respect. I was to observe later that in the Court of Appeal he used only one forensic tool. It was his voice, rich and vibrant, effortlessly filling the chamber without overwhelming his audience. He had few gestures, contenting himself with raising one partially closed hand and moving it almost indolently as he made his points. He stood in one spot. He avoided any histrionics. He kept to his carefully scripted text without ever appearing to read from it. He answered questions briefly and respectfully, never departing from the theme of his presentation. Moreover, he was a storyteller. He knew the facts of his case, and he knew the law that was applicable. He moved seamlessly from one to the other and kept his audience riveted to his argument, his issues, the Court's concerns, and his solution.

The appeal was heard over the days January 9, 10, 13, and 14. Robinette's opening to the Court was curious. He said that the three accused, Bohozuk, MacLean, and the appellant, Evelyn Dick, had been charged jointly of murder and none of their counsel had asked for separate trials. It was the Crown's decision to try this appellant alone. This course had the unfortunate result that some evidence that might have come out during a joint trial — which would have put the appellant's part in the affair in its proper light — was not elicited. Robinette must have been trying to create an atmosphere of trial unfairness to invoke some initial sympathy, but it did not work. This could not have been a serious point, and it goes against all conventional advocacy to start a long appeal with your worst argument.

The Chief Justice cut in, saying, "Has it not been the accepted practice to have separate trials where an important part of the Crown's case consists of statements made by one of the accused, which would not be evidence against the others?" Robinette responded easily, "That may be, but the practice is based upon fairness to the other accused, and I mention the matter here because it has resulted in unfairness to this appellant. It is mentioned merely as a circumstance, and not as a ground of appeal."

Recovering from his shaky beginning, Robinette moved quickly to the adequacy of the trial judge's instruction to the jury, which was his main point. He was confident that the errors made by Justice Barlow were of sufficient gravity that Mrs. Dick was entitled to a new trial. He argued that the trial judge's charge to the jury was "sketchy." It did not bring home to the jury the real problem that they had to face. The accused was entitled to have the judge explain to the jury any theory based on the evidence that would assist the accused, whether or not the theory was raised by her counsel. Practically all the circumstantial evidence (that is, the evidence other than Mrs. Dick's statements to the police) was consistent with her having been only an accessory after the fact to the killing. But not only was that possibility not put to the jury, it was in effect withdrawn from their consideration. The trial judge should have told the jury that if they had a reasonable doubt whether the accused was merely an accessory after the fact, it was their duty to acquit her on this indictment for murder.

As Robinette was referring to a number of judicial decisions, Aylesworth cut in, "If there is no proper or discernible 'theory' of the defence in evidence, but a proper marshalling of the evidence would support a possible view which would lead to acquittal, is it the duty of the trial judge to put that view to the jury?" Robinette promptly replied in the affirmative and referred again to two cases that he had mentioned earlier. He then set out a theory of the defence that had not been articulated by defence counsel at trial: "A substantial part of the circumstantial evidence pointed to the appellant's father, Donald MacLean, as the person who killed Dick — particularly some of the things found in MacLean's house by the police."

Justice Henderson then interjected helpfully, "How was the finding of those articles evidence in this trial?" Robinette relied, "It was not, but since the Crown elected to prove it, I am entitled to any benefit to be derived from it. The trial judge should have pointed out the incriminating nature of this evidence as against MacLean, and also that there was no evidence that the accused was an accessory before the fact to a killing by MacLean. If MacLean killed Dick, then at the worst the appellant was an accessory after the fact, and not guilty of murder."

Robinette then turned his attention to the trial judge's direction to the jury with respect to the all-important statements made by Mrs. Dick to the police. He was later to ask that the Court of Appeal decide that these statements should not have been admitted into evidence by the trial judge. But he started with the more limited complaint that the trial judge did not give the jury any instruction as to what use they could make of these statements against Mrs. Dick. The weakness of this position is that even if it was successful, the argument could only lead to a new trial where the statements could be reintroduced with the appropriate instruction given to the jury. However, Robinette was not a gambler, and he was not prepared to ignore this valid argument even though its success would produce only a partial victory.

Robinette started off with the critical statement of April 12. He submitted that the statement was capable of being interpreted as showing that the appellant was a mere spectator in the killing of Dick by Bohozuk, and that Mrs. Dick's part involved no more than passive acquiescence. The trial judge did not point out to the members of the jury that passive acquiescence in a killing does not make the accused a party to the offence of murder according to section 69 of the *Criminal Code of Canada* (as it then read).

It was of the utmost importance, Robinette continued, that the jury should have been called on to test and decide upon the truth of Mrs.

Dick's statements, assuming for the moment that they were properly admitted in evidence against her. The jury should have been told that they could reject the statements because of their inherent inconsistencies, and also that they should carefully consider whether a later statement could be believed when it appeared that the accused had previously told the police something entirely different and untrue.

Robinette argued further that the trial judge told the jury that even though the statements were not voluntary, they might act on them if they were satisfied from the other evidence that they were true. This was clearly wrong, and was inconsistent with his previous instruction that the jury might find that the statements were untrue because they were not made voluntarily. This inconsistency in the judge's instructions could only confuse the jurors.

Robinette next turned from the general to the particular. He contended that there were many respects in which the statement of April 12 conflicted with the facts sworn to by other witnesses. The trial judge did not draw any of these inconsistencies to the attention of the jury but told them that "slight discrepancies" tended to strengthen, rather than to weaken, evidence. This may be true of accounts given by different eyewitnesses to an occurrence, but it is quite wrong to say, as the trial judge did here, that discrepancies strengthened this last statement by the accused to the police. This was the only statement to which the trial judge particularly directed the jury's attention. He told the jury that they might believe all the statements, or only some of them, but he failed to point out that they might disbelieve them all.

In concluding this phase of his argument before the Court of Appeal, Robinette engaged in a neat piece of gamesmanship whereby he enlisted the support of the Court by suggesting that the trial judge had been less than respectful of one of the Court's own decisions. He said that the trial judge drew a distinction between the position of Crown counsel and that of defence counsel in a way that the Court of Appeal had disapproved of in the case of *Rex v. Ferguson*.[24] The result of such a direction was to neutralize the effect of anything that defence counsel may have said to the jury.

Robinette then turned to the issue of items seized by the police from the various residences. Much of this evidence was inadmissible against the accused (for instance, the articles seized at MacLean's house) and was prejudicial. There should be a new trial, therefore, because of this evidence, particularly because the trial judge failed to instruct the jury that they should entirely disregard it. Instead, the judge expressly directed their attention to the inadmissible evidence that John Dick had told a witness, on the day of his disappearance, that he was going to meet his wife that afternoon. The statement by the victim was clearly hearsay and did not conform to any of the exceptions to the hearsay rules.

Having built a strong argumentative foundation for a new trial, Robinette pressed on and sought a ruling that the damning statements of his client were themselves inadmissible in evidence. Here he was on less firm ground. The law was clear that the onus was on the Crown to show that any statement made to police by Mrs. Dick was voluntary, in the sense that it was not obtained as a result of threats, promises, offers of reward, or other inducements. Robinette wanted to extend this law to say that Mrs. Dick's statements were not voluntary because of certain failures of the police: the police failed to advise Mrs. Dick that she was the principal suspect in a murder case, and they failed to advise her of her right to remain silent by warning her that she was not obliged to say anything, but that anything she did say would be taken down in writing and might be introduced in evidence at her trial. The state of the law before this case was that the failure to give such a warning was not necessarily fatal to the admissibility of any inculpatory statement.

Robinette argued that the several statements made by Mrs. Dick should not have been admitted in evidence against her: "I refer to the English 'Judges' Rules,' printed in Archibald, Criminal Pleading, Evidence & Practice, particularly no. 7.[25] These rules have not the force of law, but they accurately state the effect of the cases. The cases lay down a general rule that a person in custody, even if a caution has been given, may not be cross-examined by a police officer, and that if he is his examination is not admissible in evidence against him."

Henderson interrupted, "Is the rule limited to cross-examination? Does it not apply equally to any examination in the form of questions and answers?" Robinette seemed to have at least this important member of the panel on his side. He responded, "Yes, except where questions are asked merely as an introduction, or to obtain an explanation of something said by the person in custody." Robinette continued:

At least the trial judge, if he does admit such a statement, should warn the jury as to the weight to be given
to it. The cases are most usefully summarized in *Taylor
on Evidence*;[26] there is also a valuable article in the
Journal of Criminal Law.[27] The Canadian cases, such as
Sankey v. The King,[28] and *Gach v. The King*,[29] are none of
them cases of prolonged questioning of an accused
person by the police, but come rather within the rule
laid down in the *Ibrahim* case,[30] that one or two preliminary questions will not invalidate a statement. In
the *Gach* case the majority state the rule a little less
strictly, but Mr. Justice Taschereau [in the Supreme
Court of Canada] lays it down quite definitely that a
caution is essential before any questioning by the
police, if the answers are to be admitted in evidence.

Robinette then submitted that if any of Mrs. Dick's earlier statements were inadmissible at her trial because the police did not caution
her, the later statements should not have been admitted unless she was
given the usual caution and was also told that her earlier statements
could not be used against her at trial. Robinette said the April 12 statement was in the worst position because no caution was given to Mrs.
Dick before the questioning at the jail, and she was not told that she was
under no compulsion to accompany the officers on the drive. Also, there
is some evidence that she did not think that she was making an official
statement on that occasion. At no time after she was charged with murder did she sign any written statement.

Robinette concluded masterfully:

To sum up, the appellant is entitled at least to a new trial
because of (a) misdirection and non-direction; (b) the
wrongful admission of evidence other than the statements; and (c) the wrongful admission of the statements. Further than this, however, if all of the statements
are held to be inadmissible, the conviction should be
quashed without ordering a new trial, because there is

no evidence on which a jury, properly directed, could convict of murder. The circumstantial evidence is consistent with her being only an accessory after the fact, and a jury, properly instructed, would be bound to give her the benefit of a reasonable doubt on this point, and to acquit on this indictment [of murder]. The position is the same if only the last statement is held to be inadmissible. The only thing in the other statements which could make the appellant an accessory before the fact is her statement that she lent money to Bohozuk to give to a "gang" to murder Dick. This money, according to the statement, was repaid by Bohozuk before Dick's death. Further, the Crown did not proceed on the theory that the accused was a party to murder by a "gang", but contended that she was a party to murder by Bohozuk. The Crown is not entitled to a new trial based upon an entirely different theory.

It was now the Crown's turn. Cecil L. Snyder, K.C., the Deputy Attorney-General, represented the Crown along with Timothy J. Rigney, the senior counsel at Mrs. Dick's trial. They were not a happy combination. Snyder had considerable experience as a trial counsel but had little familiarity with appeals. This was to cost him. He opened by submitting that the statements made by the appellant to the police were properly admitted as voluntary. He then began a largely technical argument directed to showing that the statements were not "confessions" in the classic sense and thus there was no need for the Crown to show that they were made voluntarily. He referred to the decision of *Rex v. Mandzuk*[31] as authority for the proposition that an exculpatory statement does not come within the rules for admitting confessions into evidence. He went further and cited *Rex v. Van Horst*[32] as authority for admitting a statement related to one charge into evidence when the accused is charged with a different offence.

At this point, the Chief Justice decided that it was time to relate the law to the facts of the case. He observed, "The warning given to the appellant after the charge of vagrancy was laid referred expressly to that charge and she was asked if she wanted to say anything 'in answer to the charge.' The police immediately started to ask questions relating to an entirely different charge." Snyder's weak answer was, "The manner of taking the accused into custody may have been irregular, but it was justified by the unusual circumstances. Regardless of that, the facts surrounding these statements were fully disclosed to the jury, and they, acting on their best judgment, found the accused guilty."

The problem with these last comments relating to the role of the jury with respect to the statements is that these comments had nothing to do with the admissibility of the statements. As a preliminary step to determining if the jury is to be permitted to see the accused's statements, the trial judge must decide whether these statements were given voluntarily. Only then does the jury see the statements, and the jury's function is to decide whether they believe the statements (some of them, all of them, or none of them) and how much weight they should be given in the light of all of the rest of the evidence.

Snyder went on to argue that the evidence clearly showed that on April 12 the accused was anxious to see the police — they did not seek her out. Her actions and statements on that occasion were entirely voluntary and were on her own initiative. If the critical statement of April 12 is accepted, there can be no doubt that the accused was a party to the offence of murder according to section 69 of the *Criminal Code*.

The Chief Justice did not accept this statement, however. He said, "There is nothing in that story to indicate that she had any control over Bohozuk." Snyder replied, "She knew that Bohozuk had a revolver, and they got Dick and took him for a drive." The Chief Justice rejected this: "There is no evidence that she knew that Bohozuk had the revolver with him, or even that she knew that he had already obtained it."

Snyder continued by arguing that the trial judge's instruction to the jury was not lengthy but it adequately covered all necessary matters. The trial judge's remarks about the jury disbelieving the statements if they concluded that they were not voluntary are based on *Wigmore on Evidence*.[33] However, the Chief Justice had other concerns: "Were the jury properly instructed as to parties to offences? The trial judge read s. 69, but should there not have been something further, in view of the evidence in this case?" Snyder replied, "I submit he did all that was required of him."

It was at this point in his argument that Snyder made a concession that caused Robinette to stifle a gasp of disbelief and Rigney to grimace in disgust. He said, "I concede that the circumstantial evidence, apart from the appellant's statements, is not sufficient to support a conviction for murder. Even if the statements should have been excluded, however, I ask for a new trial. The position has changed since this trial, and other knowledge has come to the Crown." Henderson cut him off: "You should not refer to anything not in this record."

Snyder closed feebly, telling the Court that the jury were fully justified in believing the appellant's final statement, and finding her guilty as charged, and the Court of Appeal should not interfere.

Rigney could barely get to his feet before stating categorically, "I do not agree that the evidence other than the appellant's statements was not sufficient for a conviction of murder." It was, however, much too late. It is incomprehensible that two senior counsel would have such poor lines of communication that they could not put forward a common front on an issue so basic as this. The reason might well have been that Snyder, not being as familiar with the evidence as Rigney, did not realize how thin the case for the Crown was without the statements. Rigney now found himself fighting a rearguard action for a new trial.

Rigney started out by repeating much of what Snyder had argued — always a mistake — about the voluntary nature of Mrs. Dick's statements. Rigney then took Robinette head-on about his argument that the trial judge did not put the theory of the defence to the jury. He said, "The trial judge could not put 'the theory of the defence' to the jury, because no defence had been adduced at the trial." The Chief Justice, however, had been persuaded otherwise. He responded, "Where a material part of the Crown's case consists of statements made by the accused, and those statements suggest a possible defence, for example, that the accused was not an actual participant in the crime, is it not the duty of the trial judge to draw that to the jury's attention?" Rigney replied, "It may be, but a failure to work out such a defence and submit it to the jury is not fatal. Where the attitude of the defence is merely that the accused is not guilty, and that the Crown has not proved its case, surely the trial judge is not required to consider all possible defences and submit them to the jury." The Chief Justice was not dissuaded: "My point is that the Crown proved by the statement, if it was accepted, that Dick was killed by Bohozuk, not by the appellant. The burden was on the Crown to show additional facts that made her a party. How could the jury be properly instructed without drawing that important feature to their attention?" Rigney's response was, "The judge read s. 69, and explained it adequately."

Robinette was brief in reply. He said, "Any incriminatory statement or remark is within the rules as to confessions; it need not be a 'plenary' confession, but may be any admission of a subordinate fact going to establish the accused's guilt. *Rex v. Scory* and *Rex v. Mandzuk* both support this proposition rather than the reverse."

The Court reserved its decision. Robinette had every reason to be optimistic about the outcome of the appeal, and he was not disappointed. On January 21, 1947, the decision of the Court was delivered by Chief Justice Robertson, quashing the conviction of Mrs. Dick and ordering a new trial. Although couched in different language and reflecting different priorities, the Court accepted the three basic propositions put forward by Robinette in his opening address. The conviction was set aside because of the failure of the Crown to establish that the statements of Mrs. Dick were voluntary; the failure of the police to administer cautions before taking the statements; and the lack of precision in the trial judge's instruction relating to the theory of the defence.

In substance, the Chief Justice held on behalf of a unanimous court that a real burden rests on the Crown when it seeks to introduce a statement into evidence in the nature of a confession by an accused person in custody to a police officer: the Crown must first establish that the statement is voluntary within the accepted sense of that term. The Chief Justice commented that Mrs. Dick was taken into custody on a charge of vagrancy, which the police did not intend to proceed with. She was then given a caution referring to the vagrancy charge, but was questioned by the police not about vagrancy but about murder. The judgment ruled that the answers she gave to those questions could not be admitted in evidence against her as a voluntary statement on her ensuing murder trial.

The most important finding from the point of view of the defence was the Chief Justice's criticism of the circumstances under which Mrs. Dick gave her most incriminating statement about how the killing took place during her famous car ride with police on April 12:

Whatever may be the proper view to take of the morning interview on 12th April, I am strongly of the opinion that what was said in the course of the drive to which the police invited the appellant on the afternoon of that day was inadmissible in evidence. No caution whatever was given. The invitation to a drive, following upon the opening given by the morning's conversation, has the appearance of a shrewd device on the part of the police to get the appellant to make unguarded statements, contrary to the advice of her solicitor which she had told them plainly it was her intention to follow, and it may reasonably be concluded that she was induced to talk without any apprehension on her part that what she said might be used in evidence. That nothing had happened to remove the pressure that naturally arose from her arrest and custody, and to incline her to tell the truth, is evidenced by a number of untrue statements made by her, and by Inspector Wood's interjection at the time, that her story of the murder did not "add up".

The Chief Justice continued that the accused, charged with the murder of her husband, had made a statement to the police in which she admitted that she had driven a car containing Dick and one Bohozuk, that during the drive a quarrel had developed between the two men, and that Bohozuk had shot and killed Dick. The Court held that in these circumstances (and in others more fully set out in the reasons for judgment), the trial judge should have fully explained to the jury the terms "abetting," "counselling," and "procuring," as they were used in section 69 of the *Criminal Code* relating to who in law are parties to an offence and the applicability of section 69 to the facts of the case as the jury might find them. And he should have told the jury that if they found that the accused was no more than passively acquiescent at the time of the shooting, and that she had no reason to expect that there would be any shooting until it actually occurred, then section 69 did not apply to make her culpable of murder.

Ordinarily, when the Crown concedes that the evidence would not support a conviction without inculpatory statements made by the accused and the Court concludes that these statements should not have been admitted into evidence, a verdict of not guilty is substituted by the appellate court. However, in this case the Court also had to deal with differences between the two counsel for the Crown regarding the ability of the circumstantial evidence to support the conviction for murder. Chief Justice Robertson had this to say on the matter:

> Counsel for the appellant contended for the acquittal of the appellant, arguing that there was no case made out against her on the admissible evidence. Mr. Snyder, who led for the Crown on the argument of this appeal, stated definitely that, in his opinion, if the statements of the appellant — the admissibility of which was disputed — were wholly excluded, there was not sufficient evidence on the record to convict the appellant of the charge of murder. Mr. Rigney, who had been senior counsel at the trial and was associated with Mr. Snyder on the hearing of the appeal, said just as definitely that he did not subscribe to Mr. Snyder's view. I do not think this Court, in a criminal case, is entitled to take refuge behind the opinion expressed by any counsel as to the effect of the evidence, but must act upon its own opinion. After having given the question much consideration I am of the opinion that the case is not one that the trial judge should have withdrawn from the jury, even if he had rejected all the statements of the appellant that are objected to. What remains for consideration is, therefore, whether the appellant had a fair and proper trial, and, in particular, whether her statements to the police while in custody were properly admitted in evidence, and whether there was misdirection or non-direction of the jury in the charge of the learned trial judge.

The reasons of the Chief Justice are very full and give a detailed account of the evidence. This is unusual. When an appellate court orders a new trial, it is the practice not to say too much about the facts so as not to influence the new trier of fact. This is so even where the jury is the trier. The concern is that the appellate court might be thought to be signalling the disposition that it thinks is appropriate on the new trial. In this case, one gets the firm impression that Chief Justice Robertson *was* advocating a result that gives effect to the theory of the defence as articulated by Robinette. For example, after dealing with the relationship within the MacLean and Dick families, the Chief Justice made this observation:

> Other than the several differences and animosities that I have indicated, there does not appear in evidence anything to indicate any motive on the part of the appellant for desiring to bring about the death of John Dick. The trial courts of the Province are kept busy with divorce cases that commonly reveal quite as much as the evidence in this case discloses, of quarrels and jealousies and marital misconduct, but divorce, and not murder, is the usual outcome. It is difficult to see anything in the relations between the appellant and John Dick, as disclosed in evidence, to explain his murder only five months after their marriage.

So much for motive. However, lest Robinette become too cocky, the Chief Justice left this for his consideration:

> It is not difficult to reach the conclusion, free from all reasonable doubt, that John Dick was murdered by some person or persons, on the 6th March 1946, and that his body was then mutilated and disposed of in a most inhuman way. This much would seem to be clearly established by the evidence without resorting to the statements of the appellant, the admissibility of which in evidence is disputed. It is also a fair conclusion, upon the same evidence, that the appellant knows a good

deal about these matters. The vital question is what, if any, part she had in the crime itself.

Another reason the Court was reluctant to enter a verdict of not guilty may well have been that the case had already generated a great deal of publicity. It is difficult for the public to understand why a woman who has been convicted of murder by a jury should be found not guilty by an appellate court on the basis of legal arguments that led to incriminating statements being removed from the evidentiary record. Chief Justice Robertson addressed this concern:

> The principles that, in my opinion, are applicable in this appeal are among the fundamental principles of the administration of justice in criminal cases. Whatever may be the character of the appellant and the iniquity of her conduct, the presumption of innocence of the crime with which she is charged, until she is proved guilty by due process of law and after a fair trial, is applicable in her case as in any other. To deny her the same fair trial that every prisoner is entitled to is to make the right to a fair trial dependent upon the pre-conceived notions of the Court in the particular case. Nothing could be more foreign to the proper administration of justice, or more destructive of the liberty of the subject, than to permit any such conception of its duty to determine the action of the Court in the cases that come before it. Whether the appellant is innocent or guilty of the crime with which she is charged is a matter to be determined by a jury. The duty of this Court is to see that there was a fair trial.

In any event, whatever the intentions of the Court of Appeal, the Crown did not approach Robinette to resolve this murder case by a plea bargaining process, an approach that would have been strictly off the record in those days. Evelyn Dick prepared herself for a second trial and asked Robinette to represent her. He agreed. Before that could take place, the Crown made one last desperate attempt to salvage the guilty verdict. It applied to the Supreme Court of Canada to hear an appeal from the Ontario Court of Appeal's decision. The matter came on before Mr. Justice Taschereau in his chambers on February 5 and 6, 1947. The application was dismissed on October 16, with Taschereau holding that even if there was some error on the part of the Court of Appeal relating to the admissibility of the statements, Mrs. Dick was still entitled to a new trial because of the misdirection of the jury by the trial judge relating to the theory of the defence. The point argued by the Crown about the admissibility of the statements was, in effect, moot.

Chapter Four
Evelyn Dick Retried

B Y THE TIME OF THE Evelyn Dick appeal in 1947, John Robinette was already well known and highly respected in the profession. But now, with his involvement in the second trial of the alleged murderess, he was to become famous and would remain so the rest of his life. I did not know him before he was famous (indeed, I was one of his admiring public when, as an arts student at University College, I first read and heard about him in the media), but I have no difficulty in accepting the judgment of his friends that his instant celebrity never changed him. He remained modest and self-effacing and discussed the Dick case, when it inevitably came up in conversation, with detachment and humour.

If Robinette was looking forward to the second trial with confidence, he was to receive two surprises during the trial, as will be seen below.

Mrs. Dick was arraigned again on February 24, 1947, in Hamilton for her second trial along with her two co-accused, Bohozuk and MacLean. The presiding judge was James C. McRuer, Chief Justice of the trial division. Once again, and without objection, the Chief Justice allowed the Crown's application to sever the trials of the three co-accused and ordered that the Crown proceed first against Mrs. Dick. The Crown was again represented by Rigney and McCulloch but had added Clifford R. Magone, K.C., as a third counsel. Robinette appeared alone for Mrs. Dick. I cannot imagine that three senior counsel were required for the conduct of this case, particularly when two of them had the experience of conducting the first trial. Certainly, the three "silks" appearing for the Crown stood in stark contrast to the youthful Robinette sitting alone at the counsel table on behalf of the even younger Evelyn Dick. This perception of David battling Goliath, shared by the public, which saw Robinette as a young, untested lawyer up against experienced counsel, was tempered by an advantage Robinette had, which he was not aware of until the trial was over. It was Chief Justice McRuer, whose persistent interruptions on behalf of the Crown alienated the jury. The jurors were also taken aback by the tactics of Rigney, supported by McRuer, which they thought were most unfair to Robinette, for whom they developed a great admiration during the trial.[34] Robinette and other lawyers were convinced that the jury acquitted Mrs. Dick despite the best efforts of the Chief Justice to intimidate them into finding her guilty.

The relationship between McRuer and Robinette has always fascinated me. I will deal with it again when I recount my experience in watching Robinette spar with Chief Justice McRuer at the murder trial of Steven Suchan and Leonard Jackson. But it seems that at least by the time of the second trial in the Dick case a tension had developed between Robinette and McRuer that was evident to spectators of the trial, and, more importantly, to the jury. For the record, Robinette consistently maintained that the animosity began here. Certainly, the transcripts of this trial demonstrate that McRuer appeared convinced that Mrs. Dick was guilty and that the judgment of the Court of Appeal with respect to her statements was wrong. In the circumstances, he tended to revert to his earlier days as a Crown prosecutor and to side with the Crown. This failing is referred to by Patrick Boyer, McRuer's official biographer:[35]

> McRuer was not without his faults as a judge. At least in his early days on the bench, he seemed incapable of ridding his mind of the attitudes and practices of the advocate. His failing was sometimes revealed by his practice of questioning witnesses himself after counsel had completed their cross-examinations. More seriously, his lawyerly instincts led him to ignore judicial impartiality and jump into the courtroom fray. In the Evelyn Dick case ... McRuer repeatedly took sides and stepped outside his allotted function to offer advice

that only a lawyer consulted by the party in question could properly give. Apparently the chief justice did not appreciate or entirely accept the well-known axiom that "the Crown never wins and never loses."

Robinette had been proceeding on the assumption, understandable I would have thought, that the issue of the admissibility of the statements made by Mrs. Dick had been unequivocally resolved by the judgment of the Court of Appeal. That was not the view of the Crown, and in the first surprise to Robinette in the case, it was not the view of McRuer. In fact, the Crown proposed to introduce not only the seven statements that had been introduced at the first trial but also the four that had not. Technically, the additional four were not part of the appellate ruling, but they fell within its judicial umbrella. Interestingly, as with the original seven, most of the additional statements were not inculpatory.

Magone, who apparently had been brought into the case to argue that Mrs. Dick's statements were admissible, seemed to think that the fact that her statements were not inculpatory was helpful to their admission into evidence. He stated[36] that up to April 12, all of her statements were exculpatory and were intended to be self-serving in nature; she was trying to excuse herself. Therefore, all of the statements made up to April 12 were not subject to the admissibility of confessions rule. Even though some of the statements ended up being inculpatory, they were not so intended by the accused. There is no law, he said, to require that every time an accused desires to say something she must be warned that her statement can be used against her. The only issue is whether the statement is voluntary. None of Mrs. Dick's statements was subject to the confessions rule since they were not intended as confessions. And second, if they were inculpatory, they were made voluntarily. The same analysis applied to the accused's decision to go on the motor trip. The fact that her lawyer advised her "to keep her mouth shut" and that she still voluntarily called on the officers to visit the places described in the evidence placed the statements she made in a more admissible light.

This, of course, was the very argument that was made and rejected in the Court of Appeal. Robinette was indignant. He said,[37] "All of the Crown's arguments were put before the Court of Appeal and your

Lordship is bound by the careful consideration of a unanimous five judge decision." He pointed out that leave to appeal to the Supreme Court of Canada had been denied.

But Chief Justice McRuer was having none of that. He replied, "Whatever decision I come to, I am sitting at the trial, and I have a discretion to exercise according to law. I must find the facts, I cannot have them found by proxy. I have the duty to apply the facts and then I must apply the law, and, as I see it, I must investigate the whole thing fully in the light of the decision of the Court of Appeal [as if it were] another case."

Robinette tried to interject, "In this case —"

McRuer overrode him: "No, in this case I am presiding and the witnesses have testified before me. All of the facts and inferences are to be drawn by me, not by any other person ... So if you have any cases I want to hear them."

Robinette then countered, "May I, with the greatest respect, take the sharpest issue with your lordship's statements in two respects? I say there is no discretion in the trial judge, and the Court of Appeal in this case quite properly said it is not a discretional matter for a trial judge at all."

McRuer responded, "Now, Mr. Robinette, you must know that I am using discretion in a strictly legal sense. We have all read the cases that discuss that matter — and do not please misinterpret my language."

The discussion between the two then focused on the discretion to admit a voluntary statement, and McRuer asked counsel to refer him to the cases that assisted the Court of Appeal to come to its decision. Robinette pointed out that it took him more than two days to argue the cases before the Court of Appeal. The strong implication was that he did not intend to do it again. He stated, "I respectfully submit to your lordship the Court of Appeal's judgment is a judgment of law." McRuer replied, "Then I will have to do the best I can without counsel's help."

Robinette then repeated what was said in the Court of Appeal's judgment that where an accused is detained for one charge, i.e., vagrancy, and illegally detained in custody, any statements made while under the pressure of the illegal arrest cannot be considered voluntary. Further, while detained for one charge, the police cannot ask questions about an entirely unrelated crime: any statements made in that respect are inadmissible. These are questions of law, Robinette explained.

Further, any statements made without a warning to the accused will also be inadmissible.

McRuer was not impressed and responded, "I have seen a great many cases, and that is new law. If that is to be interpreted that broadly, it is new law in the Dominion I think." The discussion continued back and forth with McRuer questioning Robinette about what he regarded as "this new state of the law" and the weight to be given to "the old authorities" in this context. McRuer said, "I am trying to get my mind clear on this law now." And later, "We should have a definitive statement of what the law is on this subject." Robinette replied, "I do not agree with your lordship that the Court of Appeal's judgment is something revolutionary. I thought it was an application of quite well established principles."

Robinette was quite correct in his submission that the Chief Justice, as a trial judge, was bound in law to follow the decision of the Court of Appeal. It was an impertinence to demand of counsel what authorities were submitted in argument to the appellate court. The judgment, as lawyers say, spoke for itself.

In the end, the Chief Justice did accept that he was bound by authority to follow the judgment of the Court of Appeal. In lengthy reasons he made it clear that he did not agree with the decision and set out a list of English authorities that he thought would have permitted him to admit the statements. His theme, which he took from an English House of Lords case decided in 1914, would bring forth applause from some modern thinkers who think the courts are too soft on accused persons. He quoted from Lord Sumner in *R. v. Ibrahim*:[38]

> I think there has been too much tenderness towards prisoners. I can not look at the decisions without some shame when I consider what objections have prevailed to prevent the reception of confessions ... justice and common sense have too frequently been sacrificed on the shrine of mercy ... The English law is still unsettled ... If, as appears even on the line of authorities which the trial judge did not follow, *the matter is one for the judge's discretion, depending largely on his view of the*

*impropriety of the questioner's conduct and the general
circumstances of the case ...*" [Emphasis in transcript.]

After this ruling, the Crown closed its case. I have not set out the
facts led by the Crown because the evidence called at the second trial was
the same as that presented at the first, with one notable exception. In the
second surprise of the trial, though Robinette quickly prepared for it, the
Crown called a witness who had not testified at the first trial.[39] His name
was Francis Boehler, a nineteen-year-old farmhand who worked near
Glanford Station Line on a farm owned by a family named Hamilton.

Boehler's evidence was electric. He said that one of his helpful side-
lines was providing either a horse or a tractor to pull cars out of ditch-
es in the vicinity of his farm. He vividly recalled the afternoon of March
6, 1946, when he pulled a large black car out of the mud between two
and three o'clock. He remembered the incident because it was the only
time he was not paid for helping pull a car out of the mud in the six
months he had worked on the farm. His testimony was somewhat confused as to detail, but in overview he testified that he saw the large black
car as he was going out either to milk the cows or check on the condition of a sick cow. He said that a man came to the farm and informed
him that his car was stuck in the mud. Suddenly, he heard two gunshots,
spaced about thirty seconds apart, coming from the direction of the car.
He was not sure if the sounds of the gunshots came from the car or from
a northerly direction. From the time he first spotted the car to the time
he heard the gunshots, thirty to forty-five minutes had passed. The car
was fifty yards from the farm. He hooked up a team of horses and went
to the large, dark car.

There was a man standing beside the car and a woman sitting in the
driver's seat. The woman was young, with dark hair, and had a fresh-lit
cigarette in her mouth. She had a handbag on the seat beside her with
half a gun handle sticking out of it. The woman was wearing a glove on
one hand; on the finger of the other hand was a large diamond ring.
After pulling the car to the top of the hill, Boehler glanced in the car and
caught a partial view of a man's leg on the floor in front of the rear seat
of the car. The leg displayed a black oxford shoe, a black sock, and one
dark blue trouser leg. After he finished towing the car to the top of the

hill, one of the men slid into the driver's seat, and the woman slid over to the passenger seat. She tossed a Hamilton Street Railway conductor's cap into the back seat. The witness identified Evelyn Dick sitting in the dock as the woman in the car on March 6. The witness also said that he kept a log of all the cars he had pulled out of the mud.

The faces on the Crown's side of the counsel table were smug when Boehler finished his testimony, but in reality they had made a serious tactical mistake. Crown counsel were pressing so hard for a conviction that they did not recognize that this witness's evidence was too good to be true. Had they taken the trouble to check into his background, as Robinette had, they would have realized that this man was well known to the police in the town of Dundas, near Hamilton. When Robinette was notified that the Crown was going to call this new witness and was told what in substance he was going to say, he was of course very concerned. But he had some good connections in Hamilton. One was Henry Schreiber, who was assisting Arthur Martin, counsel for Bohozuk. The other was his law student, John Bowlby, later a very good counsel and a judge of the High Court of Justice. They both asked around about Boehler and learned from the Dundas Chief of Police, Earl Jack, that Boehler was in his view a psychopath. As remembered by Robinette, the Chief said, "My God. We have had more trouble with that man coming in to us to solve our crimes."

In a carefully orchestrated cross-examination, Robinette destroyed Boehler's credibility.

> Q. Now, Mr. Boehler, when did you first tell that story
>   to anybody?
> A. To Inspector Charles Wood, sir.
>
> Q. Yes, when?
> A. I don't know the date, sir.
>
> Q. I suggest it was just a month or so ago. Is that right?
> A. No, sir.
>
> Q. How long ago?

A. About two months, two months ago.

Q. Did you tell the Hamiltons anything about it, the people you were working for?
A. No, sir.

Q. Did you read the newspapers during the first trial?
A. Yes, sir.

Q. Did you ever see a picture of Bill Bohozuk?
A. Yes.

Q. Did you ever see a picture of Evelyn Dick?
A. Yes, sir.

Q. And I suppose the man who was there that day was Bill Bohozuk?
A. Yes, sir.

This was the aspect of Boehler's evidence that was most likely to disturb the jury. His evidence, if true, was obviously relevant. He must have heard about this high-profile case featuring the strikingly photogenic Evelyn Dick. Why did it take him so long to come forward? Robinette was to return to this point, but first he took the time to show the jury something of the quality of the man who was testifying.

Q. Where were you born?
A. Hamilton.

Q. When?
A. April 26, 1927.

Q. Married?
A. Yes, sir.

Q. Not living with your wife?

A. No, sir.

Q. Did you ever threaten to shoot your wife?

A. (No response.)

Q. Did you ever threaten to shoot your wife?

A. No, sir.

Q. Did you ever point a gun at her?

A. No, sir.

Q. Did you ever clean a gun in her presence and tell her you would shoot her with it? Come on now, did you?

A. I cleaned a gun in her presence.

Q. Yes, when you were fighting with her.

His Lordship: Now Mr. Robinette —

Mr. Robinette: I am cross-examining this witness, my Lord.

His Lordship: You must let him answer one question before you ask the next one.

Mr. Robinette: But I am going to cross-examine this witness, my Lord.

His Lordship: You must let him answer one question before you ask the next, that is all.

Robinette then took the witness through his work record, which was horrendous. Boehler was only nineteen years of age at the time he testified, and he had had, by my count from the transcript, ten different employers, for whom he worked from two weeks to two or three months. Then Robinette switched back again to the witness's failure to report the incident involving Evelyn Dick.

Q. When you were working for the Hamiltons did they take any newspaper there?
A. Yes.

Q. The Hamilton Spectator, in fact?
A. Yes.

Q. And you can read?
A. Yes.

Q. And you did read about the first trial?
A. Yes.

Q. You did not give any evidence whatsoever at the first trial?
A. No.

Q. The first trial was in October, 1946. You knew the trial was going on. You read about it?
A. Yes.

Q. Read it quite carefully, the evidence?
A. I wouldn't say that, no.

Q. You read it?
A. I read it, parts of it.

Q. Pretty much in the public eye at that time, wasn't it — the case?
A. Yes.

Q. And the first person you told this story to was Inspector Wood?

A. That is correct.

Q. About when?
A. About six or seven weeks ago.

Q. Six or seven weeks ago?
A. Yes.

Q. Had you told it to anyone else — your friends or anyone?
A. No.

Q. You didn't tell it to the Hamiltons?
A. No.

Switching gears again, Robinette turned to Boehler's army record, which, if anything, was worse than his work record. Remember this was 1946, and the memory of the war was still fresh in everyone's mind. I can recall that as late as the early 1950s, I watched Robinette remind a jury that his client, accused of murder, and with a lacklustre military record, "still had enough of the fire of patriotism in his veins to enlist in the army in defence of his country." When Boehler was asked how long he had been in the army, he replied, "Around five months and twenty-eight days." It developed that the reason he remembered the twenty-eight days with such clarity was because that was the number of days he was AWOL. He was discharged because of what he described as a nervous condition.

Robinette broke off this cross-examination to start on a totally unrelated matter in which it appeared that Boehler had made up a charge against another person.

Q. Did you see a newspaper account a week or ten days ago, reporting that you had been stabbed by a Chinaman?
A. Yes.

Q. That was published, wasn't it?

A. Yes.

Q. Any truth in that?
A. Yes.

Q. By a Chinaman?
A. Yes.

Q. Where did this happen?
A. On Walnut St. in Hamilton.

Q. Where were you stabbed, what part of your body?
A. I was not stabbed, sir.

Q. Did you tell the police you were stabbed?
A. No, I said I was attacked.

Q. Did you report it to the police?
A. Yes.

Q. Any charges laid?
A. Not that I know of, sir.

Q. How were you attacked?
A. I had come out of my apartment on King St. — I had come up King St. to the corner of Walnut and King, and turned left on Walnut St. to go up to the Selective Service, and I got about half way between King and Main Streets, and I saw this fellow coming towards me, and he stopped and asked me for a match.

Q. Who — the Chinaman?
A. He was either a Chinaman or a Jap,[40] yes, sir. I reached in my pocket, pulled out a package of cigarettes — a book of matches to give him a light,

and as I brought my hand up to give him a light, he brought his right hand up like that [illustrating].

Q. His right hand up like what?
A. Like this.

Q. What with, a gun?
A. With a knife.

Q. You were stabbed then, were you?
A. No, I was not stabbed.

Q. That is a pretty dramatic episode. How did you ward that Chinaman off?
A. I saw it and I knocked the hand aside like that. It went in through my leather windbreaker, through my sweater and through my shirt.

Q. Did you report it to the police?
A. Yes.

Q. Hamilton police?
A. Ontario Provincial Police.

Q. What man in the Ontario Provincial Police did you report it to?
A. Sgt. Carl Farrow.

Q. No charge was laid? You have not heard of any charge being laid?
A. No, sir.

After a short recess, Robinette once again returned to the failure to report the supposed incident involving Evelyn Dick.

Q. You say that you heard how many shots?

A. Three.

Q. How many?
A. Three. [Note that in his examination-in-chief he said two.]

Q. And then you went upstairs and read a while after that happened?
A. I went into the house and took a magazine and went upstairs.

Q. What time of day was that that you were reading?
A. Around half-past three.

Q. What were you reading?
A. A magazine.

Q. What magazine?
A. A western magazine.

Q. How long were you reading that?
A. About half an hour. I went up about 20 minutes after three — a quarter or 20 minutes after three and I read till about around 20 minutes to four.

Q. I think I asked you if you had seen pictures in the newspaper of Bohozuk and you said yes, didn't you?
A. Yes.

Q Of course, you have seen pictures of Mrs. Dick; there have been lots of them around?
A. Yes.

Q. You have been convicted of a criminal offence, having a gun?
A. Yes.

Q. Just three or four weeks ago here in Hamilton?
A. Yes.

Q. Are you fond of guns?
A. Yes.

Q. Interested in guns?
A. Yes.

Robinette returned to the army discharge and established that the witness had received a medical discharge after undergoing a Pulhems test for psychological stability. He then concluded his cross-examination:

Q. Your wife's family's name is what?
A. Venator.

Q. Your mother-in-law's name was Mrs. Venator?
A. Yes.

Q. Was your mother-in-law in receipt of baby bonus cheques?
A. Yes.

Q. You forged her signature on a couple of those cheques, didn't you?
A. (No response.)

Q. I say you forged your mother-in-law's signature on two baby bonus cheques in August and October. I am right, am I not?

His Lordship: Just a moment, Mr. Robinette. Before you answer that question it is proper for me to tell you that you may refuse to answer the question on the ground that it may tend to criminate you. If you do refuse to answer the question on that ground, I may direct you to answer, and your answer cannot be used against you in any subsequent prosecution except a prosecution for perjury in giving such evidence. Do you understand that?

Witness: Not quite, my Lord.

His Lordship: That is the sort of question that, when it is put to you, you can refuse to answer, if it will tend to criminate you; that is, if it tends to subject you to further criminal proceedings for that offence. Do you want to claim that privilege?

Witness: Yes.

His Lordship: You will be compelled to answer but any answer you make cannot hereafter be used against you in any prosecution arising out of the giving of the evidence. Your answer cannot be used against you.

Witness: Thank you, my Lord.

Mr. Robinette: Are you going to answer my question?

His Lordship: I direct you to answer.

Witness: Yes.

Q. You did?
A. Yes.

Q. You forged your mother-in-law's signature to two
   baby bonus cheques. That is correct, isn't it?

A. Yes.

Q. More than two or just two?

A. Just two.

Q. And as a result of that you subsequently repaid the
   moneys that you obtained on the forged cheques?
   You repaid the moneys to your mother-in-law?

A. Yes.

Q. Mrs. Venator. Is that correct?

A. Yes.

Q. That is all, thank you.

I have set out this cross-examination in some detail because it illustrates the style that I was to witness so many times. Robinette rarely made a frontal attack on a witness. He did not have the "go for the jugular" approach of well-known lawyers G. Arthur Martin and Charles Dubin, I think because he recognized that he could not do it effectively. Martin and Dubin, by persistently attacking the accuracy of details in a witness's testimony, by challenging the witness with internal inconsistencies in what he or she said, by confronting the witness with documents and conflicting evidence of other witnesses and pressing their verbal attack without letting up, managed to make the witness look foolish and, most valuable of all, unreliable. But it is very difficult to accomplish this. A full-blown frontal attack raises expectations in the Court and in your client. If it fails, a lot of wind is taken from the sails of your case. Too many counsel today try to emulate Martin and Dubin's approach, but they do so by hurling themselves at the witnesses and attempting to browbeat them into submission. This seldom works, but unfortunately a number of modern trial judges have had so little effective trial experience that they seem impressed by a cross-examination that is in reality little more than a shouting match.

The approach demonstrated in the above excerpt from the transcript has the major advantage of not getting the cross-examiner into trouble. By the use of limited open or closed questions that could only be answered by short responses, Robinette controlled the witness and gave him no opportunity to make a speech or repeat what he had already said in his examination-in-chief. In critiquing Boehler's cross-examination, it is important to note what Robinette did not do. He did not ask Boehler a single question about the substance of his testimony even when he had the opportunity to confront him with inconsistencies in his testimony-in-chief. There were no questions such as "How far were you from the car when you first saw it?", "How close were you to Mrs. Dick when you first saw her?", or "Where is this logbook of other cars you have pulled out of the ditch?" Robinette's position was that the witness's evidence had been made out of whole cloth. He was not going to give the evidence any semblance of veracity by suggesting that Boehler might simply be inconsistent as to detail. For the same reason there was no confrontation of the witness. Robinette would not give him the opportunity to insist that he saw and heard what he said he saw and heard. His stance was that the witness was a pathological liar and his testimony was worthless.

To make an analogy to pitching in baseball, Robinette was a control pitcher, not a power thrower. He relied on knowing the batters and knowing his pitches. He would not try to overpower a batter; he would try to get him to go after a bad pitch. He would keep his pitches on the corners of the plate and never throw the ball down the centre of the plate. Just as an experienced pitcher will not try to do too much with his pitches, relying on his defence to help him out, Robinette never counted on his cross-examination to win a case. He used it to move his case along by setting the groundwork for the witnesses that he was prepared to call. He lived by the number one rule of cross-examination — that it should never cost your client the case.

When it came time for the defence, Robinette called Earl Jack, Chief of Police of Dundas, as a witness.[41] He testified that he knew Frank Boehler. Anticipating what was to follow and not waiting for the Crown to object, Chief Justice McRuer asked the jury to retire. He then asked Robinette what the nature of Jack's evidence was. When told it related to the character of Boehler, McRuer insisted that he wanted to hear, while the jury was absent, the questions that would be asked of Jack. This is called a *voir dire*, "a trial within a trial," and is designed to decide controversial evidentiary problems in the absence of the jury so that if the evidence is ruled inadmissible in whole or in part, the jury will not have been tainted by having heard the evidence. In practice, one of the counsel alerts the judge that he will be leading evidence that he understands "his friend" objects to, and the judge then asks the jury to withdraw. Counsel proffering the witness then describes the challenged evidence. Sometimes it is actually given in evidence. Both counsel submit arguments as to the admissibility of the evidence and the trial judge makes a ruling.

What happened in this case was truly amazing. The Chief Justice simply took over the conduct of the *voir dire* without any encouragement by the Crown. The following reflects a pattern of paternalistic intervention by McRuer that we will see repeated later in the Suchan and Jackson murder trial. In answer to a question by Robinette, Jack stated that he had been chief of police for eight years and had known Boehler for seven years as a resident of the outskirts of Dundas. The questioning proceeded:

Robinette:	Do you know [Boehler's] reputation for truthfulness in the community?
Witness:	I can only speak from my personal contact with him myself.
Robinette:	What is the reputation?
McRuer:	Oh, no. Personal contact is one thing; reputation in the community is quite another.
Robinette:	I think the witness should be given an explanation.
McRuer:	No, he is asked a question; does he know his reputation for truthfulness

in the community. We can get into an investigation that is quite irrelevant. [McRuer then puts Robinette's initial question to the witness.]

Witness: I can't speak for the community.

Robinette: I am only asking the witness to speak as to his knowledge of what the reputation is. He is not called upon to speak for the community. I think the witness misunderstands it.

McRuer: [To the witness] Do you know his reputation in the community?

Witness: Should I take that both good and bad?

McRuer: You are first asked if you know what his reputation is in the community for truthfulness, if he has one at all?

Witness: Yes.

Robinette: You said yes? What is that reputation of Boehler in the community for truthfulness?

Witness: It is none too good.

Robinette: Would you believe Boehler's testimony on oath?

McRuer: No. [And then reconsidering] It will do no harm on this voir dire.

Robinette:	Let us go back. You say not so good.
Rigney:	[Coming alive at last.] None too good, he said.
McRuer:	This is a very narrow compass, this sort of evidence.
Robinette:	There are three questions that can be asked. I think I am entitled to put to the witness now: Would you believe Frank Boehler under oath?
Witness:	I would be very skeptical of his truth under oath.
McRuer:	[To Robinette] Have you got your authorities on this? Probably it would be better to exhaust the voir dire first before we discuss the questions that might or might not be put. Have you finished your examination?
Robinette:	Yes.

Rigney, in cross-examining Chief Jack, established that Dundas had a population of about six thousand and was an industrial town with a fairly large foreign population. He got the Police Chief to agree that his knowledge of Boehler's lack of truthfulness was based on his own experience and on conversations and rumours he had heard. These latter included things he heard from Boehler's in-laws, who said he had fraudulently cashed their cheques, and from the Powell Company after it alleged that Boehler had broken into their store at night and discharged him from his job. Boehler also claimed $35 from a taxi company for a lost diamond ring that was later found on his finger. The Police Chief finally said that his conversations with the townspeople suggested "they do not put too much credence in what Boehler says."

What followed next was an argument on the admissibility of character evidence regarding Boehler. McRuer was finally persuaded that three questions could be put to Police Chief Jack, and he did so himself:

McRuer: Now, witness, be very careful and get in your mind what I am putting to you, not from individual experiences, except as they may apply to your general knowledge. Do you know the reputation of Boehler for truth and veracity in the community in which he resides?

Witness: Yes.

McRuer: You know his reputation?

Witness: Yes.

McRuer: What do you say as to whether his reputation is good or bad? That is the reputation, not your opinion that you have formed from your particular experiences.

Witness: I would have to say bad, sir.

McRuer: And then what do you say from that reputation, would you believe him on his oath?

Witness: I would be very skeptical of that, sir.

McRuer: That is not very clear. I will permit you to ask the questions, Mr. Robinette.

The jury was recalled, and Robinette asked the witness the questions that McRuer permitted and received the exact same answers. By sanitizing the testimony of Chief Jack throughout this *voir dire* and determining the questions and answers in advance, McRuer denied the jury access to the process of determining those questions and answers, in particular the impact of the cross-examination of Rigney, which he was wise enough not to repeat. Instead Rigney restricted himself to the approved questions.

Rigney: What is your understanding of the meaning of "skeptical"?

Witness: I am leery, in other words.

McRuer: You take it with reservations?

Witness: Yes. I was skeptical in this way, that I am not here to judge as to his honesty in this particular case; I am skeptical if I were dealing with him personally as to his honesty.

Rigney: As to his honesty? And that is all you wish to be understood as speaking about?

Witness: That is right.

Chief Jack was re-examined by Robinette:

Robinette: I asked you what the opinion of the community was for truthfulness. My friend has emphasized honesty. What do you say about truthfulness?

Rigney: Is my friend allowed to go over this a second time?

Robinette:	I am allowed to re-examine.
McRuer:	I would have thought an honest person and true person ...
Robinette:	It may be the same thing.
Witness:	That is the interpretation I got; honesty and truthfulness was the same thing.

That is how the evidence ended. The last testimony that the jury heard was the testimony of the discredited Boehler, the Crown's only eyewitness. In a tactical role change, Robinette built up Boehler's importance in his closing address to the jury. He said, "All this circumstantial evidence is ambiguous, but the linchpin of the Crown's case is this man Boehler, he is their important witness. What do you think of Boehler?"[42] Judging by their verdict, the jury's answer was, "Not much!" They acquitted Evelyn Dick.

It was McRuer's practice to thank jurors for their careful attention to the evidence and for the serious public duty they had performed. This time he did not do so.

This was not the end of the matter, though. The Crown appealed the jury's verdict of acquittal and raised again the question of the admissibility of the statements of Mrs. Dick. The appeal came on before the same panel that heard the first appeal. This was not good news for the Crown when its sole ground of appeal was the admissibility of the statements that this panel had unanimously ruled were inadmissible. And now, Robinette had a friend in court. Chief Justice Robertson and McRuer shared a healthy dislike for each other, and the former never missed an opportunity to straighten the latter out. In this instance he was offended by McRuer's treatment of his, Robertson's, judgment in the first Dick appeal.

The argument proceeded on April 23 and 24, 1947.[43] A new Crown Counsel appeared in addition to Clifford Magone. He was William B. Common, K.C., who was soon to establish himself as the lead counsel

The author standing by the Cleve Horn portrait of mentor and friend
John J. Robinette.

Robinette's father, T.C. Robinette, a well-known criminal lawyer in Toronto at the turn of the twentieth century.

Robinette's Osgoode Hall Law School graduation photograph, 1929.

Robinette suddenly becomes famous as the defender of Evelyn Dick in her murder trial.

Accused murderer and media cause célèbre Evelyn Dick.

William Bohozuk, Evelyn Dick's lover and co-accused, entering the courthouse.

The curious crowd at Evelyn Dick's first trial, October 19, 1946.

*Robinette with Evelyn
Dick's mother, Mrs.
Alexander MacLean.*

*Mrs. MacLean and
daughter, in 1947.*

Renowned Boyd Gang members Steven Suchan (left) and Leonard Jackson.

Sergeant of Detectives Edmund Tong of the Toronto Police, who tracked down fugitives Suchan and Jackson.

In happier days, detectives Roy Perry (left) and Edmund Tong.

Robinette's first press photo, c. 1940.

An uncharacteristically pensive Mayor Alan Lamport appears with Robinette's associate, John Brooke, before Toronto City Council.

A stylish Leo Landreville scowls for the press.

Work never far from his reach, the lawyer relaxes at home, c. 1950.

for the Crown in appeals in criminal cases. In my opinion he developed into the quintessential deputy attorney general. He was a good, not a great, counsel but deeply wise and infinitely fair. In the second Dick appeal he received a sympathetic hearing with his opening remarks, but the atmosphere became frostier when Magone started to speak.

Magone said that the Court of Appeal directed a new trial without restrictions. The sole issue at the trial was the guilt or innocence of the accused. It followed, he said, that all necessary facts must be found at that trial by the appropriate tribunal. The question of fact as to the voluntary nature of the statements was for the trial judge, without any restriction resulting from the judgment of the appeal court. While the facts may be "identical," as stated by him, the evidence on which he found those facts was different, and it was therefore open to him to admit the statements. Chief Justice Robertson interjected, "Did this Court not have to decide, as a matter of law, that these particular statements were not admissible, and was the trial judge not bound to follow that decision?" Magone replied, "I submit not, because this Court's finding as to their admissibility was based on a finding that they were not voluntary, and that finding was for the new trial judge to make, unfettered by any previous decision."

Robinette was quick to point out the inconsistencies in the Crown's position on this appeal as opposed to the first appeal and at the second trial. He stressed that at the last appeal, counsel for the Crown definitely took the position that the statements other than those of April 12 were not confessions, but only self-serving statements, not subject to the rules of confessions. Counsel for the Crown at this trial took precisely the same position. That being so, he said, the Crown cannot seek to have a third trial, based upon a different theory. "The Crown's right of appeal is limited to questions of law alone, and if the question here involved is not one of law alone, there is no right to come to this Court. Additionally, in considering a Crown appeal … the appellant should show that there would probably have been a different result."

Robinette then dealt with Evelyn Dick's statements:

> As to those statements which were dealt with by this
> Court on the first appeal, the trial judge was bound in

law to follow the judgment on that appeal. That judgment held the statements to be inadmissible because of the cumulative effect of many factors, which the trial judge here did not even consider in saying what he would have done. As to the statements, which were not before this Court formerly, there are only three which have any relevance to the charge. Two of them were wholly exculpatory, and the Crown is not entitled to a new trial for the purpose of giving them in evidence. The trial judge, in his discretion, rejected the third on quite different grounds. As to the statement of the 12th of April, the trial judge would have rejected it independently of the judgment on the former appeal, because no caution was given.

Robinette concluded, "The decision of this Court as to the admissibility of the seven statements constitutes *res judicata* [the matter has been heard and decided] as between the Crown and the respondent on this charge."

On July 16, Chief Justice Robertson, speaking for the entire five-man court, gave the judgment dismissing the appeal. He went into the facts in great detail but said:

I do not propose to discuss the question whether the learned Chief Justice of the High Court was bound to follow (not infrequently against his own opinion) the judgment of the Court of Appeal on the former appeal. Neither do I intend to discuss in detail the numerous reported cases cited by the Chief Justice in support of his own opinion. In the main, the reasons that, in my opinion, support the rejection of the statements in question are to be found in the reasons for judgment on the first appeal.

Towards the end of the judgment the Chief Justice gave a carefully worded warning to the police to the effect that the pressures they were under to solve serious crimes of the nature of the Dick case did not excuse them from following established rules with respect to confessions. He said:

> There has been, in recent years, a marked increase in the number of cases of serious crimes in which incriminating statements of the accused have been tendered in evidence, and dispute as to the admissibility of such evidence in the particular case has required the hearing of witnesses on the *voir dire*. Such a proceeding was formerly a rather rare event. In part, no doubt, this increase is due to an increase in the number of cases of serious crimes that come before the Courts. In part, however, it is due, particularly in some of the larger centres of population, to the adoption by the police of new methods of obtaining the evidence necessary to a conviction. It is important that the Courts should see that the practice is exercised within proper limits, if they are to act upon evidence so obtained. This is not to establish any new law. It is nothing more than the application of long-established principles of the law of evidence to new conditions or practices.

As an end note to these appeals I must relate that according to Patrick Boyer,[44] when Chief Justice McRuer read the decision he met privately with the Crown lawyers and suggested to them how they could strengthen their arguments on an appeal to the Supreme Court of Canada. This was egregiously irregular, but fortunately, wiser heads prevailed, and the case against Evelyn Dick for the murder of her husband was closed.

Still outstanding on her docket was the charge of murdering her infant boy, Peter David White MacLean. She appeared with William Bohozuk to answer to this charge before Justice Arthur LeBel at the spring court session in Hamilton. Once again Rigney and McCulloch appeared for the Crown, Martin and Schreiber for Bohozuk, and Robinette for Mrs. Dick. These regular meetings of counsel were beginning to resemble a series of bar reunions. The Crown again elected to proceed first against Mrs. Dick.

The Crown's case was very simple. There were no inculpatory statements by Mrs. Dick. The evidence against her was entirely circumstantial — but it was damning. Robinette, while keeping alive the possibility that the baby boy may have died of natural causes, was fighting from the outset for a reduced verdict of manslaughter. The hopelessness of the suggestion that the boy might have died of natural causes was highlighted by Justice LeBel in his summation to the jury of the circumstantial evidence on the cause of death. He said:

> Are children who die from natural causes encased in cement and kept locked in a suitcase? Is an eighteen inch child stuffed into a thirteen inch zippered bag, kept sealed, one that is likely to have died from natural causes? These are the questions, gentlemen, that you have to consider in the light of the evidence. Consider the cord around the neck of this infant. It is significant, you may think, or you may think otherwise. Its value is for you to determine. The loop was five inches in circumference: a normal child's neck, seven to ten inches, and this was a large child. The cord in Dr. Deadman's opinion was evidence of death by strangulation. Pathologically he could not support strangulation as the cause of death, but it is not absolutely necessary that he give the cause of death from pathological findings. He could not say that the cord was put about the child's neck before or after death, and therefore his opinion is subject to that very important qualification.[45]

So much for death by natural causes. The real question was whether the evidence connected Evelyn Dick to the death of her child beyond a reasonable doubt. The evidence established that the baby boy was perfectly healthy when he left the hospital with his mother. Evelyn arrived at her Rosslyn Avenue home without the baby. He was never seen alive again. She told her mother that the Children's Aid Society was going to take the boy in for adoption, but this was proved a lie by the society, which had not received an application for adoption. The police officers found at the Rosslyn Avenue house the suitcase, the cement, and a Red Cross uniform that belonged to Mrs. Dick. All these items were associated with the dead body of the baby.

No defence witnesses were called. Robinette relied solely on his considerable powers of persuasion with the jury to raise a reasonable doubt. He was successful in part, and it was a significant part. The jury returned a verdict of not guilty of murder but guilty of manslaughter. Robinette had undoubtedly saved his client's life, and largely on the strength of his arguments in the two appeals.

At the sentence hearing, Robinette called Dr. Robert Alexander Finlayson, a practising psychiatrist from Hamilton, who testified that he had examined Mrs. Dick and gave his opinion that she had a mental age of thirteen years with a mental capacity of "dull normal," near the borderline between "dull normal" and "moron." This must have come as a surprise to the police officers who interrogated her, because there was nothing in their testimony to suggest that they were dealing with a woman of diminished mental capacity. They were perhaps overly impressed with the fact, agreed to by Dr. Finlayson, that she had a very good memory. Justice LeBel took this evidence into consideration in sentencing Mrs. Dick to life imprisonment. She was to be released on parole in eleven years.

Next it was Bohozuk's turn. He was arraigned for the murder of the infant boy and pleaded not guilty. The Crown called the same evidence as in the Evelyn Dick case but added the appearance of Mrs. Dick in the witness box as a Crown witness. True to form, she refused to be sworn or give testimony and was found in contempt. In the circumstances, the Crown proffered the transcript of the evidence given by Mrs. Dick at Bohozuk's preliminary hearing in the infant death case. Over objection, the transcript was admitted. Bohozuk took the stand in his own defence and denied both that he was the father of the infant boy and that he had murdered the infant boy. While he was at it, he denied that he had murdered anyone. He swore that his relationship with Mrs. Dick did not arise until after she was married and that the relationship was never more than a casual friendship. His wife also testified and

John J. Robinette

supported him in this version of the relationship. The jury was apparently impressed by the vigour of the defence, and took only ten minutes to find Bohozuk not guilty.

There were still some loose ends in what the media had described as the "torso case." Bohozuk was arraigned with Donald MacLean for the murder of John Dick. The familiar routine of calling Mrs. Dick as a witness was repeated, and she ended up with another finding of contempt. She seemed to regard these contempt findings as a badge of honour: this time she thanked the trial judge before being escorted away. However, without her testimony, the Crown was forced to concede that it had no case against Bohozuk. Justice LeBel directed the jury to bring in a verdict of not guilty against Bohozuk, which they did. The trial continued against MacLean alone.

MacLean's trial proceeded apace, but MacLean's counsel, Walter Tuchtie, decided that this matter needed closure, to use an expression that is currently popular. He had discussions with Rigney, who then presented a fresh indictment to the hastily recalled grand jury, charging MacLean with being an accessory after the fact to the murder of John Dick. There had been a plea bargain. MacLean had agreed through his counsel to plead guilty to this reduced charge in return for the Crown dropping the more serious charge of murder. The mechanics of this judicially sanctioned arrangement were carried out by Rigney's announcement to the Court that he was offering no further evidence on the murder charge. Justice LeBel, who had been advised of this arrangement, instructed the jury to bring in a verdict of not guilty on the murder charge. The jury did this without leaving the jury box. MacLean was then arraigned on the new charge to which he pleaded guilty. The jury was discharged, and evidence was led before LeBel as to sentence. Taking into his consideration the age of the accused, his failing health, and the fact that he had already served a year in custody, Justice LeBel sentenced MacLean to five years in the penitentiary.

And so the great torso murder case ended with a whimper, not a bang. No one had killed John Dick so far as the institution of justice was concerned. And as Arthur Martin was to later say in a tribute to Robinette's achievements at a dinner at the Four Seasons Hotel in

Toronto on October 23, 1989, "The theory that John Dick committed suicide and then decapitated himself seems rather unlikely."[46]

The identity of the killer of John Dick remains a mystery that continues to fascinate the public. My wife, Joan, and I attended the Winter Garden Theatre in November 1991 to watch a stage play written by Douglas Rodger, *How Could You, Mrs. Dick?* I did not need the explanation in the program to understand the title. It came from a piece of doggerel chanted by Hamilton schoolboys in 1946 and 1947:

> You cut off his head.
> You cut off his arms.
> You cut off his legs.
> How could you, Mrs. Dick?

The play was very well performed and I particularly enjoyed the characterizations of the principal players as presented by the actors. It soon emerged that the twin fascinations of the author of the play were the suggested incestuous relationship between Evelyn and her father and the question of her involvement in the murder of her husband.

Robinette began living at Central Park Lodge during the summer of 1991, and I visited him there regularly. At that point, although his mental condition was deteriorating, he was lucid and great company so long as the visitor did not tire him by staying too long. I very much enjoyed these visits in his early days at the lodge. My wife used to tease me that I had him all to myself for the first time since I met him. Sadly, as his dreadful disease overwhelmed his faculties and he was reduced to child-like incomprehension, the visits became increasingly painful. However, 1991 was a good year.

After watching the play, I had an inspiration. Arthur Martin was now a colleague of mine on the Ontario Court of Appeal. Like many people who learned of the nature of Robinette's illness, he became distressed to the point of denial. Martin did not want to see his old friend because he did not want to see him in a reduced mental state. After all, Robinette was the man Martin had praised only two years earlier as "the peerless advocate, at home in any court, before any tribunal in any kind of case and pre-eminent in every facet of advocacy."[47] By grim irony, Martin himself was to suffer from the same or similar mental illness, one that made him a prisoner of his own body, sheltered from his friends during the extended period before his own death by his loving and protective sister, Arlene. However, Martin had repeatedly asked me about Robinette, and I gave him descriptions of my visits that I thought were upbeat. On more than one occasion he had assuaged his conscience by asking me if he could come with me on one of my visits "when I thought it would be a good time." This was the time.

The meeting of the two true brothers in the law still evokes nostalgia in me. I had seen both of them together in happier years and shared with them the zest of their companionship. They were fast friends who enjoyed the easy camaraderie and mutual self-assurance of those who are at the top of their craft. This meeting started out with both men feeling uncomfortable. Martin did not know what to say, and Robinette was embarrassed because he knew that Martin knew why he was at the lodge. However, I cheerily introduced the subject of *How Could You, Mrs. Dick?* and said that Joan and I had been to see the play a few nights earlier. They both perked up and asked about the play. Soon they were deep in their own reminiscences of the real trials of Evelyn Dick and the events that surrounded them. It was an enchanted moment. The two aged warriors remembered with astonishing clarity this old battle that was pivotal to both of their careers, Robinette's more than Martin's. They described the players: the judges, the lawyers, the accused, and the principal witnesses. They both chuckled over Frank Boehler and agreed that he was a disaster for the Crown.

When they appeared to be running down, I brought up that one of the themes of the play related to the question of Evelyn Dick's intelligence. This had led in the play to speculation over her guilt in the murder of her husband. Martin and Robinette were happy to talk about Mrs. Dick — they thought that she was not too bright and a pathological liar to boot — but they left the subject of her guilt alone. After more conversation, sensing that Robinette was tiring, I suggested to Martin that we take our leave, and we did. Martin never visited Robinette again.

This was not the end of the topic so far as I was concerned. On my next regular visit, which was about a week or ten days later, I reintroduced the subject of the play. I pointed out to Robinette that he and Martin had said a great deal about the trial and about Mrs. Dick, but neither had said anything when I raised the question of whether she was guilty. I paused and looked straight at Robinette. He said nothing. I kept looking at him. He finally said, "No, we didn't." When I continued to wait, he added, by way of explanation, "It wasn't relevant."

Chapter Five
McCarthy & McCarthy

W HEN JOHN ROBINETTE JOINED McCARTHY & McCarthy as counsel in 1949 at the age of forty-three, the firm was over ninety years old. If it wasn't the oldest continuous law firm in Ontario, it was certainly close to it. It was founded in Barrie, Ontario, in 1855 by D'Alton McCarthy, Sr., and D'Arcy Boulton under the name of Boulton and McCarthy.

D'Alton, Sr., was born in Dublin, Ireland, in 1805. The official history of McCarthy & McCarthy[48] notes that the McCarthys, like all Irishmen, were descended from kings. I was intrigued to learn that the founder of my old law firm traced his lineage back to Dermot McCarthy, king of South Munster, who built the original Blarney Castle, the present home of the famous Blarney Stone.

D'Alton, Sr., practised law successfully in Dublin and was looking forward to an early retirement when the financial losses of his partner depleted his modest fortune. He decided to start a different life in the newly formed Province of Canada, and in 1847 he emigrated from Ireland and arrived in the Barrie area with his wife and children. He tried farming initially, but he was not a farmer and was forced to return to the practice of law. He received his call to the bar in his new homeland in 1855 at the age of fifty. His son, D'Alton McCarthy, Jr., who had come with him from Ireland as a boy, joined him at Boulton and McCarthy in 1858. D'Alton, Jr., was twenty-two at the time. He had spectacular ability, and he used it to combine a brilliant career in the law and in public life as a member of Parliament. The firm became

McCarthy & McCarthy in 1870 and retained the name until the death of D'Alton, Sr., in 1873. Thereupon it became McCarthy, Boys and Pepler.

As this is not a history of my old firm, I will skip over a lot of interesting material in the firm history describing the fascinating lives of members of the McCarthy clan. D'Alton, Jr., fulfilled his promise and became one of the best-known courtroom lawyers in the country. He built a large and busy practice in Barrie, but the pressures of his professional and public life continually brought him to Toronto, and he finally relocated there in 1876 with his firm, then named McCarthy, Hoskin and Creelman. The next step was a merger with a firm founded by Britton Bath Osler, a litigator with a reputation almost as impressive as that of D'Alton, Jr. A new firm emerged in 1883 known as McCarthy, Osler, Hoskin & Creelman and later in 1903 as McCarthy, Osler, Hoskin & Harcourt. It was the second-largest law firm in Canada, behind Blake, Lash and Cassels. It existed in this form until 1916.

Both the McCarthy and Osler law firms that were behind this merger were family dynasties. The next generation of the McCarthy clan consisted of D'Alton McCarthy's son, D'Alton Lally (Lally), his nephew, Leighton, and B.B. Osler's nephews, H.S. Osler and Britton Osler. The untimely death of D'Alton, Jr., in 1898 at the age of sixty-two following injury in a horse-drawn carriage accident changed the leadership of the firm. Ultimately the merger could not be kept intact; Leighton McCarthy decided that he could support his own firm and in 1916 he left with his brother, Frank, and his cousin, Lally, to form the nucleus of the McCarthy & McCarthy firm that was so prominent in the profession when I joined it as an articling student in 1951. He also took with him the Canada Life Assurance Company, which was probably the pre-eminent client of the firm in 1951 and for many years after. The Osler branch of the firm remained as Osler, Harcourt and Harcourt. What is interesting to me is that at the time I joined McCarthys, Blake Cassels & Graydon, Osler Hoskin & Harcourt, and McCarthy & McCarthy continued to be the three largest law firms in Canada.

Rare as continuity is these days, it is worth observing that in the case of my old law firm, it has had a McCarthy in its name from its inception. It is also significant that the sizes of the firms remained relatively constant in those days. I do not think that any one of them had more than a dozen solicitors in 1916; by 1951, on my headcount, McCarthys and Oslers each had about sixteen lawyers, and Blakes had one or two more. This was to change, but the change was gradual until recently. I remember my horror at attending a dinner for a retiring partner and good friend, Peter Beatty, in May 2001. He was the only one retiring, but as a sort of by the way we were told by Neils Ortved, the chairman of what is now McCarthy Tétrault, that the occasion would also celebrate the introduction of new associates to the firm: *ninety* of them. I was reminded that following its merger with Clarkson, Tétrault in 1990, some five years after I had left the firm to accept an appointment to the bench, McCarthy Tétrault had become a truly national law firm and was the largest in Canada with a complement of some 740 lawyers.

Frank McCarthy was the McCarthy presence when I started with the firm in 1951, at the age of twenty-three. I remember him well. He was a wonderful man who was blunt to the point of rudeness, but he represented an integrity and sense of duty that was an inspiration to a young law student who had come to his articles-at-law with the suspicion that lawyers were interested pretty much in looking after themselves. He taught me to put the client and the firm first and in that order.

Frank had no interest in public life and was content to become a highly respected corporate and commercial lawyer looking after work generated by the more entrepreneurial Leighton. Frank was, I am told, a gregarious and jovial man before he was devastated by two terrible losses in his family life. The first was the loss of his beloved wife in 1930. He then turned his full attention to his son, William Francis, who by the early 1940s was an articling student at the law firm and finishing a brilliant academic career. Young McCarthy joined the RCAF as a pilot officer and was stationed in England. He was killed in action in 1942 at the age of twenty-two.

Frank had lived in the shadow of his brother, Leighton, fourteen years his senior, whose active public and business life, as well as his life in the law, merits a book by itself. But by 1946, at the age of seventy-seven, Leighton was fully retired from McCarthys and almost retired from business. He died in 1952 at the age of eighty-three. Lally, too, had since left the firm, after some disagreements with the McCarthy brothers. Matters came to a head with Lally in 1931, when the firm decided to move with Canada Life from 46 King Street to the new Canada Life Building at the northwest corner of Queen and University Avenue. Lally said he did not want "to move out to the country" and remained behind.

At about the time I arrived at the firm, Frank was concerned about another problem that bothered him greatly: one that would involve Robinette and, to a much lesser extent, me. The problem concerned a will that he had drawn for an old family friend and the president of Canada Life, Herbert C. Cox. Cox wanted to leave the majority of his estate to a charitable trust to be administered for the benefit of employees and former employees of Canada Life. The provisions of the will relating to the charitable trust were under attack on the grounds that they were directed to a non-charitable purpose. I will return to this again.

Frank McCarthy had a great sense of the firm as an institution and was totally dedicated to its best interests as a firm and not just a place for individuals to practise law. Some younger lawyers, Salter Hayden, Beverley Matthews, James Walker, and Jack Blain, joined him in this sentiment. However, the Second World War intervened, and Matthews, Walker, Blain, and others enlisted in the armed forces and served overseas. It fell on Frank McCarthy, along with Senator Hayden, Bill Terry, and "Duke" West, to carry the load at home. It was decided that in fairness to those who served, the firm would remain unchanged until their return.

Frank and his partners were true to their word. The firm did not change at all. Matthews, Walker, and Blain returned from the war in 1945, and Matthews and Walker became partners, along with Bill Terry, in 1947. In the spirit of what had always been intended, Frank gave up his role as senior partner the same year and continued as counsel until his death in 1964 at the age of eighty-two. However, he was still a force in 1951 and for a few years thereafter.

This was unfortunate in a way, because he and those who had kept the home fires burning still seemed dedicated to the status quo as far as the development of the firm was concerned. Matthews complained to me on more than one occasion that Frank, backed up by West and Terry, thought the firm was big enough. When Matthews said we needed new clients, Frank's reply was, "We have no one to do the work." When it was suggested that the firm take on new lawyers, Frank asked, "What would they do?"

However, this was all to change under the patient prodding of Matthews, who is justifiably credited with being the architect of the post-war McCarthy & McCarthy. He had a distinct vision for the future of the firm as a full-service law firm with a national and even international outreach. To this end he started recruiting talent and soliciting clients — big clients. I can remember walking into his office one day where he sat as usual behind a clean desk with a single piece of paper on it. It was a list of the most prominent corporate clients in the firm. "George," he said, "we don't have a railroad as a client." A railroad was the prestigious type of client that Matthews cherished. John Clarry told me that on one occasion, Matthews approached him to write an article for the business section of the *Globe and Mail* criticizing excessive corporate and personal income taxes. "We want to be known as 'the friend of the rich,'" he said.

We never did get a railroad, as far as I can recollect, but Matthews certainly got the equivalent of one in his talent hunt when he persuaded John Robinette to join the firm in 1949. Matthews recognized that McCarthy & McCarthy had a well-earned reputation as a litigation firm, thanks to the near celebrity status of counsel such as D'Arcy, Jr., and Lally McCarthy. That reputation had been sustained through the war by the young Salter Hayden. However, Hayden, now Senator Hayden, had pretty much transferred his considerable talents from the courtroom to the boardroom. As we shall see later in the libel action he handled for Mayor Alan Lamport, the transition was a wise one. Only the belated retainer of Robinette to argue the appeal in that case prevented a complete disaster.

Matthews was a year younger than Robinette, and they had gone through UTS together. Robinette has laughingly described his hockey experience as the goalie for the UTS entry into the juvenile hockey league. The manager of the team was Matthews. I never dared ask either of them how good a team it was. The important thing was that they became good friends and remained so until Robinette died. Matthews followed Robinette through law school at Osgoode Hall, and in 1930 he received the Gold Medal, one year after Robinette had accomplished the feat.

And so when Matthews was looking around for a counsel to kick-start the somnolent McCarthy litigation department, he needed look no further than his old friend. Robinette credits Matthews with persuading him to join the firm as counsel. In hockey parlance, Matthews had signed a franchise player.[49] As an unexpected bonus, Robinette brought with him his junior, John Brooke, a promising young counsel in his own right and soon to be a very close friend of mine.

McCarthy & McCarthy was to expand by leaps and bounds, but it was not altogether because of Matthews's activities. Other firms, including our perennial rivals, Blakes and Oslers, participated in the boom that followed the war, continuing unabated to the present time. Its impact was first felt in the 1950s when we witnessed a great growth in the scope, diversity, and complexity of the practice of law. The expansion and diversification of McCarthy & McCarthy was matched by a number of its clients and reflected the abundant growth in the Canadian economy, the development of new technology, the increased sophistication in public financing, and the emergence of massive capital projects. In some of these areas, McCarthys was in the forefront of adapting legal concepts and precedents to the new age.

By the simple act of joining McCarthys, Robinette gave the firm enhanced credibility. His legal opinions on behalf of the firm were vital to the implementation of the resourceful legal initiatives by the real estate and commercial departments, which in turn were a necessary part of the firm's participation in the residential, commercial, and manufacturing resurgence starting in the 1950s. Illustrative of the challenges we met is the story of one client, Northern Ontario Natural Gas Limited.

In the early 1950s, the development boom in Western Canadian oil and gas created demands for greatly increased new capital for Western Canada and led to the tapping of American financial markets for both debt and equity. This involved the development of joint Canadian and American public offerings, which necessitated concurrent compliance with the requirements of the Securities and Exchange Commission in the U.S. and the various Canadian securities commissions, notably the Ontario Securities Commission. McCarthy & McCarthy participated in these activities from the outset.

Increasing discoveries of natural gas in Western Canada led to proposals for a trans-Canada pipeline, and, in anticipation of the building of the pipeline, the establishment of local distribution utilities in the Ontario communities that would eventually be served with gas. A very simple and limited procedure for approving municipal franchises and authorizing the construction of gas works had existed since pre-war days. However, the advent of massive new supplies of natural gas saw the reinvention and rejuvenation of the Ontario Fuel Board (soon to be renamed the Ontario Energy Board), under the chairmanship of the former gas commissioner, Archie Crozier. A race began between rival interests to procure natural gas franchises in municipalities in Northern Ontario where the line was expected to go and in many other parts of Ontario as well. This was a new field for lawyers, particularly for me, fresh out of law school.

McCarthys was retained at the outset to act for the interests that later formed Northern Ontario Natural Gas Limited, popularly referred to as "NONG." NONG was the brainchild of Ralph Farris of Calgary and Vancouver and Spencer Clark of Seattle. Their Vancouver lawyers, the Farris law firm founded by Senator Farris, referred them to Beverley Matthews. Ralph Farris was the son of Senator Farris and the brother of John Farris, who later became the senior partner in the firm. The members of the Farris family were all headstrong, and this was to cost Ralph Farris in the years to come. However, he was a man of great personal charm and considerable magnetism. He was a born leader and tended to dominate any meeting he attended. I can remember meeting with him and Spencer Clark in Matthews's office when the two promoters first came to Toronto to explain what appeared to Matthews and me to be a somewhat visionary venture. They intended to have NONG enter into franchises for the distribution of natural gas with municipalities starting with Kenora near the Manitoba border and continuing eastward through the northland to pick up communities on the route of the Trans-Canada Highway all the way to Barrie, just north of Toronto.

Matthews was initially not much impressed with these "western cowboys" and placed their corporate affairs in the hands of John Lawson, a very able corporate lawyer, but one who did not have many more years at the bar than I did. He and I grew up together on this client's file. John looked after the corporate affairs and I was involved as counsel in representing NONG at public hearings and in administrative law proceedings before the Ontario Fuel Board, seeking to acquire these franchises and obtain approvals. In pursuing the franchises, Farris and Clark found that they had stiff competition from a local company at the

Lakehead, Twin City Gas. They also faced competition from local interests in Sudbury that wanted to have Sudbury operate its own municipal distribution utility, with its important industrial loads at International Nickel and Falconbridge Mines. From the south, the well-established Consumers Gas of Toronto, a former manufactured gas utility that was in the process of converting to natural gas, started an aggressive campaign to acquire distribution franchises moving up through Barrie, Huntsville, and other Muskoka municipalities.

McCarthys also acted for Lakeland Natural Gas Limited, which obtained franchises along Lake Ontario and the St. Lawrence River between Toronto and Montreal. Lakeland too was in competition with rival interests, notably Consumers Gas. The driving force behind Lakeland was George Gardiner, who along with his father, Percy Gardiner, had been clients of Senator Hayden's for many years. Since I was now one of the few lawyers in Ontario with experience in natural gas proceedings before the Ontario Fuel Board, and certainly the only one at McCarthys, I acted as counsel for Lakeland. There was no conflict of interest by the standards of the day. NONG was Matthews's client and Lakeland was Hayden's. I simply had to be careful to charge my time to the correct client's docket.

These proceedings before the Fuel Board were hotly contested, but in the end, NONG was to prevail in Northern Ontario. It acquired Twin City Gas through a share swap and persuaded the Sudbury City Council under the leadership of its politically ambitious mayor, Leo Landreville, to withdraw its support for a local gas utility and sign with NONG. In the end NONG acquired all the franchises it had initially sought except Barrie, which fell to Consumers Gas. Consumers did succeed in its eastern reach by acquiring Lakeland Natural Gas. Trans Canada Pipelines became the official carrier of the gas from Western Canada and everything appeared to be going smoothly.

Matthews and I were of a mind that NONG was a success and we both purchased stock in the company. Matthews also became a director of NONG. He did not realize what an embarrassment this share purchase would later prove to be for him. It was later to surface in the media that Landreville was alleged to have accepted shares in NONG in return for his assistance in obtaining the critical Sudbury franchise. Criminal charges were laid against NONG, Landreville, and Farris. I will deal with the fall-out to these allegations and Robinette's involvement in due course.

Following these regulatory fights in the mid-1950s, the challenging job of financing the huge capital investment needed to build the distribution systems and the cross-Canada transmission lines began. The public financing of NONG was the biggest coordinated operation conducted by McCarthys up to that time. It involved the participation of several of the lawyers engaged in commercial practice in addition to John Lawson and Jack Blain, who had done the corporate work for Lakeland. Jim Walker led the team of lawyers and the title searchers, whose searches covered much of Northern Ontario. The operation required, not surprisingly, legal opinions on some very difficult and important issues from John Robinette. This was the beginning of the development of a type of service that McCarthys equipped itself to provide as it grew in size and diversity, coordinating in one very large project the talents of different specialist portions of the firm. The pattern was followed in many subsequent financings.

Robinette became the cornerstone of what turned out to be the most formidable litigation department in Canada, but his relationship with McCarthys went beyond that. He enhanced the reputation of the entire firm. In this fluid era, when adjustment to the demands of a growing economy was an imperative, McCarthys' creative solicitors were modifying and expanding the traditional instruments of the common law relating to real property and working within the outmoded corporate structures to make these megaprojects a reality. They were resourceful in the use of conventional conveyancing instruments to permit the necessary land assemblage. They were obliged to develop strategies for encouraging the assistance of municipal and provincial land use authorities to assist in these acquisitions and they prepared careful and persuasive briefs to present to regulatory authorities.

Above all, they prepared the financial documents that secured the huge sums that had to be raised in domestic and international markets. The lenders of these moneys insisted on security, and security involved more than the issuance of a bond or a debenture; it also involved a validation of the process whereby the projects were assembled, constructed, and financed on an interim basis. Put simply, the legal initiatives required credibility, and it was credibility that Robinette's opinions brought to the process. With his solid record as a civil counsel, his background of academic excellence, and his years as a lecturer in the subjects of real property, mortgages, and equity, he had the credentials to command the respect of the profession and was able to support the bold initiatives put forward by the commercial and real estate branches of the firm.

In looking back on this era, I am reminded of an expression used initially, I believe, by Oka Jones, president of Consumers Gas. In describing the efforts by his company to introduce natural gas from the Eastern United States into Consumers' old manufactured gas distribution system, he said, "We are putting new wine into old bottles." This is what McCarthy & McCarthy was doing to the legal system that supported the commercial endeavours of its clients. I am thinking of such projects as the Toronto Dominion Tower and the Eaton Centre. The former, the product of the architectural genius of Ludwig Mies von der Rohe, preserved King and Bay as the financial capital of Canada. The latter created a spectacular shopping centre that is still one of the foremost drawing cards in Ontario for tourists.

Interestingly enough, while the firm placed the highest value on Robinette's opinions, Robinette himself did not give them high priority on his personal calendar of legal matters. I can remember Matthews descending on me one time demanding to know where Robinette was. A problem had come up in connection with a very large financing through a trust company whose business was very much coveted by McCarthys. An opinion on a critical legal question was required of Robinette immediately. I told Matthews that he was involved in a criminal jury case. His client was a restaurateur charged with arson in allegedly burning his own restaurant for the insurance. I could not say when the trial would be over. The senior partner was not amused and seemed to think the scheduling problem was my fault. Fortunately, time was not of the essence, as we lawyers like to say, and in due course Robinette delivered his opinion, and the trust company and my senior partner were mollified. The restaurateur was acquitted, but we did not press him to remain as a client.

Confidentiality concerns prevent me from giving specific examples of Robinette's opinions to which I have referred, although, for the most part, they are matters of public record. But I am not too sure that identifying some of them as bold, even though they have withstood the test of time and then some, would be appreciated by the members of my old firm who solicited these opinions. However, I will refer by way of illustration to one opinion that Robinette gave in relation to a matter that concerned me once we began working together in the early 1950s.

The Board of Education for the Township of Etobicoke was a client of the firm, and our office manager, Jack Parker, was the chairman of the board. I had been asked to look after its expropriation procedures for the acquisition of school sites. There was a great deal of school expansion in the 1950s in this prosperous and rapidly growing township, now part of Toronto proper. Through my work in this area I came to know Doug Emond, the business administrator of the board, very well. His confidence in me grew, and my area of advice expanded to the point where I was advising the board with respect to its legal powers generally.

Doug telephoned me one day to say that there had been a vigorous debate among the board members at their regular meeting the night before over the board's power to determine what school a particular pupil could attend. I forget the details of the controversy but remember that its genesis lay in a continuing conflict with separate school (Roman Catholic) supporters. They paid lower property taxes than public school supporters and yet opted to pay public school taxes when their children were of school age so that their children could attend the public schools, which were of a higher quality than their equivalents in the separate school system. This option could only work one way, because to qualify as a separate school supporter, a parent of the pupil had to swear an affidavit for the assessment commissioner in which he or she deposed that the parents were Roman Catholics. To qualify as a public school supporter, the Catholic parents simply declined to furnish such an affidavit until the pupil graduated from the public school system.

I might say in parenthesis that the Etobicoke Separate School Board did not favour this tactic either, pointing out to its constituents that it was the board's lack of a tax base that resulted in lesser funds being spent on the separate schools and that Roman Catholics who did not consistently support the separate school system were exacerbating the problem. I would also emphasize that the relationship between the two boards was excellent, to the point where the public school board arranged for a member of the separate board to sit on the public board in order to coordinate the activities of both boards in addressing common problems. It is of considerable interest that during my term as its legal adviser, the public board elected the separate school member, in recognition of his outstanding ability, as its chairman.

The immediate problem facing both school boards was that some parents, not only separate school supporters (although they triggered the controversy), were sending their children to schools that were outside the school district in which they paid their school taxes. The members of the board were divided on what they could or should do about it. The expedient, and it turned out to be no more than that, was to ask for a legal opinion. My opinion, which was sent in letter form, was that there was nothing in the relevant statutes governing the conduct of public schools that prohibited parents from making such a choice.

My letter was not well received, especially by the chairman of the board. While he was not a lawyer, he had been confident that my legal opinion would support his position that the children were restricted to the school districts in which their parents resided. He went over my head and complained to the senior partner responsible for this client, Bill Terry. Terry spoke to me and explained the practical implications of my opinion, including the fact that the Etobicoke Board of Education was a very good client that contributed substantial fees to the firm. I was insulted, but, aware of my junior status, I restricted myself to saying that I would change my opinion only if I could be shown some statute or other authority that I had overlooked. Terry thought about this, and taking a broader view of "authority" than I had in mind, asked me if I would take offence if he were to ask John Robinette for a second opinion. Having no basis for responding otherwise, I agreed.

Robinette's opinion was detailed and contrary to my view of the matter. He was of the opinion that the controlling *Public Schools Act* did give the board the power to restrict a pupil's attendance to the school district in which his or her parents owned property — for all practical purposes, where the parents lived. Robinette was very gracious in stating that he had the benefit of my opinion, and while acknowledging in effect that there was room for informed disagreement, he had his own view of the matter.

I had seen or been advised of Robinette's opinions in the important matters that I have referred to above. I thought some of them were pretty gutsy, to use the vernacular, but then I had not been involved in setting out the problem or doing any preliminary research, and I recognized that my observations were grossly uninformed. However, the Etobicoke board case was entirely different. I was familiar with all of the facts and references to authority in Robinette's opinion letter.

What was confirmed for me was that Robinette's opinions were indeed bold and, moreover, they were shaded in favour of the needs of the client. My opinion represented a strict construction of the statutory authority of the board of education. Robinette's was what we would now call "purposive," a word I do not fully understand, but one that is used freely by our Supreme Court of Canada to describe a statutory analysis that produces a desired result. Whereas I resented the suggestion that I should mould my opinion to accommodate the result that the client wanted, Robinette was fully prepared to help the client if he could give an opinion that he was prepared to defend.

With this background, the reader will perhaps understand my reaction to the remarks of my colleagues, not unfriendly by any means, asking how it felt to be wrong. The matter was never put to the test. The board acted on Robinette's opinion and ignored mine. But as I told myself, and the few in whom I confided my resentment, that does not mean that Robinette was right and I was wrong. It did however foreshadow coming events when Robinette's stature as a counsel had been elevated to such unrealistic levels that his opinions were treated as a remedy unto themselves. I can remember reading about a municipal council that was embroiled in some controversy or other that they were manifestly incapable of resolving. The vote that terminated the debate was a unanimous vote to solve the problem by retaining John Robinette: period.

In any event, this was the legal firm that I joined in 1951. I had not been there very long before Senator Hayden dropped by and introduced himself. He gave me a piece of good advice: "Put your head down and work. When you look up it will be fifteen years later." He was right. The time flew by as he predicted. But now it is more than fifty years later.

Chapter Six
Apprenticed to the Law

I HAVE GOTTEN A LITTLE AHEAD of myself with the foregoing description of McCarthy & McCarthy, but this information does serve as useful background to understanding John Robinette. But how did I come to be a lawyer, and how did I meet Robinette in the first place?

I would like to be able to say that I was inspired to become a lawyer because I had read about Robinette and his exploits in the Dick case, or even that I had been inspired by biographies that I had read of legends of the law like Marshal Hall and Sir Patrick Hastings, but the fact is I became a lawyer because I decided that there was nowhere else for me to go. My father, Roderick K. Finlayson, K.C., was a lawyer who practised in Winnipeg, where I was born, but I was not impressed with his career as a lawyer, and as it turned out, neither was he. He spent most of professional life as a legal and political adviser to successive leaders of the Conservative Party, later the Progressive Conservative Party, starting with Prime Minister R.B. Bennett in 1930 when I was three years old and ending with George Drew when I was attending university.

My first choice for earning a livelihood was to "go into business," and the selection was no better defined in my own mind than the quotation marks indicate. In the late spring of 1945, I was headed to the registrar's office of the University of Manitoba on Broadway Avenue to register in commerce and finance. My father asked if I would drive him downtown, and during the trip he advised against such a nebulous choice, stressing that I should enter a profession. If law was unpalatable, how about medicine? So I registered in pre-med.

The year in pre-med was a self-inflicted disaster. The fact is that I was not ready for university. I was used to the regimentation of high school with its compulsory attendance and regular testing. I did not have the discipline required of a successful university student, particularly one enrolled in a science course where activities were unmonitored and students were judged solely on their final examinations. However, I did love the social life and made many friends. They were not included among the teaching faculty, however, and I failed my year.

At this time, 1946, my parents decided to move to Ottawa, where my father was spending most of his time. My choice of university then became University College at the University of Toronto. After three more years of socially exhilarating and academically unrewarding attendance at this school of higher learning, I scraped through to graduate in the spring of 1949 with a pass bachelor of arts degree, the lowest rung on the university's ladder of achievement. By this time I realized that my father had been right when he advocated a professional career, and I am forever indebted to him for that piece of advice. But by now my choices were restricted, and I decided that there was nothing else to do but follow the lead of my older brother, Kenneth Duncan Finlayson,[50] and enter Osgoode Hall Law School, where the only requirement at that time was a university degree of any nature.

I enjoyed the study of the law. I found it stimulating and invigorating. I decided that I had better start attending all of my classes and concentrate on passing the examinations. I had run out of options. It is surprising what hard work can accomplish, and very soon I found myself back near the top of the class, a position that I had not enjoyed since high school.

By attending Osgoode Hall, I became a student member of the Law Society of Upper Canada. In order to qualify for a call to the bar and entitlement to practise law as a barrister and solicitor, I was obliged to attend two full years of academic study followed by one full year of articles to a practising lawyer and a fourth year divided between service under articles and academic instruction.

Towards the end of my second year the question came up as to whom I would apply to serve my articles. This problem prevails today, but the application process is much more structured. In 1951 it was informal and pretty much handled through an old boy network, at least as far as the established Toronto firms were concerned. My father, through politics, had many connections, and he recommended to me that I should article at McCarthy & McCarthy, which had a solid reputation. He knew Beverley Matthews there from the time Mathews served as a young man on the Bennett campaign train in the ill-fated 1935 election. Indeed, Matthews had been something of a "gofer" for my father. However, Matthews remained a staunch Conservative and became the national fundraiser for the party, a position he held for twenty years before relinquishing the role to my former classmate and later my partner at McCarthys, Patrick Vernon.

My father wrote to Matthews asking him to consider me for articles at the firm, and Matthews accepted me sight unseen. I was precisely the type of young man he was recruiting for the firm. Of Scottish heritage like himself, a Protestant, the son of a man he knew and respected, and, moreover, a Tory to the bone. As an added bonus I was also a member of his fraternity, Phi Kappa Pi. I was later to learn when I was established at the firm and looking for lawyers to help in the litigation department that (absent the fraternity) this was still the template for recruiting. It cost us some good people before I and others persuaded Matthews that this policy was anachronistic and hurtful to the quality of the firm.

In any event, I reported in early June of 1951 for my first day of articles. I was still interested in business, and to me the appeal of McCarthys was its reputation as a commercial firm. I also had my mind directed to income tax law, a field that I correctly anticipated would become more and more important and financially rewarding and in which there were then few specialists. My interview with Matthews was brief. He was very genial and asked me about my father. I said he was well and sent his best regards. My credentials validated, Matthews proceeded to tell me that I would be paid $50 per month and I would share one room with three other law students. For secretarial services we would have access to Miss Maclaren, secretary to Frank McCarthy, when she was available. The four of us would be rotated through the various departments in the law firm, and I would start in the litigation section.

As I left Matthews's office and headed towards the reception area, I noticed the name "Mr. Robinette" on an office door. There was no one there, so I stuck my head in the door and saw a spacious but not ostentatious office, tastefully decorated to match faux French provincial furniture covered with green leather upholstery. The desk was a table with no drawers. There was a filing cabinet in the corner. I introduced myself to the person who was sitting across the hall from this office. She was Elizabeth "Liz" Hudson, the secretary to John Robinette, and, yes, he was the selfsame lawyer who had defended Evelyn Dick. This was the first time I realized that he was with this law firm.

A few days later I met him. I was sitting in the law students' office with my fellow students Donald Sim, Patrick Vernon, and Frank Smalley when Robinette walked in. Typically of him, I was to learn, he did not ask his secretary to summon one of us or even telephone us. He came himself to ask who the litigation student was. I identified myself, and he said, "I want you to come to court with me." It was the start of a long and satisfying professional relationship that changed the direction of my career in the law.

Robinette has been described accurately as a shy and withdrawn man, but he was very much at ease with young people, probably because of his experience as a law teacher. He seemed to take a liking to me from the outset, principally because I made him laugh. I was soon to learn that laughter is a great antidote to stress, and the workload that Robinette carried would have crippled a man who lacked a sense of humour. I learned, too, that while Robinette was a loner in his practice, he liked company as long as it did not interfere with what he was doing. He never ate a meal or travelled with a client if he could avoid it, and he did not encourage solicitors who retained him to spend more time with him than was necessary to obtain their instructions. But time spent with a student or junior lawyer from McCarthys was easily controllable.

I remember Liz Hudson coming to me late one afternoon in March 1953, when I was still a student, and saying that Robinette had called and wanted me to join him in Cornwall. I had done some legal research on the case and knew that he was representing Mayor Aaron Horovitz, whose recent election was being challenged by a municipal elector called Robert Revie for alleged irregularities under the election provisions of the *Municipal Act*.[51] The principal irregularity was in authorizing the clerk of the City of Cornwall to send out a notice to the electorate immediately before election day giving an explanation for a notice of assessment that had unexpectedly been sent out by an independent firm responsible for determining the new assessment. However, as I knew, there was also a challenge to the validity of some of the ballots that were cast. I assumed my talents were required because there were some ballots that needed counting. I took the overnight train to Cornwall and arrived eager to perform any task set for me. I asked Robinette, "Has something happened?" He looked surprised. "No," he said, "I just wanted some company."

The case took the better part of a week, and I enjoyed every minute of it. There is nothing more agreeable than watching a good civil trial, the facts of which are familiar to you, when at the same time you have no responsibility for the outcome. I was invited to attend the traditional dinner given by the local bar association to celebrate the opening of the Cornwall Assizes because they wanted Robinette to appear. Regrettably, "our" plans did not include that dinner, but "we" were feted royally by the extensive Horovitz family when victory for the mayor was secured.[52] The highlight of the trial for me occurred when Robinette stood to address the Court in closing argument. He had my research memo in his hand. He had asked me to see if the cases distinguished between mere irregularities that could be excused in a judicial review of the election and conduct by a candidate or his agents that was fatal to the validity of the election. When I saw the memo, I said, "You're not going to rely on that, are you?" "Why not?" he replied. "It is a good memo." *And he read from it!* I had spent a good deal of time in my research and could not have felt more rewarded for my efforts. We had an agreeable ride home together on the train. From that day forward, I knew that I had a friend in John Robinette.

In the 1950s, air travel was not much resorted to when your destination was within Ontario. Short trips were by car and longer ones by train. I frequently travelled with Robinette as a student and junior lawyer and never ceased to enjoy his company. He was not a great talker; he was more of a good listener who kept the conversation going with penetrating questions or appropriate outbursts of humour. My trips with him to Ottawa on the afternoon train were pure gold. They were for appearances in the Supreme Court of Canada. My standing instructions from Robinette were to reserve two chairs in the club car for the four o'clock train, purchase a twenty-six-ounce bottle of Canadian

Club, and pick up a pouch of Imperial Mixture pipe tobacco. Robinette brought the legal briefs.

Since all the perfected Ontario cases were called from the Supreme Court's calendar at the same time, it was a rare trip when we did not meet other counsel headed for the court. If the criminal list had been called, we might meet Arthur Martin, Arthur Maloney, Bill Common, Joseph Sedgwick, or all four. If the civil list had been called it could be Charles Dubin, Arthur Patillo, or Walter Williston. No matter what the company, the drill was always the same. I would order "set ups" from the steward. Since the train was not licensed to serve liquor, the patrons of the club car were encouraged to bring their own bottles and were supplied with ice, mix, and tall crystal glasses. After a few drinks, the stories emerged and conversation flowed. I would be a rapt listener throughout the trip.

I became aware at this juncture how gossipy the profession is, among advocates at least. They love to reminisce about cases, the counsel who appeared in them, and the judges who tried them. The profession was smaller then, and there was a small number who acted as counsel to the exclusion of any solicitor work. They were an elite group, although not necessarily compatible with each other, and the stories they told about counsel who were not present were not always flattering. I so enjoyed these discussions that the actual hearings before the Supreme Court were almost an anticlimax. But I loved the court hearings, too. It was fascinating to be exposed to advocacy at that level. I was beginning to feel that I wanted to return, but with my own cases.

The arrangement Robinette had with McCarthy & McCarthy as counsel was very generous. He was not a partner in the firm and did not have to invest any capital in it. He was given a prime office and secretarial space. He selected his own secretary, and McCarthys paid her, although I understood from Liz Hudson that in her case and perhaps in those of her successors, Robinette supplemented the wages with generous bonuses. As indicated earlier, he brought John Brooke with him, and the financial arrangements between them were not a concern to the firm. McCarthys did, however, supply Brooke with an office suitable to his status, and with a secretary. In addition to this Robinette had access without cost to the firm library and all other support services such as law students, messengers, copying devices, and the like. If he required the services of a junior lawyer, the lawyer would keep track of the hours he spent on the assignment, and every quarter or so Matthews would meet with Robinette and settle these "docket entries." For his part, Robinette sent out his own bills to his clients and was not obliged to report or account to McCarthys for any of them. If he did work for a McCarthy client he would bill McCarthys for those services. Brooke would bill for his work on Robinette's professional billing forms.

As is readily apparent, Robinette had no overhead of any consequence. Everything he billed was net to him before income taxes. When lawyers who retained him marvelled to me about how low his accounts were, I had to bite my tongue. Mind you, not all of these lawyers were happy about these modest accounts; they made their own proposed billings appear proportionately high. The client was bound to measure them against the illustrious Mr. Robinette and question them. This was brought to my attention in the Horovitz election case I described briefly above. Just before leaving Cornwall for Toronto, we were sitting in the offices of M.J. Fitzpatrick, the lawyer who retained Robinette and a member of the law firm who would expect to receive his account for services. Fitzpatrick, who had advised Horovitz throughout and sat as Robinette's junior at the counsel table, said that he thought it wise to send out his account while the client was still euphoric about the result. He asked Robinette what he proposed to bill. Robinette said that in the light of the work he had done and the result achieved, he was thinking of charging $1,500. Fitzpatrick was aghast. "John!" he said. "I have internal docket charges that amount to much more than that. I was thinking of charging $5,000, and I could never justify that if you charge only $1,500."

I was amused by this exchange at the time, but Fitzpatrick was quite right. He had been advising the client on a continuing basis, and he was entitled to charge a fee that would recover his overhead and return some profit to share with his partners. Robinette's bill was unrealistically low for the reasons that I have set out above, reasons that were not known at the time to Fitzpatrick or me. Horovitz, who had been dazzled by Robinette's performance in the courtroom, would never understand why his own lawyer, whose contribution to the ultimate win was substantial although not highly visible, should charge so much more than Robinette. Ever agreeable, Robinette raised his account by $1,000.

Any number of lawyers were to comment on how modest Robinette's fees were: too many. Some years into this financial arrangement with McCarthys, Revenue Canada became intrigued. In examining Robinette's financial statements, their accountants had noted that virtually nothing was entered for overhead. When they spoke to Robinette about it, he of course told them the entire arrangement he had with the firm. Revenue Canada then started talking about assessing this lack of overhead as a "benefit" to him that should be treated notionally as income and therefore taxable in his hands. In reality, the notional overhead was not a benefit in any gratuitous sense because it was part of the *quid pro quo* for the substantial prestige Robinette brought to McCarthys as opposed to another firm. He was a beacon attracting business.

Robinette told Revenue Canada that McCarthys valued his services to the extent of supplying his overhead without charge. His inherent modesty prevented him from embellishing this point, but he did not intend to pay taxes on his diffidence. Accordingly, he gave to Revenue Canada the names of Matthews and me as references: Matthews because he was the author of the arrangement and me because I was a daily witness to its operation. Robinette spoke to the two of us separately, and I assured him that I would say all the right things. As it turned out, the Revenue Canada accountants spoke to Matthews first and were persuaded that they need not investigate the matter further. The problem disappeared for all time in 1970 when Robinette was persuaded by Matthews to become a partner. From then on, his secretary, Muriel Reid, was responsible to keep track of his time and ensure that it was charged to the proper client and at a rate set by our accounting office. However, Robinette was so efficient in the office work he did for clients that he was still a bargain even at rates that properly reflected his overhead. I suspect that he held back from Muriel the full amount of time he spent in preparation at home.

If I seem to dwell on this matter to a point beyond its importance, it is because these early financial arrangements had an unexpected benefit to me. It put me in the position where I could accept work assignments from both Robinette and Brooke on the same basis that I did from partners in McCarthys. This was important because when I first went to the firm these two counsel were by far the most fruitful source of interesting work assignments. Accordingly, I could work freely for them both and charge my time to the JJR docket.

There was litigation work from the McCarthy partners, and Senator Hayden made occasional forays into court and before administrative tribunals, but in 1951 there was only one lawyer at McCarthys who worked at litigation on a full-time basis. He was John Clarry, and he had received his call to the bar the year before in 1950 as a silver medallist. Clarry had come to the attention of Matthews and Walker during the war when Clarry served overseas from 1940 to 1946 in the Royal Canadian Service Corp and as a decorated staff officer.

John Clarry is the best lawyer I have ever met, and yes, that includes John Robinette. He could do anything and do it well. McCarthys must have thought so, too, for they transferred him to the commercial section in the spring of 1953, and I took his place as the only full-time member of what we were pleased to call the litigation department. Matthews's need for Clarry in the commercial section blinded him to his potential as a counsel. However, much as he was missed in litigation, his contribution to the commercial section was enormous. He was one of the truly creative minds in major financings undertaken on behalf of our clients. His expertise was known and respected well beyond the confines of the firm. The high opinion that he garnered from his colleagues made him the unanimous choice to replace Matthews as managing partner when that great builder felt it was time to step down.

Law school is a difficult time for a young person. You have reached the end of the period of your life that is supposed to be preparatory to taking your place in society. It is time to earn your own way, meet the person who will be your life companion, and think of raising a family. Accordingly, it is a time of great frustration. You want to get started on your career, and yet you know that you are not prepared. If you have a checkered academic history like mine, you also fear the final examinations. However, life as a student at McCarthy & McCarthy was fun. We four students were all good friends, although that harmony was strained in my case by an unexpected event involving Frank Smalley, which I will save for later in this memoir.

Our work activities all revolved around the library in the Canada Life Building. It was a comparatively small room with a large conference

table and at one time it had served as the joint office of all the law students. It was across the hall from Robinette's office, and he was a regular user of it. It was more than a reading room and became the focal
point of many discussions involving the students and any lawyer who
happened to be around. Discussion was not limited to matters of law
but also included current sporting and political activities. Debate could
become very lively and often was highly entertaining.

Like court offices throughout Ontario, the office was open on
Saturday morning. Even if it was not officially open, there was enough
work for everyone that Saturdays were mandatory workdays. We hear so
much today about the unrealistic hours law students and associates are
obliged to bill, but I can assure you that I have yet to hear of one who
put in the number of productive hours that Robinette did. When I met
him, he was in his early to middle forties and at the height of his professional powers. The hours he worked were staggering. Invariably, he
was in the office most nights of the week and all day Saturday. Sunday
work was almost a matter of course, either at the office or at home,
where he had what he described as a useful working library of his own.

I took full advantage of my opportunity to work in this relatively
unstructured professional environment. The fact was, Robinette was
overworked, and as a result so was his junior, Brooke. They did not hesitate to give me cases often at a high level of responsibility for a student.
Brooke in particular had the engaging habit of having his secretary,
Margaret Radzik, a former U.K. police constable, call me at the last
minute and state in her plummy English accent that brooked no argument, "Mr. Brooke wants you to go to Sudbury [or anywhere] to take a
discovery [or whatever]."

It was a wonderful experience for a student, and it carried on after
I received my own call to the bar in June of 1953. I was then the focal
point of all McCarthy's litigation files and received the overflow from
Robinette and Brooke. I appeared with both counsel as a junior, and the
learning experience was beyond comparison. The work was evenly
divided between criminal and civil, and it was assumed of me that as a
lawyer I would be comfortable in either discipline and in any court.

Probably the turning point in my professional career was a murder
case I took in the early spring of 1954 when Brooke, who had been

retained as counsel in the matter, broke his leg very badly while indulging himself in his great love of skiing. The case deserves some brief comment because it demonstrates the camaraderie and support I enjoyed as a young counsel.

Brooke's client was a young man called John Robertson, who in company with an even younger youth planned to play up to and then rob a closet gay who worked at a major investment firm. Homosexual conduct in those days was a criminal offence and was diagnosed by the medical profession as a mental illness. The intended victim was very vulnerable to blackmail and not at all likely to complain to the police if it would reveal his interest in these two young boys. However, the robbery went very badly. The victim was driving the two boys around the outskirts of Toronto in his car when the younger boy drew a gun and demanded the money and expensive watch that they knew the victim always carried with him. However, the two young men did not intimidate the victim. There was a fight, and the victim was beaten unconscious with a tire iron. He was then placed in the trunk of his car and driven to a remote area outside Barrie, north of Toronto. When the boys opened the trunk, the victim came after them and was beaten again and shot six times, dying as a result of his injuries.

One night in the winter of 1954, I received a telephone call from Brooke's wife, Elizabeth ("Libby"). John was in the hospital with a badly shattered leg and would not be released for some time. Would I call Robinette and tell him about John's condition and warn him that John would not be able to take some cases he had, including the one involving Robertson? I called Robinette. To my surprise, he was angry. It took a few moments to calm him down to the point where he expressed some sympathy, not much, for John's condition. His theme was that he should not have been skiing. To my further surprise, this attitude was common to almost all the senior counsel that I telephoned the next day to arrange to put off Brooke's court engagements. "A young lawyer should not be skiing" was the typical response by irritated counsel who found themselves obliged to rearrange *their* court schedules because of Brooke.

I knew all about the Robertson case, of course, including the fact that Robertson had made a full and complete confession to the police about the plan to rob the victim. While he agreed that he had beaten the victim, he denied that he had shot him, a point that was later to be disputed by his co-accused. The case was a difficult one. As a legal proposition, the fact that only one of them fired the gun was irrelevant: causing the death of a human being while carrying out the offence of armed robbery meant that both young men were guilty of murder, and hanging was still the penalty for murder.

The case was strictly pro bono, and I assumed that it would be sent back to the sheriff's office where an informal legal aid program was administered and another lawyer would be assigned. Imagine my surprise when Robinette called me into his office and asked me to take it. On second thought, surprise did not describe my reaction. I was stunned. I had never addressed a jury in my young life. I felt totally inadequate. I foolishly blurted out that these two young men could hang. Robinette nodded, and I asked for a few minutes to think it over. I was genuinely concerned about my lack of experience and the importance of the case. I reminded myself that this was not like the case of Suchan and Jackson (which I will describe later), in which two professional bank robbers had shot down and killed a police officer in the performance of his duty. They had hanged, but it was unlikely that these teenage boys would actually suffer the death penalty; they were ideal candidates for the Crown's prerogative of mercy. I was also aware of another hard fact. If I refused to take this case, I could not expect to be taken seriously as a counsel by Robinette.

Accordingly, with considerable trepidation, I agreed to take the case. I interviewed Robertson in the jail and then discussed the facts with Robinette. I expressed my opinion that my own assessment of him was that he would make a terrible witness. I wondered if he could stand up under cross-examination even though he insisted that he had never fired a shot. Robinette picked up on the denial of the shooting and interjected, "Surely to God he can remember that!"

After listening carefully, Robinette assured me that I could do the job and told me that even if the jury convicted the accused of murder, it was likely that the Minister of Justice would intervene to prevent the death penalty being carried out. While the boys were tried as adults because they were older than sixteen (juveniles were sixteen years and younger under the then *Juvenile Delinquents Act*), they were still teenagers and absent any criminal record would not likely be hanged. However, Robinette stressed, it was important that I get the trial judge to charge the jury that on the evidence they could bring in a verdict for the lesser offence of manslaughter. I was to ensure that the trial judge told the jury that they could find on the evidence that the two young men had embarked on a "joint venture for manslaughter." I said, "What's a joint venture for manslaughter?" "Never mind," Robinette replied, "just make sure the trial judge says this to the jury."

I still do not know what a joint venture for manslaughter is, and when I mentioned the legal proposition to my very experienced co-counsel and former Crown Attorney, Norman Borins, K.C., he did not know what it was either. The trial judge, the Honourable Mr. Justice Aylen, looked blank when I insisted that he so instruct the jury, but he did so. Justice Aylen was a very kind man, and he had no enthusiasm for sentencing two teenagers to death by hanging. He jumped at the chance to give the jury an alternative verdict to murder. The reality of the situation of these two young men was that without this creative instruction of Robinette's, there was no foundation on the evidence for a verdict of manslaughter. Constructive murder was an accepted principle of the criminal law in those days. A homicide is constructive murder irrespective of whether it is planned and deliberate by both parties where it is caused while committing certain enumerated offences, one of which was robbery. Once both youths testified that they each knew the younger one had a gun and that it was to be used to carry out their plan to rob the victim, and it transpired that its use caused the death of the victim of the robbery, the Crown had a classic constructive murder case. However, these two youths revealed themselves in the witness box as frightened boys, and the jury was looking for an opportunity to show them mercy. Manslaughter was a way out for the jury, and after lengthy deliberation, they took it. Aylen sentenced the two accused to a lengthy term in the penetentiary for manslaughter. I have never since felt such a sense of relief at a jury's verdict.

When I look back on this case, two memories are vivid. When I told Robinette that I had heard a number of his jury addresses in murder cases and noticed that he introduced them all with a boilerplate recitation of the role of the judge and jury and the importance of understanding the burden of proof the law imposed on the Crown and other non-controversial matters, he reached into a fold in his notebook and pulled out a number of handwritten pages of lined note paper and said, "You can borrow these." I examined them later and realized that they were his notes from his first murder case, that of Evelyn Dick.

The second memory is of an act of pure friendship on the part of Brooke at a point when the case in Barrie had taken a turn for the worse. The two young boys, who were in enough trouble when they stood together, turned on each other and insisted that contrary to both their confessions there was no common plan and the shooting was solely the responsibility of the other fellow. I was becoming rattled and had trouble sleeping at night. I sought advice from Robinette, and he said he would speak to Brooke. Brooke had been released from hospital but was on crutches and had a full cast on his leg from his toes to his hip. Nonetheless, he managed to get into his car and drive to Barrie. He watched the balance of that day's hearing, and that night he reviewed the whole case with me. He gave me sound advice as to how to proceed, but more than anything he made me feel that I was not alone in the case. I was much more at ease from that point on.

An important case that was preoccupying the senior lawyers of the firm when I arrived in the spring of 1951 involved a will that Frank McCarthy had drawn for Herbert C. Cox in 1938 when Cox was president of the Canada Life Assurance Company. In the will, Cox had attempted to set up a charitable trust in favour of employees of Canada Life. Herbert Cox died on September 17, 1947, and his wife, Louise Bogart Cox, made a similar provision in her will dated November 2, 1948. She died shortly thereafter, on November 18, 1948. The controversial clause read as follows:

> Subject as hereinbefore provided, and with respect to the balance of my residuary estate which may remain in my trustees' possession, my said trustees shall hold the same upon trust as follows: *To pay the income thereof in perpetuity for charitable purposes only; the persons to benefit directly in pursuance of such charitable purposes are to be only such as shall be or shall have been employ-*

ees of The Canada Life Assurance Company and/or the dependants of such employees of said The Canada Life Assurance Company; subject to the foregoing restrictions, the application of such income, including the amounts to be expended and the persons to benefit therefrom, shall be determined by the board of directors of the said The Canada Life Assurance Company as they, the said board of directors, in their absolute discretion shall from time to time decide. The trust fund is to be known as "The Cox Foundation" in memory of the family whose name has been so long associated with the said company.

Herbert Cox and his wife were childless, and so it was fitting that the two would leave their considerable wealth to the people who were their real family, the employees of Canada Life. The operative clause creating the Cox Foundation appears straightforward, but it was the product of a lot of thinking. Frank McCarthy was so concerned about its validity as a charitable bequest that he sought the advice of counsel in England who had a reputation for expertise in this area.

Frank was justified in his concern. The next of kin of Hebert Cox who were either excluded from participating as beneficiaries under the estate or received less than they anticipated challenged the validity of the bequest. It was impractical to administer the charitable trust with these challenges outstanding. Accordingly, by an originating notice of motion issued in the Supreme Court of Ontario in March 1949, the administrators of the Cox's will, the National Trust Co. Ltd. and Alfred Herbert Cox, sought the determination of the Court whether the bequest of his residuary estate was a valid charitable bequest and further sought certain consequential directions. The executors of Louise Bogart Cox took out an originating motion seeking similar relief at the same time. The case was literally to proceed throughout every court in the land and end up at the foot of the throne. It was to give Robinette his first and only opportunity to argue a case in London before the Judicial Committee of the Privy Council, the final level of appeal from the King's Dominions who were members of the Commonwealth of Nations.

The two motions for directions were heard first by Justice Wells of the Supreme Court of Ontario, who delivered judgment on January 27, 1950,[53] then by the Court of Appeal for Ontario,[54] and then the Supreme Court of Canada,[55] and finally with leave by the Judicial Committee of the Privy Council.[56] Had he been alive to witness the court proceedings, the late Herbert Cox could not have complained that his law firm did not show up to represent him.

When the matter came on before Wells in the spring of 1949, Beverley Matthews and Bill Terry appeared for the trustees, Salter Hayden for the trustees of Mrs. Cox's estate, Robinette and Jack Blain for the directors of Canada Life and its employees, and even Lally McCarthy returned to the fold to represent Alfred H. Cox. Frank McCarthy was the solicitor of record. Those objecting to the validity of the bequest were represented principally by John D. Arnup, who had a stature in civil matters on a par with that of Robinette. The Official Guardian and the Public Trustee were also represented. Curiously, they were on different sides of the issue, the Public Trustee supporting the will and the Official Guardian opposing it.

On this first outing, the McCarthys prevailed, Wells holding that the bequest made by each of the testators, Mr. and Mrs. Cox, was a valid charitable bequest for the relief of poverty. This was to be the firm's only victory. Wells was to be reversed by a unanimous Court of Appeal on February 16, 1951, composed of Justices Roach, Aylesworth, and Bowlby. The Supreme Court of Canada in its judgment of December 22, 1952, affirmed the Court of Appeal by a majority (Justices Kerwin, Taschereau, Kellock, Estey, and Fauteux, with Justices Rand and Cartwright dissenting). The Judicial Council upheld the Supreme Court.

By way of background to the legal issues in this case, the reader should be aware that the state, represented by the King of England at this time, did not encourage bequests in perpetuity or ones that created estates that were exempt from taxation. Historically, these estates involved the devolution of estates in land and were intended to perpetuate vast land holdings in the hands of the barons. These barons were properly considered by the king or queen of the day as a threat to the monarchy.

For not dissimilar reasons, the state in modern times discourages the creation of financial estates such as charitable foundations that are exempt from taxation in perpetuity because they deprive the state of tax revenues that are necessary to sustain it. Accordingly, His Majesty's judges very early propounded a rule known as the rule against perpetuities to the effect that a testator or a settlor of an estate cannot postpone the vesting of his or her property beyond a specific number of lives in being plus twenty-one years from the death of the testator or settlor (see *Duke of Norfolk's Case* in 1681).[57] While the rule applied to the creation of trusts, there were exemptions, and one was the charitable trust.

However, there are strict prerequisites established by law before the courts will recognize as valid a bequest in perpetuity to a charitable foundation. The beneficiaries of the trust cannot be chosen at whim. Only trusts with accepted charitable objects will qualify. Appropriately, it was in England that the scope of acceptable charitable objects was settled in a case called *The Commissioners for Special Purposes of the Income Tax v. Pemsel*.[58] Lord Macnaughten of the House of Lords set out four categories of authorized charitable trusts:

> "Charity" in its legal sense comprises four principal divisions, trusts for the relief of poverty; trusts for the advancement of education; trusts for the advancement of religion; and trusts for other purposes beneficial to the community not falling within any of the preceding heads. The trusts last referred to are not the less charitable in the eyes of the law, because incidentally they benefit the rich as well as the poor, as indeed every charity that deserves the name must do directly or indirectly.

Speaking for the majority in our Court of Appeal, Roach quoted from the above passage in *Pemsel* and said:

> A proposition of law for which there is ample authority carries me the next step. That proposition is as follows, that a trust cannot be a valid charitable trust within any of the four divisions described by Lord Macnaughten unless it is for a public purpose, that is to say, unless it is for the benefit of the community or an appreciably important class of the community.

In the case of the Cox foundation, the bequest did not fit the standard mould because the direction "to pay the income thereof in perpetuity for charitable purposes" did not specify which of the four charities the trustees were entitled to advance with respect to employees of Canada Life. More seriously, the argument was made that the bequest was not made for the benefit of the community but to employees of a private employer. Both arguments were to prevail in the end.

Wells, the judge of first instance, had reached the conclusion that the bequests created a valid charitable trust limited to the relief of poverty among the beneficiaries, namely and solely the employees of Canada Life and their dependants. There is no language in the will restricting the charitable objects to the "relief of poverty," and in any event it was the view of Roach in reversing Wells that he was not prepared to say that there is in effect a fifth category, "namely, trusts for the relief of poverty among a group of private individuals who are chosen by the donor by reason of another type of personal relationship, namely, their relationship as employees or dependants of employees of a named employer."[59] Roach concluded his judgment by stating:

> My conclusion therefore is that these appeals should be allowed because these trusts are not trusts for general public purposes; they are trusts for private individuals, a fluctuating body of private individuals but still private individuals. Because they are not for public purposes they are not charitable and therefore void as offending the rule against perpetuities.[60]

I arrived at McCarthys a few months after the decision of the Court of Appeal was rendered. Frank McCarthy was still in shock. It seemed to me that he spent much of his time worrying about the matter. He certainly spent a good deal of time in Robinette's office discussing the appeal to the Supreme Court of Canada. That court upheld the decision of Roach in the Court of Appeal in December 1952. Robinette girded his loins for battle in his first and only appearance in the Privy Council, an experience that he very much looked forward to. It was also the last appeal but one[61] to be argued in the Privy Council from Canada, since they had been abolished by an amendment to the act governing the Supreme Court of Canada effective December 10, 1949.[62] The amendment excluded judicial proceedings commenced prior to the coming into force of the amendment and so excluded the Cox Estate litigation. It was an historic occasion. It was also an unsuccessful one, from Robinette's perspective.

Lord Somerville of Harrow delivered the judgment of the Privy Council. In my opinion it was the most unsatisfactory judgment of all. We need feel no nostalgia for having restricted our appeals to Canada. Lord Somerville appears to have blended two points. One is that in order to qualify as a bequest to charity a gift must be for the benefit of the community or at least an appreciably important class of the community. The second point is that the bequest was "for charitable purposes only" without specifying which of the four valid objects was to be the object. In directing the trustees in this general way, the testator Cox left it open to the trustees to make funds available for any one or all of the four charitable objects approved by the House of Lords in the *Pemsel* case as long as the recipients of the gifts were employees of Canada Life or their dependants.

Accordingly, it was wrong to interpret the language of the charitable trust to limit it to the relief of poverty only. The latter designation might have qualified the trust as falling within the acceptable category of the relief of poverty, which on some authorities has been interpreted as making acceptable gifts to employees of a particular employer. The proposition is put awkwardly, but I take it that Lord Somerville was saying that Wells was incorrect, in effect redrafting the will to limit the charitable purpose to the relief of poverty so that he could then find the bequest valid.

One of the reasons I remember this case so vividly is that it was referred to by Allan Leal in our course of lectures in wills and trusts at law school. In fact, it was a question on the final examination. I was happily able to ace that question and received one of my best marks in this subject. Another benefit was that I was asked to accompany John Clarry on the reference to determine who was entitled to participate in the residue of the Herbert C. Cox Estate because of the intestacy that resulted from having the Cox Foundation struck down. It was an interesting exercise and taught me a great deal about the conduct of references and the commercial resources that were available in the United States allowing us to search for, find, and validate the claims of far-flung relatives of Herbert Cox who did not even know he existed. Unfortunately, I was the only one at McCarthys who received any satisfaction from the case.

There was, perhaps, one other exception. While the result of the case was a disappointment to Robinette, it was not a surprise. The fact is, Frank McCarthy had been badly served by English counsel, and it is hard to disagree with Roach's judgment in the Court of Appeal. However, the trip to London and the appearance before the Judicial Committee of the Privy Council was very much a highlight to Robinette. He had a great deal of respect for the British system of justice and indeed the English practice where the separation in principle and practice of the roles of barristers and solicitors was firmly drawn. I was surprised by how deferential he was to the English judges and how respectful he was of the judgments of the House of Lords and the English Court of Appeal. On reflection, I recognized that this made sense given that he had taught and practised law for twenty years under a legal regime where the final authority on any aspect of the law of Canada was the Privy Council and English authorities were cited routinely as setting out the law of Canada.

The Cox Estate was not exactly red meat for a young lion of the law, but it did give flesh and blood to the history of the common law, which was and is the bedrock of our system of civil law. This history was difficult to follow in our lecture in the subject at law school, I suspect because our lecturer did not understand the subject that well himself. However, the subject came to interest me more and more as I developed my own practice, and it was essential to the understanding I required as an appellate judge. And never mind, there was great excitement in store. Robinette was retained to defend Steve Suchan on a charge of murdering a police officer. It was to be another *cause célèbre* and, in my opinion, one of the most important criminal trials in Canadian judicial history.

Chapter Seven
Steven Suchan of the Boyd Gang

Sometime in the early spring of 1952, John Robinette was working late in his office when one of the cleaning staff asked to talk to him. He knew her to speak to but was surprised to learn that the woman, Elizabeth Lesso, was the mother of a notorious member of the Boyd Gang, Valente Lesso, or Steven Suchan, as he was now universally known.

Mrs. Lesso closed the door to Robinette's office. In somewhat of an understatement, she remarked that her son was a good boy but had got into trouble. She began to cry. "My son has been charged with murder. Would you take his case for me?"

Robinette felt sorry for her and said yes.

"He is charged with another man, and the other man is a very bad man," she said.[63]

Many lawyers would have jumped at the chance to become involved in such a high-profile criminal case. Whatever the outcome of the trial, its publicity would have made anyone associated with it a household name. Robinette did not shun publicity, by any means, but he did not crave it. Besides, he had quite enough on his plate as it was. In agreeing to take the case, he made his retainer conditional upon receiving an advance fee of $7,000, hoping this figure, which was large by 1952 standards, would discourage Mrs. Lesso. Far from doing so, she appeared again in his office the next night with the money, in cash.

In the early 1950s, Toronto witnessed a spree of bank robberies orchestrated by members of the now infamous Boyd Gang, Suchan among them. This band of bank robbers was named after its leader, Edwin Alonzo Boyd.[64] The gang attracted a good deal of notoriety and became the darling of the Toronto press, which then, as now, was engaged in a circulation war. The contestants then were *The Globe and Mail, The Toronto Star*, and *The Evening Telegram*. The Boyd Gang provided the sort of underworld coverage that was associated with Chicago, not Toronto the Good. The gang's membership included Leonard Jackson and Steven Suchan, two young toughs who were to become notorious after they were charged with the murder of Sergeant of Detectives Edmund Tong of the Toronto Police Force.

The shooting of Tong and the wounding of his partner, Detective Sergeant Roy Perry, simply heightened public outrage in the ongoing saga of the Boyd Gang. In death, Edmund "Eddie" Tong became a police hero. He had come to Canada in 1929 from England and began his police career at the Claremont Street Police Station. He was not in uniform for any length of time before his superiors recognized his ability to pick up clues. He was on plainclothes duty in 1933 and an acting detective until 1949 when he became a full detective. He later became a detective-sergeant, and he was a sergeant of detectives in 1952 when he was gunned down.[65]

The newspaper coverage began in earnest on November 4, 1951. Boyd and two of his gang members, who were being held in custody at Toronto's Don Jail on charges of bank robbery, managed a daring escape by sawing through the bars of a cell window with a smuggled hacksaw blade and lowering themselves to freedom using a number of bed sheets tied together. Escaping with Boyd were Leonard Jackson and Willie Jackson, who were not related. The man waiting in the getaway car was Steven Suchan.

Willie Jackson was best known as "Willie the Clown." He does not appear to have been acquainted with Leonard Jackson or Alonzo Boyd before meeting them in the Don Jail. However, he was also a bank robber and after the escape joined with Suchan, Leonard Jackson, and Boyd to rob two banks. The second robbery netted over $46,000 and was at the time the largest single robbery of a Toronto bank.

The robbers lived high off the hog for a few weeks until Willie the Clown was recognized in the washroom of a bar and arrested on December 18. A second misfortune befell the gang when much of their loot was stolen. They had stashed it with Steve Suchan's parents, which turned out to be a major mistake: Suchan's father took off to Florida with much of it.[66]

During this period, Suchan and Leonard Jackson had been living in Montreal under assumed names — Jackson with his wife, Anne, in a one-room basement apartment at 1930 Lincoln Avenue and Suchan in the luxury Croydon Apartments at 3455 Cote des Neiges. However, they would return to Toronto on occasion to join Boyd and the other members to rob banks.

Suchan, who was a handsome young man and much attracted to women, had two girlfriends in Toronto. His steady girlfriend was Mary Mitchell, a half-sister of Leonard Jackson. But he was also carrying on an affair with Anne Bosnich, a married woman who was separated from her husband. She was a real estate agent and went by her maiden name, Camero. She had been seeing Suchan for two years and had a child by him. She knew him by his true name of Valente Lesso. Bosnich lived in a rented house at 190 Wright Avenue in the Parkdale district of Toronto.

On Monday, March 3, 1952, Suchan and Jackson headed to Toronto. Suchan left on the morning train and Jackson on the evening train. Because he did not want to be seen in Toronto's Union Station, Jackson got off the train at Oshawa and telephoned Suchan at about six o'clock in the morning to ask that he come get him in Oshawa. Suchan agreed, borrowing Bosnich's car. The pair returned to 190 Wright Avenue and stayed there for three days until March 6.

It is not clear from the evidence at trial exactly what happened during this time, but it appears from Bosnich's evidence that Suchan and Jackson were heavily armed and conducted target practice on the torso of a dressmaker's dummy in the basement of her house on Wright Avenue. The neighbours complained to the landlady about the noise caused by the shooting, and she reported the disturbance to the police.

March 6 was to be a fateful day for a number of people. Suchan and Jackson left the Wright Avenue residence at one o'clock that afternoon in Bosnich's Buick sedan. Suchan was driving. Both men were armed, Suchan with a Smith & Wesson .355 revolver and Jackson with a .32. Meanwhile, Sergeant of Detectives Tong, who was now the head of the holdup squad, was hot on the men's trail. Having received word about the shooting noises on Wright Avenue, he and his partner, Detective

Sergeant Perry, drove in an unmarked car towards Parkdale in search of the culprits.

Leonard Jackson was on Tong's wanted list. The two had met while Jackson was in custody, and Jackson was very much aware of who Tong was. The suggestion, never pursued at trial by the defence for obvious reasons, was that the holdup squad used brutal interrogation methods and that Jackson had been the victim of mistreatment at the hands of either Tong or one or two of the members of his squad. Jackson did not want to experience a repeat performance.

Tong did not know Suchan, and it is not clear to what extent he associated him at that time with the Boyd Gang. However, Tong did know Suchan's other companion, Mary Mitchell. As a detective, Tong believed in keeping in touch with friends and relatives of persons on his wanted or suspect list. He knew Mitchell because she was the half-sister of Jackson. Mitchell was jealous of Anne Bosnich and resentful of Suchan because of his ongoing relationship with her. It is believed that Mitchell is the one who gave Tong a description of Bosnich's black 1951 Buick sedan with Quebec licence plate 324-385.

Perry was a nineteen-year veteran with the Toronto Police Force and Tong's partner.[67] Cruising the Parkdale area, Perry at the wheel, they saw Bosnich's car with two male occupants in it. They had seen this car before and were curious about its occupants. Perry did not know Suchan, but he and Tong both knew that Jackson was unlawfully at large.

The Buick proceeded east on College to a point between Lansdowne and Dundas. By this time Tong had radioed in the licence plate and knew that Bosnich owned the car. When Suchan stopped at a red light at College and Lansdowne, Perry pulled alongside and Tong ordered Suchan to pull over. He complied, and Perry pulled the cruiser in behind. Tong was approaching the vehicle on the driver's side when the driver's side door opened. Shots were fired, and Tong fell to the ground.

The driver of Bosnich's sedan then got out of the car and fired a bullet into the windshield of the cruiser. As Perry opened his door to get out, the driver of the suspect vehicle raised his right arm. Perry covered his face just before a shot was fired. His arm absorbed a bullet and went numb. In the meantime, the passenger in the suspects' car had also exited the vehicle with a pistol and fired shots. Perry was not sure who had shot him. He blacked out. A citizen shook him awake just as the suspects' car was fleeing. Perry reported the shooting on his police radio. Perry and Tong never used their pistols. In the end, Perry was shot twice but recovered from his wounds. Tong died of his about two weeks later.

The shooting of two police officers in the line of duty was featured in one story after another in the Toronto press and elsewhere across North America. Thanks to some good investigative work and material they found at 190 Wright Avenue, the police traced Suchan and Jackson to their apartments in Montreal. After the shooting, the two had abandoned Bosnich's car in Toronto and fled first to Hamilton by way of buses and taxis. They then stole a car and drove to Montreal. Their apartments were raided within a short time of the shooting, with the co-operation of the Montreal Police.

The first to be apprehended was Suchan at the Croydon Apartments. The night following the shooting, Detective Albert Dauphin and another member of the Montreal police surprised him as he entered his apartment. When Suchan attempted to draw his revolver, the same Smith & Wesson that he had used to shoot Tong, Dauphin shot him three times. The police officer's first shot entered Suchan's chest an inch below his heart. The second caught him in the abdomen and exited by his hip. The third struck him in the left hand.

A few days later, on March 11, Detective Jack Gillespie of the Toronto police crashed through the door of Jackson's apartment. Jackson fired at him but missed entirely. Gillespie emptied his six-shot .38 revolver at Jackson and struck him four times, once in the abdomen, twice in his left arm, and once in his right hand. Suchan and Jackson's injuries were not life threatening, and both men were returned to the Don Jail where they rejoined Willie Jackson. Shortly after, gang leader Boyd was also captured and sent to the same jail.

These were the facts that presented themselves to Robinette when he began to put his mind to preparing a defence to this most difficult case. He soon realized, from a reading of the stories in the press, that it was thornier from Suchan's perspective than he had thought. Suchan had been captured with the Smith & Wesson revolver that fired the bullet that killed Tong, and Suchan had admitted to the police on arrest that this was the gun that he had emptied at the police cruiser on the day in question.

However, Robinette would get more time to prepare then he had expected. Inexplicably, the Governor of the Don Jail decided to put the four most notorious members of the Boyd Gang, including their ingenious leader, in the same section of the jail. Boyd hatched yet another jailbreak, this time involving a smuggled hacksaw blade, a copy of a jail guard's key to their four cells, and shoe black to cover up the work they did on the bars. In preparing for the escape, the four would release themselves from their cells at nighttime by using the counterfeit key and would use the hacksaw blade to cut the bars on an outside window. The four prisoners escaped on September 8, 1952, one day before the grand jury was to be called to consider the indictment of Suchan and Jackson for murder.

This time, however, the gang's freedom was short-lived. All four were recaptured without a struggle in a barn near Toronto on September 16. The presence of the four in the barn had aroused the suspicions of neighbours, who reported them to the police. Suchan had obtained a new handgun after his escape, but he did not attempt to use it. The day after their recapture, Suchan and Jackson were arraigned before Chief Justice McRuer for a trial that was set to begin on September 22.

I was in my final year at law school when Suchan and Jackson were arraigned at City Hall, now Old City Hall, in the fall of 1952. Ignoring the interruption to my lectures, I was in almost continuous attendance at the trial held in courtroom three. Despite my brief articles as a law student at McCarthys, I was no stranger to this oddly imposing structure, which was designed at the turn of the century in the Romanesque Revival style by Edward James Lennox.[68] In my early years in the profession, I considered the building as something of an anachronism. However, as time has passed and I have become more venerable myself, I have developed a certain fondness for the old lady and am pleased that it has survived the building of the present City Hall and is still used as a courthouse.

This was my first look at McRuer in action. He was an impressive figure in his robes, and he was very much at home in courtroom three. Anyone who doubted that this was his court and that the Chief Justice was presiding over it was quickly and surely put in his place. The first to be reminded of this was John Brooke, Robinette's junior on the case. The Chief Justice summarily dismissed his application made on September 17 for a one-week adjournment of the trial from September

22 to September 29, despite the fact that the application was based in part on the need to permit Jackson to retain counsel, an application that no present-day judge would have denied. Brooke had explained to the Chief Justice that Robinette had just recently been retained as counsel for Suchan and that Jackson as yet had no counsel. Brooke stated, "I cannot say that we are ready for trial [because of Robinette's other commitments]. I would ask your lordship … that there be no trial until the 29th of this month, that is, a week this coming Monday."[69]

McRuer was not sympathetic. He observed:

> I think in this case — it is some time ago — it is March the 6th the alleged offence was committed and these assizes opened on the 8th of September and it was proposed that this case should proceed on the 15th of September, not later than the 22nd of September, and I see no reason why the case should not proceed next Monday, the 22nd. I would like to meet Mr. Robinette's convenience, but I think that this is a case of sufficient importance that probably his other arrangements may be rearranged.

Reminded by Brooke that Jackson was not represented, the Chief Justice replied that Jackson had had since mid-March to retain counsel, and the trial should not be delayed on that account. In fact, McRuer had spoken that day to Arthur Maloney, a young but brilliant criminal lawyer, and asked him to represent Jackson. With Jackson's agreement, he assigned Maloney as counsel and set September 22 as the date the trial would begin.

The trial began on that day with William O. Gibson and Henry H. Bull representing the Crown, John Robinette and John Brooke appearing for Suchan, and Arthur Maloney and J. Foran for Jackson. Robinette again requested an adjournment, stating this time that he was conscious of his duty to his client to ensure that there be a fair trial and he be fairly defended. Robinette expressed his concern that the Crown intended to call between forty and fifty witnesses, many more than were called at the preliminary inquiry, and that the Crown had not complied with his request for a copy of the evidence that the additional witnesses would give. Robinette also complained that he had not received the copy of the pathologist's report that he requested at the preliminary inquiry and that the defence had been refused access to the hospital records of Detective Tong.

Robinette then fired the first shot in what was to be a prevailing theme of the defence: widespread publicity about the case, he said, had made it virtually impossible for the two accused to receive a fair trial. This publicity would make it impossible to find jurors who did not already have a view about the guilt or innocence of the accused. Immediately upon his raising the matter, McRuer leapt in, "The Crown is not responsible for the publicity." Robinette replied, "I am not suggesting that they are, my lord. The Crown is definitely not responsible for the publicity, but the fact is that there has been an abnormal amount of publicity. Whose fault it is, for the purpose of my submission, does not really matter." McRuer replied, "I think it would make a big difference if the Crown was responsible for it." To which Robinette said:

> All I am suggesting to your lordship is this, that it is exceedingly important in this particular case, having regard to that — no matter whose fault it is, it is exceedingly important that the accused be defended adequately and with complete preparation. In view of the shortness of time and the refusal and failure to obtain this information, the defence is handicapped. I am not asking for a long adjournment, because I am conscious of how your lordship quite properly feels about this matter, but what I am requesting of your lordship is this, that I am entitled — not only that, but the accused himself is entitled by way of résumé or otherwise of the substance that was not called at the preliminary inquiry. If that could be given to us today or tomorrow I would not ask for more than two days further adjournment, and I would be prepared to go on Thursday morning. But I do feel, that not having seen the pathologist's report, having not had an opportunity to see [Tong's] hospital records, not having had an

opportunity to see or know anything, except by way of gossip, of what the evidence is against the accused, I do not think it is at all an unreasonable request in the interest of the administration of justice that the matter be delayed at least until Thursday morning.

As is evident from the transcript of the proceedings, Robinette was tenacious and specific about what he required in the way of full disclosure and the time required for an adjournment to fully prepare for trial. He summed up by saying that although the proceedings should proceed expeditiously, it was equally important that the defence be adequately prepared for a fair trial.

Arthur Maloney supported Robinette's request and gave his own reasons for needing an adjournment, which arose out of his more pressing circumstances, having only been retained less than a week previously. He asked for:

[J]ust enough time to ascertain, even from an outline of the evidence of the various witnesses whose names appear on the indictment, the nature of their evidence. I have not even the remotest knowledge of what many of them are going to say ... I am handicapped by my complete ignorance of the facts of the Crown's case ... As you know, I only came into the case on Wednesday afternoon on your lordship's appointment ... I do feel I should have this information.

McRuer remained unmoved. To this point, Gibson for the Crown had little to say. We see here, as in the Evelyn Dick case, that McRuer felt confident that he could represent the Crown's interest himself. In this case, not having called upon the Crown to answer to the very full arguments of Robinette and Maloney, McRuer engaged Gibson in a dialogue that was clearly directed to build a record for the Court of Appeal in the event that defence counsel complained to that court about his refusal to grant an adjournment.

McRuer: Mr. Gibson, for the purposes of the record I wish to ask you — this Bill, the Registrar tells me, was brought on the 9th of September.

Gibson: That is right, my lord. The grand jury considered it on the 8th and it was reported to the Court at the opening on the 9th.

McRuer: Were the accused arraigned before the Court on the 17th of September according to the note on the indictment — that is last Wednesday?

Gibson: That is right.

McRuer: Was the delay in bringing the accused before the Court for arraignment in any way due to the Crown? What I want is an answer for the record.

Gibson: I understand my lord. In no sense was it.

McRuer then asked Gibson about disclosing the pathologist's report and the hospital records. Gibson responded that he had never objected to disclosing the pathologist's report and that he did not have it. As for the hospital records, Gibson informed him that neither the Crown nor the police had seen them or had any control over them. With a proper subpoena, the defence could probably have obtained them. McRuer assured Gibson that he was "in no way responsible for interfering" with the hospital's decisions. McRuer then made his rulings:

That is all I want, Mr. Gibson. This is an application to delay this trial for a period of three days in order that defence counsel may be furnished with a copy of the

pathologist's report, may have an order from me directed to the hospital to show the hospital records with
respect to Det. Sgt. Tong prior to his death, and an order
that I direct the Crown to furnish counsel for the
accused with a short statement of the evidence proposed
to be given by those witnesses whose names appear on
the indictment who were not called at the preliminary
hearing. [Several days have passed since the earliest
opportunity arose for counsel to bring an application for
an adjournment ...] I do not think I can create any
precedent by granting an adjournment of this trial
under the circumstances of this case. I know of no law in
force in Canada that requires me to direct the Crown to
give to the defence a précis or statement of the evidence
to be given by various witnesses whose names appear on
the indictment ... application is refused. Call the jury.

By modern standards, this conduct by the Chief Justice appears
high-handed and insensitive to the defence. It is true that the Crown
had nothing to do with the escape by Suchan and Jackson. But the fact
was, the two accused were not apprehended and returned to custody
until September, and Robinette had no reason to prepare for a trial until
that took place. The question might fairly have been asked, What were
the Crown law officers doing all his time? They had not presented their
evidence to the grand jury until September 8 and did not receive a true
bill of indictment until the 9th. Our present-day disclosure requirements are much more stringent than they were during the early 1950s,
but one has to wonder why so much pressure was being placed on
Robinette to get on with the case without once asking the Crown in
what way it would be prejudiced by an adjournment of three days.
Indeed, the only interchange between the Crown and the bench was to
permit the Chief Justice to obtain some self-serving statements to but-
tress the ruling that he intended to make from the outset.

As for Maloney, McRuer's treatment of his requests for an adjournment and modest disclosure of the Crown's case borders on the outra-
geous. The requests related to the most fundamental right of an accused

person to be apprised in a timely fashion of the case he was being called on to meet. After all, Maloney took the case at the behest of the Chief Justice because he felt under an obligation as an officer of the court to do so. His client was charged with the murder of a police officer engaged in the duties of his office, an offence that on conviction mandated the death penalty. The indictment indicated that the Crown proposed to call almost fifty witnesses (forty-six were called), and the Crown's theory relating to the culpability of Jackson raised complex legal and factual issues. That said, trials were conducted in those days at a speed that would astonish today's judges and practitioners.

The failure to grant an adjournment was to be the first ground of appeal following the convictions of both accused. However, a five-judge panel of the Court of Appeal would unanimously dispose of it in a short sentence in a short endorsement:[70] "Both appellants raised as a ground of appeal, the refusal of the trial judge to grant a short adjournment, but we do not consider that there was any error in that respect on the part of the trial judge."

I have other criticisms of the trial that I will deal with, but I wish to make it clear from the outset that, as the Court of Appeal held, there was no miscarriage of justice in the verdicts of either Suchan or Jackson. The case for the Crown was overwhelming, and both Robinette and Maloney faced a hopeless task in attempting to save their clients from the hangman. My reservation is that the conduct of the Chief Justice became an unacceptable intrusion into the trial process on behalf of the Crown, which, I might add, needed no assistance whatsoever. Gibson and Bull were very experienced counsel, and the case for the Crown was carefully prepared and flawlessly submitted. A less interventionist — and may I add wiser — judge would have let them carry out their duties with a minimum of interruption. The result would have been the same, but there would have been no question of the fairness of this high-profile trial.

I had been with McCarthys a little more than a year, but it did not take long for me to learn from Robinette that he had no fondness for Chief Justice McRuer. He was convinced that McRuer was furious with him for obtaining the acquittal of Evelyn Dick on the charge of killing her husband. As the reader now knows from my treatment of the Evelyn Dick case, I agree with Robinette that McRuer was convinced of her guilt and was determined to get a conviction from the jury.

Whatever its origin, the tension between Robinette and McRuer during the Suchan trial was palpable. Sparring over the adjournment was just the beginning. The next phase of the trial was empanelling the jury, and this involved the vital task of defence counsel in selecting the individual members of the jury. Counsel knew nothing about the prospective jurors except their names, addresses, and occupations. In 1952, they were all men and had to own property within the County of York. Consequently, farmers made up a substantial segment of the panel, and the rest tended to be in an age group starting at about thirty and tending towards middle-aged. Investigative reports of individual jurors were unheard of, and counsel relied on a highly subjective assessment of the individual members of the jury panel based on their appearance, a description of their calling, and a trial-sharpened instinct as to which of the jurors they preferred.

In a criminal trial, the defence is able to challenge an individual juror on two bases. The more common is a peremptory challenge — one that requires no explanation and cannot be denied. The number of peremptory challenges is prescribed by the *Criminal Code* and is related directly to the severity of the offence for which the individual accused is being tried. The number for murder in 1952 was twenty; accordingly, Robinette and Malone had forty peremptory challenges between them. The Crown, for its part, had an unlimited number of "stand asides," which it could exercise after the accused, both of them in this case, indicated through counsel that they were prepared to accept the juror. Stand asides were the equivalent of peremptory challenges in that they required no justification.

The jury selection process usually took very little time. The jury panel, from which the jury was to be selected, was assembled in the body of the courtroom. As the clerk of the court called out their names from cards drawn at random from a wooden tumbler, the potential juror approached the front of the court and stood facing the prisoner in the dock. The selection ritual began with the clerk intoning, "Juror look upon the prisoner. Prisoner look upon the juror." At this point the clerk would pause to permit counsel to challenge the juror or to indicate that he was content. Counsel for the two accused would challenge first in the order in which the names of the accused appeared on the indictment. If the juror was challenged peremptorily, he was asked to take his seat in the body of the courtroom. If he was told by the Crown to stand aside, he was instructed to take his seat in the body of the courtroom but was told that he might be recalled. If the defence and the Crown accepted the juror, he was sworn in as a juror and asked to take his place in the jury box. This process continued until twelve jurors were sworn.

However, in addition to peremptory challenges and stand asides, the *Criminal Code* provided for challenges for cause with respect to individual jurors who were not qualified. This rarely happened. If a juror was disqualified, it was a simple matter to determine. However, one of the grounds identified under the rubric of "cause" was that the juror was "not indifferent between the Queen and the accused," meaning that the juror was biased against the accused for some reason. Reflecting their common judgment that theirs was a desperate case and desperate cases sometimes call for desperate measures, Robinette and Maloney decided to challenge each individual member for cause on the basis that his impartiality had been tainted by the intense pretrial publicity about the case.

Once the first juror was challenged for cause, two other members of the jury panel were selected at random, and they tried the issue as to whether the first juror was not indifferent between the Queen and the two accused. If he was found to be indifferent, he was sworn as a juror and replaced the first juror selected to try the cause issue. This process continued until a full jury panel was selected.

To my knowledge this challenge to each member of the panel was very much a first, and as far as Robinette was concerned it was to be a last.[71]

McRuer and Robinette crossed swords on the very first of the twenty possible jurymen called forward. Robinette challenged William H. Sharpe as not indifferent between the Queen and the two accused. Two of the twenty were called forward and sworn as triers of whether this was so. Robinette examined Sharpe, who admitted that he had discussed the case with others but had not expressed his opinion as to the guilt or innocence of Suchan. He answered in the affirmative when Robinette asked him whether he had formed an opinion, but before he could answer Robinette what that opinion was, McRuer jumped in:

McRuer:	I ask you this question before you answer that: are you prepared to put out of your mind any preconceived ideas you have and try the accused according to your oath?
Sharpe:	Yes, sir.
McRuer:	The oath that will be administered to you?
Sharpe:	Yes, sir.
Robinette:	He did not answer my question, my lord.
McRuer:	Have you any opinion as to the guilt or innocence?
Sharpe:	Yes.
Robinette:	He answered that. I put the further question to him, "What opinion have you formed?"
McRuer:	What do you say about that?
Sharpe:	You asked me, sir, if I could enter the case with a clear mind, and I say I can.
McRuer:	Then have you any preconceived opinion that is going to influence you?

Sharpe: No, sir.

Robinette: You answered my question when I put
               it to you as to whether you had an
               opinion — I think you indicated yes?

Sharpe: Yes, sir.

Robinette: What is that opinion?

Sharpe: I think there is guilt.

Robinette: I will leave it at that, my lord.

McRuer: Any further evidence?

Robinette: No, my lord.

McRuer: Now, gentlemen, the question you are
               to try is whether this juror stands
               indifferent, that is, will enter the case
               with an unprejudiced mind to try the
               accused and a true verdict give accord-
               ing to the evidence. If you want to
               retire to the jury room and discuss it
               between you, you may do so. If you are
               prepared to give your decision now —
               you must discuss it anyway; it is the
               joint view of the two of you, it is not an
               individual view we ask.

Pitt (Of the triers): The two of us have come to the con-
               clusion that this gentleman would give a
               true opinion, and he would be just in
               what he said, because he said he was
               quite willing —

McRuer:	You do not need to give reasons. Your view is that he is not [sic] indifferent?
Pitt:	He is not [sic] indifferent, sir — I don't think — he is not prejudiced.

Whereupon Robinette challenged the juror peremptorily. This type of questioning by McRuer continued for the balance of the potential jurors until a full panel was sworn. The continual interventions by the Chief Justice are reminiscent of his conduct in the *voir dire* of the Chief of Police of Dundas in the Evelyn Dick case. Again, what is notably absent is any comment by Crown counsel. In the full report of the proceedings, Gibson is reported as speaking only twice, and that is to exercise the Crown's right to stand aside two jurors.

What the record only partially reveals is the full participation of the Chief Justice in the challenge proceedings. The tone was set by the Chief Justice from the outset when he leaned over the witness box as Mr. Sharpe was about to express his opinion of the guilt or innocence of Suchan. In his rasping voice, McRuer reminded him of his oath to put preconceived ideas out of his mind and try the case according to the evidence. Mr. Sharpe impressed me as a man who thought that he was being very fair by admitting that he had a preconceived opinion, but the rest of the jury panel was put on notice that his was not the proper response. They quickly learned that the test was not whether they had a preconceived notion but whether they were prepared to observe their oaths as jurors and to try the case on the evidence presented in the courtroom.

In the end, the challenges for cause did little to assist the defence. While the answers given by prospective jurors helped defence counsel decide whether to accept a juror by waiving their challenge for cause or to reject him by using a peremptory challenge, the Crown always had the last word with its unlimited number of stand asides. Thus, while the defence may have avoided a poor choice of juror in some instances, they most certainly lost the ones whose answers to questions asked on the hearing of the cause challenge made them desirable to the defence but not the Crown.

Gibson's opening address for the Crown was concise and to the point. Briefly, he stated that Suchan[72] and Jackson were driving a car that belonged to Suchan's girlfriend when they were pulled over by detectives Tong and Perry. Tong got out to speak to the driver and he was shot. Perry was also shot in the arm as he sat in the driver's seat of the police car. The two accused fled the scene and were later apprehended in Montreal. Jackson was involved in a shootout with Montreal police and was shot three times before surrendering.

While a reading of the transcript of Gibson's opening address appears to be a methodical narrative of the evidence the Crown was prepared to call, his bearing and posture added a solemnity to the event that is not reflected on the printed page. In particular the transcript does not portray his Old Testament fervour when at the end of his address he looked directly at the two accused in the prisoners' box, pointed his finger at them, and said, "In due course the accused Valente J. Lesso alias Steve Suchan alias Victor J. Lenoff, and Leonard Jackson alias Fred Wilson were arrested in their Montreal hospitals and brought to Toronto and charged with the murder of Sergeant of Detectives Edmund Tong."

Gibson did not, in his opening address, attempt to put the theory of the Crown into a legal perspective. But Robinette and Maloney were well aware what the theory was: that the two accused had acted in concert to prevent their arrest, or at least the arrest of Jackson, who was unlawfully at large. For this reason the defence was anxious to restrict the evidence to be heard by the jury to the events of March 6 alone. They were aware that accomplishing this would be difficult. However, they probably did not anticipate the extent of the heavy weather they would experience from the Chief Justice.

The battle started with Robinette's objection to what he submitted were prejudicial statements in the Crown's opening that should result in a mistrial. These included references to the firing of air pistols at the tailor's dummy, the fact that Suchan had fathered an illegitimate child, and his possession of two unrelated weapons. The Chief Justice sharply disagreed. Maloney made similar submissions and added that the Crown's opening reference to Jackson's prior arrest for bank robbery by the deceased detective was inadmissible and prejudicial. McRuer responded that he thought the issues raised were relevant and good evidence. Just how Chief Justice McRuer could have found relevance in the assertion that Suchan had fathered an illegitimate child is hard to fathom. This reference was a clear attempt to cast Suchan in an unfavourable light given the strict, formal morality of the 1950s.

The domineering way in which the Chief Justice controlled the trial can be illustrated with reference to only a few of the many witnesses. In response to questions by the Crown, Anne Bosnich testified about her relationship to Suchan. She said that he lived with his parents and worked as a doorman at the King Edward Hotel and as a violinist for night dances. He had worked at one time for the Department of National Revenue as well. She testified that Suchan and Jackson had air pistols that they fired on a tailor's dummy in her basement. Crown counsel started to ask about Suchan's whereabouts prior to the shooting when Robinette objected:

Robinette:	I do not like to interrupt my friend, but I doubt the relevancy of all this detail. It does not seem to have anything to do with this case.
McRuer:	I can only determine that later. I will be very careful to caution the jury to disregard all this detail unless it has some particular relevance to this case.
Gibson:	I may be wrong in my opinion, but I think it is material.
McRuer:	One has to trust Crown counsel a great deal in the development of a case. I do not see that it can do any harm at the present time. It is not inflammatory. It shows the relationship between these two people, at any rate. We will proceed with it.

Robinette did obtain the concession that Bosnich's evidence be scrutinized first in the absence of the jury. At a *voir dire* the following exchange took place:

Robinette: My friend indicated to me, very kindly, that he was now prepared to question the witness with reference to the incident he described in his opening to the jury: that is the possession of air pistols and the tailor's dummy in the basement. I think we ought to hear that evidence because, in my view, there is very grave doubt as to its admissibility.

McRuer: Is it necessary for us to hear the details of the evidence? Mr. Gibson has stated in his opening address the nature of the evidence that will be given. It will be admitted or refused on a matter of principle and not on the details.

Robinette: I do not know how far this might make some possible difference: as to whether she saw the firing of the air pistols at the dummy, or who was doing it, or how far away they were standing when it was done. All that would go to the question of admissibility. My principal objection is that all of that is irrelevant, that it has nothing to do with of an alleged crime on the 6th March. It is not suggested that the air pistols are connected with the commission of the offence.

McRuer: The jury will have to decide on the state of mind of these men in the application of one branch of the law. A conspiracy is a state of mind, and to use Mr. Justice Kellock's words in *Henderson v. The King:*[73]

"The question, after all, is whether the jury would conclude on the evidence that the men had sufficient reason for thinking they had rendered themselves liable to arrest for matters involving sufficiently unpleasant consequences that they had determined to resist arrest to the extent of using violence if that should be necessary."

If two men are practising shooting at a dummy while one of them is being sought by the police as one who has escaped gaol, I would think it would be evidence that would not exclude that principle laid down by Mr. Justice Kellock.

Robinette: Suppose they were playing darts down in the basement.

McRuer: That is a very different thing. Detective Tong was not killed with a dart.

Robinette: He was not killed by an air pistol. You do not fire an air gun the same way you fire a pistol — at least in my limited knowledge of firearms.

McRuer: I do not know. We will have to hear about what kind of pistols they were. I think practising shooting at a target with any kind of a gun might be rele-

vant having regard to the principle of
law laid down by Mr. Justice Kellock.

What to me is instructive about this exchange is that it is made
without reference to the Crown. Gibson was an old hand with no small
sense of importance, but there must have been times when he asked
himself, Why am I here? There can be no doubt that McRuer was correct about the law, but the problem here, as Robinette would develop in
cross-examination, was that Bosnich had not actually seen the accused
shooting at the dummies. In fact, Bosnich almost never went to the
basement, and it had been three years since she paid attention to the
dummies. Nevertheless, McRuer admitted the evidence. He ruled that
all of Robinette's concerns went to weight and not admissibility.

Maloney did not have any better luck. He proffered two cases,[74]
relying in particular on *The Queen v. Noor Mohamed,* in support of the
proposition that the Court should not admit evidence with minimal
relevance to the crimes enumerated in the indictment. McRuer's
response was:

> The evidence goes to state of mind. Even if it is weak
> evidence, it is admissible. From the evidence offered it
> is possible for the jury to infer that these two men
> were practising to shoot at something resembling a
> human form. ...
>
> I cannot try a case piece-meal. ... I cannot interfere
> with the Crown's right to present it to the Court. What
> value is to be given to it afterwards is for the jury.

Maloney: Your lordship does not mind if I try to
make myself clear?

McRuer: I think you made yourself very clear.
You usually do.

Maloney: Do I understand your lordship to say
that one can infer from this evidence a

	state of mind in either one of the accused at the time of the crime?
McRuer:	I am not going to be cross-examined and put down for future attack at this stage. I shall charge the jury as to the relevancy of the evidence in due course.
Maloney:	Still quoting one more excerpt from *Noor Mohamed.* The evidence must be "sufficiently substantial" and not of "trifling weight" … "even though there may be some tenuous ground for holding it technically admissible." "The decision must then be left to the discretion and the sense of fairness of the judge."
McRuer:	Exercising my discretion and my sense of fairness, I think the evidence is admissible.

Detective-Sergeant Roy Perry, Tong's partner, was a key witness. He was a victim and was in a position to testify about what actually occurred. He appeared pale and tense. The defence had been advised that he had been severely traumatized by what had happened that day to him and his partner. There was some concern whether he could testify at all. But he did testify, and did so calmly and effectively. He claimed that Jackson had fired his gun. This evidence was devastating to Jackson, whose defence was to be that he was little more than an onlooker.

Maloney could not let this evidence stand unchallenged. He tried to contradict Perry by confronting him with what he had previously said at the preliminary inquiry. For example, Perry testified at the preliminary that it was Suchan who had shot him in the arm. In contrast, at the trial Perry stated he was not sure who had shot him. Maloney then confronted him with the horns of the following dilemma: Was his testimony at the preliminary inquiry more accurate because it was fresher in his mind, or had he given inaccurate testimony there? But McRuer interjected constantly to protect Perry's credibility by accusing Maloney of asking unfair questions.

Two additional witnesses illustrate what would appear to be unnecessary intervention by the trial judge to assist the Crown. Crown witness Dr. Fielden was a pathologist who testified about the cause of Tong's death. In cross-examining this witness, Robinette and Maloney tried to show that Tong lived for seventeen days after the bullet wounds and that he actually died from a blood clot unrelated to those wounds. Maloney, in particular, tried to develop this theme, pointing out to the witness that Tong was breathing and resting comfortably for seventeen days. The blood clot was too remote to have been caused by the bullet wounds. He brought out that the pathologist had only seen two or three cases of spinal injuries from bullets over his twenty-five years of experience. At this point McRuer interrupted:

> Mr. Maloney, I do not want this case to be confused with the suggestion — vague suggestion — that Sergeant Tong was not properly treated, and therefore that that should be a defence. You realize what the law is about that, if you are suggesting anything of the kind.

> Maloney: I did not quite contend that suggestion.

> McRuer: Well, then, it is all right. I just wanted to be clear as to what the cross-examination is directed to, so that the jury and I may understand it.

Perhaps the most flagrant example of intervention by the trial judge concerned ballistics expert W.W. Sutherland from the RCMP Crime Detection Laboratory. Robinette, knowing that Suchan would later admit in testimony that he emptied his revolver in Tong's direction, did not intend to expend a significant part of his limited preparation time in becoming an expert on ballistics. He asked me to see what I could find that could be helpful. There was not much literature on the subject at the time, but I did find a book, the name of which I forget, in the library of the University of Toronto. It was a good read, but it emphasized what Robinette already knew: that the best cross-examination could not discredit a bona fide expert. Ballistic comparison was a science and given adequate comparables was a compelling piece of identification evidence. The major attack the author recommended was a challenge to the expert's credentials, but this was an American book in which the author had experience with some so-called experts who had very little expertise at all. Robinette was dealing with an acknowledged expert, and he knew from his client's mouth that the bullets lodged in the bodies of Tong and Perry came from Suchan's gun.

I was to learn later that Robinette did not believe in trying to "destroy" an expert witness whose qualifications permitted him or her to give the evidence that was relevant to the particular case. He simply tried to soften the opinion given and build a platform for the introduction of his own expert or experts. It was a non-confrontational strategy that stood him in good stead over the years. Another approach he used was to obtain assistance from the opposing expert by obtaining favourable answers on some collateral issue that the witness had not testified to in chief. It was this latter course that Robinette chose in the case of this expert.

Sutherland had matched the slugs from Tong's body and elsewhere to the gun found in Suchan's possession when he was arrested. Robinette sought to diminish the significance of the damning evidence of the target practice in the basement of the house on Wright Avenue. Robinette's line of questions was constructed to force the witness to concede that air pistols and revolvers have different recoils. Target practice with an air pistol would not improve the shooter's aim in firing the revolvers used on the police officers. After extracting this helpful evidence, Robinette ended his questions, only to watch McRuer begin his:

McRuer:	How long have you been making these examinations for giving evidence at trials?

Sutherland:	The past eight years. But most of the court appearances have been in the last four or five years.
McRuer:	And recognizing the serious nature of the evidence, I say to you, have you — what do you say as to this question, as to whether you have a firm conclusion that the bullet which was removed from Sergeant Tong's body was fired through exhibit No. 33 [Suchan's gun]?
Sutherland:	I have no real or honest doubt.
McRuer:	You have no doubt about it at all.
Sutherland:	No doubt.
McRuer:	That is based on all the examinations that you have made of the various ...
Sutherland:	This examination, and the whole of my experience, sir.
McRuer:	All right.

Maloney fared no better in his cross-examination of Sutherland. He asked one question about which gun the bullet came from. McRuer interrupted this solitary question with six of his own, exasperating Maloney. For example:

Maloney:	Will your lordship permit me to ask the officer about the bullet that was removed from Perry's ...

McRuer:	Yes; that was exhibit 34. He says it was eliminated from the guns that were said to have come from the possession of Jackson.

Sutherland was the last Crown witness. It was now Saturday morning and Robinette was called on to start the defence. His one and only witness was Suchan. Considering the strength of the Crown's case and the fact that the defence had been forced on with little time for preparation, one would be forgiven for thinking that defence counsel would be granted some leeway in examining his own client upon whose credibility so much rested. It was not to be.

Suchan's defence was thin. The thrust of it was that he was aware that he, along with his parents, was harbouring Edwin Boyd, who was a fugitive from justice. He also had with him in the car Jackson, who was "hotter than a firecracker because of his break from the Don." In the circumstances, he did not want to become involved in controversy with any motorist because this could attract the attention of the police. He was prepared to go to unusual lengths to prevent this from happening.

After Suchan was called to the stand and took the oath, Robinette led him through his evidence. Robinette liked to get his witnesses' evidence in quickly. As was his habit with other witnesses, Robinette set the stage for the defence with an economy of words. He guided Suchan, without leading questions, to the crucial area, which in this case was the day of the shooting.

Robinette:	Now bring your mind to Thursday March 8, 1952. Did you know Ann Camera at that time?
Suchan:	Yes.
Robinette:	At about 1.00 p.m. were you in Mrs. Camera's car?
Suchan:	I was.

Robinette: Were you driving or were you a pas-
                 senger?

Suchan: I was driving.

Robinette: Did you have any passenger?

Suchan: My passenger was Lennie.

Robinette: The other accused?

Suchan: That's correct.

Robinette: When you left 190 Wright Avenue,
                 where were you planning to go?

Suchan: I was driving Lennie to the bus depot
                 on Bay Street.

Robinette: Where had he intended to go?

Suchan: He wanted to go by bus to Oshawa and
                 get the train to Montreal.

McRuer: That is hearsay.

Robinette: What street did you drive along?

Suchan: I drove west to Roncesvalles, up
                 Roncesvalles, up Sorauren, along
                 Dundas and I intended to go along
                 College Street.

Robinette: Did you drive east on College?

Suchan: Yes I did.

Robinette:	As you approached the intersection of College and Lansdowne, did anything occur?
Suchan:	Yes it did.
Robinette:	Did you know Sergeant of Detectives Edmund Tong?
Suchan:	No, I did not.
Robinette:	Did you know Detective Sergeant Perry?
Suchan:	No.
Robinette:	What happened at that intersection?

Suchan then testified that as he was driving along College Street towards Lansdowne, he saw a car crowding him into the curb and thought it might have been a car he cut off a few blocks back. He did not know Perry or Tong and did not recognize that the car was a police cruiser. Suchan testified that he did not want to be discovered with Jackson because he had recently escaped from custody and was concerned that any police investigation would quickly link him and his parents to Boyd.

As the car tried to crowd him into the curb, Suchan fired his gun in the direction of the car's hood in an attempt to damage its engine and to get away. He stated that he never got out of his car and that he never saw anyone get out of the other car. He still did not know that it was a police cruiser. After he fired his gun, he was not aware that Jackson left the car, but he did notice Jackson when he jumped back into their car as Suchan started to drive away. He ran a red light and abandoned the car a few blocks away. He and Jackson then took taxis to Bronte, Oakville, Burlington, and finally Hamilton. In Hamilton they stole a car and drove to Montreal.

The next night, Suchan went to his apartment in Montreal and was greeted with the sound of a gun being drawn behind him. He wheeled, saw a flash of a gun barrel and a man's forehead before he felt a stinging pain in his arm and then his hip. He never drew his gun.

Robinette:	Could you indicate on your body [where you were shot]?
McRuer:	What relevance has this now?
Robinette:	My lord, the relevance is that your lordship admitted the evidence of the police detectives on the theory that subsequent conduct is relevant, and in my submission I am entitled to develop the whole of the subsequent conduct.
McRuer:	Well, all right, if you think it is important.
Robinette:	I do my lord. [Then to the witness:] Where were you injured?
Suchan:	Just below the heart, just to the left of centre. The other was in the hand and the third shot went through the stomach and out the back hip.

Suchan concluded his testimony by describing how three or four weeks prior to the trial, he had escaped from jail and was recaptured on a farm in North York without a shot being fired, even though there was opportunity to shoot and kill policemen. Robinette persuaded McRuer to accept this evidence as subsequent conduct of peaceable surrender to offset the Crown's evidence of subsequent conduct in Suchan's original apprehension, which, in the theory of the Crown, amounted to violence.

As between the two accused, both Robinette and Maloney considered Suchan to be the more vulnerable witness on cross-examination. It was vital to Jackson that Suchan be persuasive because he was prepared to take all the blame. However, Suchan stood up surprisingly well under the bludgeoning cross-examination of the skilled and forceful Gibson.

He did not change his evidence in any respect, and in particular admitted that all six bullets had been fired from his gun and that the gun was aimed at the cruiser, not its occupants.

Robinette understood that Jackson was not going to testify.[75] However, emboldened by Suchan's performance, Maloney changed his mind and was prepared to call Jackson in his own defence. He asked for fifteen minutes to confer with his client. McRuer said he could only have ten.

Jackson was called and sworn. Maloney sought to humanize him by bringing out some of his background. He wanted the jury to see him as a person, not simply stigmatized as a member of the Boyd Gang.

> Maloney: What education did you have?
>
> Jackson: 8th Grade
>
> McRuer: Is this relevant?
>
> …
>
> Maloney: What other type of work did you do?
>
> McRuer: Is this relevant?
>
> Maloney: I submit it is relevant to show something about the accused's background.
>
> McRuer: I do not know that it makes any difference what background he may have. You cannot show the background of an accused to show he is likely to commit a crime, nor can you show the background to show that he is unlikely to commit a crime. I would think it would work both ways. But be as brief as you can.

When the Crown was leading its witnesses, Crown counsel was permitted to go into the background of many of them without encountering any objection from the bench. That thought must have been in Maloney's mind because he ignored the rebuke from McRuer and continued with about another dozen background questions.

Jackson then provided his narrative of the events on the critical day. He stated that he was a passenger in Suchan's car. As he was consulting the train schedule, the car stopped and out of the corner of his eye he was alerted by someone — he was not sure who it was. He got out of the car and was about to flee because he was a wanted man. As he started towards the rear of the vehicle, he heard a volley of shots and pulled out his gun to protect himself. He never fired. He did not know the men in the cruiser as he did not see their faces. He thought it might have been a police cruiser because of the aerial in the middle. He saw a body lying on the ground when Suchan's car started moving. He decided to run back and jump in.

Robinette did not question Jackson. But Gibson's cross-examination was very effective. He established that Jackson knew officers Tong and Perry by sight. This exchange followed:

Gibson:	You got to the back of the car with your gun out?
Jackson:	I drew my gun after I had reached the back of the car approximately.
McRuer:	Just a moment. I want to get that accurately. Did you say, "I drew my gun after I reached the back of the car practically?"
Jackson:	To tell you the truth, my lord, I drew it after I heard the shots.
McRuer:	I want the answer. Give it to me, Mr. Reporter, please.

(Reporter reads back what Jackson said.)

Gibson:	And you were not going to be taken, arrested, if you could help it?
Jackson:	Sir, the reason I carried the gun was to not be apprehended, to assist me in escaping apprehension, not to use the gun but to help …
McRuer:	Just a moment. Did you have it loaded?
Jackson:	Yes, sir, I did.
McRuer:	Did you need to have it loaded just to assist you in escaping without using it?
Jackson:	Yes, sir.
McRuer:	You thought you should have it loaded to assist you in escaping?
Jackson:	Yes, sir.
McRuer:	Without using it. Is that your answer?
Jackson:	Yes, sir.

When Gibson was allowed to continue, he established that Jackson carried weapons after his escape from jail in case of violent encounters with someone trying to apprehend him. Gibson then asked about an earlier occasion when Suchan picked him up at Oshawa from the train from Montreal, so as not to be spotted at busy Union Station. He continued:

Gibson:	Lesso [Suchan] knew that is why you wanted to be picked up from Oshawa.

Jackson: I can't read another man's mind, sir.

McRuer: Did you have any conversation with him as to why he should go down at six o'clock in the morning and pick you up at Oshawa, when you could stay on the train and come through to Toronto?

Jackson: No sir, I asked if he would pick me up.

McRuer: He knew that you had escaped at that time?

Jackson: Yes, sir.

McRuer: And he came down to pick you up.

Jackson: That is right.

Gibson went on to establish that Anne Camera's car was used to avoid detection because it had an innocent plate. He also elicited that Jackson grew a moustache and started wearing glasses as a disguise.

Once Gibson had finished his cross-examination, Maloney re-examined Jackson in an attempt to rehabilitate him. I can still remember the look of relief on Jackson's face as he started to leave the witness box, the ordeal of testimony behind him. But the now familiar rasping voice of McRuer stopped him in his tracks.

McRuer: One or two questions I want to ask you. Did you go by the name of Wilson in Montreal?

Jackson: Yes, sir.

Mcruer: When you left 190 Wright Avenue on March 6, were you carrying a brief case?

Jackson:	Yes, sir.
McRuer:	Why were you carrying a brief case?
Jackson:	For a disguise, sir.
McRuer:	Was Lesso [Suchan] carrying a brief case for a disguise too?
Jackson:	I don't know sir.
McRuer:	Had you in mind what you were going to use the briefcases for?
Jackson:	No, sir. I just carried it for disguise.
McRuer:	I want to understand a little more [about your purpose for arming your-self with a loaded revolver]. Was it a revolver or a pistol?
Jackson:	A revolver.
McRuer:	Was it a .45?
Jackson:	No sir.
McRuer:	What caliber?
Jackson:	32-20.
McRuer:	That is a revolver that will cause death?
Jackson:	Yes sir.
McRuer:	No doubt about that?

Jackson: That is right, sir.

McRuer: What was your purpose in arming yourself with a loaded revolver?

Jackson: To aid me in attempting to flee if I was apprehended.

McRuer: To aid you in attempting to flee if you were apprehended. That you would fire it to assist you in attempting to flee if you were apprehended — was that the purpose?

Jackson: Not to kill, sir.

McRuer: I am saying to fire it.

Jackson: Yes, sir.

McRuer: So it is perfectly fair and perfectly clear, is it, that as you went out and got into that car and drove to the corner of Lansdowne and College, you were armed with a loaded revolver, having in your mind that you would fire it if necessary in an effort to assist you in escaping lawful apprehension?

Jackson: Yes, sir.

The transcript records what I still think today was a remarkable display of injudicial conduct on the part of the Chief Justice. This conduct is particularly offensive when dealing with the accused. It is difficult to overstate the impact of questions from the presiding judge at a jury trial. They are given more weight by members of the jury because they trust the impartiality of the questioner and assume that he is asking questions for the purpose of eliciting the truth and not as a combatant in a forensic duel. The mere physical presence of the trial judge gives him an advantage. He is speaking from the bench, an elevated position of authority and strength, literally hovering over the witness who is obliged to look up at him in giving his answers. He can expect no help from counsel in the form of objections to unfair questions. There is no one left to rule on the objections.

The questions of the Chief Justice and the answers to them sealed Jackson's fate. They also doomed Suchan because the admission by Jackson that he intended to use his gun in order to prevent apprehension made a mockery out of Suchan's testimony that he had acted alone and on the spur of the moment. Maloney's biographer, Charles Pullen, explains that it was Jackson who changed his mind and insisted that he wanted to testify and that Maloney did not have the experience to persuade him otherwise.[76] However it happened, with the benefit of hindsight, Jackson's decision to testify was a mistake. Jackson could not improve on the defence Suchan had provided to him, and as it turned out he destroyed himself by trying. As Robinette put it later in his oral history, "Jackson was terrible. He virtually said that he was guilty. McRuer asked him a question and Jackson made an answer virtually saying, 'Yes, I intended to kill him.' It was just about that bad."

The evidence was completed on the Saturday afternoon, and the trial adjourned to Monday morning for the addresses of counsel and the instruction of the jury by the Chief Justice. Unfortunately, as was customary, the addresses of counsel were not transcribed, and Robinette's file that would contain his notes cannot be found at McCarthy Tétrault.

Robinette was the first counsel to address the jury. This was not my first opportunity to hear him in such a circumstance. I had been with him in court as his student when he had acted in other criminal cases and had obtained favourable verdicts for his clients. But you cannot take the full measure of a counsel unless you have seen him with his back to the wall in defence of a client who faces the death penalty. Unlike some counsel whose eloquence and fervour are often muted and rendered hesitant by the lack of substance to their case, Robinette's performances were always a *tour de force*. His great voice, a rich baritone, he used to full effect. His was a commanding presence dominated by a handsome head and lit up by brown eyes, which could flash in anger or mist over in sorrow. When he spoke, he dominated the courtroom. The members of the jury were riveted.

Robinette carefully reviewed the facts of the case and related them to the theory of Suchan's defence. As stated, it was that Suchan did not wish to be involved in an incident arising out of a dispute with another motorist because he was in the company of Jackson, an escaped prisoner. He might then be investigated by the police and it would be discovered that he had been harbouring another escaped prisoner, Boyd. This would also land his parents in trouble because Boyd had stayed at the Suchan home. Accordingly, he fired a number of shots directed at the engine of the other car trying to immobilize it so that he could make his getaway. Suchan, submitted Robinette, did not see Tong and did not intend to shoot him. This was not to suggest, Robinette told the jury, that Suchan's conduct was not blameworthy and that he should be allowed to escape the consequences of his unlawful conduct in discharging his firearm in the direction of the two men. However, a verdict of guilty was not warranted, and the ends of justice would be met by a verdict of manslaughter.

It was an eloquent and persuasive address, but you can't make a silk purse out of a sow's ear. The desperation of this defence is what probably drove Robinette to indulge in one of his rare oratorical excesses. Referring to the shootout with the Montreal police on the arrest of his client, he referred to Suchan's serious injuries and suggested that a higher force had perhaps intervened to save Suchan's life. If the suggestion to the jury was that its members should not undo God's work, it backfired. Gibson seized on the suggestion in his opening remarks to the jury. "Gentlemen," Gibson said. "I've been working on this trial for months and months and today for the first time I've heard that divine intervention entered into the case."

When reminded about this later, Robinette was rueful. "That was a spectacular opening. He was just as scathing as he could be with that line, and I was the one who'd opened the door for him to use it."[77]

The Chief Justice's charge to the jury was very complete. After starting with the standard instruction on the duties of the jurors and the legal definitions of homicide, he charged them that under what was then section 259 of the *Code*: culpable homicide is murder if (a) the offender means to cause the death of the person killed; (b) means to cause to the person killed any bodily injury that is known to the offender as likely to cause death and is reckless whether death ensues or not; and (c) if the offender, for any unlawful object, does an act that he knows or ought to have known to be likely to cause death, and thereby kills any person, though he may have desired that his object should be effected without hurting anyone. He summed up by stating:

> Culpable homicide means blameable or unlawful death. Thus, culpable homicide is murder if the offender means to cause the death of the person killed — and I remind you that I said a man is presumed to intend the natural consequences of his acts. His intention is sometimes gathered from whether he had a motive or not, and it helps a great deal in some cases to find out, did the man have a motive to kill.

The case for the Crown was that the fatal shot had been fired by one or other of the accused in carrying out their common unlawful intention of resisting, with their revolvers, Jackson's apprehension. Therefore, both were parties to the offence of murder because of section 69(2) of the *Code*, which provided:

> 69. (2) If several persons form an intention in common to prosecute any unlawful purpose, and to assist each other therein, each of them is party to every offence committed by any one of them in the prosecution of such common purpose, the commission of which offence was, or ought to have been known to be a probable consequence of the prosecution of such common purpose.

The Chief Justice told the jury that whether the shooting happened the way Suchan said or the way others said, Suchan had conceded that his motive in shooting was to prevent an investigation into his relationship with a man known as Boyd. He turned to common intention:

> If you find Lesso [Suchan] to have committed the fatal shot, you then proceed to Jackson's guilt or innocence. Was there a concerted plan of these two accused to prosecute any unlawful purpose and to assist each other therein? Was the shooting of Tong done in the prosecution of that unlawful purpose, and was that an act which Jackson knew, or ought to have known, to be the probable consequence of such unlawful purpose? A plan to resist lawful apprehension is, gentlemen, an unlawful purpose.

The question, after all, is whether the jury would conclude on the evidence "that these two men had sufficient reason for thinking they had rendered themselves liable to arrest for matters involving sufficiently unpleasant consequences that they had determined to resist arrest to the extent of using violence if it should prove necessary."

The Chief Justice stated that carrying firearms was unlawful in the circumstances of this case. He recounted the undisputed facts of the case, for example that the fatal bullet came from Suchan's gun. He then reminded the jury of the following facts that Robinette had specifically objected to in the conference prior to the jury charge because they were not all on the record. These facts included Jackson's previous arrest by Tong on July 30, 1951; that Tong was present for Jackson's trial on September 25, 1951 (at this point McRuer stated "You may draw your own conclusion whether Jackson knew Tong on sight"); and that Jackson was taken into custody on November 3, 1951, but on November 4, he was no longer there.

McRuer then invited the jury to consider these facts as making up elements of an unlawful purpose. To all of this Robinette strongly objected. Nonetheless, the Chief Justice later returned to the same theme by suggesting that the accused's intent was also to kill Perry since he would be the only one who could identify them. He said, "Were they both covering Perry, the only living man there who might identify them? Gentlemen, it is for your judgment. Or the only man they hoped would be there that might identify them."

McRuer's final instruction was that the jury must decide if Suchan was not guilty, or if guilty, whether he was guilty of murder or manslaughter. If Suchan was found not guilty, then as a matter of law, Jackson was not guilty and the jury should so find. However, if Suchan was found guilty of either murder or manslaughter, the jury must then consider whether, when the shots were fired, the two accused were acting out of a common intention to resist Jackson's arrest with violence.

The jury retired at 5:40 p.m., and the defence made its objections to the charge. Robinette had been steaming as he listened to McRuer trivialize the defence. Now given the opportunity to voice his protest, he was brief and to the point:

> My Lord, I did think with the greatest respect that your lordship only referred to the defence to pour scorn on it, and the defence was not adequately and fairly put to the jury.

After listening to Maloney's objections, McRuer turned to Robinette:

> Mr. Robinette, I would be indebted to you if you could elucidate the matters in which you say I did not fairly put to the defence of your client.

> Robinette: In discussing the theory of the defence it was only mentioned really to be criticized. In the net result, the suggestion that it was open for the jury to find manslaughter was rather made light of; your lordship said, "If you believe the explanation you can convict of manslaughter."

McRuer: It is awfully hard for me — would you put to me what you say is your legal position of how the jury could possibly convict of manslaughter?

Robinette: The legal proposition is that the accused did not intend to cause death and did not intend to cause bodily harm and that it was not a bodily injury which was known to the offender to likely cause death, and reckless whether death ensued or not. They should be told that if they are in a state of doubt they should bring in manslaughter and not murder.

McRuer: I think that is a proper observation.

The jury returned at 5:59 p.m. and the Chief Justice addressed some of Maloney's concerns and said this about Robinette's:

One counsel suggested that I mentioned the theory of the defence to pour scorn on it. I am not here to pour scorn on any theories put forward. I have a duty to point out weaknesses of the prosecution's evidence and those of the other side. If I point out weaknesses on one side or the other, I am not pouring scorn on any theory. The jury is the sole finder of fact and if I have led you to accept evidence otherwise, disregard it completely. I only pointed things out for your serious consideration and nothing more.

With respect to the defence's suggestion of manslaughter, it is contended that the accused did not intend to cause the death of Tong and that the evidence was not established beyond a reasonable doubt that he did mean to cause bodily injury which was known to him to be likely to cause death, and was reckless whether death ensued or not. If you are in doubt, it becomes an unintentional killing and becomes manslaughter.

The jury retired again at 6:55 p.m. and returned at 7:40 p.m. with verdicts of guilty as charged against both accused. The Chief Justice sentenced the two men individually. They both were to be taken to the place of execution on December 16, 1952, and hanged by the neck until they were dead.

McRuer thanked the jury: "I cannot see how you could have arrived at any other verdict upon the evidence." He thanked Maloney "for accepting this difficult assignment on such short notice and for performing it in a very distinguished manner." He also thanked all of the witnesses and the officials of the administration of justice. He thanked the press for their co-operation in playing the role of informing the public and in informing witnesses so that they could come forward. He did not thank Robinette.

When I left the courtroom that Monday night, I was not aware that I had witnessed one of the great trials of Canadian legal history. What was to follow in the proceedings against the two accused was anticlimactic and, in retrospect, inevitable.

Robinette's notice of appeal to the Court of Appeal listed six grounds of appeal, which reflected the objections made at trial: (1) the trial judge failed to grant an adjournment; (2) he erred in refusing to order the Crown to produce a summary of the evidence to be given by witnesses who were not called at the preliminary inquiry; (3) he erred in admitting evidence regarding the presence of air pistols at 190 Wright Avenue; (4) he erred in admitting evidence regarding the presence of parts of a tailor's dummy at 190 Wright Avenue; (5) he erred in admitting evidence relating to the arrest of the accused in Montreal and the finding of articles unconnected with the case; and (6) he erred in his charge by failing to present the defence's theory as fully and fairly as he presented the theory of the Crown.

Robinette and Maloney appeared in the Court of Appeal for the appellants on November 10. William B. Common, K.C., who was now the senior Crown law officer, represented the Crown. Bill Common had justified the high hopes of those who put their faith in him, becoming an outstanding appellate lawyer. He was a very fair man and presented the facts of a criminal case with scrupulous impartiality, never hesitating to concede a point against the Crown where his own preparation of the appeal indicated that it was merited. However, there were to be no concessions on this day. Common was loaded for bear. Not that it would have done them much good in this case, but Robinette and Maloney had lost from the bench McRuer's firm critic, John Robertson. He had retired on September 1, 1952, and was replaced on September 24 by John W. Pickup from Robertson's old law firm, Fasken, Robertson, Aitchison, Pickup and Calvin.

The appeal lasted two days before a panel of five justices of appeal presided over by the new Chief Justice. I was surprised that immediately following the end of the hearing and despite the lengthy arguments of counsel, the Chief Justice read a three-paragraph endorsement on behalf of the Court dismissing both appeals virtually without reasons. The Court was clearly influenced by the strength of the Crown's case to the point that it did not think that it needed to deal with the merits of the appellants' arguments except in the most summary fashion. The Chief Justice read:

> As to the appellant Suchan, there can be no doubt that on March 6th, 1952 he shot Detective Tong. He deliberately opened fire with his revolver in the direction of Mr. Tong and killed him. He was plainly guilty of murder. He had a fair trial.

That says it all. No analysis, no reference to authority; just a bald statement that amounted to a concurrent finding of guilt. As to Jackson, while conceding that it was not a shot from his gun that killed Tong, the Court said, "There is ample evidence upon which the jury could find that he and Suchan, at the time the shooting occurred, had formed a common intention to resist arrest by violence." Common grounds of appeal put forward by Robinette and Maloney respecting the admission of evidence of what took place at the arrest of the two in Montreal, of the target practice on Wright Avenue, and of the fact that they had armed themselves after their escape from the Don Jail were either ignored or dismissed without any reasons. The Court stated:

> We are of the opinion that the evidence as to what took place when the appellant Jackson was arrested in Montreal on March 11th was properly admitted, also the evidence of the so called target practice at the home on Wright Avenue on March 5th as well as the evidence as to having armed himself with guns after his escape some time before from the Toronto Gaol.

The next avenue of appeal was the Supreme Court of Canada. But an appeal to that court was available only on a question of law and only if a single judge of that court was prepared to grant the accused leave to have the appeal heard by a full panel of the court. An application was duly made and fully argued in his chambers in Ottawa before Mr. Justice Wilfrid Estey, whose son Willard Z. "Bud" Estey later became a member of that court. Here at least the appellants' counsel had the benefit of full reasons as to why their application was being rejected. Estey wrote a thirteen-page judgment that set out the facts of the case extensively and dealt with the objections of the two appellants in detail.[78] Even Maloney's favourite case, *Noor Mohamed v. The King,* was distinguished.

Robinette was later to describe Justice Estey as a kindly and conscientious man. He felt that Estey was very concerned about this case and wanted to be sure in his own mind that there was no basis for granting leave to appeal. Estey knew that if he did not grant leave, both accused men would be hanged. There was no possibility of a commutation of their sentences to life imprisonment. In Robinette's opinion it was for this reason that Estey took the rather unusual step of reserving his decision for six days and writing a judgment explaining it. His was the type of judgment that the Court of Appeal ought to have written.

In any event, good judicial writing or bad, it was the last real hope that the accused had for a review of their convictions. The application to the Minister of Justice and the federal cabinet for a commutation of the death penalty to life imprisonment was rejected. Suchan and Jackson were hanged at the Don Jail on December 16, 1952, right on schedule.

The days before the hanging were very difficult for Robinette. A defence lawyer in a criminal case develops a certain closeness to his or her client. It arises, I think, out of the knowledge that you are all that stands between the person you are defending and incarceration, or in this case, death. No matter how heinous the crime alleged, your duty is to put the best face on your client's conduct; to become a protector of his rights under the law. The client for his part looks to you as his last best chance for either acquittal or at least a diminution of his culpability. As a result, you tend to look for his best features and to gloss over his less stellar qualities.

Robinette was no exception. His natural tendency was to remain detached from his clients, both in civil and criminal cases. He brought a cerebral intensity to his professional tasks and was not one to be caught up in causes or swayed by sentimentality. However, he did care very much about Suchan. He found that he was a surprisingly sensitive man with a deep knowledge and love of music. He came to adopt Mrs. Lesso's theme that her son was a good man who fell into bad company. Certainly Suchan was a brave man and went to his death with a stoicism that very much affected Robinette. He kept telling Robinette not to worry about him, although he felt terrible for his mother's sake. Robinette described his last visit to Suchan a few days before the hanging:

> When I left him, I was in tears. He said to me, "Don't cry, Mr. Robinette, don't you cry — you have done wonderfully well — I will be all right." And then I shook hands and said goodbye. It wasn't easy. He said he had a brother, and he said to me, "One thing I would like you to do, I just want to make sure that you speak to my brother, because he has been writing to me very wonderful letters, and I have written him back — just tell him that you feel I am going to be all right." I did that. And with Mrs. Suchan. Tough, however. It still bothers me.[79]

Mrs. Lesso told Robinette, who she mistakenly believed was Roman Catholic, that her son had been baptized a Catholic, and she was anxious that he return to the church and make his confession before he died.

Robinette spoke to Arthur Maloney, a devout Catholic, and through him arranged to have Father John Kelly attend on Suchan. Father Kelly was an academic who later became the president of St. Michael's University. He had a number of discussions with Suchan about sports and books before bringing the conversation around to religion. Before he died, Suchan reaffirmed his faith, and Father Kelly took his confession.[80]

Meanwhile, Jackson, who was born Leonard Stone to a Jewish mother and an English father and had been raised as a Jew, had listened to all these conversations between Father Kelly and Suchan from his adjoining cell. He became interested in Catholicism and, with the assistance of Maloney, persuaded Father Kelly to let him take instruction and convert to the Catholic religion. In the end, Father Kelly took his confession as well.

Maloney took a good deal of solace in Jackson's conversion. He took the hanging of his client very hard. Robinette felt that it took him a long time to get over it. The conversion of Jackson to Catholicism was the one bright spot in the whole tragic affair, as far as Maloney was concerned. He said as much to Robinette, but the Huguenot in Robinette was not impressed. As he later recalled to me, he told Maloney, "You were supposed to save his neck, not his soul."

Chapter Eight
JJR Makes a Choice

L IFE AS AN ARTICLING STUDENT at McCarthy & McCarthy had been busy and stimulating. It turned out to be momentous in ways that I had never imagined. Shortly after my arrival, a pert brunette with a laughing smile and a vivacious personality turned male heads at the firm. She was Joan Helen Twilley, and she had been hired as a legal secretary to John Lawson. She was strikingly beautiful and unattached. I was determined to get to know her better. Unfortunately, mine was not the only eye she caught, and I was a little slow off the mark. By the time I screwed up my courage to ask her for a date, my fellow articling student Frank Smalley had already asked her out. However, whatever qualities I lacked as a suitor, persistence was not one of them. I managed to date the lovely Ms. Twilley, despite the attentions of Smalley.

Our friendly but serious competition for Joan's affections did not go unnoticed, particularly by the other secretaries. One observer was Liz Hudson, Robinette's secretary, a young woman whose favour I had assid-uously cultivated for other reasons. She was the key to access to John Robinette. She kept me abreast of all of his cases so that I could follow them. She even suggested to Robinette on a number of occasions that he take me with him to court. She also volunteered her secretarial services when it became obvious that Frank McCarthy's secretary, Miss McLaren, who could be as crusty as her boss, was impatient with her added assign-ment of looking after the modest typing requirements of the students.

All in all, Liz Hudson was a good friend, and when Robinette, who thrived on gossip, asked her what she knew about this office romance, she eagerly filled him in. Robinette chuckled when he heard the details and offered the unsolicited advice to Liz that Joan should give me preference because "George is going to make a good lawyer." Liz promptly passed this along to Joan and, not for the last time, I was to benefit from a Robinette recommendation. However, this was the first one and the one that I shall most cherish. Joan and I were married on August 22, 1953. It was the best move I ever made. She has brought warmth and light to my life and strength and wisdom to our entire family.

And so in the fall of 1953, I was quite smug about my situation. I was well settled into matrimony and had embarked upon my new career as a litigator at McCarthys under Robinette's leadership. However, driving home from work on the evening of October 21, I heard a bulletin on the car radio announcing that John Robinette, the famous criminal lawyer who had successfully defended Evelyn Dick, had been appointed to the appellate division of the Supreme Court of Ontario. I was shocked by this news. It made my choice of McCarthys and litigation less attractive by more than a little. Robinette was not only a leader by precept and example, he was the major business-getter in my chosen line of work. Without him, our litigation department would be limited to support services for the other departments.

The next day I arrived at the office to find that I was not the only person upset by the news. Beverley Matthews was most disturbed. It appears that the call from Stuart Garson, the Minister of Justice at the time, had caught Robinette off guard and in a somewhat "down" mood largely brought on by overwork. And the whole thing came up when Matthews was not around to be consulted. Robinette did speak to Jim Walker, but Walker did not understand, as Matthews would have reflexively, that his task was to talk Robinette out of accepting the appointment. Walker reminded Robinette that it was an important step in his professional life and worse, that if he did not accept it now, he was unlikely to receive an offer a second time.

So, when Matthews arrived back at the office from a business trip, he was faced with a *fait accompli*. However, Robinette was already having second thoughts, as I learned when I went into his office to congratulate him. He said that he was going to miss the office more than he had realized. In his oral history, Robinette remembered his state of mind at the time as follows:[81]

> This was a very embarrassing incident for me. Fortunately, everyone was very kind to me about it. And I will tell you the whole story. I was phoned one day by the Minister of Justice, the Honourable Stuart Garson, who was in the Pearson or the St. Laurent government, a Liberal government. He asked me if I would accept an appointment to the Court of Appeal. I foolishly acted quickly. I was flattered, honoured, and I was young, much younger than the other judges on the Court. They weren't appointing in those days judges quite as young as I was then. I accepted by telephone, and then he announced it. I got home, and in the next two or three days I was very worried. I had three daughters who were at school, and I went home and added up my life insurance premiums because with my young family I had a fair amount of life insurance — that was the only investment I really had except the house. And the salary was $14,000 a year then.

When his interviewer asked what his income was then, he replied, "probably $35,000 or so." This is another example where I do not accept the accuracy of parts of Robinette's oral history. As a first-year employee of the firm, I was paid $3,000 per year, which was not very much by any standard. Matthews had impressed on me that this figure was to be a matter of confidence between the two of us. I could understand why. However, I was not content to spend the rest of my professional life working for nickels and dimes, and I was anxious to know the upside of the remuneration situation. I quickly determined what the partners were making by keeping my eyes and ears open. Thanks to my friendship with Liz Hudson, I did not have to do even that when it came to Robinette's income. She was very proud of his earnings and showed me his 1952 income tax return. He had understated the figure by more than half.

In the circumstances, Matthews did not have any trouble convincing Robinette that he had made a mistake. The problem was what to do about it. John Arnup, who had become a good friend and confidant of Robinette by this time, recalls the turmoil Robinette was going through:[82]

> John had second thoughts, and he invited a number of people individually to come to his house to talk to him. He was a very distraught man at that point because he had decided he didn't want the job. T.N. Phelan was one of the people he asked to come and see him, and Mr. Mason, who was an ex-treasurer and long-time bencher, was another. I have no knowledge at all of what either one of them said to John, and I'm pretty vague about what I said to John when he asked me to come and see him. I know that I was very sympathetic to his position. I remember telling him that if he was unhappy on day one, how unhappy was he going to be from then on, for the rest of his judicial career?

John Brooke, who remembers that Robinette was "getting bluer and bluer" about the situation, says that on the Sunday following the announcement, he was at Robinette's home to assist him in winding down his practice when Matthews and Gershom Mason arrived. The reader will recall that in addition to being a former treasurer of the Law Society of Upper Canada, Mason was now the head of the firm that Robinette articled with in 1928–29. Robinette had great admiration and respect for him. According to Brooke, after listening to Robinette explain his dilemma, Mason said simply, "Robinette. If you have made a mistake you must correct it at once." Robinette went to the telephone and called Garson at home to tell him that he had changed his mind.

Unfortunately, the royal patent under the Great Seal of Canada appointing him a judge of the Supreme Court of Ontario and a member of the Court of Appeal and ex officio a member of the High Court of Justice (to give his full, albeit temporary, title) had already been issued. It was agreed that he would have to resign formally. Robinette felt it best to travel to Ottawa to hand in his resignation and explain in person why he had changed his mind. On November 11, 1953, he handed to Garson a letter dated November 9, 1953, in which he discussed the personal reasons for his decision and finished off by saying, "It is therefore with the deepest regret and solely for personal reasons that I now tender to you my resignation as a member of the Court of Appeal for Ontario and ex officio a member of the High Court of Justice." Robinette said he was sympathetically received, and Garson accepted his written resignation with regret. On December 10, the Governor General of Canada approved an Order-in-Council advising that the resignation had been accepted.[83] It is interesting to note in the light of the controversy that later arose out of Robinette's resignation that the recital to the Order-in-Council states that Robinette "has declined to accept the appointment and has tendered his resignation."

In later reporting to Earl Smith, the Secretary of the Law Society, on the circumstances surrounding his resignation, Robinette stated, "In my discussion with Mr. Garson, I made it clear that it was not my intention to accept in any way any incidental advantage which might accrue to me, as for example, the use of the title Honourable. The order in council accepting my resignation does not confer any right to use the title Honourable."[84]

One would have thought that this would be the end of the matter, but to Robinette's continuing embarrassment, this was not to be the case. Robinette's fame was such that his resignation and the effect of it on his status as a bencher of the Law Society of Upper Canada became a story in itself, with the newspapers writing about it for public consumption. Robinette had been elected a bencher at the quinquennial election in 1946 (he stood third out of thirty elected), and he was elected again in 1951 (he stood first). He was thus a bencher at the time of judicial appointment.

The benchers constitute the directing minds of the Law Society of Upper Canada, which is the governing body of the legal profession in Ontario. The Law Society was intended by its founders to replicate the authority and practices of the Inns of Court in London, England. Those Inns in turn traced their origins to the reign of Edward I. The Law Society was recognized in Upper Canada in 1797 at a meeting of barristers at Newark, Ontario, now Niagara-on-the-Lake, following the passage of "An Act for the better regulating of the Practice of the Law" at a sitting of the House of Assembly and Legislative Council of Upper Canada.[85] The newly formed society continued the traditions of the Inns, including the designation of its directors as benchers, reflecting the practice of reserving benches in the dining rooms of English Inns for the governing members.

To those who wonder why the person who would ordinarily be the president of the Law Society is called the treasurer, this, too, finds its roots in history. The original Inns of Court were boarding houses for barristers and aspiring barristers. The landlord of the Inns insisted on dealing with only one representative for payment of the rent. That barrister, who was selected by the lodgers to represent them to the landlord in this important matter, collected rents from the lodgers and remitted payment to the landlord. He became the treasurer and the accepted leader of the group, which in time constituted the membership of an Inn of Court.

In 1953 there were thirty benchers elected every five years by lawyers who were members of the society. None was a woman. In the event that a bencher died, resigned, or was appointed a judge, the remaining benchers replaced him for the balance of his term. Accordingly, with his judicial appointment, Robinette would no longer be a member of the Law Society and therefore was ineligible to be a bencher. However, if he was a retired judge and a practising member of the bar, he would be a bencher ex officio. The practical effect on the benchers would be that Robinette's appointment as a judge would create a vacancy among the elected benchers, and he would have to be replaced. However, Robinette had never been sworn in as a judge and had been one in name only, and very briefly at that.

It is a measure of the workload of Convocation at the time that this matter should get so much attention. Convocation placed it on its agenda and resolved it by appointing a special committee composed of John Arnup, Joseph Sedgwick, and Roland Wilson to look into it further. The committee's answer was to make an application to the Court for its opinion.

Robinette was totally unconcerned about the matter. As he told me, he was either a judge who had resigned, in which case he was entitled to attend Convocation as a bencher ex officio, or he was not a judge and therefore reverted to his status as an elected bencher. He instructed John Clarry to appear for him on the return of the application before the judge in Weekly Court and to advise the presiding judge that he was taking no position in the matter and was submitting his rights to the Court. Clarry was then to ask for permission to withdraw. When Robinette gave these instructions, I do not know if he was aware that the judge hearing the application was to be his nemesis, Chief Justice McRuer.

I should pause here to sum up my assessment of the relationship between Robinette and McRuer. To my mind, they were at that time the two dominant figures in the legal profession in Ontario. They were the two biggest dogs on the street, and at times they behaved that way. Both had brilliant legal minds, but McRuer was a control freak who insisted on getting his way in his courtroom. Patrick Boyer's biography of McRuer is titled *A Passion for Justice*, which is a good description of the subject but does not address the significant limitation in McRuer's character. It was McRuer's own view of justice, and not justice under the law, that he showed a passion for. In many respects, McRuer showed little judgment in recognizing the limits of his authority and, as we have seen, he did not hesitate to overstep the proper bounds of judicial restraint and strive to force a result that he regarded intuitively as the correct one.

For his part, Robinette was not without sin. He had a very sure sense of himself and strove to dominate the courtroom to advance his clients' interests. There were times when it appeared he not only wanted to dominate the courtroom, but also to run it. As a student, I saw more of Robinette in action than I did any other counsel, and I assumed that his peremptory objections to the questions of counsel or the answers of the witness were the way things were done. I was to learn otherwise when I started conducting my own cases. I can recall one of my first civil trials in the High Court before Justice Gale, later chief justice of the High Court, and later still, chief justice of Ontario. When my opponent's witness said something that I considered hearsay and thus inadmissible, I, still sitting in my chair, said, as I had heard Robinette say many times, "He can't say that!" Well! I quickly learned that when counsel has an objection to make, he gets to his feet and addresses the judge, not the witness. He respectfully makes submissions as to the nature of his objection and asks the judge to instruct the witness on how to proceed. If the judge agrees with the submissions, he tells the witness, "You can't say that."

I should add parenthetically that Gale was very much of a stickler for protocol and did not hesitate to enforce the rules of court, even for Robinette. For example, despite the fact that he was a close friend of Robinette's (they had summer cottages at Southampton and played golf together regularly), Gale made him stand down to the bottom of the list in Weekly Court on one occasion because he was not in his place at the counsel table when Gale, as the presiding judge, entered the courtroom. I have often wondered what went on in the mind of Robinette's opponent, who had not violated protocol and was punished along with him. He would have to wait with Robinette until late in the afternoon for the list to be exhausted so that the case they shared could proceed. However, nobody was late again in Weekly Court when Gale was presiding.

But to return to McRuer. In his oral history, Robinette played down his grudge with McRuer to the point that it disappeared. He said that McRuer was always kind to him, and he respected his decisions as being correct, even singling out as an example this application on his status as a bencher. I, on the other hand, have a vivid recollection of Robinette's reaction on receiving that decision. "He did that deliberately to embarrass me," he muttered. He repeated his belief that McRuer had never forgiven him for winning the Dick case. I remember another instance when Robinette was scheduled to appear before McRuer in Ottawa but was unable to do so because of a meeting he was obliged to attend in Toronto in his capacity as treasurer. He asked a local lawyer who was involved in the case to ask for an adjournment, assuring him that McRuer was aware of his dilemma and was sympathetic to his scheduling conflict. McRuer, however, took the opportunity to tear a strip off senior counsel who take too many cases and cause great inconvenience to the courts and their clients. Local counsel got the adjournment, but the reprimand was published in the press. Robinette was furious and fired off a letter to McRuer chastising him for the public criticism. McRuer sent a semi-apologetic response that Robinette mocked. "He addressed the letter, 'My dear John,'" he sneered.

Robinette was a good hater, as befits a prototypical Scorpio, of those he considered, for one reason or another, to have unfairly bested him. In referring to one of these adversaries he frequently explained that he found him (there were no hers) "a difficult person." I remember asking him how he was getting along with Crown counsel in his appeal in the case of *Regina v. McNamara*,[86] better known as "the Dredging Case," and one I shall return to. The Crown, Roderick McLeod, Q.C., now in private practice, is one of the ablest counsel I have ever seen in a courtroom, but he could be zealous to the point of becoming "a difficult person." As trial counsel for two of the accused who were not involved in the appeal, I had some run-ins with McLeod, as had other defence counsel, during a lengthy and sometimes acrimonious trial. When I asked Robinette how he was getting along with McLeod, cheekily adding that he would hardly be doing full service to his client if he had succeeded in avoiding controversy, Robinette was not amused. "He," meaning McLeod, "was so patronizing to me." While Robinette was essentially a modest man and was irritated by admirers who were effusive in giving voice to his praises, he had a sure sense of his position in the profession and resented any person who failed to show him the proper respect.

In his oral history, however, Robinette was not about to appear vengeful about McRuer on a record that he knew would be available to the public. Robinette's protestations to the contrary, the frequent references in that history to McRuer's being "kind" to him are a laugh. McRuer was kind to me as he was to all young counsel who appeared before him well prepared and respectful of his authority. You never had a problem with McRuer unless you challenged him, which is just what Robinette did consistently. Kindness implies paternalism, and Robinette would not have thanked him for that. Robinette's example of McRuer's kindness to his daughter, Joan, emphasizes that Robinette was using the word in the same vein as I am. Joan Robinette was McRuer's law clerk for two years beginning in 1957. She liked working for him and to no one's surprise found him patient, understanding, and helpful in his role as her principal. He was generous with his time and encouraged her to become involved in the work of the court. She learned a great deal from him and thought enough of him as a person that she invited him to be a guest at her wedding to Dick Sadleir. But Joan never challenged his authority. There was no confusion in her mind as to who was the pupil and who the teacher. I might add that Joan confirms my recollection that her father disliked McRuer.

I will give one more example of the conflict between these two legal titans before returning to the court proceeding over Robinette's position as bencher. As a law student I sat with Robinette when he undertook the pro bono defence of a man charged with vehicular manslaughter. In his closing address, after making the usual disclaimer that the jury was to take the law from the Chief Justice and where his version was to conflict with anything Robinette should say, the jury was to ignore his comments and accept those of the Chief Justice, Robinette outlined what was required of the Crown to establish criminal negligence beyond a reasonable doubt and thus convict his client. He was describing criminal negligence as being a departure from a standard of driving beyond gross negligence and amounting to reckless and wanton disregard for the lives and safety of other persons, when suddenly McRuer interrupted him and stated that this was not the law. I have never before or since heard a trial judge interrupt counsel in his address to the jury. This is counsel's last opportunity to persuade the jury of his client's innocence. While a trial judge can and should correct counsel's statements later in his charge to the jury, the address itself is not to be interfered with. Robinette was outraged. He wheeled and practically shouted at the Chief Justice, "I have authority for every one of those statements." McRuer was rather condescending. "Oh, yes. But the words you used appear in separate authorities and you have used them cumulatively." The good news was that Robinette's client was acquitted.

The conflict between these two never abated so far as I could discern, and I am not in a position to declare a winner. Robinette did outlast McRuer, who left the bench in 1964 at the age of seventy-four to head the Royal Commission Inquiry into Civil Rights.

The application before McRuer to determine Robinette's status as a bencher was heard on April 8 and 9, 1954. C.H. Walker, Q.C., who took no position on the matter, represented the Law Society. The merits of the case were argued by Arthur A. Macdonald, Q.C., who represented those members of the profession who took the position that Robinette was an ex officio bencher, and J.L. Stewart, Q.C., who represented those members who took the position that he was not. McRuer, with his usual single-minded approach to problems in his court, came up with an answer that no one had suggested to date: that Robinette was neither a judge nor a bencher. In his reasons at the close of argument, McRuer lost no time in disposing of the argument that Robinette was a retired judge. He said:

> There is no express provision in the Act [*The Law Society Act*, R.S.O. 1950, c. 200] that, once a bencher has been elected, in order to continue to be a bencher he must be a member of the bar, but I do not think the Act

is capable of any other construction than that the qualification of a bencher at all times is that he be a member of the bar in good standing. Otherwise, it would lead to the absurd result pointed out by Mr. Macdonald in his argument, that if a bencher should be disbarred after his election and before the next quinquennial election he would continue to be a bencher notwithstanding his disbarment. The benchers constitute the governing body of the Society and as such must necessarily be members of the Society and members of the bar in good standing.

That brings me now to the question whether Mr. Robinette, upon his appointment by the Governor General of Canada to be a judge of the Supreme Court of Ontario, ceased to be a member of the bar of Ontario so that, upon his appointment, a vacancy was created among the benchers. Mr. Stewart contends that it is not necessary for me to decide this. In the first place, I think it is, and in the second place, I think the whole proceedings here would be quite useless if I did not decide it, because the purpose of these proceedings, as I view them, is to ascertain what is the legal position of the Law Society with respect to Mr. Robinette's position, and it is just as important to know whether a vacancy has occurred to which a bencher must be elected as to know whether Mr. Robinette is an ex officio bencher, for both these reasons I must enter upon the consideration of that subject.

The Chief Justice then addressed the following issue:

Can a judge who has been duly appointed but who has not taken the oath of office and has not entered upon his official duties, but who has resigned before doing so and whose resignation has been accepted, be said to be "a retired judge of the Supreme Court of Ontario"?

McRuer looked at the limited number of precedents on the matter and concluded that since Robinette had never taken the oath of office, he had never entered on his judicial duties. Accordingly, when his resignation was accepted, he did not acquire the status of a retired judge. A "retired judge" meant a person who had fulfilled a judicial office and who, at his own request, was relieved from the discharge of his duty. He wrote:

> My opinion therefore is, and I so declare, that when Mr. Robinette was appointed by the Queen's patent to be a judge of the Supreme Court of Ontario a vacancy occurred among the benchers but, notwithstanding that he ceased to be a bencher, he did not become an ex officio bencher when his resignation was accepted.

In the result, Robinette was neither a judge nor a bencher. The benchers, being of a practical bent, solved this problem by appointing him a bencher to fill his own vacancy. This was on May 21, 1954.

As it turned out, McRuer did Robinette a favour with his ruling. This designation of retired judges as ex officio benchers, since abolished, was intended to honour judges who after retiring were prepared to come back and assist Convocation in its deliberations. They had no vote. Robinette was in his prime and had a lot to contribute. Moreover, as an ex officio bencher he would not have been eligible to stand for election as treasurer. He stood for election at the next general election of benchers in 1956 and again headed the polls. He was to be elected treasurer in May of 1958 and would serve four one-year terms ending in the spring of 1962.

I observed two immediate consequences of Robinette's decision not to accept the judicial appointment. The first was that those solicitors who had had their files returned to them when Robinette wound up his practice called to congratulate him on his return to the profession and expressed their eagerness to retain him anew. They were not all successful. Robinette was a lawyer who had trouble saying no, and he had taken on far too many cases, some of them not worthy of a counsel of his standing. As the junior lawyer, I had had the unhappy task of stalling these lawyers and making excuses for Robinette's neglect of their clients' affairs. I also became very proficient at "speaking to the list," that is, explaining to the Registrar or his assistants and sometimes a judge just why it was that Mr. Robinette could not proceed with cases that had been placed on the "ready list" for trial. With this second opportunity to decide whether he would take on files with which he was now familiar, Robinette became uncharacteristically selective and refused to accept the return of those he knew to be troublesome and unrewarding. I rejoiced. An appointment to the bench turned out to be a unique way for Robinette to thin out his practice.

The second consequence to me was that I became Matthews's agent charged with ensuring that the firm was never again caught off guard by a judicial appointment for Robinette. Matthews instructed me to keep my ear to the ground for any rumours of possible appointments to the bench that might interest Robinette. I took this assignment seriously because I had a stake in Robinette's remaining at the firm. I not only reported on rumours, of which there was an abundance, but I also briefed Matthews on arguments that he could make to Robinette as to why he should not accept a particular appointment if it were offered. Two examples come to mind.

Both Matthews and I recognized that Robinette was unlikely to accept an offer of an appointment at the same level as that which had caused him so much grief to decline. However, one day in the spring of 1967, I heard that Dana Porter, the Chief Justice of Ontario, was in hospital suffering from bone cancer in his spine. His prognosis, I heard, was poor. I told Matthews that this was one appointment that Robinette might be interested in. It was a prestigious office, a better one in my view than an appointment to the Supreme Court of Canada, and one that did not involve relocating or travelling outside of Toronto. Matthews listened intently as I spoke and after reflecting a moment said, "Dana is an old friend of mine. I will go and visit him and see how he is coming along." He did so almost immediately, and reported that Dana had said he was simply suffering from a sore back and would be out of hospital shortly.

I do not know how much Porter knew of the true state of his health, but he died in that hospital on May 13, within weeks of this conversation. However, our fears about Robinette were assuaged when we learned that the front-runner as Dana's replacement was Robinette's good friend "Bill" Gale, at that time the chief justice of the High Court and a man whose elevation Robinette undoubtedly supported. Gale was appointed chief justice following Porter's death and served with distinction until his retirement in 1976.

The next alarm bell sounded in March 1970 when John Cartwright, then chief justice of Canada, was obliged to retire from the court at age seventy-five. He was one of the three Ontario appointments and by tradition was to be replaced by an Ontario judge or a member of the practising Ontario bar. I warned Matthews of this impending vacancy and suggested that Robinette would be reluctant to leave Toronto where his family was still largely situated. Based on my own parents' lives in Ottawa, I painted for Robinette's benefit a bleak picture of a stilted social life that revolved around the government of the day: an unexciting city that was the biggest small town in Canada. (I remind my Ottawa friends, if I have any after this tirade, that these remarks represented an advocate's brief, not a considered personal judgment.)

This appointment was offered to Robinette. In his oral history he recalled that he bowed to his family's wishes in not pursuing the appointment: "My family did not wish to leave Toronto … particularly my wife … and the children were in private school here." Robinette said he had his own reservations. "But I had to balance it all, and looking back, I think I made, now, at my age, the right decision. If I had been a judge I would have had to quit at seventy-five. In all events, I have had a very happy family life, which is the most important thing … I am close to my children and the grandchildren. I didn't make a mistake."

The question naturally arises whether Robinette would have made a good judge. Just as many athletes excel at their chosen sport and find later that they have neither the temperament nor the teaching skills to coach players or manage a team, so a significant number of counsel are unable to make the transition from fearless advocate to patient adjudicator. I think we need have had no concern about Robinette's abilities as a judge. He had demonstrated that he was pre-eminent in every facet of the law in which he engaged: as a student, as a teacher, and as a counsel. He had the intellect, the mental discipline, the work habits, the non-confrontational disposition, and the overall good manners to make a superb judge. My only caveat would be that he would become impatient at the inevitable repetition of argument and the slow pace of appellate courts, which in those days took a passive role in the scheduling and hearing of appeals. That certainly was his concern when he was asked about being a judge: he was afraid he would become bored.

That said, I am glad that he did not take an appointment. It would have been a waste, particularly in the decade that preceded 1982 and the introduction of the *Canadian Charter of Rights and Freedoms*. Before the Charter, the work of the appellate courts was largely problem-solving. It was interesting work and important, too, but it did not require the direction and leadership that it was to require (and has not always received) post-Charter. When I was a counsel, I thought that while there were some outstanding judges on the court, the talent pool was thin, and the court included a number of timeservers. The hard fact was that an appointment to the Ontario Court of Appeal was not much sought after until John Arnup joined that court in 1970 directly from the profession. His prestige matched that of Robinette's, and he was followed in succession as vacancies occurred by four leading counsel: Charles Dubin, Willard "Bud" Estey, and Arthur Martin in 1973, with Bert McKinnon following in 1974. It was only then that the court, under the forceful leadership of Chief Justice Gale, began to acquire the enviable reputation throughout Canada that it enjoys to this day.

Robinette would have been an ornament on any bench, but the profession would have lost an advocate of irreplaceable talent, and I am not sure that the trade-off favoured the public interest. Robinette was in a class by himself. He had come to be recognized as the quintessential counsel. He was the advocate who did everything and did it effortlessly well. I doubt that he could have had a greater influence on the development of the law as a judge than he did as a lawyer. He had a reputation that transcended the craft of the advocate, which shone like a beacon until the last days of his practice. As for his not wanting to be forced to retire at seventy-five, I can attest that when I accepted an appointment to the bench in December 1984, Robinette was still going strong at the age of seventy-eight and making it look easy. He was still the leader of the profession, the man whom the bench and bar turned to first when confronted by a critical problem and, as we shall see later, counsel to governments both provincial and federal.

Chapter Nine
First Among Equals

I HAVE SPENT ALL OF my professional life in or around Osgoode Hall at the corner of Queen Street and University Avenue in downtown Toronto. I attended law school and received my call to the bar there. I took practice courses there, which I later tutored. It was at Osgoode that I argued motions before masters and judges as well as appeals before the justices of the Court of Appeal. I was elected to serve as a bencher of the Law Society of Upper Canada in 1970 and met regularly with my fellow benchers in the society's quarters at Osgoode. I was elected treasurer of the Law Society for two terms in the years 1979–80 and 1980–81. During those two years I had my office on the ground floor of the original building at Osgoode Hall. In December 1984, I was appointed to the Court of Appeal and occupied chambers at Osgoode Hall until my retirement. I know the building well, and I love it.

I am thoroughly familiar with its history. In 1829, the Law Society purchased six acres of pastureland at what are now Queen and York Streets. The property was so far removed from the mainstream of the then Town of York that the society had to fence the entire property to keep local cattle off the land. A simple wooden fence accomplished this initially, and that structure was replaced in style in 1868 by the erection of an ornate iron fence with its famous cow baffle gates. The society completed construction of what is now the east wing of the premises in 1832. It was named Osgoode Hall after the first chief justice of Upper Canada, William Osgoode.

In 1846, the society entered into an agreement with the government of Upper Canada to house the Superior Courts of Justice. For that purpose, it built what is now the west wing, which adjoins the east wing through the main entrance on the ground floor and through the Great Library on the second floor. In 1874, the society transferred ownership of the west wing and the main entrance to the province to eliminate its obvious conflict as landlord to the courts of justice where so many of its members appeared as advocates. The building complex has since been enlarged, the latest addition being in 1958 to provide space for offering the Bar Admission Course to law students.

Nobody had a greater love for this building than did Robinette. This was the first theatre for advocacy in Canada, and it was here that Robinette took centre stage and performed his electrifying feats of forensic persuasion for more than fifty years. Even more than for me, it was a second office for him. As indicated in earlier chapters, he maintained an office there as lecturer from1929 until 1937 and as editor of the law reports from 1932 until 1942. He was first elected a bencher in 1946 and was re-elected several times until he became treasurer in May 1958, serving four terms ending in May 1962. The benchers had quarters reserved for them, and as treasurer, Robinette occupied the same office that later was available to me. As a retired treasurer, he was an ex officio bencher for the rest of his life. A special office was set aside for former treasurers following a renovation in 1978.

Robinette's terms as treasurer were for the most part uneventful. These years appear to occupy a hiatus in the often busy history of the Law Society. The most significant happening of the period between the late 1940s and late 1950s was the slow recognition by the benchers that the society could no longer dictate the curriculum for legal education in the province.

The universities, led by the vociferous Caesar Wright, who was then the dean of the University of Toronto Law School, were demanding that the society recognize their perceived mandate to operate their own law faculties. The University of Toronto was the only university that had such a law school, but the other major universities were clamouring for the right to start their own. There was a stumbling block that prevented the universities from proceeding alone in this initiative: university law schools could grant academic diplomas, but the Law Society determined who would be admitted to the practice of law — only those who were graduates of its own Osgoode Hall Law School. The tension was really between the need for an academic-oriented law school and the society's preference for its own practice-oriented law school.

For people who were seeking legal training in the late 1940s, as I was, the choice between a law school that only granted a diploma versus a school without the degree but with a ticket to practise law was a no-brainer. Wright was not getting enough students to justify the size and expense of his faculty. The extended and at times vicious public debate over this issue fortunately ended in a compromise in March 1957. Robinette played some part, but not an important one, in resolving the debate while he was a bencher.

The resolution of the problem involved the creation of a Bar Admission Course by the benchers. This course consisted of a period of service under articles to a lawyer for fifteen months followed by a further six months of practical and clinical training at Osgoode Hall, supervised by members of the Osgoode Hall Law School staff and practising members of the profession. To be admitted to the Bar Admission Course, an applicant would have to be a graduate of the Osgoode Hall Law School academic course *or* (and here was the compromise) of an approved law course in an approved university, provided that the applicant could also satisfy further requirements prescribed by the benchers such as citizenship, good character and fitness, and payment of fees. The society was empowered to approve the law course and the university that provided it, although an agreement was reached in advance on the acceptable core subjects and the length of the academic term. Upon the certification of the staff of the Bar Admission Course that an applicant had served his or her articles and had passed prescribed oral or written examinations, he or she would be eligible for the call to the bar in the usual way.

However, Robinette, certainly as treasurer, had little to do with this significant development in legal education. The Minutes of Convocation record that the creation of the new regime was initiated by the acceptance by the society of the University of Toronto, Queens University, the University of Ottawa, and Dalhousie University as the universities from which the Law Society accepted academic degrees as qualifying its recipients to enrol in the Bar Admission Course. These universities had been approved prior to Robinette's election as treasurer. During his tenure, the following law school faculties were approved: University of Western Ontario (June 26, 1958); University of New Brunswick, conditional approval (September 19, 1958); University of British Columbia (January 16, 1959).

A review of some of the entries in the Minutes of Convocation illustrates that events during Robinette's time as treasurer consisted mainly of housekeeping and no real initiatives. Examples include: implementing the agreement between the universities and the Law Society with the blessing of the government at Queen's Park; supporting Metropolitan Toronto's request to the government of Canada that the University Avenue Armouries be sold to the municipality as a site for the new courthouse — all benchers were urged "to use any influence they had in support of the request"; and obtaining information regarding the condition of the original iron fence surrounding Osgoode Hall, which had stood since its completion in 1868, and about the cost of repairing it (the report was not forthcoming during Robinette's time as treasurer).

The minutes also describe special events and guests of the society. In November 1959, the Prime Minister of Canada, the Right Honourable John G. Diefenbaker, was invited to become a member of the Bar of Ontario and an honorary bencher. Diefenbaker's acceptance was noted on January 15, 1960, and it was stated that he would be attending on February 19. However, "due to a severe blizzard in Ottawa," Diefenbaker was not able to attend and the event was postponed to March 18. The Honourable Leslie Miscampbell Frost, Q.C., LL.D., D.C.L., Prime Minister of Ontario,[87] received an invitation in November 1960 from the Treasurer to become an honorary bencher of the society and received the title in January 1961. John Keiller McKay, Lieutenant Governor of Ontario, was awarded an Honorary Doctor of Laws on June 22, 1961.

In February 1959, the Law Society established Honorary Life Memberships. This category was composed of "all members who are paid up on the books of the Society for fifty years or over." They were to remain full-time members of the society but "were liable to the payment of no further fees." This policy was to come into effect on

December 1, 1959. In January 1960, the minutes noted that the original terms of the life membership policy precluded judges from being eligible. The terms were thus altered so that "members are not disqualified from life membership by reason only of their membership in the Society having been interrupted by service on the bench, and the time spent in such service may be included for the purpose of determining eligibility for life membership." The Treasurer informed Convocation that "the establishment of Honorary Life Memberships in the Law Society had given great satisfaction to the senior members of the Bar and their families, and that many interesting letters had been received from life members."

Robinette does come into focus in the minutes of the society during his time as treasurer, but in a way that must have embarrassed him. Two references to missing books occur, one in the minutes dated February 19, 1960, and the other on March 16, 1962.

> Your Committee reports that 55 text-books disappeared from the library in the year 1959 as compared with 71 taken away in 1958. Your Committee recommends that a notice be inserted in the Ontario Weekly Notes advising the members of the profession of this loss and appealing to them to return any library books which may be in their possession.

> ...

> Your Committee recommends that a suitable notice to the members of the Society and students at the Osgoode Hall Law School be inserted in the Ontario Weekly Notes, drawing their attention to the serious shortage resulting from the unauthorized taking of books from the library and advising that where books taken out without authority are found in the possession of any member or student, the matter will be brought to the attention of the Discipline Committee or the Dean of the Law School for action, and that

copies of this notice, on Law Society stationery, be posted on the notice boards in the Great Library and the Phillips Stewart Library.

I do not know how Robinette could sit through the reading of these reports without turning crimson. I vividly recall being sent by Robinette when I was student to the Great Library to get out books that we did not have at McCarthys. But I do not have nearly as vivid a recollection of returning them. I should not have been surprised that the librarian of the Great Library, George Johnston, was reluctant to lend them out.

Robinette's reputation for not returning borrowed books, a reputation that I learned about in stages, came to light during a minor crisis at McCarthys relating to the firm's one and only copy of the current edition of *Tremeear's Criminal Code*. It was found to be missing from the library at a time when a senior lawyer in the commercial section wanted to look at it, for reasons that are lost in the mists of time. He was quite agitated over its unavailability and made quite a fuss about the matter. Now everyone knew where the book was — Robinette must have taken it home and forgotten to bring it back. But office protocol being what it was, no one was permitted to ask him if he had the book. Instead, memos were distributed to all solicitors and students asking them to search their offices and return the book if found. Robinette received the memo but was unresponsive.

The next step was to have Robinette's secretary search his office and his attaché bags for the book when he was in court. No results. Finally, a discreet telephone call was made to Mrs. Robinette at a time when her husband was away from home. She was asked if she would look for the missing book in his library. She did and reported that it was in fact there. She was asked to wrap the *Tremeear* in brown wrapping paper and secure it with a string. Pat Vernon, the only student with wheels, was then dispatched on his motorcycle to pick up the package. However, he was not told of the contents of the package. Pat placed the package on the carrier of his bike and raced back to the office. No student was permitted to witness the opening of the package in the library, which is just as well. I could not have restrained myself if I had been present. The package contained a genuine *Tremeear* all right, but unfortunately, the flyleaf disclosed that its true owner was the Phillips Stewart Library. Robinette had borrowed his *Tremeear* from the Osgoode Hall Law School's student library.

I recounted this story about the missing *Tremeear* with appropriate embellishments at the dedication of the John J. Robinette Library at McCarthy Tétrault on April 3, 1996. Robinette's personal legal texts, abridgements, and law reports were being donated by his family to the firm. At the close of my remarks, the chief librarian at McCarthy's approached me and said she had not said anything about this to anyone, but I should know that the bulk of the books obtained from Robinette's home after his death came from the Phillips Stewart Library. I suspect that this was a cache from his days as a lecturer. The provenance of the "useful working library" at McCarthys is apparently suspect.

Another matter that piqued my interest was a note in the minutes of November 18, 1960, that "the Treasurer referred to newspaper comments in connection with the case of *Abiscott v. Abiscott and Simpson* and Mr. Justice Wilson's criticism of the conduct of the case by Mr. Elliot R. Pepper, the Queen's Proctor for the Attorney General."

I remember this incident. It revolved around the duties of the Office of Queen's Proctor, an anachronistic office whose holder examined the circumstances surrounding petitions for divorce to ascertain in the public interest whether the parties were guilty of "collusion, connivance or condonation" in seeking to obtain a divorce. In 1960, and for some time thereafter, the only grounds recognized in Ontario for divorce were adultery or bestiality — adultery, for all practical purposes. The narrowness of the basis for dissolving marriage invited abuse. The evidence of adultery was not always available, and the party seeking the divorce could not assert his or her own adultery; rather, the spouse responding to the petition had to be the party guilty of marital misconduct.

This situation tempted the parties to agree that one of them, usually the husband, would "commit adultery" for the purpose of supplying the wife with the necessary grounds for divorce. This amounted to collusion. Another option was to engage in conduct short of an agreement whereby the so-called wronged party might know that the petitioning spouse's adultery was committed solely for the purpose of obtaining a divorce, thereby giving tacit consent to the wrongdoing. This was connivance. Condonation involved adultery that was real enough, but the innocent party had by words or conduct forgiven the erring spouse. As a further aspect of the moral rectitude of the proceedings, the rules provided that in the event that the petitioning spouse was also guilty of adultery, it was necessary for that spouse to ask forgiveness by filing, in a sealed envelope, a wonderfully titled "prayer of discretion" in which was described the circumstances of the adultery. The petitioning spouse would request the trial judge to exercise his discretion to grant the divorce notwithstanding his or her own marital misconduct.

The Queen's Proctor was to ensure that the rules of court governing the conduct of divorce proceedings were observed and that none of the above improprieties tainted the integrity of the process. Procedurally, the injured party commenced the proceedings by issuing a petition for divorce alleging adultery by the respondent spouse with a named person, who was known as the co-respondent. A hearing before a High Court judge followed, at which the petitioner had the onus to prove the adultery. The vast majority of these proceedings were uncontested and almost invariably resulted in a judgment nisi, that is to say, a conditional decree of divorce that could be made absolute by another High Court judge no less than three months later. The theory of the three-month waiting period was to permit the parties to the marriage to reconsider the divorce and perhaps reconcile. It was also intended to give an opportunity to the Queen's Proctor to investigate the circumstances surrounding the granting of the decree nisi to determine whether any of the dreaded three Cs had been perpetrated.

It takes very little imagination to recognize that the role of the Queen's Proctor was not much appreciated by those in an unhappy marriage who were simply trying to rectify their mistake by getting divorced. One would also not be surprised to know that the office of the Queen's Proctor was not much sought after. The parties and some judges treated the office-holder as a nuisance. He was not highly regarded even by the Attorney General who appointed him and who failed to provide him with sufficient investigative resources to carry out his duties effectively. He was pretty much reduced to following up on complaints by busybodies or more usually by a party to the divorce proceedings who for one reason or another wanted to prevent the divorce. In the result, the appearance of the

Queen's Proctor at hearings before a judge for a decree absolute was almost invariably a formality.

However, there was one judge who took the office of Queen's Proctor seriously. He was Justice John L. Wilson, a stickler for protocol (he was famous for a story that may well be apocryphal — that he did not permit a certain lawyer to appear before him because he was not wearing striped trousers beneath his gown). Wilson thought that the Attorney General was not taking the office seriously enough. The specific ground of complaint he voiced in the case of *Abiscott v. Abiscott and Simpson* was that the Attorney General had not appointed a senior counsel to fill this illustrious office, but instead had chosen young Elliot R. Pepper to carry out its ancient duties. Now Pepper was bright, energetic, and of proven ability, but he was undoubtedly young, a quality over which he had no control. Wilson made some comments about him that many members of the profession considered an unfair, personal attack based on Pepper's alleged inexperience. Some background is necessary to understand why the judge's comments gave rise to so much publicity.

Joan Abiscott was the plaintiff in an action against Ivan Abiscott for the dissolution of their marriage on the basis of Ivan's alleged adultery with a woman named Laura Simpson. It appears that after a decree nisi for divorce had been obtained, a number of issues were raised as to the bona fides of the proceedings. Mrs. Abiscott was said to have stated publicly that she had acted as a professional co-respondent in a number of other divorce proceedings. This statement sparked immediate media attention on divorce proceedings generally and led to an investigation into cases in which Mrs. Abiscott had been named as a co-respondent. Mrs. Abiscott's own divorce came under scrutiny, and questions were raised as to whether the picture of Laura Simpson shown in the affidavit of service of the petition for divorce was truly her photograph. Also questioned was whether Mr. Abiscott had in fact committed adultery with her.

Because of the newspaper notoriety generated by these allegations, Justice George T. Walsh directed that there be a trial of these issues. The Office of Queen's Proctor had the Attorney General intervene to oppose granting a decree absolute to finalize the divorce. The specific questions placed before Justice Wilson at the trial were: (1) whether the plaintiff Mrs. Abiscott was a credible witness at the trial leading to the granting of the decree nisi; (2) whether the alleged adultery with Laura Simpson actually took place; (3) whether the picture was that of Laura Simpson; (4) whether a prayer of discretion should have been filed by the plaintiff asking to be excused for her own adultery committed in the course of her career as a professional co-respondent; (5) whether the decree nisi was obtained by collusion, fraud, or other wrongdoing; and (6) whether the decree nisi was against the evidence and the law. Pepper as Queen's Proctor appeared in opposition to the granting of a decree absolute finalizing the divorce.

Wilson was most unhappy with the manner in which the proceedings before him were conducted. He said that the evidence did not justify setting aside the decree nisi and refusing to grant a decree absolute. While he did not make any findings of impropriety on the part of the parties to the divorce action, he complained that this was only because the Queen's Proctor had simply failed to prove the facts alleged in its intervention. In the course of these reasons, Justice Wilson said the following about Pepper:

> Unfortunately, in the light of what has taken place in this case I feel I have not had the assistance of sufficiently senior counsel to give this matter the consideration its importance justifies. Unfortunately for the young man who appeared as counsel for the [Queen's Proctor], he has not had, in my opinion, adequate experience to handle a case of this nature and for that he is not to be criticized in any way. He has come here and done the best that he can when, in my opinion, the services of one of the most competent, experienced and skilful counsel is needed. This is a difficult type of case. The public interest certainly ought to be protected but the task of the trial judge in difficult matters is increased beyond the comprehension of any person who has not been in the trial judge's position when he hasn't got the help that he needs. My critical remarks have not been intended as personal to counsel. He is well liked; he has done good work in other fields and I have already made

known yesterday, without any suggestion on anyone's part, to one of his superiors that in the publicity that was given to the remarks that I made that they should not be construed as detrimental to this young man.

In discussing the question of costs, Wilson went on to say:

I think it is a foregone conclusion on the material that the Attorney-General thought he had reasonable grounds for believing he should intervene. Whether or not he would have succeeded at the trial with more experienced counsel of course I am unable to say but certainly the issues would have been much more thoroughly investigated from the procedural point of view. It would have made my task much easier, and that of any other judge much easier, in arriving at a conclusion but, of course, I cannot say whether the outcome would have been any different.

Convocation considered the matter on November 18, 1960. After a full discussion, Robinette as treasurer was authorized to issue the following public statement:

The Benchers of the Law Society of Upper Canada in Convocation assembled deem it to be their duty in the interests of the administration of justice and of our profession to make a public statement concerning the observations made by The Honourable Mr. Justice John L. Wilson, in a case which recently received widespread publicity, with reference to the presentation of the case by a junior but highly respected member of our Bar. In our view it is not a part of the function of a Judge to upbraid publicly a counsel who respectfully and in good faith is presenting a case to the Court. All cases in our Courts cannot be presented by senior counsel, and both in Ontario and England it has been the tradition and practice for the Bench and senior members of the Bar to assist and guide, with constructive criticism if necessary, the junior members of the profession. It is only thus that there can be an even administration of justice and a training of the profession in the work of a barrister. We deeply regret that on this occasion the learned Justice departed from a salutary practice which has been followed almost uniformly by our Judges and senior members of our profession.

This statement was not to be the end of the matter. If the bar did not like the bench criticizing its members, the bench liked the criticism of one of its members even less. The minutes of February 17, 1961, disclose that the benchers received letters from the Chief Justice of Ontario, Dana Porter, and the Chief Justice of the High Court, James McRuer, protesting what they considered to be an attack on the independence of the judiciary. Robinette reported that he had personal interviews with the chief justices and received a second letter from the Chief Justice of Ontario. McRuer's second letter to Robinette reveals his views on the merits of the bar's complaint:

As I said in my previous letter, there may be cases where it is wise and kindly to refrain from public criticism of counsel but there are many cases when it would be an injustice both to the public and to the legal profession for the Judge to refrain from publicly stating his views as to the presentation of the case. The particular case in question was surely one of the latter sort. It was the first of its kind in this jurisdiction. The intervention was for the purpose of bringing to light any corruption in the administration of justice that might have been concealed in the original trial. The plaintiff had publicly declared that she had made a profession of corrupting justice. In those circumstances if the trial judge found, as he did on ample grounds, that the case was one which demanded more experienced counsel and more competent presentation, surely it was his duty to say so publicly.

The minutes record that Robinette appointed a special six-bencher committee to look into the matter, which met on two occasions. Convocation authorized him to send a letter explaining the position of the benchers while at the same time acknowledging the validity of the judges' concerns about their independence. It reads in part as follows:

> The Benchers regret that their action should have been the occasion of deep concern to the Judges and they have placed first, in their consideration of the matter, the maintenance of the good relations between Bench and Bar in the province.
>
> ...
>
> It was not our intention to assert any jurisdiction or power over the Judges whose independence must be respected and for whose good name we have the highest regard. We fully recognize that Judges may in proper cases and within proper limits publicly criticize counsel who appear before them, but we are of the opinion that we have the privilege and the duty to speak for the Bar and to comment when we feel that those limits have been exceeded. By so doing we are not attempting to define the powers, rights or duties of the Judges and, of course, we agree that we can not do so.

I suspect that Robinette had a great deal to do with the drafting of this letter. The language certainly reflects his strongly held views that counsel should not be subject to gratuitous abuse. I would have liked to have been a fly on the wall when he explained this to Chief Justice McRuer. I also note from the Law Society's file that while Robinette, in his capacity as treasurer, received two letters from McRuer addressed "My dear Treasurer," he did not answer them directly and simply asked Chief Justice Porter to pass along to McRuer a copy of his letters to Porter.

Porter's last letter of February 24, 1961, seems to have put the matter to rest. He wrote:

> I have given consideration to the suggestion of a joint committee to deal with the relations between the Bench and the Bar. I do not think that such a committee would be appropriate or necessary. I feel sure that the action taken by Convocation will go far to restore the excellent relationship that has existed between the Bench and the Bar. The Chief Justice of the High Court has asked me to say that he agrees with the views expressed in this letter.

Robinette sent this letter along to W. Earl Smith, the Secretary of the Law Society, with the comment, "There is peace in the land." For his part, the Attorney General responded to the criticism of having appointed a junior counsel as Queen's Proctor by naming Pepper in the Queen's next New Year's Honours List as a Queen's Counsel so that he became one of "Her Majesty's Counsel Learned in the Law of Ontario" and was entitled to precedence over barristers who had not been so honoured.

Looking back at this incident, which was taken very seriously at the time, I cannot help but think that if Convocation had continued to this day to be as active in monitoring the conduct of bench and bar, we might have avoided the lack of civility among counsel and, to a lesser extent, between the bar and the bench that we now too often witness. The current acrimony between counsel engaged in litigation and the judges who attempt to run their courts is destructive to the administration of justice and hurtful to the interests being represented in the particular case. The bench and the bar fulfil different roles directed to the same end: the resolution of disputes under the law and within an appropriate timeframe. Gratuitous personal criticism of counsel who is doing his or her best furthers none of these goals and in turn invites a response from counsel to the judge that is disrespectful and, just as importantly, does not advance the interests of the parties to the dispute.

The above review of the minutes confirms that Convocation was not burdened by a heavy agenda during Robinette's stewardship as treasurer. At that time, there was no comprehensive legal aid program, compensation fund, or errors and omissions insurance fund, which were to later impose heavy burdens on the Law Society. The casual workload accords with my own recollection that Robinette did not spend much time at this job. In fact, his attendances at the Law Society administrative offices were so sporadic that "Alf" Bennett, the financial assistant to the secretary, became a fixture in the waiting room at McCarthys, where he attended to obtain the Treasurer's signature on even the most routine cheques for the society.

I discussed my memories on this topic with John Arnup, who was to succeed Joseph Sedgwick as treasurer in 1963. We had this conversation about the business of Convocation:[88]

>
> GDF: I've Robinette's *curriculum vitae* which was put together by the Law Society from its archives. It shows that he became Treasurer on May 16, 1958. Could you tell something about the problems he faced when he was the Treasurer? My own recollection is that there wasn't a great deal going on in his four years.
>
> JDA: That impression of yours is accurate. The main problem that he acquired was the opening of the Bar Admission Course as a result of the agreement of 1957 with the universities, but that was more my problem than John's.
>
> GDF: You were the Chairman of the Education Committee at that time?
>
> JDA: Yes. And, in my second, third and fourth years in that post, I had asked for and got Bill

Howland as vice-chair of the Education
Committee and he was a great asset in making
the Bar Admission Course work.

My one criticism of both Robinette and
Sedgwick as treasurers was that they did not
realize and most of the benchers did not realize
that there was a lot of defalcation going on [by
lawyers from their trust accounts] which had
not come to light except in one or two instances
and, when I became treasurer in 1963, it was a
case of inherit the wind. News of defalcation
was breaking out all over the place, and I don't
blame John for letting this happen — it should
have been reported to other benchers and to
staff — although, at that point, we had no staff
to do serious investigations, and we hired an
accountant, the first one ever in the pay of the
Law Society, to look into lawyers' trust accounts,
both on complaints and on suggestions made by
benchers or other lawyers.

GDF: When was this? During your tenure?

JDA: Yes.

GDF: In those days, back when Robinette was
       Treasurer, how long would Convocation last,
       and what kind of business would be done at
       Convocation?

JDA: Present benchers would find it hard to believe
       how Convocation acted. At 9:30 a.m., George
       Walsh's committee [later the first Justice
       George T. Walsh], which was Unauthorized
       Practice, and largely in pursuit of unlicensed
       conveyancers, had a meeting. Convocation as a

rule did not start until 11:00 a.m., although
later on, I think towards the end of John's term,
it was advanced to 10:30 a.m., but almost
always — unless something very special intervened — Convocation was through by lunch,
1:00 p.m. The chairman of each committee
read a report which had not been circulated in
advance to other benchers and that probably
had something to do with the fact that the
extent of debate was quite limited unless somebody had prior wind of a contentious matter
and had come ready to speak about it. Also, the
work of the Discipline Committee was not significant although it developed towards the end
of the 1950s.

GDF: There was no Legal Aid program?

JDA: There was no Legal Aid program. The compensation fund and legal aid both had their
origin later on. Legal Aid had its origin in my
time and actually at my initiative. The compensation fund was a little later and was not
unanimously accepted by Convocation but a
substantial majority was in favour of a fund to
compensate clients of dishonest lawyers, but
neither of those problems was a problem for
John Robinette.

GDF: Convocation met on a Friday, and there were
meetings September through to June.

JDA: Yes, and at the June Convocation, all the
benchers were gowned. That was a tradition. But
one of the differences started in my case which
was in 1952 when I first became a bencher: a

number of the benchers wore morning coats. The treasurer, of course, was gowned, but a number of benchers wore morning coats, and a number of others, including me, wore directors' coats and striped pants to all Convocations so there was an air of solemnity about the thing that was perhaps a hangover from the days when the benchers were a good deal older than they were by the time I was finished as Treasurer.[89]

Robinette's limited interest in administration — whether at the Law Society or McCarthys — should not have come as a surprise to anyone who had seen him operate in an office setting. He was a loner and concerned himself only with what affected him directly. That is not to say that he was not fully capable of looking after himself. Rather, he simply did not have a larger view of the firm or its future. He left that to Matthews, whom he trusted completely in planning matters. If he had a specific problem, he would ask his secretary to do whatever was necessary to solve it. On larger issues he would enlist the support of persons like me. This of course was a blessing. The last thing we wanted was this superstar to take an uninformed interest in office management.

I think this is what his fellow benchers wanted of him as well. He was to be their leader in public relations, not an administrative zealot who would awaken them to some unfortunate shortcomings in their conduct of the affairs of the profession, such as mass defalcations (misappropriations of monies) by lawyers and the glaring need for a comprehensive legal aid plan. Convocation received a splendid champion, a person who related well to the public. Not only did Robinette have a great presence, he also had an infallible feeling for the occasion.

One of my favourite examples, perhaps because I organized the event when I was treasurer, was an address he gave at a memorial service for the Right Honourable John R. Cartwright in the Great Library at Osgoode Hall on May 14, 1980. The Great Library was a brilliant setting for this tribute. This magnificent room, housing the largest private collection of legal material in Canada, is simply extraordinary for a working library. It stretches from east to west along the front of Osgoode

Hall, its etched and stained glass windows looking to the south. Its ceiling, sculptured and intricately decorated, is more than two storeys high and is supported by fourteen columns. Two galleries cling to the north wall. The west end contains a fireplace, and set above it and dominating that end of the room is a huge portrait in oils of Sir John Beverley Robinson, Chief Justice of Upper Canada from 1829 to 1862. The east end projects a more sombre image. It has a statue of a young man, eyes heaven-raised, standing before a plaque with the names of members of the Law Society who fell in battle during the Great War. It was before this memorial that Robinette stood. He recognized the significance of the forum. He opened with:

> I am privileged to say a few words this afternoon in the presence of the relatives of John Robert Cartwright and his loving friends and admirers. It is peculiarly fitting that a service in his memory is being held in this gracious and distinguished library. The setting here will remind us of his love of English literature and of his devotion to the law and that it was in this room and in the adjacent chambers that his professional career was nurtured. And for yet another reason it is apt that the service is being held here because behind me in this room stands the Law Society's sculpture and plaque in memory of many of John's friends and associates who died in the First Great War.

Robinette went on to describe Cartwright's outstanding war record. Cartwright enlisted at the outbreak of war as a private at age eighteen, was twice wounded in France and received the Military Cross for gallantry, became aide de camp to three Canadian generals, two of whom were killed in action, and returned to Canada with the rank of captain. Robinette also reviewed Cartwright's brilliant legal career, which culminated in his appointment to the position of chief justice of Canada. Along the way, he touched on a facet of Cartwright of which I was not aware, but that in no sense surprised me:

He was always a keen student of English literature
and of the derivation and precise meaning of words.
While sitting on the Supreme Court of Canada he
would send for a book which one might contemplate
was some law report but frequently it was the Oxford
English Dictionary so that he could clarify his mind
as to the proper use and meaning of a particular
word or phrase. As you know his favourite author
was G.K. Chesterton and there was probably no one
of his era who had a greater knowledge of the works
of Chesterton.

I knew Cartwright as a member of the highest court and to a much
lesser extent as a person. I had some slight association with him as a fraternity brother, and he was generous in his support and encouragement
as I struggled to become a counsel. His treatment of me was by no
means singular — he was helpful to all young counsel whom he thought
were trying — but to me he was something special. As I sat and listened
to Robinette on the occasion of this memorial to Cartwright, I congratulated myself on having asked him to be the speaker. It is difficult to
imagine a more gracious tribute to a true gentleman who distinguished
himself in both war and peace.

After his tenure as treasurer, Robinette was not particularly active as
an ex officio bencher. It was the accepted courtesy for former treasurers
to absent themselves from Convocation so as not to give the impression
that they were looking over the shoulder of their successors. Robinette
invoked this protocol with more enthusiasm than perhaps was necessary. But I must say I was relieved that during my tenure Robinette
never attended meetings of Convocation, although he frequently
appeared for lunch. Even so, I was harried by some senior benchers who
seemed to greet all my initiatives with the query, "Have you spoken to
John Robinette about this?"

The Minutes of Convocation recite as Robinette's contribution to
Convocation that he remained active on the Professional Conduct
Committee for the years 1972–74, he became a Life Member in June
1979, and he received an honorary doctorate in Ottawa in April 1982.

Of special interest is a note in the Law Society's minutes that Robinette offered to make funds available on an annual basis to establish a prize of $150 in honour of his late father, Thomas Cowper Robinette, K.C., to be awarded to the third-year student of Osgoode Hall Law School who obtained the highest mark in the subject of criminology. The minutes note that the Dean of the law school accepted the offer with gratitude and that the prize, to be known as the Thomas Cowper Robinette Memorial Prize, was to be established with the first award to be made in 1963–64.

Chapter Ten
Taking in Our Own Laundry: Ross v. Lamport

O
NE OF THE MORE DISAGREEABLE duties that befall counsel in a
large firm is having to give advice to members of his own firm.
There is nothing more tiresome than returning to the office
after an exhausting day of trying to persuade a reluctant court to accept
your arguments only to find that a partner of the firm has been await-
ing your arrival impatiently because he wants your advice on a matter
of transcending importance to him. While you are looking distractedly
at a host of pink telephone slips that demand your immediate attention,
the partner is bludgeoning you with facts about a matter that your tired
mind has difficulty absorbing.

Robinette was not exempt from this treatment and, in fact, probably
received more of it than anybody in the firm. He was very patient about
it, but was not averse to giving a quick and not necessarily accurate
answer just to get rid of the bothersome partner. However, in his case, the
massaging of senior partners went well beyond mere listening and opin-
ion-giving; he was often asked to step into the breach and get involved in
a matter that had gone seriously wrong. One of these cases was the ill-
fated defamation action conducted by Senator Hayden (reported as *Ross
v. Lamport*[90]), which was to occupy a good deal of Robinette's time.

In the early 1950s, staid old Toronto was blessed with the election of
a vigorous and flamboyant mayor named Alan Lamport. Lamport was
determined to shake the city out of the doldrums and take it to where it
belonged in the mid-twentieth century. Most of all, he wanted to do
something about Toronto's somnolent Sundays by legalizing sporting

events on the Christian Sabbath. He was successful in this and other ventures, and "Lampy" is still remembered fondly in Toronto as the mayor who brought Sunday sports to the city. Lamport sought the public eye and courted the press assiduously. He always provided a lively quote, and the press loved him. He was also a bit of a loose cannon, and this was to be his undoing with respect to an unassuming and previously unknown taxi driver named Thomas A. Ross.

Ross owned and drove a taxicab and needed a licence to function in both capacities. The responsibility of issuing licences to taxicab owners and drivers under the City of Toronto bylaw rested with the Board of Police Commissioners. The members of the board at that time were Judge Barton, a County Court judge; James MacFadden, a sitting magistrate; and the Mayor of Toronto, who acted as chairman of the board.

In the spring of 1953, these board members rejected Ross's application for a cab owner's licence. In the board's view, based on its earlier experience with Ross, Ross was actually in the business of buying and selling taxi licences, which was contrary at least to the spirit of the regulatory policy of the board. However, Ross persisted. He appealed the board's refusal to grant him the licence by invoking the provisions of the *Municipal Act*.[91]

Ross's appeal was heard by Justice LeBel of the High Court of Justice. On May 20, 1953, he allowed Ross's appeal and ordered the board to issue a cab owner's licence to Ross forthwith. The substance of Justice LeBel's reasons was as follows. Although there was some suggestion in the questions asked by members of the board that Ross had profitably traded in cab owners' licences in the past, this allegation was hotly denied by Ross, and no evidence was presented to the board to contradict his denial. As a result, there was no factual basis for the board's decision to refuse the licence that Ross sought. LeBel concluded that the board must act judicially and must not refuse the application without giving due consideration to Ross's position by allowing him to state his case and by permitting him to call evidence if necessary. The need to act judicially is particularly strong where allegations have been made which, if true, would justify the refusal of a licence.

The Board of Police Commissioners did not obey Justice LeBel's order. In October 1953, two motions were made in Weekly Court at

Toronto before Chief Justice McRuer. One was a motion on behalf of
Ross to have both Lamport and Judge Barton (MacFadden was out of
the country on vacation) cited for contempt of court in willfully refusing to obey the order of Justice LeBel. The other was a motion on
behalf of Lamport and the other members of the board to reverse or set
aside LeBel's order.

These motions came on for hearing on October 29, 1953. It would
appear that Lamport and his fellow board members got a frosty reception. After the argument on the morning of October 30 and before the
Chief Justice delivered judgment, the board met again and decided to
issue a cab owner's licence to Ross, conditional on his withdrawal from
the contempt proceedings. Counsel re-attended before the Chief Justice
of the High Court, and on consent of the parties, he permitted the contempt proceedings to be withdrawn and ordered the issuing of the
licence. Ross was entitled to his legal costs throughout the judicial proceedings.[92] However, before the licence was actually issued, Lamport
exploded to the press about the matter.

In a move that he would very much regret, Lamport spoke to three
newspaper reporters that day: Lee Belland from the *Toronto Star* and
Grey Hamilton and Lee French from the *Globe and Mail*. Torontonians
awakened on Saturday, October 31, 1953, to the banner headline on the
front page of the *Globe*, LAMPORT CHARGES CHIEF JUSTICE DID-
N'T READ EVIDENCE IN CASE. Over that headline and in smaller
print were the underlined words, "Funny Ethics in My Book": Mayor.
The story continued on the front page with pictures of McRuer and
Lamport cheek by jowl and a picture of Ross below. The following
words were quoted and attributed to Lamport:

> Mr. Justice McRuer's statement that the police commis-
> sion was depriving Ross of a living indicated he had not
> read the evidence. The truth never came out. It was
> never shown why we did this. The facts are that here is
> a fellow who has been trafficking in licenses to make
> himself some money and the court upholds him while
> others can't get them. There has never been a more fla-
> grant case of trafficking ... Chief Justice McRuer's

statement that we were depriving a man of his living shows favoritism. He preferred Ross' viewpoint.

Evidently, Lamport's abuse was really directed to McRuer, but McRuer was not about to do anything about it. When asked for his comments by a *Globe* reporter, he replied loftily (and properly), "I do not give interviews on my judgments." Lamport was in a sense blindsided when the unobtrusive Ross came forward and instituted an action based on both slander and libel: slander arising from the expression by Lamport of these words to the reporters, and libel in the reporters' publication of the interview with Lamport in the *Globe* and a similar story in the *Star*.

On receiving the writ of summons, Lamport rushed over to McCarthys to see his old friend and supporter, Senator Salter Hayden, a man, as I indicated earlier, who at one time enjoyed a formidable reputation as a barrister. Convincing evidence of this reputation is provided by an experience I had as an articling student when I visited Sir Lyman Duff, the former chief justice of Canada and legendary legal icon, at his home in Ottawa. I was with my father, who was a friend of his, and during drinks (none for Sir Lyman), I was asked with whom I was working at McCarthy & McCarthy. At the time, I was involved in a case with Senator Hayden and said so. Sir Lyman was most generous in his praise of him and said that he was the best-prepared counsel to have appeared before him. This reaction astonished me, because my experience with Hayden was quite the opposite. However, Sir Lyman was speaking of the past.

I found working with Hayden to be hectic to the point of unsettling. He had astonishing self-confidence and had no hesitation in relying on my work completely. He accepted my explanations of all documents and events without question and would even permit me to hand him judicial authorities during the course of argument, which he would read aloud, and for the first time. On the other hand, he was very quick on his feet and was one of the best cross-examiners I have ever watched. However, I was not prepared to regard him as a mentor.

One thing I did know about Hayden was that he was a poor fit in Ross's action against Lamport. He and Lamport were too much alike. They both were arrogant and quick to take offence. They were impatient and lacked discipline. They were not prepared to take Ross seriously, and they grossly underestimated Ross's lawyer, R. Nelles Starr, Q.C.

Starr was a very good lawyer. He had developed a specialty in defamation law, though by no means did he restrict his practice to this comparatively narrow field. He had acted for Ross in his applications for a taxi licence as well as the subsequent appeal and contempt motion. He was a formidable and tenacious forensic foe. He also had the knack of getting under the skin of opposing counsel, sometimes just by being spectacularly rude. My own experience with him is illustrative.

In the case of *Crump Mechanical Contracting Ltd. v. Toronto Dominion Centre Ltd.*,[93] Starr was suing the new Toronto Dominion Centre on behalf of the plumbing and heating subcontractor, which maintained that it was entitled to extra payment for authorized extras for work performed on the main tower. It was a long and tedious piece of litigation, as most construction cases are, and there were plenty of opportunities for counsel to rub each other the wrong way. So after Starr had asked me such questions as, "Did you dye your hair?" and inquired of me about "fat Robinette" and "that little crook, Hayden," I realized that I would have to come up with a strategy to counteract these obvious attempts to throw me off my stride. I decided that I would tell him what a wonderful fellow he was and how he was one of my favourite people. Starr looked puzzled by this non-violent counterattack. He was not used to being told that he was nice. I was glad I took this approach because it allowed me to enjoy one stunt he pulled that was truly funny.

We were both in the middle of the *Crump* trial at the University Avenue courthouse before Justice Samuel Hughes. Starr was in good form. During one of my arguments to the Court, he pulled on my sleeve, and when I bent over to hear what he had to say, he whispered, "How can you be such a fucking liar?" I apologized to the Court for the interruption, thanked "my friend," and carried on. Shortly thereafter, we adjourned for lunch. I headed for the University Club, which was just across the street from the courthouse. As I was well aware, Hughes and Starr were both members of the same club. As it turned out, both independently were going there that day for lunch.

I should explain that the University Club had a large circular club table where members sat and chatted informally. Hughes, Starr, and I were regulars at this table, and when I arrived first, I sat down there as usual. Starr came in and hesitated when he saw me, but sat down just the same. When Hughes came in, he looked at both of us and decided that he would sit by himself at a small table away from the club table.

Now Hughes was a very meticulous man and was totally predictable about his lunch. He always had a pint of Labatt's beer "off the shelf," white rolls and cheddar cheese, nothing else. On this occasion, anticipating trouble, a steward hovered nervously by. He went over to Hughes with the mandatory bottle of Labatt's and said, "I'm sorry, Your Honour, but there is no cheddar cheese." Judges of the Superior Court were entitled at that time to be addressed as "Your Lordship" when in court or their chambers. "Your Honour" was restricted to County and District Court judges. In neither case was the honorific to be used in a gentlemen's club.

Hughes was clearly irritated by the form of address and certainly by the news about the cheese. "There must be some cheddar in the club," he said. "Check upstairs if you would." "Yes, Your Honour," replied the waiter, who meekly departed to the upstairs dining room. He returned shortly with the announcement, "I'm sorry, Your Honour, but there is no cheddar cheese in the whole club. We are out." Hughes was clearly annoyed. "This would never have happened in an English club," he said. "Very well, show me a menu and I will order something else."

These exchanges between the waiter and Hughes had been monitored with some amusement by the regulars at the club table, who were all aware of Hughes's eating habits. In any event, the waiter finally got Hughes settled down, and Hughes reluctantly engaged in eating his second choice for lunch. Shortly after, Starr finished his lunch and got up from the club table. As he was leaving, he went by Hughes's table and declared, "Finlayson took the last of the cheddar cheese." Nobody laughed louder than Hughes.

Unfortunately, Senator Hayden was very thin-skinned and he reacted negatively, and not always effectively, to Starr's every barb. For instance, Starr referred to him as Senator Hayden in court to make sure the jury did not forget that they were dealing with two people of rank and privilege in both Lamport and his counsel. Instead of ignoring this breach of protocol (no titles are to be used in court for lawyers), Hayden was reduced to complaining unsuccessfully about this to the trial judge in chambers.

Defamation actions are very technical and, until relatively recently, they were invariably tried by a jury. This meant that counsel in their preparation must be aware of the complexities involved in drafting the pleadings of the claim of defamation and in drafting the defences to such a claim. At the same time, they must be aware of the need to simplify the issues for trial purposes so that the issues will be clear to the jury. Hayden did not do this drafting exercise well, while Starr did it extraordinarily well.

Counsel must also have a clear strategy from the outset so that the client is sure of where the evidence is going and the significance of his or her testimony on the issues. Such a strategy is necessary because it is a perfectly sound technique to plead defences in the alternative. For example, one can plead that the statements that the plaintiff alleges are defamatory were never uttered; alternatively, if the statements were uttered, they are incapable of being defamatory; in the further alternative, if the statements are capable of being defamatory, they are true; and finally, if they were uttered and they were not true, the statements are a matter of fair comment. But counsel had better decide which position the defence was prepared to live with before the client entered the box to testify. Pleading in the alternative is one thing; testifying in that way can lead to ridiculous positions.

In this case, the defence pleaded that Lamport did not make all the statements attributed to him by the three newspaper men and that he did not authorize the stories in the newspapers containing the defamatory words revolving around the phrase "trafficking in licences." The defence pleaded alternatively that the statements were a matter of fair comment and were not actionable.

Starr explained this contradictory position to the jury in his opening address, as reported in the *Globe and Mail* on September 21, 1954:

> Mr. Lamport denies the statements were made and says
> if they were they were not disparaging. He did not
> know or desire that they would be written down and
> published and they were made in reply to questions

from the reporters. He pleads fair comment on policy
as chairman of the commission.

This is a difficult stance for the mayor of Toronto to adopt in testimony, and Lamport did not make a very good witness. He was taken through the stories in the *Globe* and the *Star* by Senator Hayden and asked which statements attributed to him he agreed with and which he disagreed with. Lamport took exception to some of the statements and not to others. But the stories in the two newspapers were very similar, and it was difficult to believe that the reporters had made the same mistakes coincidentally. This was particularly so when all three of the reporters testified and referred to their notes on what Lamport had said.

Starr had a field day in cross-examination and was allowed to get away with some editorializing that was very effective. According to the *Globe* report of September 24:

> Mr. Starr asked him if he saw any significance in his "desire to admit the words that are innocent and deny those which are vicious." Mr. Lamport went into a long explanation that ended with, "I had a very high sense of responsibility to my oath of office and to the people I represented. I had no regard for my personal interests." He was referring to his dual role as mayor and chairman of the board of police commissioners.

In addition to giving long-winded and unresponsive answers, Lamport was combative to the point where Justice McLennan had to remind him and the jury, "This is not a personal contest between Mr. Starr and Mr. Lamport." His Lordship had earlier said to the witness, "Please conduct yourself in the witness box so that there will be no competition."[94]

Over and above Lamport's belligerence, it is difficult to determine just what it was that he was trying to say. If you have to concede that you addressed three men who you knew were reporters and made remarks about a matter of civic business, what is the point that you are trying to make to the jury? That you as the mayor can shoot your mouth off at will to newspaper reporters but take no responsibility for what they wrote even though you have never complained to the newspapers about the accuracy of the subsequent stories?

Starr was an effective cross-examiner and made very good use of the pre-trial examinations for discovery. I learned a lesson that I would never forget. In these discoveries, which take place in special examiners' rooms, no one is present but the parties, their counsel, and a shorthand reporter. This fosters a sense of informality. Lamport and, to a lesser extent, Hayden conducted themselves as if the transcript would never see the light of day. Lamport was argumentative and unresponsive to proper questions, and Hayden kept telling him that he did not have to answer certain questions without bothering to give a reason for his position. He also lectured Starr on his behaviour. When these passages were read out in open court, they could only have strengthened Starr's argument that Lamport did not think he was obliged to explain himself to anyone. In the result, as Robinette was to later say about the senator's handling of the case, "The jury didn't like Hayden's client, and they didn't like Hayden too much either."[95]

However, Starr had his own brand of hubris, and it brought him down at least temporarily. He overstated his case to the jury, delivering an address that the Court of Appeal was later to agree was inflammatory. The following excerpts are from the *Globe* of September 28, 1954:

> R.N. Starr, for Ross, referred to the founding of the judicial system in Magna Carta, and said: "We are not going to allow it to be destroyed by arrogant conduct on the part of boards and commissions. This is a deliberate and calculated attempt to strike at the foundations of the system in which we believe.
>
> "One would expect that a man occupying a position of responsibility and trust would have gone to the Chief Justice and apologized, would have gone to Mr. Ross and apologized, or to the newspapers to complain about the stories.
>
> "The Board had its ears pinned back thoroughly by Mr. Justice Lebel and didn't like it," Mr. Starr went on.

"Then [the decision] went to the Chief Justice. Mr. Lamport's statement was designed in the first instance to discredit the courts and the second instance to destroy Ross."

…

"The whole thing was a shocking attack on a man's honesty," Mr. Starr said. "The decision by the board was the most shameful and disgraceful capitulation by a group of men that I have ever seen in the annals of the country."

The *Globe* report continued: Mr. Starr described the activities of boards set up by the government across the country and said, "The time has come to put an end to it. Let's not have it in this country as they had it in England in the case of Archer-Shee or the Winslow boy.[96] Let's not have any more of this arrogance, *this self-imposed sitting on the right of the Almighty*. It's justice we are after — not Lamport law," he added. "Some of us seek fame, power or money, but most of us just want a decent reputation to pass on to our children." Mr. Starr ended on an eloquent note from Shakespeare: "Good name in man or woman, dear my lord, is the immediate jewel of their souls: who steals my purse steals trash: 'tis something, nothing: 'twas mine, 'tis his, and has been slave to thousands. But he who filches from me my good name, robs me of that which not enriches him, and makes me poor indeed."

The jury was out for almost three hours. I had been dropping in and out of the case between my own assignments, and I went into the courtroom at Old City Hall on the evening of Monday, September 27, 1954, to await the verdict. It came down at 8:10 p.m. It was a disaster. The trial judge had asked the jury to answer eight questions of fact and to assess the damages if they found for the plaintiff. Every question was answered adversely to Lamport, and the damages, totalling $40,000, were the highest award in Canadian legal history and stood as a record for many years thereafter.

In their answers to the questions put to them, the jury found:

(1) that the words complained of as having been spoken to the *Globe and Mail* reporters Hamilton and French were in fact spoken by the appellant to them;

(2) that the words complained of as having been spoken to the *Toronto Star* reporter Belland were in fact spoken to him;

(3) that Lamport authorized or intended the publication of the words that were published in the *Globe and Mail* and in the *Toronto Star*;

(4) that the words spoken by Lamport referred to Ross in the way of his trade or calling;

(5) that the words were defamatory of Ross in their natural and ordinary meaning and also in at least one of the meanings attributed to them in the innuendo pleaded by Ross in his statement of claim;

(6) that the words in their natural and ordinary meaning were not true in substance and in fact;

(7) that, in so far as the words were comment, they were not fair comment on facts truly stated;

(8) that there was express malice on the part of the defendant.

The jury dealt with the amount of damages under four headings. They allowed $2,500 for slander in respect of the words spoken to Belland; $2,500 for slander in respect of the words spoken to Hamilton and French; $25,000 for libel in respect of the article published in the *Globe and Mail*; and $10,000 for libel in respect of the article published in the *Toronto Star*. The total amount of the damages was thus $40,000, and the trial judge entered judgment for that sum.[97]

Senator Hayden was devastated by this result and never appeared in court again on a contested matter. He asked Robinette to take the appeal.

At first blush it appeared to be a hopeless undertaking because of the answers given by the jury to the specific questions put to them by the trial judge. Fortunately, Hayden had insisted that the official court reporter report the closing addresses of counsel to the jury, something not ordinarily done. Robinette read Starr's address and saw a ray of hope. While the Court of Appeal had traditionally avoided interfering with the conduct of counsel in a civil case ("a lawsuit is not a tea party" was their customary response), in Robinette's view, Starr's closing address was clearly inflammatory and had crossed the line of permissible exhortation to the jury. As he said to me at the time, he did not think that the members of the panel of our appellate court would be comfortable with Starr's reference to Lamport sitting on the "right of the Almighty." This was blasphemy to an overwhelmingly Christian community. Robinette licked his lips when he found that Wilfred Roach, a devout Roman Catholic, was to be on his panel of appellate judges. "Wilf won't like that remark," he said.

Of course, running against this distaste for religious references in a secular court and the natural reluctance of the Court of Appeal to accept such a large defamation award against the mayor of the city were the truly insulting remarks that Lamport had made against one of their own, Chief Justice McRuer. Judges are always sensitive to their vulnerability to uninformed criticism (too sensitive, in my view) and feel helpless to respond effectively to it. However, while offensive, the remarks were irrelevant to Ross's cause of action, despite Starr's attempts at a linkage in the Court of Appeal. Robinette planned to direct the Court's attention to the language of Starr's jury address. The address appeared to invite the jury to punish Lamport not only for his part in the conduct of the Board of Police Commissioners in denying Ross a licence, but also for the alleged arbitrary actions of others and of administrative bodies generally. But first Robinette had to get a leg up on a substantive legal issue revolving around innuendoes that Ross had pleaded in his statement of claim.

Robinette opened his appeal — which was heard on May 9, 1955, by a court consisting of Chief Justice Pickup and Justices Roach, J.K. MacKay, F.G. MacKay, and Shroeder — with an argument about how the trial judge had misdirected the jury on the issue of the innuendoes pleaded by Ross.[98] Innuendo is a technical term in libel and slander actions and refers to a secondary meaning that is to be inferred from the words that were spoken or written. In this case, Ross did not rely solely on the words, "here is a fellow who has been trafficking in licences to make himself some money," for their plain and ordinary meaning. He also pleaded that the words spoken were meant and understood to convey the innuendo that Ross "in his personal capacity and in his capacity as a taxi driver and owner, had been dishonest with the Honourable the Chief Justice of the High Court, the Board of Commissioners of Police for the City of Toronto, and in his relations with the public, that he was concerned only in 'trafficking' in licences at a profit to himself in preference to serving the public in his trade, and that he had obtained in some way the good offices of the Honourable the Chief Justice of the High Court."

Robinette developed his arguments before the appellate court in the following way.[99] Ross had not called any evidence to establish that the words uttered by Lamport were understood by anyone in a sense other than their natural meaning, and he had failed to establish any of the innuendoes pleaded. Nor had Ross called any evidence to show that he had been held up to hatred, contempt, or ridicule as a result of the words uttered by Lamport. Ross did not suggest or prove that he had suffered any damages as the result of the publication of either the alleged slander or the alleged libel. On the contrary, Ross admitted that he had not suffered any loss of business or any damage related to expanding his business. He had admitted that he did not own any taxi-cabs and was not engaged in the business of being a cab owner or driver when the alleged slanderous words were uttered.

Robinette's argument was based on the fact that, subject to strict and narrow exceptions, slander is not actionable without proof of special damages, i.e., damages such as are referred to immediately above, which must be specifically alleged and specifically proved. Since Ross did not prove any damage, he attempted to fit his case within the established exception of words spoken of a man in relation to his trade or calling. However, to come within this exception to the normal rule that a plaintiff in an action for slander must prove special damages, Ross was required to prove that he was actually carrying on the trade or business in question at the time of the alleged slander. At the trial, Ross had admitted to the contrary. Furthermore, for the words to come within the exception, they must impute to Ross ignorance or incompetence in carrying on his calling. This requirement relates to claims for both libel and slander, and primarily concerns the innuendoes pleaded. The trial judge did not distinguish in his charge between the words alleged to have been spoken to different groups of reporters.

Robinette argued that each innuendo is to be regarded as a separate allegation. When any innuendo has been improperly left to the jury by the trial judge there must be a new trial, because it is impossible to say what part of the damages awarded was based on the innuendo that should not have been left with them. Here, there was nothing in the evidence to support some of the innuendoes pleaded by Ross, but they were all left with the jury.

Robinette pointed out that Lamport's trial counsel had objected to the form of the questions put to the jury by the trial judge and had requested him to ask the jury specifically which of the words that Ross complained of were spoken to each of the different reporters. According to Robinette, the evidence of the reporters indicated that the jury should have been told to disregard at least one sentence that appeared in the *Toronto Star*. That sentence referred to what police officials stated. The reporter testified that he could not swear that Lamport made any reference to that topic. However, the trial judge left it up to the jury to determine whether Lamport had made any such statement to the reporter. It was particularly important in a case such as this, Robinette argued, that where the newspapers expanded on what Lamport said, the jury should be directed with care and precision to determine which words were spoken by Lamport, as distinguished from words introduced into the articles by the newspaper staff.

Robinette had set the table with his legal arguments on substantive matters and now was able to turn the Court's mind to the inflammatory jury address. Robinette watched the Court carefully as he read out the offending remarks and noted, as he had predicted, that Justice Roach frowned when he heard the statement about Lamport sitting on the right of the Almighty. Robinette argued forcefully that Nelles Starr's entire address to the jury was inflammatory, and was calculated to lead them to consider matters that they should not have considered. In particular, in referring to the assessment of damages, Starr invited the jury to consider matters that were quite irrelevant and were calculated only to inflame the jury and cause them to render a perverse and unreasonable verdict. Robinette referred to his comments about the Magna Carta and his plea not to allow the judicial system to be destroyed by arrogant conduct on the part of boards and commissions. He also played up the reference to the infamous Archer-Shee case. Robinette's submission to the Court was that the inflammatory address alone required that there be a new trial. Robinette conceded that trial counsel had not objected to Starr's address at the trial. But he argued that when this ground of appeal was considered in conjunction with the trial judge's improper jury address, the failure of trial counsel to object should not be fatal to the success of the appeal.

Robinette ended on the note that the jury's award of $40,000 as damages was fantastically extravagant, perverse, and unwarranted. The trial judge did not really assist or guide the jury on the appropriate quantum of damages. He failed to direct them that there must be some reasonable relation between the wrong done and the sanction applied, and did not caution them with regard to the inflammatory nature of counsel's address. In the result, Robinette argued, the jury brought in an award that no reasonable jury could properly bring in. The conclusion must be that they considered matters in connection with the damage award that they should not have considered.

The Court of Appeal accepted the substance of Robinette's arguments and ordered a new trial on all matters including the assessment of damages. Chief Justice Pickup, speaking for the Court, came to the following conclusions: (1) not all of the innuendoes should have been placed before the jury as the words published were not capable of bearing the meanings assigned to some of them by the plaintiff; (2) the words spoken were not in relation to Ross in his calling and thus no actual damage to Ross was shown; (3) the jury address by Ross's counsel had been inflammatory; and (4) the damages were excessive.

Robinette could not have asked for anything more. There was unrestrained joy at McCarthy & McCarthy. However, Starr was not through yet. He launched an appeal to the Supreme Court of Canada, which he was entitled to do as of right. The Supreme Court, consisting of Chief Justice Kerwin and Justices Rand, Locke, Cartwright, and Abbott, heard the appeal over three days from December 13 to 15, 1955. On March 2, 1956, the Court released three sets of reasons in which they all agreed that a new trial was necessary, but only on the issue of damages.[100] It is surprising that so many sets of reasons were delivered because the thinking of each member of the Court seems to have been the same.

Regarding the innuendo problem enunciated by the Court of Appeal, Justice Cartwright expressed the view that although the manner in which the innuendoes were submitted to the jury was not satisfactory, he was not satisfied that a different ruling by the trial judge would have assisted Lamport's case.

The Chief Justice, with whom Justice Rand agreed, stated that in view of the position taken by Lamport's trial counsel — in which he sought to use all the innuendoes in order to strengthen his argument that Lamport had brought himself within his claim of privilege and was therefore entitled to comment fairly on a matter of public interest — his counsel could not change his position on appeal and complain that one or more innuendoes were not capable of the meaning ascribed.

What really did surprise me was the highest court's attitude to the inflammatory address argument. They simply disagreed with the reaction of the Court of Appeal that the address was inflammatory. In the end, the Court allowed the appeal and limited the new trial to determining the amount of damages.

The new trial was an anticlimax. The new jury was also unhappy with Lamport, despite the fact that Robinette now represented him. They went through the heads of damage in the same way as the first jury had done, but having been instructed that the first award had been struck down as too high, they were careful to pare a little off each head of damage. The result was a net award of $25,000, still very high for the time.

The real relief to Lamport came through the efforts of Robinette's colleague, John Brooke. Lamport, for all his excess of zeal, was acting in his capacity as mayor and without the city's backing would be unable to meet his legal obligations and pay the damage award. Brooke went to the Toronto City Council with Lamport and in essence persuaded the members that there but for the grace of God, go they. Council accepted the argument and agreed to indemnify Lamport for his legal costs and the amount of the final damage award. It was a messy ending, but lawsuits frequently have that quality.

Chapter Eleven
Taking in Our Own Laundry Part II: NONG and Leo Landreville

MY EXPERIENCES WITH NORTHERN ONTARIO Natural Gas (NONG) and its two principals, Ralph K. Farris and C. Spencer Clark, were part of my maturation process as a lawyer. Looking back at it from my present perspective, I cannot believe that I failed to realize at the time the significance of the NONG project and how huge the consequences of success or failure were to its entrepreneurs.

At the outset of this chapter, I would like to acknowledge my indebtedness to William Kaplan's excellent book, *Bad Judgment: The Case of Mr. Justice Leo A. Landreville*,[101] which I read when it was first published and reread before writing this chapter to refresh my memory about the chronology of events related to the early history of NONG and the involvement of the former mayor of Sudbury.[102]

When I first met Farris and Clark in the offices of McCarthy & McCarthy sometime in the early spring of 1955, I knew nothing more of the natural gas industry and the discussions about the various competing projects to bring natural gas from the West to Eastern Canada than I had read in the newspapers. These discussions were to culminate in Parliament during what was called the "pipeline debate" in May 1956, which some credit with bringing down the Liberal government that had reigned undisturbed in Ottawa from 1935.

During this period of intense political interest in government policy on natural gas, Farris and Clark managed to convince sixteen municipalities in Northern Ontario, including Cochrane, Timmins, and North Bay, to sign franchises granting NONG the exclusive right to construct facilities and distribute natural gas within the boundaries of their respective municipalities. The founders of NONG had not yet won distribution rights from the Lakehead cities of Port Arthur and Fort William (now collectively Thunder Bay) or Sudbury, but they had assembled an important nucleus for a distribution system and achieved a big jump on the competition.

Early in the acquisition stage, Farris and Clark needed counsel to act for the company in an application before the Ontario Fuel Board to obtain orders under the *Municipal Franchises Act*[103] to approve granting the franchises and to dispense with the statutory requirement that franchise agreements be submitted to the municipal electors for their approval. They turned to their all-purpose law firm, McCarthy & McCarthy, and that firm designated me. I was excited at the challenge, little appreciating that in the process of completing their goal of a single natural gas distribution system stretching from the Manitoba-Ontario border through the northland and ending at a point near Toronto, the promoters of NONG would create as much political havoc in the Ontario legislature at Queen's Park as did the founders of Trans Canada Pipelines Limited in Parliament. I was to be a first-hand witness to this turmoil and an assistant to Robinette when he was called in to act as counsel.

My selection by Beverly Matthews as NONG's counsel reflected an engaging quality shared by all of my seniors at McCarthys that even though I was "the last boy out of school" (Frank McCarthy's expression), they expected me to know everything there was about the practice of law. I, brashly, had no difficulty in taking that notion to heart. But unfortunately it was sometimes a hard to sell to the clients. Farris and Clark were no exception. My youthful appearance was particularly offputting to Clark, who as president of a natural gas utility in the United States, Cascade Natural Gas Company of Seattle, was familiar with regulatory proceedings in the United States before state regulatory boards and the Federal Power Commission. He was used to dealing with veterans of a bar that specialized in public utility work. However, there was no established private sector bar of that nature in Eastern Canada in 1955.

I was used to the sight of the dropped jaw when I showed up unexpectedly at a hearing or meeting in the place of Robinette. I learned to counter my unfavourable first impression by hard work and thorough preparation. After my initial hearing before the Ontario Fuel Board, where I obtained the necessary approvals for the original sixteen franchises, I felt that I had achieved a satisfactory rapport with Farris and Clark and, at a different level, of course, the respect of the two members of the board — the chairman, Archie Crozier, and the member, Ralph Howard — who were to hear all the applications involving NONG with which I was involved.

Obtaining these and other orders from the board involved considerable travelling with Farris and Clark and other members of NONG, including J. Chester Grey and John Tomlinson. I took advantage of this propinquity to learn as much as I could about the natural gas industry. From them I learned that the basic problem confronting any project designed to deliver natural gas from Western Canada to Northern Ontario was the formidable presence of the prehistoric rock formation running north of the Great Lakes through Northern Ontario and Quebec known as the Canadian Shield. The most immediate obstacle related to increased construction costs in this difficult terrain because of the need to bury the thirty-six-inch-diameter high-pressure natural gas pipeline. Compounding these increased costs was the lack of proven markets in Northern Ontario, which discouraged any forecast of a reasonable economic return for such significant expense.

It was this twin reality that encouraged western gas producers to propose two ventures that would yield immediate returns to them and still provide gas to the east. One was the straight swap of western gas exported to Western U.S. and California for eastern American gas imported from the Texas panhandle. In short, no cross-continental pipeline at all. The other was the construction of a pipeline from the Alberta border to Winnipeg, dropping it south and proceeding east through Michigan and below the Great Lakes to re-enter Canada in southern Ontario. Neither alternative left any room for NONG or the northern communities.

Fortunately for NONG, Clarence D. Howe, who was pretty much running the country from an economic point of view in his role of minister of munitions and supply in the federal Liberal government of the day, decreed that there would be no western gas sold in Eastern Canada directly or by displacement except via an all-Canadian route. The Government of Canada assumed the responsibility of constructing the pipeline from the Manitoba border to Kapuskasing through a Crown corporation called Northern Ontario Pipelines Crown Corporation, which was later subsumed by Trans Canada Pipelines.

The primary task confronting NONG was to satisfy the federal government that there was a market worth serving in Northern Ontario, while at the same time convincing the northern communities that NONG was the best vehicle for distributing gas from a cross-Canada pipeline. Great projects often have small beginnings, and the genesis of the plan to deliver gas to Northern Ontario was small to the point of being humorous. The plan was hatched by Phillip Kelly, the Minister of Mines for Ontario. He used his nephew, Gordon Kelly McLean, as his messenger. McLean approached Farris in his home of Vancouver armed with no more evidence of economic feasibility than a Shell Oil road map of Northern Ontario. He had carefully circled the towns and cities that were served by the Trans-Canada Highway and explained that this should be the route of the proposed Canadian pipeline. He also pointed out the obvious — that there was no gas utility service in Ontario north of Toronto. The way was open for a new venture.

Farris was basically in the oil business, not natural gas, and certainly not natural gas utilities. However, he was a visionary and an enthusiast. He spoke to his friend, Spence Clark, at Cascade Natural Gas, and Clark became interested. Seed money was obtained through mutual friends in the oil and gas business, NONG was incorporated, employees were hired, and the co-venturers were off and running.

The obstacles to a viable natural gas distribution system were the same as for the trans-Canada line: a sparse population and an abundance of rock. However, an examination of the market by the knowledgeable Chester Grey, a field representative and advance man for NONG, revealed that there were substantial industrial loads available from the producing mines and the major pulp and paper mills, which virtually sustained the working population of Northern Ontario. By balancing the high residential winter loads with heavy industrial summer loads, the pipeline could be kept full, and a distribution system would be economically feasible. Particularly attractive was International Nickel at Copper Cliff, a separate municipality adjoining Sudbury. While not on the Trans-Canada Highway, it was such an attractive industrial load that it justified the construction by NONG of a separate spur line to bring it into the NONG system. Additionally, Sudbury was verging on being a boom community and presented attractive commercial and residential loads.

NONG rounded out its franchise holdings by acquiring a 50 percent interest in Twin City Gas, a local company controlled by a local contractor, which had acquired the franchises in Port Arthur, Fort William, Dryden, and Kenora. NONG picked up other franchises, such as Gravenhurst and Bracebridge, but there is no question that NONG needed Sudbury and its nickel loads to complete the viability of its venture. I was not involved in any of the negotiations with the municipalities for franchise rights except for the open hearing discussions at the Ontario Fuel Board proceedings. I was specifically kept out of the matter of the Sudbury franchise. Farris made it very clear that he had become a friend of the mayor, a lawyer named Leo Landreville, whom he much admired, and that any negotiating as to franchise terms was to be left to the two of them. I will return to this subject shortly when I deal with the substance of the criminal charges brought against Landreville and Farris arising out of the granting of the franchise by the City of Sudbury.[104]

The bulk of the franchises having been obtained and approved, I applied on NONG's behalf for certificates of convenience and necessity authorizing the construction of the facilities to implement NONG's obligations to supply natural gas to the various franchised communities. The hearing before the Ontario Fuel Board commenced on June 21, 1956. However, the solicitor for Sudbury, John J. Kelly, had some concerns that he expressed to the city council and the board about the terms of the proposed franchise agreement with NONG. We proceeded with the evidence on convenience and necessity, which was really quite speculative as to the feasibility of the venture, simply because there was no experience to compare it with. But the board's decision whether to approve the NONG franchise was postponed because of two adjournments obtained by Kelly. During one of these hearing breaks, the chairman of the board went to Sudbury to address the city council and suggested that there was urgency in having the bylaw passed granting the franchise to NONG.[105] In the end, the certificates were granted on August 15, 1956.

The proceedings before the Fuel Board often were informal to the point of approaching perfunctory. I commend the chairman of the board for that. This was not a Sudbury project or even a Northern Ontario project. It was the implementation of a national policy formulated by the Government of Canada, and strongly supported by the governments of Ontario and Quebec, to permit Eastern Canada to obtain the full benefit of the abundant gas supplies in Western Canada through a secure source of supply that remained fully within the jurisdiction and control of Canada. The so-called northern route that NONG relied on for its gas supply was vital to this national policy, and the Ontario government was quick to realize that it would not be an economically feasible venture unless, first, the whole of the North was served by one supplier and, second, its entire system was treated as one delivery point from Trans Canada Pipelines for pricing purposes. Archie Crozier was thoroughly versed in the requirements of the gas industry. He used his position, properly in my view, to explain the realities of the economics involved to the various municipalities whose distribution franchises were required. They all wanted natural gas (which was a boon to them, in fact more than a boon, a bonanza), but their representatives sometimes permitted local politics and personal interests to confuse the issues.

The work before the Fuel Board having been completed, the next step was to raise public money. NONG was well connected in this regard through its directors and their relationships with Bear Stearns & Co. and Lehman Brothers, two merchant bankers from New York, and Bankers Bond Corporation Ltd. of Toronto. The original shareholders in 1954 apart from provisional directors were Farris, Clark, Farris's development company, Charter Oil, a Matthew M. Newell and, most significantly, Gordon Kelly McLean, who had 200 of the original 500 founders' shares.

A list of shareholders shows that prior to the first public offering dated May 30, 1957, and filed with the Ontario Securities Commission on June 4, 1957, approximately 19,000 NONG shares had been distributed and were being held by an unknown number of persons.[106] I was one of them. I had bought 250 shares from John Tomlinson, an officer of NONG, at $2.50 per share. I did so with some reluctance. Not because I considered there was anything unethical about the purchase; Beverley Matthews had bought 1,500 shares at $1.00 on April 11, 1956. My concern arose out of my lack of faith in the prospects of the company, and I was most reluctant to pay out $625 from my meagre portfolio for a stock that did not interest me as an investment. However, I was working closely with Tomlinson at the time on various matters relating to the business of the company, and I did not want him, and through him, the other officers of the company, to know of my lack of confidence in NONG's future. I was originally offered 500 shares but was relieved when Tomlinson later told me that he could only deliver 250 shares because he had over-committed.

The stock was not listed on any stock exchange, and I had no idea what was happening to it. I was surprised and delighted when Tomlinson told me a few months later that the stock was trading over-the-counter at $18 a share. When I told Matthews the news, he was even more surprised and equally delighted. He promised to buy me a drink if the report turned out to be accurate. I made inquiries of a broker friend about ten days later and when he said NONG shares were selling at $21, I told him to sell. It was the only windfall I have experienced on the market and I am still enjoying the fruits of it, in that it provided the downpayment on the first house Joan and I bought for our expanding family. I also received a bottle of Scotch whisky from Matthews.

The first public offering of NONG shares was made on May 30, 1957, when a prospectus prepared by McCarthys was issued listing 400,000 common shares on the Toronto Stock Exchange. While the directors of the company anticipated a good public response, they were overwhelmed by the enthusiasm with which the shares were received. The original shareholders were sitting pretty. One of them was MPP and Cabinet Minister Phil Kelly, who turned out to be the beneficial owner of many of the shares held by his nephew, Gordon. Unfortunately for all the newly rich, Kelly allowed his newfound money to show. He was also indiscreet about the source of his wealth. There was no reason in law why members of the legislature, even cabinet members, could not own shares in a utility such as NONG, but the premier of the day, Leslie M. Frost, had given instructions to all his cabinet members that they were not to hold shares in any pipeline because the provincial government had a bill before the legislature to supply $35 million in public funds to support the construction of the northern gas pipeline. The moneys were never called for, but the edict was never rescinded, and when the Premier learned of the secret holdings of his Minister of Mines, Kelly was forced to resign his cabinet post. During the course of the intense media scrutiny that ensued, it turned out that two other cabinet members, Clare Mapledoram, the Minister of Lands and Forests, and Colonel William Griesinger, the Minister of Public Works, also owned shares. The media were not mollified, and Frost reluctantly had to order an independent inquiry, or rather he instructed Attorney General Kelso Roberts to do so.

The public inquiry was conducted under then section 23 of the *Securities Act*[107] through an emanation of the Ontario Securities Commission chaired by Gordon W. Ford, Q.C., a prominent Toronto barrister, and including Harry S. Bray, Q.C., the senior in-house counsel of the Securities Commission, and W.H. Chisholm, the senior commission auditor. It was broad-based and authorized the investigation of possible infractions of the *Securities Act,* the *Corporations Act,* or the *Criminal Code.* The panel was to inquire into whether there was evidence of bribery or corruption among elected officials including members of the legislature and municipal councils, whether any elected official having any dealings with NONG had owned shares of NONG, and finally whether there were any irregularities with respect to the issue of NONG shares.

At the hearing, I appeared for NONG, Farris, Clark, Beverley Matthews, and John Lawson. Lawson was there as a formal witness to prove the incorporation of the company, identify the minute and accounting books, and testify on other non-controversial matters about the company. Matthews did not have much of substance to say either, but being a prominent Tory who made a great deal of money out of the sale of his shares, he had been exposed to a lot of publicity, which he intensely disliked. Farris and Clark were the people the commission really wanted to hear from.

NONG had waived solicitor-client privilege over correspondence with my office. In preparing for the hearing, I read all the letters before producing them to the commission. The fruits of my scrutiny did not so much surprise as amuse me. The letters almost without exception were from John Lawson and me to either NONG or Farris and Clark. In those days, McCarthy lawyers and staff wrote all their letters on firm letterhead using typewriters with blue ribbons. The blue text looked very pretty and, in our view at least, lent an elevating distinctiveness to our correspondence. However, the blue ink was a pain in the neck to the recipients of the correspondence because the duplicating and copying machines of the day did not react to blue ink, which did not contain carbon particles. I remember sitting in a conference room looking at file after file of blue letters to which there were no responses. In fact, the only non-blue letter I can recall was from Farris to Matthews confirming the first appointment that he and Clark had with him.

My letters mainly confirmed things I had done in connection with the Fuel Board hearings. I remember asking Farris why he never answered my letters. He said he did not believe in correspondence — if a reply was required, he made it by telephone or on the next occasion that he and the letter writer met. He said that he had found from experience that letter writing was a nuisance in his line of business and that the problems raised in the letters largely disappeared by themselves; certainly without the help of a reply. I thought this rather strange at the time. In the light of future developments, I am sure that Farris devoutly wished that he had maintained his unique writing policy, particularly with respect to his dealings with Leo Landreville.

I thought the hearings before the commission went reasonably well. But that was because I had not been told about the distribution of 14,000 NONG shares issued on January 17, 1957, in the name of Convesto & Co. The following question of Farris by the chairman and his answer seemed innocuous enough.

Q. Now, one further question with reference to this meeting of January 17th, Mr. Farris, with reference to the issue and allotment of those 14,000 shares to Convesto. They, of course, were issued to Continental Investments Corporation Limited and you were directed to issue them in the name of Convesto, I take it?

A. Yes, that is right.

Q. Are you aware of the disposition of those 14,000 shares issued and allotted to Convesto under date of January 17th, 1957?

A. No, I am not.

This answer was to turn out to be untrue and would ultimately lead to a perjury charge against Farris.

The problem of the Convesto shares did not arise immediately, and from an interim report released by the commission dated July 2, 1958, it looked as though Farris, Clark, and NONG had pretty much weathered the storm. The company and its principals were cleared of any suggestion of bribery and corruption at the municipal and provincial levels, and there was a finding that there was no substance to the allegations of misuse of NONG stock. However, there were recommendations that charges be laid for breaches of the *Ontario Securities Act* relating to the distribution of NONG shares to the public before the issuance of a prospectus.

Such charges were indeed laid against Farris, Clark, and NONG after the release of the interim report, and we asked Robinette to represent them. Cyril Carson was retained to act for the Crown. He was at this time a very senior lawyer and a noted authority on the Canadian Constitution because of his many briefs on behalf of the Government of Canada, which took him to every court, including the Privy Council. Of course, we were not operating in the Privy Council in dealing with these charges, only Magistrate's Court, where I was very much at home in those years. One look at the charges told me that the Crown could not succeed on most of them. The accused were charged with summary conviction offences that were subject to a six-month limitation period. They included failing to keep proper books of account and (embarrassingly to McCarthys) failing to make full disclosure in a prospectus. Only one charge on the list had a statutory limitation period that could exceed six months: making a primary distribution of NONG shares without filing a prospectus. The limitation period on that charge did not begin to run until one year from the date when the facts upon which the charge was based came to the knowledge of the Ontario Securities Commission. I took the limitation period defences up with Robinette and he agreed with me. There was no defence to the primary distribution charge in light of the facts about the distribution of stock before the issuance of a prospectus.

The accused went to trial in September 1958 before Senior Magistrate Thomas Elmore. The merits of the charges were hardly touched on. Robinette moved to quash all the charges on the basis that they were null and void as being out of time. Remarkably, Carson had not anticipated this challenge, and I recall he requested an adjournment for a few minutes, whereupon he phoned whoever retained him for instructions. Robinette had no difficulty in persuading the Magistrate that those charges subject to a simple six-month limitation period had to be quashed. As we predicted, Magistrate Elmore took a different view of the primary distribution charge. Robinette had argued that the charge should be dismissed because the prospectus issued on June 4, 1957, brought to the knowledge of the Ontario Securities Commission the facts upon which these proceedings were based. However, Elmore ruled, "In my opinion, the prospectus did not do this. I do not think it was necessary in order to constitute a proper prospectus that it contain such information nor do I think it did." Accordingly, he convicted NONG, Farris, and Clark on this one count.[108]

Magistrate Elmore did not regard the offence as serious. His views are expressed during the following dialogue with counsel:

MR. ROBINETTE: I will not take more than a moment. My submission Your Worship, with reference to the charge on which Your Worship has registered a conviction is as Your Worship said in your reasons for judgment, it is a difficult point and after all, it was pretty much a lawyer's fight and a matter of interpretation. There was no moral wrong doing. As far as the company and its directors are concerned, they throughout acted with the knowledge and on the advice of a solicitor and a secretary of the company and it couldn't be said there was any moral wrong doing. It was a highly technical charge and I remind Your Worship it is not the normal case where someone is coming into Court and in fact complaining he has lost money because he didn't have a prospectus. There is nothing of that in this case at all. The 57 people — I have forgotten the exact number — 40 after you eliminate the people who could be considered as promoters, the 40 odd people who purchased the shares were principally out of the jurisdiction and they have not complained in fact as Your Worship knows, they have made a profit on their shares, their shares are worth a great deal more to-day than they were then. It is a technical question, whether a prospectus under those circumstances, if a prospectus was necessary. Your Worship has found legally there was. I suggest Your Worship might be the first to admit the matter is arguable. I do think under the circumstances that really it is a case for suspended sentence or some nominal penalty. No one has been hurt.

MR. CARSON: There is nothing I want to say, it is a matter which should be left to your discretion. The provision which is relevant to this question is 63, the latter part of subsection 1 and subsection 2 in the case of – 63-1 applies to the individuals and 2 to the company.

MR. ROBINETTE: Those are very flexible provisions which are designed for a variety of cases. I will leave it to Your Worship.

THE COURT: Yes. It is kind of strange, a fine is so much higher against the company; you impose a heavy penalty against the company and you are taking the money out of the pockets of the people that you were endeavouring to protect.

MR. ROBINETTE: Who have not lost anything anyway.

THE COURT: Well of course I suppose it will be rather demeaning to the accused if they were not fined a substantial amount.

MR. ROBINETTE: They will not mind.

THE COURT: Well it does not appear to me — I have found that the prospectus was quite all right. It does not appear to me that there was anything done or any effort to mislead these people and they have all profited. On the other hand of course, the future of this stock might have been vastly different and they might have lost. Again it is a question on which there is a great deal of difference of opinion as to whether or not I am right and it appears that it was the opinion of their solicitor that they didn't need to file so there was nothing deliberate about it. I think the penalty against the company will be $150.00 and costs or a writ of distress and the

> penalty against the individuals will be
> $500.00 each or one month, $500.00
> and costs each or one month.

These sanctions were of a magnitude of those handed out in police court for traffic offences. This case was a good example of damage control as demonstrated by Robinette.

However, the bad news about NONG kept trickling out, and Robinette was to become much further involved. The scandal that revolved around NONG's early days was kept alive because those in public office who had profited from their dealings with the company tended to be sanctimonious and hyper-resistant to any suggestion that they had shown even bad judgment in their participation in the development of this important public utility. This attitude offended the public. The result was that when irregularities or even the perception of improprieties emerged, the public and others involved in the administration of justice overreacted and, in the case of Leo Landreville at least, treated him unfairly. Put another way, the participants in this windfall were their own worst enemies.

The scandal broke with Phil Kelly who flaunted his money while at the same time expressing resentment at having to give up his cabinet seat. He spitefully suggested that reporters take a closer look at the NONG list of shareholders. Attention quickly focused on the 14,000 shares issued to Convesto for $2.50 at a time when the shares were selling over-the-counter for much more. John W. McGraw of Vancouver owned Convesto (an abbreviation of Continental Investment Corporation Ltd.), and he declined an invitation to attend the earlier OSC hearing. He was well aware that he was not a compellable witness in Ontario before the OSC, although he did offer to make himself available for an interview in Vancouver. In the result, he was not examined at the first inquiry, and he declined to volunteer any information thereafter. The more he stonewalled on disclosing his dealings in NONG stock, the more persistent became Donald C. MacDonald, the leader in the Ontario legislature of the CCF Party, predecessor to the NDP, in insisting that there should be a full public inquiry.

Without getting too much into the details, it appears that the RCMP investigated the accounts of Convesto with respect to an unrelated matter, and the books disclosed that 10,000 shares of NONG stock had gone to Leo Landreville. Landreville, who had resigned as mayor of Sudbury on September 30, 1956, to accept an appointment to the trial division of the Supreme Court of Ontario, declined to co-operate with the police and explain the transaction. Under constant pressure from the opposition and the media, the government at Queen's Park instructed the OSC to convene a second inquiry. This time, Harry S. Bray, Q.C., was the chairman. He began his sittings on August 13, 1962.

Landreville appeared before the OSC on October 3 and 4 with Barry Pepper, Q.C., as his counsel. It was at this hearing that the truly remarkable correspondence between Landreville, NONG, and Farris emerged. The letters were to send Farris to jail for perjury, result in criminal charges against Landreville, and create a constitutional crisis for the Government of Canada.

The four letters that follow are the most damning of the collection. They demonstrate a surprising lack of discretion for one who did not like writing letters and a remarkable lack of judgment for one who subsequently became a Superior Court judge. They are reproduced here in their entirety.[109]

Toronto, Ontario
July 20th, 1956

Mr. L.A. Landreville
250 Elm Street West
Sudbury, Ontario.

Dear Mr. Landreville:

You have recently expressed an interest in our company indicating that when free to do so you would like to assist us in some capacity, particularly with reference to representing us as we face the many problems ahead of us in the Sudbury area and Northern Ontario generally. You have indicated your faith and interest in us by expressing also a desire to purchase stock in our company. We greatly appreciate this twofold approbation of us by you.

At a director's meeting held the 18th of July following a shareholders' meeting on the 17th, your participation in our company was discussed. The shareholders' meeting had approved a change in capital whereby the authorized capital was increased to 2,000,000 shares and the outstanding shares split five for one to bring the total issued shares to approximately 660,000. The directors resolved to offer existing shareholders the right to subscribe for 40,000 additional shares of the "new" stock at a price of $2.50 per share.

At the same time it was resolved to offer you 10,000 shares at the same price of $2.50 per share. This offer is firm until July 18th, 1957. Should you wish to purchase portions of these shares at different times that will be in order.

At your convenience and when you are free to do so we would welcome the opportunity to discuss our relationship for the future in greater detail.

Yours truly,

NORTHERN ONTARIO NATURAL GAS COMPANY LIMITED

Ralph K. Farris,
President
C. Spencer Clark,
Executive Vice-President

* * *

Sudbury, Ontario
July 30th, 1956

Mr. Ralph K. Farris, President,
Northern Ontario Natural Gas Co. Ltd.,
2308-44 King Street, West,
TORONTO, Ontario

Dear Mr. Farris:

I have your very kind letter of July 20th at hand.

I fully appreciate the advantages of the offer you outline to me and I fully intend to exercise this option before July 18th, 1957.

There is the additional question of the personal interest I will devote to your Company in Northern Ontario. While all the management questions may be at a problematic stage in your Company, I would like to assure you of my interest in promoting the welfare of your Company in the time to come.

My present Office, as Mayor, does not permit me to a definite committal but in the course of the months following January next, I feel sure we may sit down and see if your Company and I have something which we could exchange to our mutual benefit.

Yours very truly,
L.A. Landreville

* * *

Sudbury, Ontario
September 19th, 1956

Mr. Ralph K. Farris, President,
Northern Ontario Natural Gas Co. Ltd.,
44 King Street, W., Suite 2308,
TORONTO, Ontario.

My dear Ralph:

On the early morning of Tuesday following our meeting in North Bay, I was in conversation with the Minister of Justice and some other high official. I made my decision — I accepted.

After the dilemma of whether to have my appendix out or not, the dilemma of remaining a bachelor and happy or get married — this was the biggest dilemma! I feel that given three or four years and with my ambition, I would have squeezed you out of the Presidency of your Company — now I have chosen to be put on the shelf of this all — inspiring, [sic] unapproachable, staid class of people called Judges — what a decision! However, right or wrong, I will stick to it and do the best I can.

I want to assure you that my interest in your Company, <u>outwardly aloof</u>, will, nevertheless, remain active. <u>I am keeping your letter of July 20th carefully in my file</u>.

Sincerely,
Leo

* * *

October 1st, 1956.

Mr. L.A. Landreville, Q.C.,
Landreville, Hawkins & Gratton,
22 Elm Street East,
SUDBURY, Ontario.

Dear Leo:

Please accept my congratulations on your appointment
to the Ontario Supreme Court. I know that your decision
was not an easy one and those of us who have learned to
appreciate your many facets will understand what a difficult decision it was. There can be no question as to the
wisdom of the appointment and I hope that time will
show that there was equal wisdom in its acceptance.

I am hoping to see you in a few days in either
Ottawa or Sudbury where perhaps before your status
becomes more formal we can have a toast or something together.

Best regards.
Ralph

The timing of these letters takes on special significance when compared with the operative dates of By-law No. 56-58 of the City of
Sudbury, which authorized the City to execute the franchise agreement
with NONG. The bylaw was given first and second reading in May 1956.
On June 11, the Fuel Board ordered that it was unnecessary to refer the
franchise agreement to the electors for their consent. On June 21, the
hearing before the board for a certificate of public convenience and
necessity was held. On July 19, the board adjourned its hearing until
July 31. On July 20, the date of the first letter, NONG returned to the
City a signed copy of the franchise agreement.[110] On August 3,
Landreville prepared a memorandum for the Sudbury council report-

ing favourably on the hearing before the board. On August 15, the board issued the required certificate. On October 10, Landreville's appointment to the Supreme Court of Ontario, which had been announced on September 14, took effect.[111] Providing the final link was Landreville's testimony at the subsequent perjury trial of Farris that he had a conversation with Farris in the first week of July and asked Farris to make it possible for him to acquire 10,000 shares of NONG stock. The price of $2.40 to $2.50 was discussed.[112]

Following the hearing before Harry Bray, and before his report was issued, perjury charges were laid against Farris arising from both of his attendances at the two OSC hearings. The perjury in both cases related to his denial of knowledge of the ownership and disposition of the 14,000 Convesto shares. He appeared before Justice Dalton Wells and a jury, and this time Farris was represented by Joseph Sedgwick, Q.C. Despite a sympathetic jury charge by the trial judge, the jury convicted Farris and he was sentenced to jail for nine months.

Attorney General Frederick Cass then decided to lay municipal corruption charges against Farris and Landreville. Farris was not tried on these charges. He contracted Hodgkin's disease and was too sick to participate in a trial. He was forced into early retirement because of his conviction and sickness and died at the age of sixty in January 1970.[113] The charges laid against Landreville were that within two years of February 1, 1957, he, as a municipal official, offered or agreed to accept from a person (Farris) a benefit, being stock in NONG, as consideration to aid in procuring the adoption of a measure, motion, or resolution of the City of Sudbury providing for a franchise agreement between the City and NONG. He faced a companion charge relating to providing aid in procuring the signing of the franchise agreement.

Pepper, who had represented Landreville throughout the second OSC inquiry and beyond, recommended that Robinette be retained on the criminal charges. The matter started as a preliminary hearing before Magistrate Albert Marck in October 1964 and lasted six days. A preliminary hearing in those days was usually a perfunctory affair with the Crown putting in only enough evidence to satisfy the test for committing a person to trial. The threshold, not high to meet and well below the trial standard of guilt beyond a reasonable doubt, is whether there is sufficient evidence upon which a properly instructed jury could convict. Ordinarily, the accused's counsel uses the preliminary hearing as a form of examination for discovery and asks questions to receive clarification or to pin down a critical witness in preparation for a full-blown attack on his or her credibility at trial. Because of the low standard of evidentiary proof, credibility is not an issue at a preliminary hearing. It is for the trier of fact at the full trial to decide whether to believe any or all of a witness's evidence.

This was not an ordinary trial, however. Effectively it was a political trial, and I doubt that the Crown would have proceeded with the charges if the provincial government of the day had not been so badly embarrassed by NONG and those who profited from its ventures. Unlike the Farris trial, in which the accused was convicted of lying under oath, this case required the Crown to show that the former mayor of Sudbury, now a Supreme Court judge, had done something corrupt in return for receiving 10,000 shares for $2.50 per share, which he sold shortly after and realized a net profit of $117,000. Despite his public assertions that he paid $2.50 a share for a total of $25,000, Landreville in fact had paid no money for the shares. And they were offered to him at a time when they were worth more than $10 a share. The mechanics of the transaction were that Convesto, on the instructions of Farris, sold 2,500 of the shares at a price in excess of $10 per share, credited Landreville with $25,000 to pay for the share allotment at $2.50 and delivered 7,500 of the shares to Landreville without charge on February 12, 1957. Landreville promptly sold 5,500 shares the next day and the remainder in two lots, 1,500 in 1958 and 500 in 1961, for a total net profit of $117,000.[114]

Robinette recognized that, ethical considerations aside (and these were irrelevant anyway in a criminal trial), Landreville's defence was that he had done nothing in return to receive this windfall. Robinette submitted to Magistrate Marck that there was no quid pro quo for the shares and therefore no offence. The Magistrate accepted his argument in its entirety. In very full and careful reasons, he stated:[115]

> Prior to the third reading of the by-law, Mr. Crozier Chairman of the Fuel Board had attended at City Council and suggested there was urgency in having the

by-law passed granting the franchise — the franchise agreement was fully explained. Mr. C.D. Howe during this period expressed urgency in the passing of the by-law. Surely after the efforts of Mr. Crozier and Mr. Howe it became quite obvious that there was some degree of urgency for the passing of the by-law.

Viva voce evidence was given by John J. Kelly, Patrick Henry Murphy and Thomas L. Hennesy, James Cormack, Peter Guimond who were all employees of the City of Sudbury or elected members of Council. *Not one* of these said or intimated that the accused ever tried to influence him directly or indirectly subtly or otherwise. Each of them swore on oath that they acted independently of the accused and had never been subservient to the accused as Mayor or directed in any manner by the accused.

Evidence has been adduced that the accused as Mayor did not vote on any by-law. Where is the influence used by the accused? Where is the criminal act by the accused Mayor?[116]

The Magistrate concluded that a properly charged jury could not find Landreville guilty, and he discharged him on both counts.

Robinette regarded this as the end of the matter. He told me that there was no evidence whatsoever that Landreville had used his influence to assist NONG in obtaining the Sudbury franchise. Apparently, the Attorney General, then Arthur Wishart, Q.C., agreed. He issued a press release in which he stated that after a thorough study of the NONG report prepared by the OSC, his department had laid charges and all relevant evidence had been placed before Magistrate Marck, who, after a full hearing, found that the evidence did not warrant Landreville's committal for trial. The Attorney General rejected the suggestion made by critics that he should nevertheless proceed to prefer a Bill of Indictment before a grand jury.[117]

Despite the dismissal of charges against him, Landreville had misjudged the public's perception of his action in making so much money in such a short period of time for doing nothing. To complicate his problems, in the seven or eight years he had spent on the bench as a judge, he had not endeared himself to his colleagues or to the bar. He was not a very good judge and his flippant and arrogant manner made him few friends. My own view of him was that he had never been a particularly good lawyer and his judgment, extending even to the handling of his personal life, was seriously flawed. Following Marck's decision, there was a great deal of grumbling throughout the profession about his conduct.

John Arnup was the treasurer of the Law Society at the time and had a number of things to say in his oral history to the Law Society about what was referred to as the "Landreville Affair." He recalled:[118]

> A number of Benchers approached me to say, "How long are we going to sit silent as the representatives of the legal profession in Canada, while a Supreme Court judge before whom we are appearing, here, there, across Ontario, is now shown to have indulged in practices which were to say the least suspect and to say the worst may have been criminal?"

The legal profession is hopelessly gossip-prone, and it became an open secret that benchers and senior members of the profession weren't the only ones who felt uncomfortable with Landreville remaining a judge; the federal government wished he would resign as well. Arnup gave into pressure from members of his Convocation and appointed a committee, chaired by one of Landreville's more vociferous critics, Arthur Pattillo, Q.C, to look into the matter. This, I think, was an unfortunate decision because Landreville was no longer a member of the Law Society and his conduct was not subject to discipline or review by the benchers. The committee produced a curious report dated March 17, 1965, that made serious allegations of misconduct against Landreville without having heard from him or anyone on his behalf. The committee simply read the public record and, after making some very specific findings of impropriety, concluded:[119]

> The fact that Landreville was given an opportunity to acquire shares at the same price as the original promoters of the Company and that the option was given immediately following the passing of the third reading of the by-law and for no apparent consideration, and that subsequently without any exercise of such option by Landreville he received 7500 shares free and clear, which he subsequently sold for $117,000, and that when Farris was first questioned about the matter he deliberately lied, support the inference that the acquisition of shares by Landreville was tainted with impropriety.

And then, without any authority to do so, the committee recommended to Convocation that the benchers deplore the continuance of Landreville in office and that the Secretary of the Law Society be authorized and directed to forward a copy of the report to the attorneys general of Canada and Ontario, the chief justices of Ontario and the High Court of Justice, and finally to "The Honorable Mr. Justice Landreville." The Treasurer was also authorized to issue copies of the report "to the press at such time thereafter as he may in his direction deem fit." Convocation adopted this report on April 23, 1965, by a strong majority, according to Arnup.

Arnup as treasurer wrote a confidential letter to Minister of Justice Lucien Cardin, outlining the content of the report and Convocation's adoption of it. The letter was obviously reviewed by cabinet because Arnup's next informal discussion was with the new attorney general, Guy Favreau (Cardin had died suddenly), who asked him for his opinion on appointing Ivan Rand, a retired justice of the Supreme Court of Canada, to be named as a commissioner to inquire into whether Landreville's dealings in NONG shares while mayor of Sudbury constituted misconduct such as to disqualify him from continuing to sit as a judge. Arnup responded that he thought this was a good idea.[120]

In light of my early association with NONG, its principals, and some municipal officials (not including Landreville, whom I had met only briefly while he was mayor), it should not be surprising that I maintained an intense interest in following all media and other reports about the

NONG scandal. As a former treasurer and present ex officio bencher, Robinette knew all about these proceedings, although he was not asked to participate in them. Robinette kept me apprised of the activities of the benchers and of Arnup as treasurer. My own opinion, which Robinette shared, was that Landreville had brought much of this on himself by proclaiming from the rooftops his innocence of the faintest impropriety and demanding that the Minister of Justice convene a committee of inquiry of some kind to establish this fact. At that time, there was no vehicle for bringing complaints against judges as we now have in the Canadian Judicial Council. Only a joint address to both Houses of Parliament could result in the removal from office of a federally appointed judge, a truly draconian and rare step. However, this was a step that the Minister of Justice was prepared to take unless Landreville accepted an inquiry headed up by a retired judge. He suggested Ivan Rand.

Robinette, who was to represent Landreville at the inquiry, spoke to me about the strategy that he should pursue, not so much for advice but as a sounding board. I was very much against agreeing to a proceeding before a joint committee of the Senate and Parliament because of some unhappy experiences I had with legislative committees in Ontario. The lack of discipline in the hearings was disturbing enough to discourage participation, but the political positions that often underlay the proceedings in the first place tended to taint them and obscure the issues.

In contrast, Rand had been a very distinguished judge and was very much respected. Mild-mannered and soft-spoken, he appeared to me to be the ideal choice. I knew Rand personally on a limited basis. On retiring from the Supreme Court of Canada, he moved to Toronto and lived for a time at the University Club. I spoke with him on numerous occasions and found him interesting, stimulating, and intensely curious about matters with which he was not already familiar. I liked him very much. My father knew and liked him, as well. He had lunch with him and his fellow judges from time to time at the Rideau Club in Ottawa. My father was concerned that Rand was a teetotaler, which he always took as a bad sign. "Never trust a man who doesn't drink," he often said. Perhaps I should have remembered this caveat when asked about the suitability of Rand's appointment as commissioner. I enthusiastically endorsed the idea of going the inquiry route before Rand. How wrong I turned out to be. On the other hand, I was dead right about the joint committee, for reasons that I will soon discuss.

The authority for the inquiry to be held by Rand was the *Inquiries Act*[121] of Canada, which did not relate to the conduct of judges as such. The terms of the Rand Inquiry highlighted the jurisdictional problem of holding an inquiry on the conduct of a judge in office. Rand was authorized to inquire: (a) into the dealings of the Honourable Mr. Justice Landreville with Northern Ontario Natural Gas or any of its officers, employees, or representatives, or in the shares of the said company; and (b) to advise whether, in the opinion of the commissioner, anything done by Mr. Justice Landreville in the course of such dealings constituted misbehaviour in his official capacity as a judge of the Supreme Court of Ontario, or whether the Honourable Mr. Justice Landreville has by such dealings proved himself unfit for the proper exercise of his judicial duties.

Robinette approached the hearing before Rand with some confidence. He was sensitive to the jurisdictional issues and recognized that the federal government's jurisdictional problem was the converse of that of the benchers of the Law Society. Whereas the latter had no authority over a sitting judge and therefore attempted to criticize his conduct as a lawyer before his appointment, the Minister of Justice had no authority over his conduct as a lawyer and was attempting to show that those actions had rendered him unfit to accept judicial office. Robinette was to emphasize throughout the inquiry that Landreville's alleged misconduct was committed before he was appointed a judge, and in any event, Magistrate Marck had found unequivocally that there was no evidence of impropriety by Landreville in his capacity as mayor of Sudbury. Robinette even had the unsolicited letter of Marck to Earl Smith, the Secretary of the Law Society, taking issue in the strongest language with the report of the Law Society that endorsed the findings of Arthur Pattillo's committee. Marck's letter, dated June 12, 1965, states in part:[122]

> The misunderstanding of this case by you and some press comments arises from two unfortunate incidents. Firstly, the judgment I rendered could not possibly encompass, review and bear on all the facts heard during a five day hearing. Wherefore certain facts may not

appear to have been considered by me. I wish to assure you all facts have been taken into consideration and they do not allow certain inferences your Report draws. Secondly, I have used in the judgment these inaccurate words: "I cannot find sufficient evidence to place him on his trial". As you well know the established law, in a preliminary hearing is not a question of *sufficiency*. If there is any evidence on which a jury properly charged *could* convict, the magistrate *must* commit to trial.

In the Landreville case, *not only was there a total absence of evidence* he had been guilty of municipal corruption, my decision points out findings that disprove that possibility or necessity.

Robinette did not think that he would need to use this letter because he could not see how the damning Pattillo report, which was based on hearsay, could be evidence on the inquiry. To his astonishment, the former Supreme Court of Canada judge did admit it into evidence, although he professed later to have given it no consideration:[123] "It is perhaps unnecessary to say that the resolution of the Benchers of the Law Society of Upper Canada submitted to the Minister of Justice has played no part whatever in arriving at the conclusions of fact set out in this report."

Notwithstanding this disclaimer, Rand did think that the Pattillo report had some relevance in that it indicated that the governing body of the legal profession had demonstrated considerable interest about this "subject of wide public concern." He annexed it to his report, thus republishing it for all the world to see.

As it turned out, Robinette's biggest problem at the inquiry was his client. Landreville saw the proceeding as being directed not at him, but at his accusers. In the opinion of David Humphrey, Q.C.,[124] who represented Landreville before the joint committee of Parliament, Landreville was expecting the Rand Inquiry to be pretty much of a whitewash, designed to exonerate him and restore his reputation at the expense of his carping critics. He seemed to perceive, in Humphrey's judgment, that the then minister of justice, Favreau, was as anxious as Landreville to protect the good name of the court by once and for all clearing the air of any hint of scandal associated with this appointment.

Instead of appearing before the commissioner as a chastened man who had not recognized how others might perceive his conduct, Landreville practically lectured Rand on the injustices he had suffered at the hands of his critics. And Rand did not like this a bit. Robinette told me that Rand had taken an instant scunner to Landreville. "He hated him," he told me. He found Landreville cocky and arrogant and just too full of himself for his own good. Robinette tried to give Landreville advice on how to conduct himself, but he would not listen. Robinette suggested that at some stage in the proceedings, Landreville should show some contrition. He should acknowledge that, with the benefit of hindsight, he may have made a mistake in going through with the share "purchase" after he had accepted an appointment to the bench and would no longer be able to be active in NONG's affairs as originally planned. Landreville rejected the advice of his eminent counsel out of hand. "I've been a counsel myself, John," he retorted.

One really does not need Robinette's insight to read into Rand's reasons that he did not like Landreville. Rand seemed to think that it was part of his duty as commissioner to provide character sketches of the leading protagonists in this drama, including Farris and Gordon McLean. Of Landreville he wrote,[125] "In short, he presents the somewhat versatile character of a modern hedonist of vitality whose philosophy is expressed in terms of pragmatic opportunism for public prominence, financial and social success, tinctured with arrogance towards subordinates and confidence in his ability to move around."

It is now popular to refer to subsequent events designed to conceal past misdeeds as the cover-up. The media seize on this part of any investigation, and it becomes the investigation itself. Never mind how trivial and inconsequential was the original conduct that is said to have justified the investigation. The more unsubstantiated the original allegations of impropriety, the more important becomes the conduct of the investigated party subsequent to those events. While the term "cover-up" postdates the Landreville Inquiry, the commissioner needed no precedent for recognizing that if Landreville were to be pronounced unfit to be a judge, it would have to be on the basis of what he did when he was a judge with respect to his acquisition of the NONG shares. Accordingly, the denigration of Landreville's general character was only the first step. The *coup de grace* was the cover-up, which was in two stages as described by Rand:[126]

> Drawn from the foregoing facts and considerations, the following conclusions have been reached:
>
> ***
>
> I.   The stock transaction between Justice Landreville and Ralph K. Farris, effecting the acquisition of 7,500 shares in Northern Ontario Natural Gas Company, Limited for which no valid consideration was given, notwithstanding the result of the preliminary inquiry into charges laid against Justice Landreville, justifiably gives rise to grave suspicion of impropriety. In that situation it is the opinion of the undersigned that it was obligatory on Justice Landreville to remove that suspicion and satisfactorily to establish his innocence, which he has not done.
>
> II. That in the subsequent investigation into the stock transaction before the Securities Commission of Ontario in 1962, and the direct and incidental dealing with it in the proceedings brought against Ralph K. Farris for perjury in 1963 and 1964 in which Justice Landreville was a Crown witness, the conduct of Justice Landreville in giving evidence constituted a gross contempt of these tribunals and a serious violation of his personal duty as a Justice of the Supreme Court of Ontario, which has permanently impaired his usefulness as a Judge.
>
> III. That a fortiori the conduct of Justice Landreville, from the effective dealing, in the spring of 1956,

with the proposal of a franchise for supplying natural gas to the City of Sudbury to the completion
of the share transaction in February 1957, including the proceedings in 1962, 1963 and 1964, mentioned, treated as a single body of action, the concluding portion of which, trailing odours of scandal arising from its initiation and consummated
while he was a Judge of the Supreme Court of
Ontario, drawing upon himself the onus of establishing satisfactorily his innocence, which he has
failed to do, was a dereliction of both his duty as a
public official and his personal duty as a Judge, a
breach of that standard of conduct obligatory
upon him, which has permanently impaired his
usefulness as a Judge.

By examining the actions of Landreville and others after the term of
his office as mayor and into the time when he was a judge, the
Commissioner was able to assume a tenuous jurisdiction over the stated purpose of the inquiry, that is, to determine whether anything done
by Landreville constituted misbehaviour in his official capacity as a
judge. The continuing cover-up was the answer.

With the express finding that "Landreville has proven himself unfit
for the proper exercise of his judicial functions," Rand drove the last
spike into Landreville's coffin.[127] Either Landreville had to resign, or the
Minister of Justice would have to refer the matter to a joint committee
of Parliament with the recommendation that he be removed from
office. It came as no surprise to those who knew him that Landreville
refused to resign. The federal government, which I am satisfied would
have done anything within reason to make this matter go away, had no
choice but to strike a special joint committee of the Senate and of the
House of Commons respecting Mr. Justice Landreville. It was jointly
chaired by Senator Daniel A. Lang and Ovide Laflamme, MP. Its first
hearing date was February 1, 1967.

Landreville was prepared to fight on, but Robinette had had more
than enough of him. According to David Humphrey, whom Robinette

persuaded to take over the brief, "John just had it with Leo. He did everything that Robinette would never do."[128] Apart from consistently ignoring his advice, Landreville persisted in arguing his case in the media and even, to Robinette's horror, spoke to Magistrate Marck out of court during his preliminary hearing. As it turned out, Humphrey did not have any better luck controlling Landreville. Humphrey recalls in his interview with me that on the occasion in Robinette's office when he handed over the brief to him, Robinette told Landreville in Humphrey's presence, "Leo, let David do the talking for you." Humphrey arrived in Ottawa for the hearing before the joint committee to discover that Landreville had been on the French radio network stating that the only reason the government wanted to get rid of him was because he was French Canadian.

This was the end of Robinette's official involvement in the Landreville saga, although he did offer to appear as a witness before the joint committee and testify about procedural unfairness that occurred during the Rand Inquiry. However, the joint committee had its own rules and it did not think that a review of the Rand report was relevant. Similarly, it was not interested in character evidence because it was not prepared to give any consideration to the character assassination by Rand. Finally, it was not interested in evidence as to Landreville's record as a judge because Rand had found that there was no judicial impropriety with respect to the performance of his judicial functions.

The hearings before the committee, as I had feared, were a mess. They took place sporadically over nineteen meetings. There was no consistent core of members who heard all the evidence. There were times when there was no quorum. To give some semblance of a homogeneous hearing, Landreville had to be recalled on a number of occasions to repeat his testimony. He testified at eleven of the meetings.[129]

I hesitate to say this, but the fact that the hearings themselves were so unstructured makes baffling the committee's decision to simply uphold the Rand Commission's recommendation to remove Landreville. One is drawn to the reluctant conclusion that the committee hearings played no part in the ultimate decision. In its Second Report, dated March 17, 1967, the committee issued two disclaimers:[130]

4. The report of the Honourable Ivan C. Rand states:

    "No question is raised of misbehaviour in the dis-
    charge of judicial duty; the inquiry goes to conduct
    outside that function."

5. The reflections of the Honourable Ivan C. Rand on
    Mr. Justice Landreville's character were not consid-
    ered pertinent and thus played no part in the
    Committee's decision.

Notwithstanding that the committee had almost disemboweled
Rand's justification for his report, the committee accepted his conclu-
sionary recommendation without reasons:[131]

> After hearing the testimony of Mr. Justice Landreville
> and considering the report of the Honourable Ivan C.
> Rand, the Committee finds that Mr. Justice Landreville
> has proven himself unfit for the proper exercise of his
> judicial functions and, with great regret, recommends
> the expediency of presenting an address to His
> Excellency for the removal of Mr. Justice Landreville
> from the Supreme Court of Ontario.

What happened thereafter is clouded, although William Kaplan
does review the record and makes a good deal of sense of it.[132]
Humphrey told me that Landreville wanted to address the Senate when
the bill to impeach him was introduced, but he was persuaded privately by one of the joint chairmen, Ovide Laflamme, to consider resigning.
Landreville was prepared to do this if he received a judge's pension pro-
rated by the ratio of the number of years he had served as a judge.
Laflamme told him, according to Landreville, that a pension was officially out of the question, but there was money buried in the budget
estimates that could be made available off the record. In the end,
Landreville did resign, citing permanent infirmity arising out of physical illness and mental stress. He was later adamant that it was the unof-

ficial promise of this pension that induced him to resign. But no pension was forthcoming.

Landreville received some measure of vindication when through a new lawyer, Gordon F. Henderson, Q.C., of Ottawa, he brought proceedings before the Federal Court of Canada, which resulted in a 1977 decision quashing the Rand Inquiry Report[133] because of procedural irregularities arising out of Rand's failure to comply with the provisions of the *Inquiries Act*. This was followed by a declaration in 1980 that the governor-in-council (the cabinet) must hear and determine whether Landreville was entitled to a disability pension.[134] Ultimately, he did reach a monetary settlement with the government.

Chapter Twelve
The View from Olympus

T HE TITLE TO THIS CHAPTER may seem over-elevated, but there is no question that Robinette operated at a different level from that of any other lawyer of his generation. There are undoubtedly a rare few who could match his quality in a specialized field, but none who displayed his diversity in achieving excellence in all areas of the law. As he said in answer to the question whether he would have made a good judge, "I don't know. You can say I had a very wide experience. Not only was I an academic lawyer, but I had been through the tough mill of criminal cases with a jury, and serious ones, so certainly I had the experience."[135]

This self-assessment sheds light on why he was such a good counsel. In addition to his reputation as a criminal lawyer, a reputation that mildly irritated him in that it suggested that his abilities were narrowly focused, Robinette was a skilled civil lawyer with experience gathered from a broad range of cases, both jury and non-jury. He excelled in trial work and was at home in the Court of Appeal. He was as good a trial lawyer as he was an appellate counsel, another uncommon attribute. Add to this an extensive practice before administrative tribunals both federal and provincial, and you have the complete lawyer.

Robinette owned the Supreme Court of Canada over a period of fifty years, from his first appearance as a second junior counsel for the Crown in *Reference Re: Adoption Act (Ontario)*,[136] to his last appearance in *Clark v. Canadian National Railway Co.*[137] Taking 1942 as a starting point for cases in which he was lead or sole counsel, he appeared in 176 appeals before the

Supreme Court, an achievement no other counsel has been able to match. Justice Ian Binnie of the Supreme Court of Canada recalls:[138]

> By chance I was in the Supreme Court when Justice Ronald Martland retired. John Robinette was present in court to speak on behalf of the Law Society of Upper Canada (or perhaps the Canadian Bar Association). In any event, in the course of his amusing remarks, Martland J. said words to the effect, "When I arrived here on January 15, 1958, Mr. Robinette was here to greet me. Now, twenty-four years later, as I take my leave, Mr. Robinette is here to say goodbye, now as then the Dean of the Supreme Court bar." It was a very moving tribute.

No other name with a comparable forensic background comes to mind. Bora Laskin, his old friend from his teaching days who was later to sit on the Court of Appeal and then serve as the chief justice of Canada, perhaps put it best when, on presenting the Advocates' Society Medal of Advocacy to Robinette on June 29, 1976, he said:

> To me he has always been the complete professional able to make any case, whatever its complexity, understandable by the Bench, never wedded to a textual submission, using the English language as Churchill used it, to find eloquence in the simplest of its words, no polysyllables for him when a common word would do. When I think of John Robinette I think of what Harold Laski wrote to Holmes in one of his letters. "You can have a manner," said Laski, "without having anything to say, but you can have style only when you have a fond (a depth) of substance." J.J. has style, and the many lawyers who have worked for him, or watched him know this, as do members of any Bench before which he has pleaded.

I think it was because of his diverse skills and experience that he was the acknowledged leader of the bar, a judgment made ungrudgingly by those with considerable reputation as counsel themselves and by virtually everyone who had contact with him in a professional way. The fact that his excellence was conceded is not so unusual, considering the longevity of his career as an advocate, but the universality of his admiration speaks to something else.

Robinette was very well liked. He was a tall, handsome man, good humoured, and courteous to everyone, particularly young counsel. The office staff at McCarthys loved him. For them he always had a friendly hello, a thoughtful remark, or a quip to set them at ease. He was a likeable guy, and he commanded a great deal of personal loyalty. Rather oddly, considering how well liked he was in the firm, at McCarthy & McCarthy his social life was a source of speculation among the junior lawyers. It seemed to us that he was working constantly except for the long judicial holiday of July and August when he disappeared to his cottage and did not surface again until September. While he had an abundance of friends who would have jumped at the opportunity to have lunch with him, when he was not recessing from a court attendance he preferred to have a sandwich in his office or go out by himself to God knows where. He belonged to the University Club, which was just a few buildings north on University Avenue from the office at the Canada Life Building. I became a member of that club in due course and I cannot recall ever seeing him there for lunch. Curiously, while he and Beverley Matthews remained fast friends to the very end, Robinette did not make new friends among any of his new colleagues at McCarthys who were in his age group.

As indicated earlier, Robinette was rarely mentioned by those who knew him without their volunteering that he was a gentleman. However, he was not one to suffer fools gladly — or at all. Mistakes on the part of secretaries or junior associates were greeted with impatience and even anger. I can attest to that personally. He was a hard-working man and a brilliant lawyer and he had difficulty in adjusting to a lower standard. As I indicated earlier, he was an elitist and he could be quite contemptuous of some of the senior lawyers in the firm whom he considered "stupid." However, he avoided personal controversy to the point of absurdity and this, along with his natural courtliness, protected him from projecting an intellectual arrogance that comes all too readily to the truly gifted.

Robinette could be a bugger in court on occasion, and I cannot but wonder why those he treated roughly there did not resent him more. I can remember that my friend Bert MacKinnon, a distinguished counsel in his own right before being made a judge of the Court of Appeal, was critical of Robinette because of the way he played on the prejudices of some of the judges, notably Walter Schroeder. This tendency will be discussed later. But MacKinnon still thought Robinette was the best counsel ever, an opinion stemming largely from his manner out of court. In this regard, Binnie relates a small but telling story:

> I was acting for the City of Hamilton in the late 1970s in a dispute over land use regulation of Hamilton Harbour. The case was heard by Griffiths J. (I believe it was his first trial). Griffiths decided in favour of the City. Robinette was retained to argue the appeal for the Harbour Commissioners, but there were too many findings of fact against him and he lost.[139] Shortly after the judgment was released, he called me and said words to the effect, "My clients have instructed me to seek leave to appeal the decision to the Supreme Court of Canada, and I wondered if you would be free to argue the motion in Ottawa on [some date well into the future]."
>
> I of course had a virtually blank engagement book that far ahead. He was well aware of the radical difference between our respective schedules, but instead of simply serving a Notice of Motion with a peremptory date, or delegating the phone call to somebody else in his office, he called himself. This reflected his professional courtesy, but more than that showed his sense that everybody at the bar is essentially equal to everyone else in an ancient and honourable profession and should be treated as such. It is certainly a lesson I never forgot, but in the heyday of people like Walter Williston and Cyril Carson and other "entourage" leaders, it was just a different approach.

A colleague on the Court of Appeal, David Doherty, tells a similar story.

When he was student serving his articles at the Crown Law Office of the Ministry of the Attorney General, a businessman named Norton Cooper was charged with paying secret commissions to a government official. He was not represented by Robinette at trial and was convicted by a jury. Clay Powell acted for the Crown and Doherty, as a student, worked for Powell during the trial.

Cooper appealed his conviction to the Court of Appeal and retained Robinette. That court ordered a new trial.[140] By this time, Doherty was taking the teaching portion of the Bar Admission Course, but he attended the hearing of the appeal anyway. The Crown obtained leave to appeal to the Supreme Court of Canada, and a date was set for hearing in the spring of 1976. Doherty had received his call to the bar the spring before but was selected by Powell to argue the case in the Supreme Court of Canada. It was to be his first appearance in that Court. The Court, in a four to three split, allowed the Crown appeal and restored the conviction.[141] I will let Doherty tell the rest of the story himself.[142]

> I don't remember speaking with Mr. Robinette before the appeal, although I may well have. I do remember seeing him in the gowning room and thinking that it was odd that he was all by himself. Based on what I had seen to that point, I thought that lawyers from big law firms always travelled in groups of at least three. After the oral argument was completed, the Court reserved judgment. I was getting changed in the gowning room, and Mr. Robinette came over and started to speak to me about what seemed to be really nothing in particular. We spoke for ten or fifteen minutes, and it was only when I reflected on the conversation later that I realized that he was really talking to me about the way I had presented the argument and things that I could have done differently. For example, I remember him talking about the value of a prepared argument but the need to keep focused on the Court. He didn't say it in

so many words, as if he was saying, "This is the first thing or the second thing you did right or wrong." He somehow worked it into a normal conversation we were having so that when I thought about it later, I thought, "He was really saying to me, 'You know you have to keep your eye on the Court, and you can't lock yourself into a prepared argument without regard to what interests the Court.'"

The other comment I remember was about listening to the questions and thinking before you answered them. Again, he didn't talk about it in so many words, but we talked about pace and how quickly you speak and how it's not a race and things like that and, again, when I thought back on it, I thought, "You know, what he's really saying is, 'Listen to the question. Take your time. Answer the question.'" All of this was done in the most informal and friendly manner as if both he and I had been in the Court a hundred times before and we were sort of equal, chatting away about the art of oral advocacy.

I'll certainly never forget, firstly, that a person of his stature was prepared to take the time to talk with me and, secondly, the way he did it to make me feel so much as his equal and a fellow member of the bar and as someone who he found interesting and significant — if that's the right word — enough to talk to. It just struck me, in retrospect in particular, as such a humble and generous thing to do.

Another example of the Robinette's generosity comes from Colin K. Irving of Montreal, a counsel whose reputation extends well beyond the Province of Quebec. He writes:[143]

[In the middle 1980s], I represented a woman who had been imprisoned at Kingston for some ten years of a twenty-five-year sentence having been found guilty as a party to the murder of a policeman in Calgary. Our application, based on the fact that the twenty-five-year no parole provision was enacted after the murder, was for a declaration that she be made immediately eligible for parole. At the time I had little experience in the Ontario courts, and I went to Mr. Robinette for help. He was enormously generous with his time and invaluable advice in the High Court proceedings (where we lost), the Court of Appeal (where we also lost), and finally in the Supreme Court of Canada, where we succeeded. He would not think of accepting a fee.

I had great affection for him and remember him as the finest advocate I have ever heard. He combined a determination to win and skill of the highest order in doing so, with a rare degree of graciousness and courtesy.

In order to refresh my memory about Robinette's style as a counsel, I went looking for a videotape of an old Canadian Broadcasting Corporation program called *A Case for the Courts*, which was shown in 1962. One broadcast of this series featured Robinette. Regrettably I could not find the original, but Mary Lou Finlay of the CBC replayed substantial portions of it in a half-hour television interview of Robinette in 1976. *A Case for the Courts* consisted of a number of half-hour programs about fictional court cases starring real judges and practising lawyers. The format is now familiar to fans of the *Law and Order* series. The first segment showed the commission of a crime or the facts that constituted the basis for a civil action, and the second segment showed parts of the trial resulting in a resolution of the problem. The guiding force behind this series, from the point of view of the legal profession, was Justice C.D. "Carl" Stewart, a member of the High Court of Justice. He appeared as the judge in the majority of the cases and was very good in this role.

The finale of the series was a ninety-minute special, to borrow the jargon of the trade, and it was to feature a criminal case with Stewart presiding over a jury trial. Henry Bull, Q.C., was the Crown attorney, and John Robinette and George D. Finlayson appeared for the defence. Yes, I was there and played just as active a part in the film version as I would have in a real trial. I said nothing. I took notes (or pretended to), looked alert and interested, and nodded my head sagely when my learned senior made compelling points. My performance impressed at least one of my friends, Sanford "Sandy" World, Q.C., who wrote congratulating me on reviving mime theatre in Canada.

But Robinette's performance was a *tour de force*. He was forty-six years of age at the time and at the height of his powers. His hair was jet black and, while he was heavy, about 250 pounds on a six-foot frame, the weight made him look more impressive in his flowing silk gown. He was used to being heavy and knew how to control his movements so that he at no time appeared clumsy. Indeed, he used his size and his great mahogany voice to dominate the stage. In this tape, he was in front of a jury, albeit a make-believe one, but he played up to it constantly. He spoke firmly, authoritatively, and pointedly. His client was an alleged bank robber. The principal witness for the Crown had given an unsatisfactory description of the accused as being at the scene of the crime. The witness, in a burst of inspiration that he obviously thought was helpful, declared that the robber "looked like Jimmy Cagney." In his closing address, Robinette picked up various inconsistencies in the witness's description of the accused and used them to good effect. And then, reminiscent of his approach to the Crown witness Boehler in the *Dick* case, he built up the importance of this disappointing witness as being the bulwark of the Crown's case. At the end of his address, he turned from the jury and, pointing dramatically to the prisoners' box, said, "Look at him. Does he look like Jimmy Cagney?"

The production of this show fascinated me. Apart from a brief review of the scripts at the home of Carl Stewart, the principal actors — the judge and the two lawyers (I was not there) — had but one rehearsal, and that was the dress rehearsal just before the shooting of the show in the main CBC studio on Jarvis Street on a Sunday morning. There was one run-through with very few interruptions for directions to the players, and then we broke for lunch at our respective homes. Stewart demonstrated a deft touch by saying that he was going home "to read Livy to his children." Hard to one-up that.

We returned in the early afternoon, and the show was shot in one continuous take. Despite Henry Bull having dropped his glasses (which he picked up without missing a line), the director was satisfied that the first take was the finished product. Apparently he had come to expect this display of thespian prowess from the legal profession because of earlier productions in the series. He simply shook his head in admiration and gushed, "Lawyers make the best actors." It was certainly true of these three hams. They enjoyed themselves immensely. Robinette was particularly at ease and treated the day's outing as a lark.

Robinette did in fact put on an act when he was appearing before a jury. He never relaxed when the panel was in the courtroom. There was no chit-chat or inside jokes with opposing counsel, no matter how well he knew them. He was on display at all times. He looked serious and concerned, the way a responsible counsel should look. He made a great show of taking notes when he did take them, usually finishing off the last line with a period that was delivered with some flourish. He would nod his head in agreement with a witness who had said something helpful and shake it vigorously if he said something unfavourable. Often he would lean forward quickly, make a note, and throw his pen down authoritatively as if indicating the real truth was in what he had just written. The jury could not take their eyes away from him. Sometimes even the witnesses were so transfixed by his antics that they would keep looking at him, more concerned about his reaction to their answers than about the next question from examining counsel.

The thought had occurred to me early in my association with Robinette that his fame might make jurors reluctant to accept his arguments — they might well be thinking that they would not let this big-time lawyer further enhance his reputation by pulling the wool over *their* eyes. This, however, did not appear to be the case. Jurors liked Robinette and were delighted to be on his jury. They followed his every move and listened intently to his arguments. In the days before talking to jurors after they rendered their verdict was prohibited by the *Criminal Code*,[144] individual members of the jury panel would come up to Robinette and congratulate him on his performance.

Charles Dubin tells a story about Robinette that may be embellished but is so typical that it deserves to be true. Dubin, Arthur Martin, and Robinette were acting along with other distinguished counsel (the list of appearances reads like a who's who of the profession) for a number of accused corporations engaged in the dental supply business. The case was heard by a jury and presided over by Justice Frederick Barlow during September and October of 1948. The corporations were charged substantially with conspiring to unduly lessen competition. The case was called *The King v. The Ash-Temple Company Limited et al.*[145]

Suppliers of dental equipment charged with price-fixing and represented by high-priced lawyers — I cannot imagine, from a defence perspective, a less attractive case to be tried by a jury. It invites the presumption of guilt. That aside, it was agreed among counsel that they should give the jury panel maximum exposure to Robinette by allowing him to sit next to the jury box. The case for the prosecution depended almost entirely on documents (some 4,000 in number) that were being read to the jury by the prosecution team, which was led by the formidable D.L. "Lally" McCarthy, K.C. The documents were very damning and made for difficult listening at the defence counsel table when Lally McCarthy read them.

Robinette was unperturbed. When the first unhelpful document was read, he murmured, just loud enough for the jurors to hear him, "That is a good letter." Dubin, who was sitting on Robinette's left, heard him, but Martin, on Dubin's left, did not. "What did John say?" asked Martin. "He said it is a good letter," Dubin replied. Another letter was read, even more troubling to the defence. Robinette murmured, "That's another good letter." Once again, Martin did not hear. "What did he say, Charles?" Dubin replied, "He said that's another good letter." Still later, the most damning letter that the prosecution had was read to the jury. Robinette, looking more confident than ever, said, *sotto voce,* "That's a very good letter." Once again a frustrated Martin did not hear him and asked Dubin what Robinette had said. Dubin told him, "He says it is a very good letter." This was too much for Martin. He turned away muttering, "Is John at the same trial as the rest of us?" Unfortunately for students of the jury system, the jury never tried the matter. It was taken away from them by the trial judge, who was not satisfied that the Crown had made out a *prima facie* case of guilt. He directed the jury to enter a verdict of not guilty. His ruling was upheld on appeal.[146]

Robinette's success as a counsel appeared innate, but in reality it was the product of intense work. To the outside world, Robinette presented himself as unhurried and effortlessly in command of his brief. However, one of the great qualities that he demonstrated for the eternal benefit of those young lawyers like me who were associated with him was a work ethic that may have been matched by a few lawyers at McCarthys but was surpassed by none. Robinette's public display of self-assurance was genuine because it was earned by his personal attention to the facts and to the legal principles central to his brief. And I stress personal attention. Robinette did his own preparation for the most part and delegated as little as he had to. I can remember being asked to prepare a memorandum on a discrete point of law or to interview a particular witness who was not available at a time or place convenient to Robinette. But I was never asked to work up one of his cases for him or prepare his memorandum of fact or law. I think that he had confidence in his own work product and preferred to do his own research because he knew he could rely on it. However, I also accept his statements on more than one occasion that he felt ethically obliged to do his own work because the clients who paid his fees were entitled to receive the benefit of his, and not someone else's, preparation.

This work ethic never changed. John Honsberger, Q.C., a knowledgeable observer of the profession in his capacity as editor of the Osgoode *Gazette* and other publications, recounts the following:[147]

> Towards the end of his life I saw Mr. Robinette reading law in the Great Library. I made some kind of remark that it was strange that he read his own law. He answered that he always did. As a surgeon would not operate based upon an examination by an intern, he would not take a case which he did not prepare. He added that if he were to instruct a junior to read the law, it would take so long to dictate a memorandum on what to look for and what he might find or not find that it was easier to do it himself.

I can say that Robinette was not at his best when he shared a case with another counsel, as I was to find out when I appeared with him in the Supreme Court of Canada. When Willard "Bud" Estey was appointed to the Court of Appeal, he had a portfolio of blue chip litigation to distribute. I was flattered that he recommended to Imperial Oil that I take over a piece of litigation it had with Nova Scotia Light Heat and Power Corporation alleging breach of contract of a long-term supply contract for bunker "c" fuel oil. The issue was the ability of Imperial Oil to pass on to the customer what was referred to in the industry as "host government take," by relying on the definition of taxes in the contract.

The parties had entered into an agreement whereby Imperial was to supply the power company with its entire requirements of bunker fuel oil for the years 1970 to 1976. The agreement provided that any increase or decrease in "tax, duty, charge or fee applicable to the product or its manufacture, sale or delivery" or "any imposition of any new tax, duty, charge or fee on the product or its production, manufacture, sale or delivery," that was to be borne by Imperial would be reflected in a price adjustment. The clause did not apply to a tax on income or profits. The oil itself came from an Exxon subsidiary in Venezuela called Creole Oils and was notionally delivered by Creole to a subsidiary of Imperial in Bermuda called Albury Corporation before its actual delivery to Imperial at Halifax. Venezuela was not only a member of the international oil cartel known as OPEC, but also was its founder. As a result of the government of Venezuela's imposition of new taxes on crude oil production and export, the prices Imperial paid for crude oil rose. Imperial sought to pass on these additional costs under the terms of the agreement. Both the trial judge and the appeal division decided that the agreement contemplated passing on only Canadian taxes borne by Imperial and not by other companies in the Exxon group.

The case was very interesting and was an education to me on the pricing practices of the OPEC cartel, which during the first few years of this contract had increased the world price of oil from about $2 a barrel to $18 and rising. The financial consequences to both Imperial Oil and the power company were immense. I had taken the trial and lost it.[148] An appeal was inevitable, and during the course of discussing its ramifications, the general counsel for Imperial Oil diffidently raised the issue of whether I would mind if John Robinette came into the case. I had no choice but to agree, but I really was not in the least offended. My relationship with Robinette was such that I had no difficulty in deferring to him on any subject relating to the law, and I was quite comfortable appearing with him as his junior, a role I would not have assumed for any other counsel at that stage in my career. The year was 1975, and I had been a Queen's Counsel in my own right for well over ten years.

The case was complex and involved issues that had been painstakingly developed in the evidence. Robinette decided that he would limit his argument to the issue of the interpretation of the contract and leave the other issues to me. The separation of issues seemed to work satisfactorily in the Nova Scotia Court of Appeal, and the members of that court gave us a good hearing, but a losing one nonetheless. After reserving, they delivered full reasons dismissing the appeal.[149]

Imperial Oil was anxious to appeal to the Supreme Court of Canada. However, at that time leave to appeal to our highest court was required. I anticipated that there would be some difficulty in obtaining leave for the same reason that Imperial was so anxious to obtain it: there was an awful lot of money involved — literally millions. The members of the Supreme Court suffered then and now from a reverse elitism, affecting an air of disdain when the amount at risk to the parties is considerable. However, I reasoned that the local provincial Court of Appeal might well be conscious of the amounts involved and not wish to be seen as protecting consumers of electricity in the province from international monitory pressures. I read the *Supreme Court of Canada Act* and observed that an order permitting leave was not restricted to the Supreme Court itself, but could also come from the provincial appellate court that was being appealed from. I made such an application and was successful.

My triumph was short-lived. The appeal came on May 25, 1977, before a panel of only five Supreme Court justices and without the Chief Justice — always a bad omen. The Court was annoyed that I had made an end run on its control over the court docket, and the members of the court quickly demonstrated that in their view I had been too clever by half. They could not wait for Robinette to sit down before venting their disapproval of the case and the burden they carried as a result of having to hear it. Unlike the Nova Scotia Court of Appeal, which respected the division of advocacy between Robinette and me when Robinette explained it to them, this court was quick to fire questions at Robinette that had nothing to do with the interpretation of the contract, and Robinette did not have the answers. This was the first time I had ever observed Robinette receive an unfriendly hearing by any appellate court.

Robinette held on until the bell, as they say in boxing, and that evening we reviewed our position. Robinette, employing another sports metaphor, said, "It's time to bring in the long reliever." He said, "George, I am not getting a good hearing, and frankly I do not know what to do about it. I think you should start your part of the argument tomorrow." I did and was able to answer the questions that Robinette had not answered, plus a few more dingers, but it was much too late. The Court was solidly against us. While it called on the respondent, I sensed it was more out of courtesy, and perhaps apology, to Robinette than to be further informed about the appeal. Justice Martland delivered the unanimous judgment of the Court, dismissing the appeal on June 24, 1977.[150]

By way of a footnote to this case, a short time later the Supreme Court of Canada released a direction to the effect that provincial appellate courts should not exercise their concurrent statutory jurisdiction to grant leave to appeal to the Supreme Court of Canada because it made it difficult for the top court to control its workload.

There are many counsel still alive whom I could cite in support of Robinette's excellence as a counsel, but I will content myself with one who in my opinion was his equal in the civil field. John Arnup said this of him:[151]

> I regarded John as the paramount advocate of his day, and comparisons with other days were not appropriate because the style of advocacy had changed. I had seen Mr. Tilley on a number of occasions and D.L. [Lally] McCarthy on a number of occasions, but John was the leader of the sober, methodical advocacy. Clarity as a lecturer had been his *forte*, but this was true in the Court of Appeal and in the Supreme Court of Canada — we had two or three cases in the Supreme Court of Canada.
>
> It has been said many times that he was the greatest advocate of his day, and I accept that, and friends of his and mine like Barry Pepper and Joe Sedgwick would agree with that assessment of Robinette.

Robinette would be pleased to have his name linked with Tilley, whom he mentioned in his oral history as a counsel he wanted to emulate. When asked why, Robinette said:[152]

> He was in my view the best counsel of that era. He had a wide practice, thoroughly prepared his cases. He didn't do any criminal work, all civil work, and he took a lot of cases in the Supreme Court of Canada and some in the Privy Council. He was very successful. A big man. Watching him then in his early days, and watching him later on, he built his cases up brick by brick. He would get the court to understand one point and then go on with the rest. He wasn't what you would call a sensational lawyer; he was out to persuade the court. And I always thought he was good.

Arnup made reference to a practice of Robinette's of which I was well aware, but which initially surprised me considering his otherwise easy-rolling eloquence.[153] This practice was his use of scripted notes for appellate purposes. Arnup said of it:

> On appeal, he was always scripted, as I was, with his notebook. He didn't read from his notebook, but he followed it fairly closely. I never was in a case with John Robinette where I thought he was ill-prepared. As far as I was concerned, he was always prepared and, if you had a case against him, you had to proceed on that assumption and cover all the bases. He had juniors in a number of cases, but basically, I think, he was a lone worker who liked to do his own preparation. He had others read law for him, no doubt, but that notebook with his legible longhand outline of his argument was always his strong point and I, on a number of occasions, wished that I could peek at it for the next day's sittings. But he was not hidebound to the notebook and, to use a perhaps inappropriate expression, he

could roll with the punches if something happened
that was unexpected.

I am indebted to Arnup for mentioning these detailed notes because
it reminds me of an experience I had when I took over an appeal from
Robinette that he had been prepared to argue in a matter of days in the
Court of Appeal. He was apologetic for giving me the matter at the last
moment, but he had a case that was unexpectedly called in the Supreme
Court of Canada and, as was the custom in those days, he had to give it
priority. He warned that the appeal he was giving me was a difficult one
and added, almost deferentially, that I might receive some assistance
from his notes that were in the file.

The case was *Hood v. Hood*,[154] and it was indeed a difficult one.
Moreover, I was appearing for the appellant, and argument was scheduled in the last week of June of 1970, bad news because the Court would
be looking forward to its long vacation (July and August) and would be
reluctant to pick up any reserve judgments.

Jack Hood was the owner of Harlequin Books, but his marriage to
Nancy Hood did not match the fairy-tale romances he was so successful
in selling. He and his wife married in 1963 but had not lived together
since October 1966, when Mrs. Hood left the matrimonial home and on
the next day laid an assault charge against her husband. Shortly after,
she commenced proceedings against him, alleging cruelty on his part.
She later amended the pleadings to allege desertion. Prior to the trial,
Mrs. Hood, through her solicitor, made overtures about reconciling
with Mr. Hood, which were fruitless. Her action was dismissed by the
trial judge, Justice Moorhouse, who found that Mrs. Hood's disruptive
attitude throughout the period of cohabitation was planned and deliberate, that she had left the matrimonial home, that there was no desertion by her husband, and that the charge of assault had been laid for the
purpose of founding a cause of action for alimony.

While the appeal from Justice Moorhouse's decision was pending,
Mrs. Hood made a further offer of reconciliation, which also failed. The
appeal was dismissed, and a few days later Mrs. Hood withdrew the
assault charge. Later that month, she wrote to her husband offering to
resume cohabitation. I quote the letter in its entirety:

I should like to talk to you about our getting back together again. I know if we had our differences in the past but I think we could resume our lives together successfully now that we have been apart for a while.

At our ages there are many years ahead that we could enjoy together if we took up our marriage again. I am willing to come back and try, and I know we can make a go of it if we both work at it. I was very sorry that you wouldn't meet with me last December when I asked my lawyer to speak to your lawyer so that the trial had to go ahead in January. I think we could have talked things over at that time and resumed our married life. It would really be more rewarding for both of us to have each other for the rest of our lives. Remember you told me when I tried so hard to get you to make up after a quarrel that if I hadn't done it you never would. You said you just couldn't give in, it was your nature. Well, I'm trying again and I'd like you to think about it seriously and to think what we are both missing by not being together. I will look forward to hearing from you in the meantime.

Love,
Nancy

Jack Hood was not moved. He not unjustifiably saw the letter as insincere and nothing more than an attempt to overturn the effect of Moorhouse's judgment. By effecting a reconciliation, she would overcome the finding that she had deserted her husband and would be able to resume her litigation. He should have had his lawyer draft an appropriate response, but chose instead to return the letter after writing on it, "No. Thanks just the same."

Predictably, Mrs. Hood then sued her husband a second time. She alleged that his refusal to resume cohabitation constituted desertion, which entitled her to live separate and apart from him, and to receive alimony from him. The second trial judge, Justice Donohue, took a different view of the letter than did Jack Hood. He found: "As I read it, it is conciliatory in tone, affectionate to a degree appropriate to mature persons, apologetic without being abject, constructive and clearly sets out that the plaintiff wishes to resume cohabitation with the defendant." Accordingly, Donohue declared that by reason of having been deserted, the wife was entitled to live separate and apart from Mr. Hood. And, for as long as she lived separate and apart from him, or until further ordered, she was entitled to alimony in the sum of $750 per month.

This factual scenario seems strange by modern standards and serves as a reminder of how recently the law has been changed to eliminate the element of fault from matrimonial proceedings. No matter that the Hoods had been living apart for three years; Mrs. Hood, who had no independent means, could not claim support payments from her wealthy husband without demonstrating that she had been entitled to leave the matrimonial home because of his misconduct, such as adultery or physical abuse. However, while the law was not sympathetic to Mrs. Hood, judges were because they recognized the anachronism of attempting to preserve the institution of marriage by compelling the wife to remain with her husband through economic necessity. As Jack Hood's counsel, I recognized that the appellate court would feel less than benevolent towards him and would be reluctant to overturn the trial judge's finding that Hood's cavalier refusal to entertain his wife's offer of reconciliation effectively made him guilty of deserting her.

The view I took of the case when I first read it was that the central issue of the appeal revolved around the genuineness or sincerity of Mrs. Hood's offer to reconcile. In taking this view of the case, I would be asking the Court of Appeal to reverse the findings of Justice Donohue. This would be a difficult argument to win in light of the fact that Mrs. Hood had given evidence that the trial judge accepted, while her husband did not testify.

But then I looked at Robinette's notes. I can still see them in my mind's eye. They were on three-holed notepaper suitable for the notebook that he always carried. They were typed, double-spaced, and neatly paragraphed. They read like a dime novel and could have been handed to the Court as a written argument. More important, once I read

Robinette (left) greets popular New York senator Robert F. Kennedy.

At a reception during an Advocates' Society jaunt to Dublin in 1971: Justice Brian Walsh (left); Sean Flanagan, a solicitor who was a famous Gaelic footballer; Lois Robinette; Mícheál O Moráin, Irish Minister for Justice; Robinette; and John Arnup.

Robinette receives the Companion of the Order of Canada medal from Governor General Roland Michener, 1973.

*Old friends
Robinette and
Michener meet
in more relaxed
circumstances.*

*The Robinettes
with McCarthy &
McCarthy postwar
leader, Beverley
Matthews.*

*Robinette with
Douglas Laidlaw,
Jack Blaine, and
David Gordon.*

*With Gregory
Evans, Chief Justice
of the High Court
of Justice.*

*With William
Howland, Chief
Justice of Ontario.*

*Robinette shares a
joke with
McCarthy lawyer
and later Justice
David Doherty.*

Holding court with McCarthy lawyers James Walker (left), Harry MacDonnell, and Peter Beattie.

Robinette receives an honorary doctorate from the University of Toronto, one of four such doctorates given to him by Canadian universities.

The newly installed Chancellor of Trent University mingles with students and faculty, 1984.

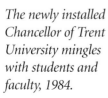

Robinette plants a tree at Campbell House to mark his fiftieth year as a member of the bar.

Sharing war stories at a dinner to mark the sixtieth anniversary of Robinette's call to the bar are Chief Justice Dickson (left) and famed criminal lawyer Arthur Martin. October 1989.

John Sopinka, counsel and later Supreme Court of Canada judge, congratulates Robinette, recipient of the first Robinette Medal, as Rob Pritchard, dean of the University of Toronto Law School, looks on.

A formal photograph taken of Robinette upon the sixtieth anniversary of his call to the bar.

Proud fathers Robinette and Bora Laskin celebrate the call to the bar of John Laskin and Dale Robinette, 1971.

Robinette with extended family.

John and Lois Robinette share a quiet moment on holidays.

Robinette making new friends.

At the inauguration of McCarthy Tétrault's John J. Robinette Library are Justice John Brooke and Robinette's long-time secretary Muriel Reid.

Lois Robinette and portrait of her husband at the John J. Robinette Library.

them, I realized my approach to the appeal was wrong. These notes informed me that I was not going to attempt to persuade the Court that it should reverse the trial judge on his finding of fact based on the uncontradicted evidence of Nancy Hood. Instead, I was going to argue that Justice Donohue had ignored the previous judicial finding made by Justice Moorhouse dismissing the wife's allegations of cruelty and desertion and finding that it was she who had deserted her husband. The Court of Appeal had since affirmed Justice Moorhouse's judgment. Mrs. Hood's letter offering to reconcile was written shortly thereafter.

Under these circumstances, I would argue, Jack Hood had ample grounds for refusing to accept the offer contained in the letter. He had good reason in light of his experience with his wife to doubt that it was genuine. But whether or not it was genuine was not the issue. Mr. Hood had valid reasons for refusing to accept the offer to resume cohabitation having fresh in his mind that Justice Moorhouse had found that his wife's attitude, which resulted in the breakup of the home, was planned and deliberate: she had threatened to harm him financially and hurt his standing in the community, and she had made it clear at the first trial that she did not wish to return to him. Certainly, I would argue, his refusal to accept the offer did not make him a deserter.

Hood v. Hood is not a significant jurisprudential case. It is so badly indexed that it is difficult to retrieve from the published law reports. However, it is a textbook example of how counsel should analyze and prepare an appeal. Robinette's approach to the case was not just a matter of a change in emphasis from mine. It was a flank attack as opposed to my proposed frontal assault. I was prepared to attack the judgment by arguing that the key finding that the offer of reconciliation was genuine was unreasonable and not supported by the evidence. In this strategy I would have most certainly failed.

Robinette's approach was to isolate this finding by conceding it, but then arguing that it was of limited value to Mrs. Hood. The issue in his mind was not whether the offer was authentic but whether Jack Hood was obliged to accept it. The ground he elected to fight on was whether Hood was justified in thinking the offer was not genuine based on the evidence of his wife's prior conduct as found by the trial judge in the first trial. This appellate strategy pointed out the weaknesses in Donohue's finding that the offer of reconciliation was genuine without placing the burden on the appellant husband of satisfying the difficult onus of demonstrating that this finding was wrong.

On the appeal, my court consisted of Chief Justice Gale and Justices Arthur Kelly and John Brooke. Brooke had left Robinette and McCarthys when he became a trial judge on October 31, 1963, and was further elevated to the Court of Appeal on March 13, 1969. The court documents before the panel indicated that Robinette was to appear as counsel, and the panel was looking forward to hearing from him. Perhaps this was why my initial arguments were not well received. All members of the panel picked up on the point that I was attempting to reverse Donohue on his findings of fact and credibility. Their reaction to the appeal was the same as mine on first impression. I was having a difficult time of it when I suddenly thought that perhaps Robinette could be more persuasive. Accordingly, I started reading from his notes — verbatim. The whole atmosphere changed. The Court was listening. It called on my opponent, Earl Cherniak, to respond, and the panel members peppered him with questions. At the end of the argument, the Chief Justice delivered judgment from the bench allowing the appeal, setting aside the judgment below, and dismissing Mrs. Hood's action. Robinette had prevailed. I was elated.

In those days, the parties could appeal as of right to the Supreme Court of Canada if the subject matter of the judgment in appeal involved $10,000 or more. Cherniak elected to take the matter further and served a notice of appeal. I was confirmed in my opinion that the panel of the Ontario Court of Appeal were disappointed that Robinette had not appeared to argue the case by a conversation I had with Chief Justice Gale. One day after he heard that his judgment was under appeal, he spotted me in the hall outside his courtroom. He called me over and said that he had heard the matter was going to Ottawa, adding, "We went out on a bit of a limb in that Hood case. I think you should make sure that Robinette argues the case in the Supreme Court."

This conversation was more than a little deflating. However, being publicly told that I was no John Robinette was not a new experience for me. On the other hand, Gale's remark was unusually crass considering he was not supposed to have any interest in whether he was upheld by a higher court or not. In any event, I had already spoken to Robinette and his instructing solicitor, Philip Isbister, Q.C., about turning back the brief and was told that Jack Hood was quite taken with me and insisted that I remain on the appeal.

Cherniak and I appeared in May 1971 before a panel composed of Justices Martland, Judson, Ritchie, Hall, and Laskin. Astonishingly, the same thing happened again. Cherniak was very well received as counsel for the appellant, but the same could not be said for me as counsel for the respondent. The Court seemed troubled by the notion that despite the judicial findings in the first trial, the Court of Appeal's reversal of the finding of Justice Donohue rested ultimately on that court's refusal to believe in the wife's sincerity because of the "shadow cast by the first action" (Laskin's words). Once again I abandoned my own prepared argument and read from Robinette's notes. Once again the mood of the Court changed radically. This time Robinette was not quite so persuasive, but he did prevail by a margin of three to two. Justice Martland wrote the majority judgment dismissing the appeal with Justice Laskin dissenting and Justice Hall concurring with Laskin.

Robinette's advice on appellate strategy was always insightful, but it did not always assist in obtaining a successful outcome. I remember, shortly after my call to the bar, receiving an appeal from an out-of-town law firm that involved a civil action arising from a hit-and-run automobile accident. The owner and driver of the car insisted that he was not involved in the accident — that it was some other car. The trial judge thought otherwise and found against him. The driver was appealing that finding.

There was some circumstantial evidence consisting of a small dent in a fender and some paint scrapings found at the scene of the accident that connected my client's car to the accident, but it was very weak and had not been subjected to proper forensic analysis. The most damaging evidence was a statement said to have been made by my client long after the accident in which he admitted that he and his car had been at the scene of the accident but denied any negligence. Our position was that the statement was made under the statutory compulsion of the *Highway Traffic Act*: while the statement identifying him as the owner and driver of the car was properly coerced, the contents of the statement could not be used to implicate him in civil liability. This point was still a live legal issue at the time. The case excited me because it was obvious, in my thinking, that without the statement there was nothing to implicate the appellant in the accident. The legal issue of how the statement could be used would have to be decided by our Court of Appeal. I was to be counsel in a leading case.

I spoke to Robinette and explained the interesting legal point in the appeal. He just smiled and said, "The members of the court will have read the incriminating statement, and they will know that the appellant was responsible for the accident. They will not want to interfere with the judgment of the trial judge." How right he was. The Court did not want to hear about the statement and my finely honed self-incrimination argument. Its members kept pointing to the circumstantial evidence, which, they solemnly intoned, was enough to support the finding below of my client's identity as the driver of the car involved in the accident. Justice Robert Laidlaw was the president of the panel and was most scornful of my submissions that the circumstantial evidence not only was insufficient for this purpose but, if anything, was exculpatory. I pointed out that the dents in the car reflected a trivial contact, whereas the pedestrian victim had been struck so violently that he was knocked clear out of his shoes. Laidlaw, an old negligence lawyer, was amused. "I had a case in my practice where that happened," he told the Court. "The explanation was very simple. The victim's shoes were too large."

The above two cases demonstrate the key to Robinette's success: his unfailing good judgment, the one quality that endured throughout his career. I have known him to be disappointed, but seldom surprised, at a result. Almost inevitably he had accurately assessed the prospects of success and determined the soundest approach to a successful presentation. That did not mean that he always expected to carry the day, but it prevented him from reproaching himself when he did not. I imagine that this is why he was able to carry on in the stressful role as advocate for so many years.

But while judgment is the *sine qua non* of the successful counsel, the advocate must have a platform from which he or she operates. There is a lot of advice given in good faith by successful counsel on the appellate advocacy, but I have never seen a more succinct exposition on this subject than the one Robinette himself delivered on January 26, 1981, in an address to the Civil Litigation Section of the Canadian Bar Association entitled "Advocacy in the Appeal Courts." I do not have the text of the address, but I am indebted to Justice Robert P. Armstrong for a copy of the minutes prepared by the secretary of the meeting, which included the following:

> Advocacy is the power to persuade a tribunal that your client is in the right by involving the exercise of your skill, diligence and knowledge to the best of your abilities. The skill in an advocate's performance is acquired by experience, study and observation. Robinette cautioned that every advocate should use their own powers of persuasion and lucidity, striving to develop their own style instead of imitating someone else's style.
>
> Robinette then laid down what he termed the "Rules" of Advocacy:

1. All rules of advocacy must yield to the particular situation the facts disclose. Communicate the facts as you see them to the court.
2. Follow the three c's: chronology; candour; clarity.
3. Organize your presentation in the order that will be the most persuasive. Set out your best points first. Avoid burdening a busy tribunal with points of law that are merely academic.
4. Use correct grammar and proper punctuation. Cite cases correctly, referring to the official reporting series where possible.
5. Cite Supreme Court of Canada cases in precedent to all others. Provincial Courts of Appeal; the English Court of Appeal; and decisions of the High Court of Australia rank successively as the next most persuasive decisions.
6. Be succinct. Go for the jugular.

> Robinette pointed out that written submissions outline the material facts and discuss applicable rules of law with reference to the particular remedies sought, while oral presentations allow the detailing of issues and clarification of points that are troubling the tribunal.

My own view is that what set Robinette above some very good counsel was his unerring ability to assess his audience and recognize what it was that did or should concern it. This applied whatever the audience: a jury, a single trial judge, a panel of appellate judges, or the Supreme Court of Canada. This insight was not restricted to "courts" in the traditional sense but embraced administrative tribunals, municipal councils, coroners' juries, and after-dinner audiences. Not only did he have the uncanny ability to make these judgments, he also had the self-confidence to live or die by them. This ability was not just a preliminary assessment; it was a flexible cerebral instrument that told him on a continuous basis how his arguments were being received. I do not know how many times I saw him sit down after arguing only one or perhaps two of the issues that were in his factum, confident that he had made his point and content to leave the matter at that. This did not mean that he inevitably won the case, because they were not all winnable. It did mean that in Robinette's judgment, he was going to win or lose on the point or points that he had argued and that no supplementary or alternative submissions were going to carry the day. This strategy, because that is what it was, was unnerving to the opposing counsel and to the Court. By restricting his submissions to one or more points, Robinette had elevated his issues to the point that they dominated the case. He had set the agenda and placed his imprimatur on a single issue or at the most two. Such an expression of confidence coming from one of his stature could not be ignored. The Court readily discarded other issues to which they might have been sympathetic and insisted that Robinette's opponent do the same. Robinette had effectively appropriated the argument by insisting that the case be argued on his terms.

Not many counsel today have the courage to make such a judgment call as to which arguments they will live or die with. There is too much fear on the part of counsel of being second-guessed, when they should only be concerned with whether the best arguments, not all the arguments, were made on behalf of the client. It is perhaps this quality of making your own bed that Colin Irving saw in Robinette when he first observed him in court. He writes:

> I first heard him [Robinette] in the Supreme Court of Canada when I was very wet behind the ears and was acting as bag carrier to John L. O'Brien, Q.C., himself no mean advocate. We were waiting our turn outside the courtroom and word came that J.J.R. was about to argue. Mr. O'Brien directed me into the courtroom. "Get in there and listen. You might even learn something." I still recall the clarity and persuasiveness of his argument. I recall even more my shock when judgment was given against him from the bench, a matter which did not seem to trouble him in the least.

Another aspect of Robinette's discipline in court was that he would not allow himself to be deflected from pursuing his forensic tactic by comments or questions from the bench. He would answer them courteously and briefly and, if the occasion called for it, firmly. But he did not make the error of expanding on the subject, which was an error as a member of the Court of Appeal I later witnessed other counsel make many times. I am referring to the situation in which a member of the panel asks a question or makes a comment that is only marginally relevant and counsel, instead of crafting a response that is short and to the point, decides to expand on the subject in the hope that by taking an interest in the justice's concern, he or she is acquiring an ally on the Court. In reality, counsel is gaining two enemies who have to listen to their colleague and counsel rattling on in an exchange that is not helpful to the resolution of the appeal. The effect of this error in judgment is compounded today by the application of time limits on the arguments of counsel.

A number of years ago, R. Jeffrey Flinn of London, Ontario, now Justice Flinn, told me a story that makes the point vividly. He had retained Robinette to act for his client, London Life Insurance Company, in an appeal from Judge Smith of the County Court, County of Frontenac, on a matter that raised an important point of principle to insurers.[155] Flinn appeared as Robinette's junior in March 1959 before a court composed of Justices Laidlaw, LeBel, and McGillivray. During the course of the morning's argument, Justice McGillivray asked Robinette about a certain case that Robinette had not heard of. He turned to Flinn, who whispered, "I have read that case and it has nothing to do with this appeal." Robinette was wise enough not to relay that answer to McGillivray, saying instead, "I am not familiar with that case, My Lord. I will look it up in the library during the lunch break and address the court on it in the afternoon."

The lunch break came. Robinette did not go near the library. In concluding his argument that afternoon, he made no mention of McGillivray's case. When he sat down, Flinn whispered that he had forgotten to deal with the mystery case. Robinette answered, "I didn't forget. The court will know that I read it and realize that it had nothing to do with this appeal." This is called touch. Robinette was not going to embarrass a member of the court by emphasizing that he had made an uninformed comment.

As alluded to earlier, Robinette had some other qualities that were not so admirable. He was capable of being a bully and was quite prepared to encourage a trial judge to browbeat his opponent. My first example is the Cornwall case involving the mayor of that city, which I described earlier.[156] Senior counsel for the relator challenging the validity of the election was P.J. Bolsby, Q.C., and he was assisted by a very able but comparatively young counsel named John S. "Jack" Boeckh. Boeckh was a very nice person when you got to know him, but he tended to be a bit waspish in dealing with opposing counsel. He once displayed this unfortunate feature of his advocacy in dealing with a submission of Robinette's. Robinette leapt to his feet and proceeded to jump all over Boeckh, much to the astonishment of the trial judge and the mortification of Boeckh.

As a student I assumed that this was all part of the give and take of the trial scene, but in conversation later with Boeckh I realized that he was surprised and devastated by this unexpected response to his argument. The judge, Morris King, was a very gentle man, I was to later learn, and he was very uncomfortable with this display of raw power. I realized very shortly that this was not a deliberate tactic by Robinette to throw a relatively inexperienced counsel off his stroke. He had simply lost his temper because of the lack of respect he was being shown by a junior member of the bar.

I have mentioned Robinette's temper on more than one occasion to friends of mine who knew him well, and they have always expressed surprise. I wondered if I had been singled out for special treatment because I had not only witnessed his occasional outbursts of unfiltered anger but had also been subjected to them. However, I could hardly have remained as close to him as I was for so many years if I were the only person he ever became angry with. Indeed, I think he only got angry with people he knew well and who would take it in good part. I emphasize that these outbursts were few and far between and, for my part at least, occurred when he was under stress from a heavy workload. But I was not a special case. When I was a student I was astonished at the running verbal battles between Robinette and his then-secretary, Liz Hudson, who had a combative streak in her makeup. His last secretary, Muriel Reid, confirmed how short and impatient he could be if her work was not done just so, but told me that she was in such total awe of him when she came to work for him in the 1950s that she would not dare answer him. As their working relationship developed, awe turned to respect, but she was still quite content to ignore any expressions of irritation on his part.

As a final witness, I call a member of Robinette's family. His wife Lois confirmed his fiery temper, which, I hasten to add again, was infrequent. She illustrated her point with a story that had become family legend about his outburst following a tennis match at Southampton. This was recounted with more than a little embellishment by Chief Justice Gale at a bar dinner. The audience was totally confused: they had difficulty envisaging Robinette as a tennis player, let alone one with a John McEnroe temperament. I later asked Robinette for clarification of the incident in question, but he was uncommunicative on the subject.

Robinette also had a practice of encouraging the bench to abuse counsel, and one example that I partially witnessed did him little credit. It involved Walter Schroeder of the Court of Appeal and an appeal that was brought to Robinette from Walkerton by Campbell Grant, Q.C., an old Southampton friend and later Justice Campbell of the High Court. It is reported as *Kennedy v. Tomlinson et al.*[157] and was a most complicated matter involving a farmer named Kennedy from the Walkerton area who had some mental problems. He brought an action for damages against multiple parties, including his wife, for breach of an oral contract requiring her to return to live with him. He also claimed damages against his solicitor, Tomlinson, for negligence and breach of his professional duty as a solicitor in not preparing an agreement between him and his wife requiring her to return and live with him. In addition, he sought damages against his father-in-law, one Chappel, for wrongfully causing him to lose the services and consortium of his wife. Kennedy also claimed damages against his wife and Tomlinson for conspiracy to defraud and for fraud. He made a further claim for damages of $50,000 against his wife, Tomlinson, Chappel, and three others, Wade, McClevis, and Freeborn, for "conspiracy to cause and for causing the plaintiff to be maliciously prosecuted and falsely arrested and falsely imprisoned" in the Walkerton jail and in the Ontario Hospital at London. He made a separate claim against McClevis, a Police Court magistrate, for damages for malicious prosecution, false arrest, false imprisonment, false conviction, and libel, and for expenses, pain, and suffering. A demand was also made in the action against Freeborn, the Crown attorney for the County of Bruce, for damages for negligence, breach of duty, malicious prosecution, false arrest, false imprisonment, and pain and suffering. A separate claim was made against Constable Wade for damages for assault, false arrest, false imprisonment, malicious prosecution, and pain and suffering.

As might be expected, this action, which was heard by a jury, received a good deal of publicity in Walkerton and beyond. Kennedy had some success at trial, and Robinette was retained by Campbell Grant to take the appeal. Grant acted as his junior. Kennedy retained a well-known Toronto lawyer, Lewis Duncan, Q.C. Duncan was very much of an odd man out in the profession and had some demons of his own. Not long after this case was argued, he shot himself in the washroom of a department store using his First World War service revolver. I knew him slightly (he was another fraternity brother) and respected his doggedness in representing persons with unpopular cases, but his constant court motions and niggling about details were undoubtedly an annoyance to those who had to deal with him professionally.

However, this case was interesting in that Duncan had as his juniors two well-known and extremely able counsel who agreed with him that the plaintiff Kennedy had been badly treated by the ruling elite of the County of Bruce. They were Andrew Brewin, Q.C., a sitting member of Parliament, and Bert MacKinnon, Q.C., my former lecturer in constitutional law at Osgoode Hall Law School and later my associate chief justice at the Court of Appeal. Kennedy's counsel decided to cross-appeal some of the issues at trial and to ask for increased damages. The appeal came on in the spring of 1959 before Chief Justice Porter and Justices Schroeder and MacGillivray.

My only interest in the case was that it was out of the ordinary. However, my curiosity was further piqued when I heard counsel in the robing room complaining about the way Schroeder was behaving, apparently with the active encouragement of Robinette. Initially, I downplayed counsel's reaction because I was well aware of Robinette's practice of shaking his head with disapproval when his opponent advanced arguments that he disagreed with and nodding his head with approval when the presiding judge or a member of the Court of Appeal said something with which he found favour. After I finished my own court motion, I dropped in to see for myself. It was not a pretty scene.

I should say at the outset that Schroeder was not a favourite of mine, nor I of his, it would appear. I do not know why he took a scunner to me, but he did. It was typical of him that he made no effort to conceal his dislike, engaging in such childish antics as deliberately misstating my name: "Do you have any thing else to say, Mr. Finlay?" He did the same thing with others, so I knew it was no accident. When I looked in on *Kennedy v. Tomlinson*, I could see that he had added Lewis Duncan to his list of *bêtes noirs*. Perhaps our fraternity had blackballed him. Whatever the reason, Schroeder was determined to make an example of Duncan and his two juniors who had the temerity to defend their leader's position on the appeal. But what made the performance ugly was that when Schroeder made what he thought was a brilliant forensic foray against Duncan's position, he would look down to Robinette for his reaction. Robinette would respond with a smile and a nod and then write something in his notebook with a flourish that connoted that the remark from the bench deserved to be memorialized. Schroeder would then smile in self-satisfaction. "Teacher's pet," I said to myself.

The scene bothered me. Robinette did not have to have someone kissing up to him this way. It was one thing to put on a show for a jury or court to distract an opponent (although I would have thought that a counsel of Robinette's stature could have shed such law school mock trial tactics), but to squander your prestige in support of a performance such as Schroeder's added no lustre to Robinette's name. What I saw and heard was typical of what happened on that appeal, and frankly I was embarrassed by it. Certainly Robinette's reputation was diminished in the eyes all those who witnessed his participation in Schroeder's disgraceful performance. I think the bitterness was revived when Schroeder wrote the unanimous judgment for the Court, allowing Robinette's appeal and dismissing the cross-appeal. The Supreme Court of Canada stated that while it did not agree with all the reasons of Schroeder, it was not prepared to grant leave.[158]

If it appears to the reader that I am stretching a bit to find something negative to say about Robinette, the perception is correct. He was certainly the easiest person in the world to deal with if he was satisfied that you were doing your level best. If he appeared insensitive to his opponents on occasion, that simply reflected the way the game was played when he entered the profession. You played to win. While he made a point of concealing any disappointment he felt about a particular result, this did not mean that he did not care. One person who noted this quality and commented is Ian Binnie, who writes:

> Another incident, which I think illustrates John Robinette's will to win, occurred in the *Churchill Industries* case[159] where the Government of Manitoba was represented by its Attorney General's department. A vast array of legal talent was hired by the various defendants to strike out all or parts of the Statement of Claim. There were several successful motions. Eventually, the Statement of Claim, as amended, was in pretty good shape but the defendants decided to have another go at striking it out. Robinette's Notice of Motion (probably drafted by one of his colleagues) was full of hyperbole about the vices of the Statement of Claim. In chatting to

the Manitoba government lawyer prior to the hearing of the motion, the lawyer looked to the great man and asked, in effect, "Do you think the Statement of Claim is really all that bad?" Robinette, sensing the opportunity, responded with a fatherly pat on the shoulder, "Oh, Fred, I think you can do better than that." As I understand the story, Manitoba conceded the motion and went back to the drawing board.

As for Robinette's practice of doing his own thing, it did have its disadvantages. Robinette was aware of the fact that he was famous, but he did not always accept the consequences. He may have felt having an entourage was ostentatious, but it can be useful in protecting the overburdened counsel from those who seek his services. But Robinette's staff consisted of one person: his secretary. Over the years, Liz Hudson, Ethel Hopkins, and Muriel Reid each filled that post. They did an excellent job of shielding him from unwelcome attention but could not be with him all the time. Robinette's reluctance to be confrontational led to a passivity that permitted people to take advantage of him. He simply could not say no when pressed to take on another matter. This led to a number of situations in which he was obliged to resort to clumsy devices to extract himself from rash commitments.

One of my favourite stories, which I have told on many occasions, relates to Robinette's ill-advised assurance to a fellow lawyer that he would see a number of that lawyer's clients and act for them in a messy family dispute. Before the meeting, Robinette came to me and said that he had committed himself to see these people, but that he would tell them that I was working with him on the case and would do the preparatory work. However, I was to understand that I would take the matter over in its entirety.

We met in Robinette's office. There must have been six people there. They all spoke at once. It was plot worthy of a Russian novel. The substance of the problem was that this extended family, in happier days, had reorganized their family wealth for tax purposes and had transferred it to what appeared to be a myriad of companies. Predictably, family unity fell apart, and some of its members wanted to unscramble this financial omelette. Robinette listened intently to what sounded to me like babble. He looked grave. He nodded his head in sympathy or shook it in concern. He appeared profoundly moved by this heart-rending tale of family betrayal. This went on for twenty minutes or so while I scribbled away trying to make some sense of what was being said. Finally, Robinette interrupted and explained my humble role in this most serious of matters, proceeding to usher all of us out of his office and into my more modest quarters. Far from being offended, the clients were most grateful. One was overwhelmed. "Isn't he brilliant?" he said to me. "Yes," I replied, "but what was it that struck you the most about his brilliance?" He replied unhesitatingly, "He sat through that whole session and didn't take a single note."

A case that did not involve me struck me as even funnier. Donald Sim was involved with Harold Fox, the leader of the bar in intellectual property law, in much the same relationship as I had with Robinette. Sim had an important patent action that the clients wanted Robinette to take over. Robinette had agreed, thinking the time for performance was well into the future. However, the clients wanted to see their star counsel in person to impress on him the importance of the matter. An appointment was made, but when the time arrived, Robinette was not in his office. Muriel Reid said he would be late. Sim, wanting to husband the limited time available for the conference, ushered the clients into Robinette's office so there would be no delay in starting the meeting when the great man arrived. Robinette did arrive. He had apparently forgotten about the appointment, and had certainly forgotten all about the case, if he was ever aware of it. However, old pro that he was, he put on his patient, concerned mask and listened intently for about ten minutes. He then arose suddenly and walked to the door. His parting words were, "I am running late and have another meeting outside the office. I have to leave now, but you people remain here as long as you wish."

To end this chapter on an appropriately positive note, I repeat the account given to me by David Brown, Q.C., of whom the reader will hear more later, involving a highly technical argument that Robinette was obliged to deal with regarding the jurisdiction of the Federal Court of Canada. To my mind, the account demonstrates the work ethic and attention to detail that were so important to Robinette's dominance. Brown recounts[160] that when he was a member of the law firm of Davies,

Ward and Beck, his client, McNamara Construction, was involved in litigation that raised an obscure jurisdictional problem.[161] I will let him describe the problem and what occurred:

> McNamara Construction had been sued by the Government of Canada in the Federal Court over alleged deficiencies in the construction of a Young Offenders' Institution out in Drumheller, Alberta. We acted for McNamara, and I was convinced that the Crown was in the wrong court. We had tried in the lower court to get the case thrown out on the ground of lack of jurisdiction and we lost.
>
> I then went over and talked to Mr. Robinette and asked him if he would take the case to the Federal Court of Appeal, working with me on it. This was probably eight or ten years after the *Leitch v. Texas Gulf* case.[162] I hadn't worked with him since then. He agreed to take it on. We lost in the Federal Court of Appeal but, at the time, the Supreme Court of Canada was hearing the *Quebec North Shore* case,[163] which was also a jurisdictional case on the Federal Court, and we were convinced decision in *Quebec North Shore* that Chief Justice Laskin was waiting for the next case to definitively determine what the jurisdiction of the Federal Court was.
>
> And so we appealed from the Federal Court of Appeal judgment to the Supreme Court of Canada, and Robinette and I went to the Supreme Court of Canada on it. I did most of the research, or a lot of the research, for him. We had a Privy Council case that made our case quite difficult and we had a number of Canadian precedents, including a Supreme Court of Canada precedent, on our side, but we appeared to have been overruled by the Privy Council, and I wasn't able to do anything to resolve this issue.
>
> I can remember meeting with Mr. Robinette in his hotel room late in the afternoon of the day before our

case was to go to the Supreme Court. We puzzled
through this issue, and he was trying to get the best arguments he could to overcome what appeared to be a bad
precedent. I got to the Court the next morning and met
with Robinette. He had a big stack of very old pleadings
with him. He had gone down to the Supreme Court of
Canada archives early that morning and he got the
Supreme Court of Canada case that had been appealed
to the Privy Council and found, in the factum of the
Supreme Court of Canada, that the way the particular
case was argued, the statements by the Privy Council
should not be construed in the way that we thought they
would be construed.

We won the case. We won it because of the little bit
of research that Robinette had done at 8:30 that morning before he got up on his feet. In what I thought was
a very complicated case, he was on his feet for only
forty-five minutes. He just laid it out beautifully, and
then the *coup de grace* was when he brought forward
this package that he had acquired from the archives at
the Supreme Court of Canada. The Crown counsel
[George W. Ainslie, Q.C.] was totally taken by surprise.
He thought that he was going to win hands down
because of this Privy Council case.

Without getting too involved with the details of the argument
before the Supreme Court of Canada, it appears that the Privy Council
case that Justice Thurlow of the Federal Court of Appeal relied on for
the jurisdictional point was *Consolidated Distilleries Ltd. v. The King*,[164] a
case in which the Crown was attempting to recover on some bonds
issued by Consolidated Distilleries in what was then the Exchequer
Court of Canada. Lord Russell of Killowen said at p. 520:

The Exchequer Court of Canada was constituted in the
year 1875 in exercise of this power [of Parliament under
s. 101 of the *British North America Act*]. It was conced-

ed by the appellants (and rightly, as their lordships think) in the argument before the Board, that the Parliament of Canada could, in exercising the power conferred by s. 101, properly confer upon the Exchequer Court jurisdiction to hear and determine actions to enforce the liability on bonds executed in favour of the Crown in pursuance of a revenue law enacted by the Parliament of Canada. The point as to jurisdiction accordingly resolves itself into the question whether the language of *the Exchequer Court Act* [R.S.C. 1927, c.34] upon its true interpretation purports to confer the necessary jurisdiction.

In reversing the court below, Chief Justice Laskin, as predicted by Robinette and Brown, relied on the *Quebec North Shore* case. He pointed out that the basis for conferring legislative power to create courts for the better administration of the laws of Canada was section 101 of the *British North America Act.* However, in the *Quebec North Shore* case, the Supreme Court had made it a prerequisite to the exercise of jurisdiction by the Federal Court that there be existing and applicable federal laws that can be invoked to support any proceedings before it. It is not enough that the Parliament of Canada has legislative jurisdiction over the matter in issue for the Federal Court to have jurisdiction; Parliament must have expressly legislated on the subject. The Chief Justice did not deal explicitly with Robinette's archival findings on *Consolidated Distilleries,* but he mentioned the case and dismissed it as having been referred to in *Quebec North Shore.* The ultimate success of the *McNamara* case on this jurisdictional point was not an academic exercise. By the time the issue was resolved by the Supreme Court of Canada, the applicable Alberta statute of limitations prevented the action being recommenced in provincial court.

Chapter Thirteen
Thar's Anomalies in Them Thar Hills

R OBINETTE WAS INVOLVED IN A very lengthy civil action that was
of intense interest to members of the mining community and
those who were interested in trading in shares in mining companies. The case commenced in the fall of 1966 and was to proceed over
164 trial days to judgment on November 19, 1968, setting a record for
longevity in its day.

Leitch Gold Mines Limited, for whom Robinette was to act, was a
Canadian company engaged in mining activities. It was to be the plaintiff in an action against Texas Gulf Sulphur, a large American corporation that had been prospecting for minerals in Ontario since 1957. The
cause of action was for breach of contract arising out of an agreement
between the two parties that was dated February 1, 1963.[165]

During the 1960s, the period of interest here, Texas Gulf was conducting geophysical exploration for mineral deposits, including performing extensive airborne electromagnetic surveying in Northern
Ontario. Texas Gulf's system and equipment for conducting such surveys
are described in detail in Chief Justice Gale's extensive reasons for judgment in *Leitch Gold Mines Ltd. v. Texas Gulf.* The process of finding and
developing a mine in the Canadian Shield is a lengthy and complex one
that begins with aerial geophysical surveys of what is thought to be
promising terrain. Then follows investigation on the ground of areas that
the aerial survey equipment indicates as potentially containing economic mineral deposits. If a mineral deposit is thought to exist after the completion of the aerial survey and the preliminary ground investigation, the

next step is to acquire the mining rights, either by staking them out or by the transfer or option of patented lands. Further ground exploration work is then done and, if deemed advisable, the area of interest is drilled. An assay of the drill core is usually the determining factor on whether or not an ore body has been found.

A mining exploration program is, therefore, an ever-narrowing process of selection, beginning with the choice of certain large areas for aerial survey and ending with the selection of a drill site. The exploration of the Canadian Shield for base metals by the Texas Gulf exploration department began with the division of northern parts of Ontario and Quebec into nineteen areas convenient for airborne geophysical surveys. The location of those areas was later shown on a map that was attached to and formed part of the contract between Leitch and Texas Gulf, which was to become the subject matter of the dispute.

There was a lot of further exploratory work to be done, but Texas Gulf had already determined that some of the surveys had shown promising anomalies — indications that valuable mineralization might be present. The promising mineralization included a variety of minerals, but in particular, copper, zinc, and silver. Texas Gulf quietly started to accumulate mining rights in some of the areas covered by the aerial surveys.

However, the aerial surveys covered a vast area of land, and Texas Gulf was receptive to a limited arrangement suggested by Charles Pegg, Exploration Manager of Leitch Gold Mines, for the development of a portion of the properties covered by the surveys. Pegg suggested that Texas Gulf turn over a large part of its data for Leitch's exclusive use with a view to Leitch's determination of whether or not there were any economic mineral deposits thereon, and if there were, to acquire such deposits by staking or otherwise.[166] The data, described as "pertinent data relating to the surveyed areas," included all maps, survey plans, diamond drill legs, and data prepared by or on behalf of Texas Gulf in respect of the surveyed areas as the result of aerial geophysical surveys and ground geophysical and geological surveys and diamond drillings. In return, Leitch was to use its best efforts to acquire the mining rights to any economic anomalies within the surveyed areas and transfer the claims or other evidence of a proprietary nature in the anomalies to a company to be formed and called "New Company." New Company was to be owned 90 percent by Leitch and 10 percent by Texas Gulf.

At this time, and not necessarily for the purpose of the discussions with Leitch, Texas Gulf prepared a sketch map and released it to Leitch. It indicated by rough outline the areas over which surveys had been flown. Also at this time, Texas Gulf indicated a willingness to turn over data for any of these areas "with a possible temporary restriction on some ground North of Timmins." No mention was made of the further fact that Texas Gulf had already begun its attempts to acquire the fee simple title to certain lands lying north of that city and within the area numbered 4 on the map. In area 4, Texas Gulf's airborne surveys had located a large electromagnetic anomaly that might indicate the presence of ore-bearing rock of commercially exploitable quality and quantity. This anomaly had been detected on flights as many as four years earlier in 1959 when Texas Gulf had begun surveying in the district. Its presence had been confirmed in the intervening years on several reflights of both area 4 and (on at least one occasion on June 21, 1960) of an area lying immediately adjacent, numbered 3 on the sketch map and designated by Texas Gulf as "Prosser Geary." This anomaly, designated "Kidd 55," although lying entirely within area 4, thus appeared on at least one aerial survey data report as being in area 3 and on several other reports as being in area 4. Ground magnetic tests of the anomaly conducted in 1961 had produced discouragingly negative results. No further tests were made in the area until after the agreement with Leitch. Eventually, Kidd 55 was developed by Texas Gulf into the enormously valuable Kidd Creek Mine, rich in copper, zinc, and silver and estimated to be worth $2 billion.

In the meantime, the parties continued to negotiate with reference to the sketch map for a transfer of data. In early 1963, they concluded an agreement under which Texas Gulf was to deliver to Leitch "all pertinent data relating to the surveyed areas" in return for a continuing 10 percent interest in New Company. All pertinent data was defined as "shown outlined in red on the plan attached hereto and marked 1, 3, 5, 6, 8, 9, 10, 11, 12, 13, 14, 18, 19 respectively." It is to be noted that area 4 is conspicuously absent from this definition. There was a suggestion by Leitch that names be used to designate the surveyed areas rather than numbers, but this was rejected by Texas Gulf on the ground that occasionally in the course of flying the surveys in Prosser Geary (area 3), Texas Gulf's helicopter had overlapped into area 4 and it was not Texas Gulf's intention to release data for any part of area 4. The plan, as eventually accepted and attached to the agreement, was based on the rough map, which had been prominent in the negotiations. It indicated the surveyed areas by number as well as by colour (coded according to the years in which the principal survey flights for each area had been conducted). It also purported to show an outline of the shape of the area intended to be covered by the flights comprising each aerial survey. The plan was, however, designated "Location Map of Areas Flown" and further identified areas 3 and 4 by the names "Prosser Geary" and "Timmins" respectively.

After the transfer of data, the parties pursued their separate interests. Leitch conducted ground exploration in area 9 at South Abitibi and in a remote corner of area 3 with portions of the acquired data, and Texas Gulf intensified its examination of the Kidd 55 anomaly. Rumours that Texas Gulf had made a valuable discovery emerged, and when they were eventually confirmed, Leitch took the position that the mine was within the area for which data had been transferred and that Texas Gulf was in breach of its contract "not [to] carry on or arrange for any further survey or exploration of the surveyed areas and ... not [to] stake or otherwise acquire claims within the surveyed areas ... without the written consent of [Leitch]." Leitch commenced an action in the Supreme Court of Ontario claiming: (1) a declaration that Texas Gulf held as a constructive trustee for Leitch all lands "in the surveyed area 'Prosser Geary' lying under or covered by the aerial geophysical survey named 'Prosser Geary'" and said to include the Kidd 55 anomaly; (2) rectification of the plan or map; and, in the alternative (3) damages for various breaches of contract in the combined amount of $450,000,000.

Robinette was retained to act for Leitch and John Arnup for Texas Gulf. The case brought into extended conflict two counsel who in my opinion were the leaders of the civil bar. They were also very close friends and coincidentally close friends of the trial judge, Chief Justice George A. "Bill" Gale.[167] As I have already indicated, Gale was a golf-playing chum of Robinette's and his cottage neighbour at Southampton. Gale and Arnup practised law together for eleven years before Gale was appointed to the bench. This certainly had the effect of making more civil a long, arduous, and technically demanding non-jury trial. In a recent interview, Arnup reminisced as follows:[168]

> The relationship between John and me was cemented in those days and, by the time of *Texas Gulf*, I regarded and, on some occasions, said that my best friend at the bar, apart from my own partners, was John Robinette and my best friend on the bench was Bill Gale, with whom I had practised law for eleven years before he was appointed to the High Court. This accounted for what some people regarded with surprise in the *Texas Gulf* case: the lack of acrimony between counsel and between counsel and the judge.
>
> It is noteworthy in my mind that, although we had 164 days of trial, neither John nor I had words with the judge on any occasion, and John and I had words only twice in the first few months of the trial. One occasion was my fault, and one occasion was John's. On each occasion, at the next recess the offender went to his opponent and apologized for what he had said in open court, and it never happened again.

I, along with everybody else at McCarthys, was aware that Robinette had been retained in this case, but, departing from my normal practice of seeking to know what Robinette was doing and discussing his cases with him, I stayed away from him on *Texas Gulf*. The financial stakes were huge, and both the plaintiff and the defendant had their shares listed on, I believe, the Toronto Stock Exchange, but certainly they were actively traded stocks. The outcome of the case, or even its perceived outcome, would drastically affect the value of the shares of the two parties to the litigation, none more than those of Robinette's client. I anticipated, correctly as it emerged, that I would be pestered by people who, knowing of my close association with Robinette, would want to know how Robinette thought the case was going. I could honestly tell anyone who asked me how Robinette felt about its outcome that I knew nothing about the case. I do not think my expressions of ignorance were believed by some of my inquisitors. I was surprised at what details they wanted to know. One person asked me if Robinette *looked* confident.

I was also amused at the efforts made by investors to forecast the result of the case. I heard of more than one instance in which lawyers who had nothing to do with the matter were retained to analyze the conduct of the trial and give an opinion about the possible result, much like the popular television lawyers in the American media. I did not realize until much later that stockbrokers and their agents attended the trial regularly to make their own assessment of its progress. One, I am told, was such a conscientious attender that on a day when his arrival was delayed, the Chief Justice asked about him and, after being told that the weather was holding him up, recessed the case until his arrival.

It would be interesting to conduct a survey about how these courtroom groupies made out in their predictions. If they were relying on their own appreciation of court theatre, they were inviting trouble. I have already pointed out what a consummate actor Robinette was once he donned his trial gown. Arnup was quite the opposite, and if he strove for any effect, it was to be unobtrusive. Furthermore, Arnup was much smaller than Robinette and any overt confrontation would make him seem overmatched. But Arnup knew his case and knew the Court. And Bill Gale was not impressed by appearances.

My principal source of information as to the conduct of the trial from the perspective of Leitch Gold Mines is David A. Brown, Q.C., now the chairman and CEO of the Ontario Securities Commission. He was a law student and later junior counsel on the case for Leitch. In an interview,[169] I took advantage of his position and asked him about the rumours of the trial from stockbrokers and others:

> GDF: There was a great deal of money involved in this case and because the shares of both companies were traded on the Toronto Stock Exchange there was a lot of speculation in the market arising out of the views investors took of the outcome of the case. Did you find yourself being

pressured by persons interested in knowing
whether Leitch was winning or losing?

DAB: Yes, although we were pretty low on people's
radar screens, so to say, because we were young
students at the time. But I know Sid Robinson,
Sr., was the public spokesperson for Leitch Gold
Mines and he was always being pestered. And it
was my first understanding of the need for
proper disclosure from public companies as
well because he spent a lot of time making sure
that the progress of the trial was being accurately reported in the press so that there would-
n't be misconceptions and rumours that would
drive the stock price one way or the other.

GDF: I was told that there were even stockbrokers who
sat through the trial thinking they were going to
pick up something.

DAB: Absolutely right. There were brokers there
every day and I think it went on for 150-some
odd days.

Brown was involved in this litigation from the outset as a result of
his friendship with the son of the senior partner of the firm that acted
for Leitch, Sidney H. Robinson, Q.C., of Holden, Murdoch, Finlay and
Robinson. Brown had graduated from university with an engineering
degree before entering law school at the University of Toronto. Sidney
Robinson's son, Sydney P. H. Robinson, Jr., was a law classmate of
Brown's and knew that he had an engineering degree. Robinson, Jr., suggested to his father that the firm should add Brown to the legal team at
Holden, Murdoch because of his engineering background. The firm
knew they were at an impasse with Texas Gulf and that they would end
up in litigation. Brown was given responsibility for case-managing this
litigation. Brown told me:

I agreed to do that and started working half-days during my second year in law school, and that carried through my third year, the bar admission course, and through to my first year as a lawyer at Holden, Murdoch. Throughout that time, I spent virtually all my time working with Mr. Robinette, seconded directly to him on the *Leitch v. Texas Gulf* trial, which took us through preparation for examinations-for-discovery, the examinations themselves, and then the trial.

When Robinette was retained to act as counsel to the Holden, Murdoch firm in connection with the *Leitch* case, Brown's association with Robinette became close. During the discovery stage of the litigation they would work either at Robinette's office or at the Holden, Murdoch offices. The firm occupied the top two floors of the old Bank of Nova Scotia building on King Street, and Robinette was at McCarthys, still in the Canada Life building at University Avenue and Queen Street. Brown remembers shuttling back and forth between those offices before the trial started.

The courtroom for the trial was located in the then-new courthouse on University Avenue at Armoury Street. It was Courtroom 20, reserved for major civil and criminal trials. Gale had been very much involved as chief justice of the High Court in the design of the new University Avenue courthouse and regarded Courtroom 20 as its showpiece and his personal courtroom. For the purposes of this trial, he divided the entire top floor of the courthouse so that the Texas Gulf legal team had one side and the Leitch team had the other side. Both parties transported a portion of their offices to the courthouse, including secretaries and other support staff. These quarters became the respective legal offices of the two parties for the duration of the trial, including weekend meetings.

In light of his extensive exposure to Robinette, I asked Brown how he liked working with him and what his first reaction to him was. He replied:

> I was quite a young man. He was one of the first lawyers that I met. I grew up in Ottawa in a family where we didn't know many lawyers. My parents didn't have in their inner circle of friends, people who were lawyers. I can't

to this day recollect why it was I decided to go to law school, but I was somehow driven to go to law school and he was the first lawyer that I really got to know.

He was absolutely delightful to work with. I could not have had a better introduction to practising law than working across the table with him. He was challenging intellectually but very much a gentleman. I had a growing family; I had one son, and then we had twins born during the course of the *Texas Gulf* case. He was always very sensitive to family needs.

We had a lot of laughs together. We spent many weekends researching points, but they were always easygoing discussions with Mr. Robinette trying to draw people out and get the best of what he could from the people working for him. I think that, even at the time, we [Brown and Robinson, Jr.] knew that this was going to be a very special time for us all in our legal careers.

I was surprised to read in Robinette's oral history that he had never been asked to give a legal opinion on the merits of the case. Holden, Murdoch had retained him solely as a barrister to conduct the trial. However, I was interested in knowing what the theory of the case was from the perspective of Leitch as plaintiff. Brown was able to give me an overview.

As mentioned, Texas Gulf had done a lot of geophysical mapping in Northern Canada, and it did this by flying a helicopter with electromagnetic brooms that would map the territory underneath the flight of the helicopter. Texas Gulf collected boxes and boxes of data with respect to the areas over which the helicopter was flying. Dr. Walter Holyk, who was their chief geologist, had a fairly small-scale map of the region on which he drew boxes with a pencil, roughly indicating the areas that had been overflown by the helicopter. The areas were at various regions around Northern Ontario and Northern Quebec on the Canadian Shield.

Charles Pegg, who was the chief geologist and exploration manager of Leitch Gold Mines, heard that Texas Gulf was withdrawing from those areas, that the exploratory survey had not found anything of interest, and

Texas Gulf was going off to do other things. "So," in the words of Brown, "Charlie Pegg did a deal for Leitch Gold Mines where he took all of the data that Texas Gulf had collected and which they had gone over in a preliminary way and not found anything of interest, and Pegg was convinced that there was mineralization in that area and that Texas Gulf had just missed it." On this understanding, Pegg entered into an agreement with Texas Gulf whereby Leitch would take possession of all of the data that had been collected on these overflights in return for a profit-sharing arrangement if Leitch indeed found anything of interest.

The agreement (of February 1, 1963) referred to Leitch's exclusive rights to the data within the areas shown on the map. In the view of Leitch, the question in the litigation was whether it had the rights to the data or only to that portion of the data that happened to be inside the lines on the sketch map. The problem was that, in some cases, the helicopter had overflown those lines in the course of simply making turns at the end of an aerial sweep. As it turned out, the Kidd Creek Mine, which was discovered in those overflights that Texas Gulf had missed in their preliminary analysis of the data, had indeed been picked up by that electromagnetic survey. Pegg found it and realized that he had the largest lead zinc mine in North America. The problem was that the mine was on a piece of the data that was straddling this line on the map and, in fact, it was probably just outside the line. So, continued Brown, it was almost a combination of errors as far as Leitch Gold Mines was concerned. If the agreement had been worded slightly differently to focus on the data, and not the area within the boxes, Leitch would have ended up with, said Brown, "a two-billion-dollar oil well."

The reason the trial took so long was that there was a great deal of technical evidence related to the interpretation of these maps in reference to the readings from the electromagnetic surveys. As Robinette put it in his oral history, "The evidence was largely documentary; that is what took so long. It wasn't a particularly stimulating case really. It was important, but you could go on for days just looking at these maps and listening to the experts talking about them."

Brown gives an example of an exercise that the parties went through with one witness:

There are a number of incidents that are firmly engrained in my mind ... but one of the most interesting and one during which Mr. Robinette and his team had a chuckle at the expense of John Arnup and his team, involved the announcement on a Friday afternoon at the close of the hearing for that day by Mr. Arnup that they had an expert witness that they wanted to bring forward on Monday. Because of the fact that the Texas Gulf jet had to go and pick this individual up and it would take about an hour to fly him to Toronto, he wanted to delay the start of the trial on Monday morning by an hour.

He wouldn't disclose who this surprise witness was, so Mr. Robinette and Sydney Robinson and I got together that afternoon and into the evening to try to figure out who this witness might be. We decided that, because the Texas Gulf jet probably flew at 500 miles an hour, this witness was coming from a location within a 500-mile radius of Toronto. So we drew that circle on a map, and then Sydney and I went to the University of Toronto School of Mines Library on Saturday and discovered that there was a very famous cartographer who lived within that radius.

Because the current portion of the trial was on cartography and where this ore body was actually located in relation to some lines drawn on a map, we thought that it was a pretty good bet that this Ph.D. in cartography was the surprise expert witness. So we discovered that this gentleman had a long and distinguished career, had written a number of books, but like so many other academics in that type of field, had changed his views considerably over the course of his career. We were able to find that some of the things that he said in his later writing contradicted things that he said in his earlier writing. We met with Mr. Robinette for a good portion of the day on Sunday, combing through his books and preparing Mr. Robinette for cross-examination, should this indeed be the correct witness.

And, sure enough, on Monday morning, we stacked all of these books on the counsel table right in front of Mr. Robinette in plain view of Mr. Arnup. When Mr. Arnup and his team came into the courtroom that morning, they immediately asked for a short adjournment, and Mr. Arnup apparently accused his team in their closed chambers of leaking information to the other side. In the result, Mr. Robinette was able to conduct a very effective cross-examination of this expert witness.

Further inquiry on my part as to the identity of the mystery witness led me to Justice Dennis Lane, who was a former member of the Texas Gulf trial team. He identified the witness as Professor Arthur Robinson of the University of Wisconsin at Madison. Lane was the lawyer who interviewed him prior to giving his testimony. His memory refreshed, Brown agreed that he was the man. However, his anecdote loses some of its force in a rereading of Chief Justice Gale's judgment, which reveals that Gale thought very highly of Professor Robinson as a witness and accepted his evidence without qualification. It does reinforce my earlier point that Robinette could look like a winner even when he was losing.

The anecdote also stimulated my interest as to Brown's perception of how readily Robinette absorbed the technical data and details that supported the various opinions of the experts. Brown answered as follows:

My recollection is that he was a very quick study, that he would master, over the course of an evening enough of the technical details to get through the next day and, by the end of the next day or, at the latest early the following day, he would have forgotten it all. I think it was more than just with technical information or technical details that he was able to do that. I think he had the kind of mind where he could focus on something intensely and then he would push it out of his mind and make room for the next issue.

He used to say to us, and it happened on more than
one occasion, "You know, there was a case a couple of
years ago – I can't remember the name of the parties –
and the issue was sort of" and he would describe in a
very general way an issue. We'd go and spend three hours
in the Great Hall Library trying to find the case. When
we ultimately found it, we found that he was counsel for
one side or the other. And he had the issue right; he
couldn't remember anything else about the case.

Cartography was one of the important subjects of expert testimony
because the map that Holyk gave Pegg was on such a small scale that
each pencil line could have been several miles wide when plotted on the
ground. A part of Leitch's case was that the parties could never have
intended such a rough instrument to delineate where Leitch's rights
began and Texas Gulf's rights left off. In the opinion of Leitch's experts,
the parties would have used a much larger scale map if they really wanted to delineate on the map an area on the ground.

Robinette accordingly argued that the obligation under the agreement of February 1, 1963, was for Texas Gulf to turn over all their data
regardless of the terrain that it purported to map on the ground. Holyk's
map that was attached to the agreement was not intended to be definitive of the rights of the parties; it was simply part of the data and intended to assist in organizing the surveys. It was, in short, merely an index.
The thrust of the agreement was that it obligated Texas Gulf not to interfere with or frustrate the examination by Leitch of anomalies, which,
under the agreement, Leitch was required to investigate. These anomalies
were the data generated by the Prosser Geary survey no matter where the
helicopter was flying when the electromagnetic survey occurred.

Robinette argued that two flights and the surveys they generated were
Prosser Geary flights, and one of them detected the Kidd 55 anomaly
twice. Accordingly, under the terms of the agreement, Texas Gulf was not
permitted to continue or renew the exploration of any anomaly detected
during the Prosser Geary survey notwithstanding that such an anomaly
had been discovered before the agreement was signed or located within
area 4. Robinette also emphasized that some of the Kidd 55 data had in

fact been turned over to Leitch in accordance with the agreement, thus fortifying his argument that this is what the parties intended at the time.

However, the weakness in Leitch's case arose in an area that counsel did not regard as a problem. The case depended on the Chief Justice accepting the testimony of Charles Pegg as to how the agreement was negotiated and the deal was closed. The Leitch team felt they had every reason to be confident that Pegg would be a solid witness. On the other hand, Arnup perceived Pegg as the Achilles heel of Leitch's case. He described his reasons in an interview:[170]

> JDA: I was aware partway through the examination-for-discovery of Charlie Pegg that he had lied about two or three very crucial matters because I had personally talked to three Texas Gulf people who had been involved with various aspects of Pegg's activities and I was satisfied that they were honest and unshakable in cross-examination.
>
> This turned out to be right, and my cross-examination of Pegg consisted in part of what was apparently low-key questions to him based on his examination-for-discovery with the classical series of questions: Were you asked that question? Did you make that answer? Was it true? To all of which he replied in the affirmative, and I spent almost a whole day in argument pointing out to Gale the aspects of Pegg's evidence that ought not to be believed, because unless Pegg was believed, Leitch couldn't win the case.
>
> GDF: What essentially was Pegg saying at the discovery?
>
> JDA: I would like to be able to give a clear answer to that question but the fact is that I don't now remember what part of the initial interview

between Pegg and Dr. Walter Holyk I later relied on as showing Pegg was not telling the truth. One night, for no particular reason, sticks in my memory having to do with an occasion when Pegg went out to Calgary where Texas Gulf had an office with a lot of documentation and the films stored. He told a story about one of the engineering staff at Texas Gulf helping him sort out paper that he was entitled to, reports and so on, and had a graphic story of this man being up a ladder taking things off the top shelf.

I remember we reached this point one day of the examination-for-discovery, saying to Pegg: "Well, we'll leave Mr. So-and-so up the ladder overnight, and we'll resume this at ten o'clock tomorrow morning." Well, I knew that the man he was talking about hadn't even been in Calgary at the time that he was talking about. The story Pegg was telling, that a Texas Gulf employee authorized to handle their documents had handed him documents, assisted Leitch's case against Texas Gulf. At the trial, discovery was, of course, proved by the cross-examination. But I called the man who was supposed to have been up the ladder and was able to prove by the records as well as his oral testimony that he hadn't even been in Calgary at the time that Pegg was there. And, while it was not a crucial point, it was a very clear, flat demonstration of Pegg lying.

One of the other aspects of Pegg's participation was that it turned out in my cross-examination that he had a contract as exploration director of Leitch Gold Mines under which he got 5 percent of the value of anything he found. Of course, I said to him, "If Leitch succeeds in

its claim of $500 million, you will become enti-
tled to $25 million." He hesitated and said he
guessed that was right. That in itself wasn't
enough as to be a killer of credibility, but it was
part of the pile of stuff that I was able to get out
of Pegg, and I knew that if Gale had made a
finding of credibility against Pegg, the case was
over. You could forget all the flight data and the
little mistakes that at one time or another had
been made. That turned out to be true.

After reading the judgment of the Chief Justice with some care, I agree
with Arnup's analysis. A lot of expensive expert testimony was ignored
once the Chief Justice made the decision that the agreement was not as
described by Pegg but rather by Dr. Holyk, whose evidence he preferred.

In the Chief Justice's view, there were two critical meetings between
Holyk and Pegg. The first was at the Royal York Hotel in Toronto on
March 11, 1963, when they met during a prospectors' convention and
worked out the basic outline of the contract that was back-dated to
February 1. The Chief Justice found that the two men were the only ones
to deal on behalf of their respective companies, and they had full authority to bind those companies. It was there that Holyk, with the critical
map before him, stated that Texas Gulf would be willing to deliver data
with respect to any area shown on the map with the exception of area 4.
The Chief Justice had already determined that Texas Gulf was highly
intrigued by the economic prospects of Kidd 55 and was in the process
of acquiring options from the owners of the land to purchase the fee
simple. Holyk and his staff were not prepared to reveal to anyone how
highly they regarded the properties for fear of jeopardizing these negotiations. It was conceded that Kidd 55 was wholly within area 4 on the
map. The Chief Justice "accepted unreservedly the evidence of Dr. Holyk
as to what occurred at the meeting at the hotel on March 11th."

This was pretty well the ball game. However, for completeness I
should refer to the meeting that Arnup recollected in his conversation
with me because it was part of the assessment of Pegg's credibility made
by the Chief Justice. The reader will recall that Robinette had relied on

the delivery to Pegg by Texas Gulf of flight data from Prosser Geary as evidence that Leitch was to receive all the data regardless of which land the map identified was overflown in making the aerial survey. The Chief Justice was not impressed with his evidence on this issue.

It appears that Pegg was in Calgary on May 30, 1963, to obtain the agreed-on data from the offices of Texas Gulf. By the time of his pre-trial examination for discovery and even more so at trial, he knew the importance of trying to prove that Texas Gulf had voluntarily delivered to him the reflight data of June 21, 1960, showing the Kidd 55 anomaly. In the view of the Chief Justice, he also knew that his assertion would not be effective unless he had the data delivered to him by some employee of Texas Gulf who was knowledgeable about the data and the significance of it to the contract between the parties. Such a man was George Podolsky, a Texas Gulf geophysicist who was responsible for ordering the photography for the 1960 aerial surveys. Pegg testified that he met with Podolsky and a Dr. John F. Macdougall, another Texas Gulf geophysicist who, unlike Podolsky, was totally unfamiliar with the material to be delivered.

As Arnup indicated, during his examination-for-discovery and later at trial Pegg narrated that Podolsky had personally mounted a ladder in the drafting room of Texas Gulf's Calgary office and pulled out from a high shelf, one by one, the cartons containing the envelopes on which were located the flight data (including the one relating to the reflight of June 21, 1960). He sorted those envelopes while Pegg and Dr. Macdougall looked on. Pegg told the Court that Podolsky was so slow and methodical in the process that he, Pegg, became impatient and offered assistance, which was declined. According to Pegg, Podolsky continued the slow business of sorting to the end.

In contrast, Texas Gulf's evidence, as testified to by Dr. Macdougall, was that because he was suffering from bursitis on the afternoon in question, Macdougall invited Pegg to mount the ladder to obtain the carton containing the envelopes. Pegg carried them down, and he and Pegg, not Podolsky, made the actual selection of the envelopes. Both Macdougall and Podolsky swore that Podolsky played no part in sorting of envelopes or, indeed, in handing any data to Pegg. The Chief Justice accepted the evidence of Macdougall and Podolsky and rejected that of Pegg. He made no finding whether Podolsky was even there. Later in reference to this meeting, Gale stated in his findings on credibility, "Even if Mr. Podolsky sorted the material in Calgary, there is no evidence that he consciously or deliberately handed over data relating to area 4 or to Kidd 55. Indeed all of the evidence on that point is to the contrary."

The Chief Justice's conclusion on the importance of Holyk's map was critical. He said, "I have no difficulty in believing that Mr. Pegg did not regard the map as a mere index, but rather he accepted it as being an important and decisive part of the agreement. That which occurred during the actual negotiation reinforces that conclusion."

Robinette summed up his feelings about the case in his oral history in response to the following questions:

Q. When you first were retained by Holden, Murdoch did you give an opinion as to whether they had a law suit, or were you just retained on the fact that you were going to go to trial?

A. Oh, definitely. I never gave an opinion.

Q. What were your feelings about your chances, when you saw the original case?

A. Well, I thought it was reasonably good. Provided our main witness stood up, and he didn't.

Q. This is Charlie Pegg?

A. Nice fellow. But he said some things in court that we had never heard of.

Q. Such as?

A. Well, I can't recall immediately what it was. All I know is, I can't recall the detail, but both Robinson

[Sr.] and I were disappointed in his performance and his cross-examination by John Arnup. And that was what really destroyed our case. It was a very narrow question as to the location [of Kidd 55]. I can't possibly carry all those things in my mind. All I can remember is that — Charlie was a prospector and he wasn't really articulate. He didn't think fast. On the other hand, Texas Gulf had a geologist [Holyk] from the United States who was one of the outstanding authorities on this and he was very good, very articulate.

The Chief Justice concluded his findings on the critical issue whether there was any ambiguity in the agreement of February 1, 1963, by holding: there was no patent or latent ambiguity in the contract; if there was a latent ambiguity, it must be resolved in favour of Texas Gulf; there was no equivocation in the contract; and if there was equivocation, it was to be resolved in favour of Texas Gulf. The contract, together with the map, was unambiguous and definitive of the rights of the parties. These findings, he said, meant that Texas Gulf did not hold the Kidd Creek Mine as constructive trustee for Leitch Gold Mines and Leitch was not entitled to damages as alternative relief.

While this was the substance of the case, the Chief Justice was also obliged to deal with several ancillary claims for damages arising out of other breaches of the agreement of February 1, 1963. The first related to the allegation that Texas Gulf had withheld data on anomalies Kidd 63 and Kidd 64, which were located within the area marked on the map as area 3. Although this information should have been delivered because it was within an area marked on the map, there was no evidence led at trial that the two anomalies had any economic value.

Along the same lines, Leitch alleged that by acquiring options and staking claims within area 3 without first obtaining Leitch's permission, Texas Gulf had violated its covenant not to carry on any further activities of this nature. In fact, and as found by the Chief Justice, Texas Gulf did further aerial photography to substitute for early photographs that had not turned out well. Once again the problem for Leitch was that there were no damages shown. A final argument, which Leitch again won on liability and lost on damages, related to Texas Gulf acquiring patented lands within area 3.

The Chief Justice solved these problems by ordering a reference to the Master at Toronto and directing him to ascertain the loss, if any, sustained by Leitch as a result of the breaches of contract committed by Texas Gulf in:

(a) wrongly withholding survey data and reports which ought to have been delivered to the plaintiff [Leitch] under clause 1 of the contract; and

(b) wrongly acquiring other land in portions of the surveyed areas without first seeking the plaintiff's consent contrary to the second part of the second paragraph of clause 5 of the agreement and contrary to clause 10 of the agreement.

These victories may appear as small beer in the contest for the Kidd mine, but they did accomplish something significant in dollar amounts. According to the oral history of Robinette, Texas Gulf was anxious to put this whole contest behind them. When Leitch announced that it was not appealing the judgment of Chief Justice Gale, the solicitors for Texas Gulf — Osler, Hoskin and Harcourt — entered into negotiations with Holden, Murdoch, and the two firms agreed to settle all outstanding issues including the payment of costs awarded to Texas Gulf. It was Robinette's understanding that the parties essentially agreed that the quantum of the costs award would be treated as equal to the damage award that was to be determined by the Master.

Robinette's decision that Leitch could not win an appeal on the substantive issue of who owned the Kidd Creek Mine was not a difficult one. As he said in his oral history, the case essentially turned on its facts. Appeal courts show great deference to findings of fact by trial judges, especially ones that involve assessments of credibility, and Chief Justice Gale was highly respected as a trial judge. I have read better judgments of his than this one, but certainly he went to great pains to hammer home the point that all data related to the lands within area 4 on Dr.

Holyk's map were excluded from Texas Gulf's commitments to Leitch under the agreement.

Speculators hoped for a "dead cat bounce" in the stock market price of Leitch from the fact of an appeal itself, but neither Robinette nor Leitch were interested in this. They were satisfied that the fight for the ownership of the Kidd Creek Mine was lost.

I ended my interview with David Brown by asking him what he thought of the performances of the leading civil lawyers whom he had the privilege of watching in action over a lengthy trial. His answer was insightful:

> Their styles were totally different. It took me practising law probably for twenty years to understand the differences and to recollect what they were. Mr. Arnup was very, very precise in his questioning, and he would ask a question that would admit of only one answer. We saw a number of times that his line of questioning would miss a point that we knew that our witness was vulnerable on from our point of view because he was so precise in his questioning.
>
> Mr. Robinette would ask questions, and even we sometimes didn't know what answer he was looking for, and we had, for the most part, written the questions for him. But he would ask very general questions and he tended to elicit from witnesses far more information than we thought Mr. Arnup did. It was quite a contrast watching the two of them.
>
> They also, the two of them, knew one another so well. I remember lamenting shortly after the case was over that I didn't think I had learned much about civil procedure because civil procedure was never an issue. Mr. Robinette never pushed Mr. Arnup beyond the Rules, and so we didn't get many arguments about hearsay or leading questions or any of the rules of evidence because they both knew them so well; they didn't attempt to test the boundaries.

So titan met titan and Arnup prevailed. It is bad enough to be saddled with a highly technical case that goes on forever, but it is most discouraging to lose when your principal witness disappoints your expectations. But this is what civil litigation is all about. Most of it is hard work and drudgery highlighted by moments of panic and leavened by occasional sparks of humour. At the end of the day you ask yourself if you would have done anything different, but whatever the answer, you turn to another file.

Chapter Fourteen
Still Cutting the Mustard

O N FEBRUARY 15, 1980, JOHN Robinette was about to argue an appeal in the Ontario Court of Appeal from a trial judgment of what was probably the most complicated criminal case ever heard in Canada. He was seventy-three years of age. The argument would consume forty-four court days, ending on April 16, 1980. The five-man panel of the court, composed of Justices Martin, Lacourcière, Houlden, Weatherstone, and Goodman, would reserve on the matter until January 15, 1981, when the Court would deliver the longest judgment in its storied history, filling 347 pages in the published report.[171]

I was very familiar with the case, having acted as counsel for two of the original accused — one an individual and one a corporation — during eighteen months of preliminary hearing and 197 days of the trial, which was presided over by William Parker, the Associate Chief Justice of the High Court. The trial spanned more than fourteen months, beginning March 1, 1978, and ending May 5, 1979. The case was officially known as *The Queen v. McNamara* but was universally referred to as the "Dredging Case."

The prosecution arose from the Crown's allegation of a long-standing conspiracy among the dredging companies of Canada to defraud municipal, provincial, and federal governments or their agencies by agreeing to whom and at what price bids would be awarded in the dredging industry. The alleged mechanics of the "bid rigging" were straightforward enough. The Crown maintained that three men were responsible for the rigging of the bids: Albin Louis Quinlan of McNamara Corporation, Robert Joseph

Schneider of Canadian Dredge and Dock Limited, and Horace Grant Rindress of J.P. Porter Company Limited. When public agencies would call for sealed tenders to be submitted in relation to dredging and marine construction projects in Canada, these three men would decide which of the companies covered by the conspiracy would be awarded the contract and adjust the tender prices accordingly.

The "unsuccessful bidders" would be offered some compensation by the proposed low bidder in exchange for submitting an artificially high bid or not bidding at all. This compensation could involve cash payment,[172] a subcontract on the project, or an agreement that a particular bidder would be awarded the next contract. The Crown maintained that the cost estimates of the successful bidder included the compensation paid to obtain this co-operation. The public agency was thus paying a higher price for the work than it would have paid if the job had been bid on competitively.

Seven counts of such bid rigging over a period of eight years were involved in this case. The formal charge was conspiracy to defraud named governments and public agencies. The corporate accused that were convicted after the lengthy trial were the companies represented by Quinlan, Schneider, and Rindress, namely McNamara Corporation, Canadian Dredge and Dock, and J.P. Porter. Also convicted were Pitts Engineering Construction Limited, C.A. Pitts General Contractors Limited, Richelieu Dredging Corporation Inc., Sceptre Dredging Limited, and Marine Industries. The individual accused convicted at trial had all been associated with these corporations in various capacities during the years at issue. Harold McNamara was president and chairman of McNamara Corporation. Jean Simard was a director of Marine Industries and vice-president of J.P. Porter, of which Richelieu Dredging was a subsidiary. Sydney Cooper was the majority shareholder and president of Pitt Engineering, of which C.A. Pitts Ltd. was a subsidiary. Frank Hamata was president and Albert Gill was vice-president of Sceptre Dredging. There were other corporations and individuals named in the indictment (including the two for whom I acted), but they were not convicted at trial and were not appellants in the appeal.

The thirteen accused, both individual and corporate, appealed their convictions on charges of conspiracy to defraud. Lorne Morphy, Q.C., assisted by Charles F. Scott, had acted for Jean Simard throughout the preliminary hearing and the trial. Simard had been sentenced to three years in penitentiary on three counts of conspiracy to defraud arising out of his conduct of various corporate offices involving Marine Industries, J.P. Porter, and Richelieu Dredging. Simard was the scion of a distinguished Quebec family who had built a considerable industrial establishment based in Quebec with interests in marine construction, real estate, lumber, a trust company, and, of course, dredging. On receiving instructions to appeal these convictions, Morphy decided, in the words of Charles Scott, "that it was a good idea to bring a fresh pair of eyes to the case." He and Scott sought out Robinette to review the material and to act on the appeal.[173]

I was apprehensive when I heard of this request to Robinette. Having lived through so much of the case, I was concerned that it would be simply too much for him at his age. Frankly, I was afraid that he might embarrass himself, a fate I had seen befall truly distinguished counsel who had stayed on after they lacked the energy and powers of concentration that had been their strengths in earlier days. Happily, I kept my mouth shut and was to be reminded, again, that I had underestimated the old master.

There were certain issues common to all the appeals. The overarching complaint was that the Crown had overburdened the case to an unmanageable degree by charging twenty accused on seven counts in the indictment and by introducing similar act evidence to show a variety of continuing conspiracies to rig harbour dredging contracts throughout Canada over a period of fifty years. The specific grounds of appeal included the following issues: (1) whether the trial judge failed to address the problem of overburdening by refusing to sever the various counts; (2) whether a special "accomplice evidence" warning was required for the jury with respect to Quinlan, Schneider, and Rindress, the three Crown witnesses who had been granted immunity from prosecution in return for their testimony; (3) whether the trial judge should have given effect to the defence objections to the evidence purporting to serve as corroboration of the accomplice evidence; (4) whether evidence of other alleged bid riggings led by the Crown was valid similar fact evidence; and (5) whether a corporation could be convicted of a criminal offence because of the conduct of its officers or directors, the so-called directing minds of the corporations.

There were additional separate issues in the cases of individual appellants, but I am concerned only about the grounds of appeal relating to Simard. Robinette not only embraced and, indeed, forcibly argued the general issues of overburdening the case and misusing similar act evidence, he also made much of a strange brand of character evidence that the Crown sprang on Simard during cross-examination.

As mentioned, Simard's family owned a number of companies in Quebec. He and his brother, Arthur Simard, held various positions in these companies. In particular, Jean Simard was an officer and director of J.P. Porter. One of the principal Crown witnesses, the admitted accomplice Rindress, was president of that company, and he testified concerning his bid-rigging activities. He also testified that he reported to Jean Simard and that Simard was aware of, and authorized, bid rigging of dredging contracts. The trial judge gave the jury the standard accomplice warning with respect to Rindress's evidence: he told them that it was dangerous to convict an accused on the evidence of an accomplice unless there is independent evidence implicating the accused in the criminal conspiracy with which he is charged. The trial judge then left numerous pieces of evidence with the jury that he described as capable of corroborating Rindress's testimony.

One item that the trial judge referred to several times as corroborative evidence was a transaction involving the sale of the Marine Building, which was owned by one of the Simard family companies, the Marine Building Company. Evidence concerning this building arose during the cross-examination of Jean Simard. As the Court of Appeal held,[174] his evidence was to the effect that the building had been sold in 1971 for $2,500,000. However, the deed and the records of the Marine Building Company indicated that the sale price was $2,000,000 rather than the real price of $2,500,000. The difference of $500,000 was deposited initially in an account in Bermuda in the purchaser's name. The funds were then transferred to an account in the name of Jean and/or Leon Simard, another brother of Jean Simard. Members of the Simard family eventually received these funds, less a real estate commission. Jean Simard admitted that the tax authorities subsequently reassessed him and his fellow directors with respect to this transaction. The Marine Building Company, which had owned the building, and Leon Simard were each charged with tax evasion and pleaded guilty.

Both Jean Simard and his brother Arthur were cross-examined extensively with respect to this transaction involving the Marine Building Company, a company of which they were both shareholders and directors. Jean Simard's trial counsel strenuously objected to this line of questioning on the basis that whatever its legality, the transaction was not an act in furtherance of the conspiracy alleged and was accordingly irrelevant and could only have the effect of making Jean Simard appear to be a person of bad character. However, the trial judge permitted the Crown to explore the matter. Jean Simard admitted knowing about the transaction, but testified that he had left the details to others. He denied knowledge of bid rigging in the dredging industry and testified that the family practice was to choose good management for their companies, such as J.P. Porter, who were then left to run the companies. He referred to them as "trusted lieutenants."

The admissibility of this evidence under the rubric of evidence capable of corroborating Rindress's testimony was vital to the credibility of Jean Simard. At the end of the case, the only live issue was not whether there was a conspiracy to rig bids, but whether Jean Simard was a participant in the conspiracy. In that regard, the only direct evidence implicating Jean Simard was the testimony of the accomplice Rindress.

As the Court of Appeal put it,[175] one of the dangers of convicting on accomplice evidence that is not corroborated by independent evidence is that since the accomplice is admittedly guilty of the crime, and since he is therefore able to truthfully relate its details, his ability to do so may lend a false plausibility to the critical part of his story that the accused authorized or condoned his offence. Accordingly, it was of the utmost importance in this case that the jury be clearly instructed that, in order for the evidence to be capable of corroborating Rindress in relation to Jean Simard, it must be independent evidence that showed or tended to show that Simard was a participant in the conspiracies charged. Robinette argued that in this case, many of the items of evidence left with the jury as capable of being corroborative did not in fact have that quality.

It was Morphy's and Scott's position at trial that where the trial judge left numerous items to the jury as capable of being corroborative of the only real issue — namely, Jean Simard's participation in the conspiracy to defraud government agencies — there was a danger that the jury would rely on items that were not capable of being corroborative on that vital issue. Further, they argued, where a group of items were cumulatively capable of constituting corroboration, they should be left to the jury as a package and not simply listed individually, as was done in this case.

Robinette was well aware that the appeal he was arguing had a built-in obstruction to success in the fact of its immense size and overall complexity. An overburdened trial record not only presents a formidable impediment to the jury's ability to understand the underlying issues, its very mass discourages appellate courts from setting aside the verdicts arrived at by the jury. This is not to suggest that the Court was not up to the task of hearing and digesting the material before it. Two of the members of this panel, Martin and Houlden, were workaholics, and the rest did not shirk the responsibilities of their office. The burden to the administration of justice and the cost to the accused become significant factors when deciding if errors by the trial judge in his evidentiary rulings or in his instructions to the jury on the relevant law are sufficiently important to satisfy the appeal court that there has been a substantial wrong or miscarriage of justice such that it is obliged to set aside any of the convictions.

It was because of the complexity of the case that Morphy wanted to retain Robinette. He had the reputation of a counsel who could manage difficult cases and prevent the Court from becoming buried in the facts. At the same time, he could make those facts appealing or at least understandable to the appellate court, which had not lived with the case through months and months of preliminary hearing and trial, unlike Morphy and Scott.

I interviewed Charles Scott about this case in my chambers at Osgoode Hall. He was kind enough to resurrect his old notes of the proceedings in the Court of Appeal and beyond. He had been a very young lawyer[176] when he first went with Lorne Morphy to see Robinette. He can still remember how overwhelmed he was at meeting the man who was then the unquestioned doyen of the bar. His own words tell it best:

It was a very daunting experience for me to work with John Robinette. He had, at the time, a towering reputation. He was regarded universally as a gentleman and as the premier counsel of the Canadian bar and here I was trying to work with him on this enormously complex case. I was a very young lawyer at the time with a very daunting proposition. Throughout the whole piece, he treated me with much more respect than I was due. He treated me with politeness; we worked through problems together. It was just from every sort of aspect a really satisfying experience and a tremendous – not introduction, because I had worked with some great lawyers; I had worked with Charles Dubin, I had worked with Lorne Morphy. It was a tremendous way of letting me know how a really great lawyer dealt with young people in the profession.

We worked really hard on that appeal and we spent a lot of time together. Your former partner, Doug Laidlaw, told me – and I have no reason to doubt it – that I spent more time with John Robinette as a result of that experience than he had through his entire career in actually working on cases. I guess that's true. Doug would know. But it was an extraordinary thing. I felt myself to be in a really very, very privileged situation to be able to do that.[177]

Douglas K. Laidlaw, Q.C., was one of the trial counsel in the Dredging Case. He acted for Canadian Dredge and Dock and for Hugh Martin, the Chairman of the Board and principal shareholder of that company. Martin was acquitted at trial, but Laidlaw continued to act for Canadian Dredge and Dock throughout the appeal process. He was unsuccessful in persuading either the Court of Appeal or the Supreme Court of Canada that his corporate client should not have been convicted because of the self-proclaimed bid-rigging activities of its operating head, the accomplice Schneider. Doug was also my fast friend and partner at McCarthy & McCarthy. He died all too soon from an automobile accident in August 1984.

This appeal was important to Robinette. He did not need to know about my doubts as to his continued ability to operate at a high level over a sustained period of time. He was hearing the footsteps of time and had his own doubts about himself. At the time I was puzzled as to why a counsel with his long and distinguished record of achievement, which even then was unmatched, would not step back and smell the roses for the rest of his life. However, now that I myself am a septuagenarian, I can understand his reluctance to stop competing in the forensic arena. His health was good and his mind alert. He wanted to keep working because he knew of nothing else he could do.

Morphy and Scott met with Robinette on June 5, 1979, and discussed the case. He agreed to take the appeal, and young Scott was assigned to look after his detailed briefing. As Scott put it, "I did a first cut of the facts," and Robinette initially concentrated on the law. However, as Scott submitted his summaries of the facts, Robinette became more and more involved with them. Scott remembers that he commented on the drafts and "toning up the advocacy in them." This partnership of ideas ultimately produced a factum of 259 pages. On the law, that area in which Robinette brought "his peculiar and enormous talents to bear," the product was sixty-five pages in length. Scott continued in his interview:

> I remember spending a good deal of time with him. I remember one afternoon I went up to see him at his house and I brought my son with me. My son, I think, was maybe three or four, and I just left him in the car for a moment and was going to drop something off at Robinette's house on Glenayr. However, Mrs. Robinette looked around me at the door and saw there was a little person in the car. She immediately brought him in, and he played quietly with some toys that she brought out of a drawer in the cabinet in their living room. Just a little vignette about what a warm individual both he and his wife were through all of that.

While Robinette argued in his factum and in his oral submissions to the Court all of the issues set out in the notice of appeal, in the final analysis he was successful on the Crown's misuse of character evidence as evidence capable of being corroborative. In Jean Simard's case, two items were improperly left to the jury as capable of being corroborative that were seriously prejudicial to the accused. One of these items was the admission that the accused knew a certain senator. This admission was described by the trial judge as capable of corroborating Rindress's evidence that Jean Simard knew that Rindress had negotiated a political payoff with this senator in order to facilitate an adjustment of the specifications of a dredging contract between J.P. Porter and the Government of Canada.

The other item improperly left with the jury was the Marine Building transaction. The Crown had argued that evidence of this transaction was admissible to rebut Jean Simard's evidence of his good character and was relevant with respect to his credibility. It was also argued, and the argument is so tenuous as to defy logic, that the fact that this transaction (which was directed to tax evasion) did not appear in the books of J.P. Porter was consistent with the absence of records about bid rigging in the same books and thus supported the Crown's theory that the Simard family had delegated the dirty work of conducting a variety of illegal activities "off the books."

Robinette submitted that the fact that the accused had left the illegal details of the Building Company transaction to his trusted subordinates did not tend to prove that the accused had given Rindress a mandate to rig bids in the dredging industry unless it was thought that because of his character or disposition, he was likely to have done so. But using the evidence in this manner would violate a fundamental principle of the law of evidence: the Crown is not permitted to introduce evidence of offences other than the one for which the accused is charged for the purpose of showing that the accused is the type of person who would commit the type of offence on which he stood charged.

In argument, Robinette contended that the cross-examination of both Jean and Arthur Simard regarding the Marine Building transaction violated the general rule that the Crown may not initially introduce evidence showing that the accused is a person of bad character and that the cross-examination could not be justified under any of the exceptions to this general rule. Robinette's first problem was that the trial judge had ruled that Jean and Arthur had put in issue both their personal characters and that of the corporations they controlled in the course of their own testimony under the guidance of Morphy. Consequently, the cross-examination was proper even though it incidentally reflected on their character. In effect, the trial judge ruled that their combined testimony placed the character of the entire business interests of the Simard family in issue because they both testified that they delegated the day-to-day operations to such trusted lieutenants as Rindress.

Character evidence is a touchy subject for defence counsel to handle. It is well accepted that in calling the accused to testify, defence counsel is entitled to ask introductory questions about his place of residence, marital status, and his employment without thereby putting the accused's character in issue. However, to go beyond that places the accused in jeopardy of exposing his whole life to cross-examination by the Crown. The results can be devastating to the defence because while the trial judge is duty bound to instruct the jury that it may use evidence of the accused's bad character only to test his credibility as a witness in this trial, the jury will take the view that the accused is an unsavoury person and one likely to have committed the crime with which he is presently charged.

In this case, Robinette argued forcefully that Morphy's questions of Simard were not made with a view to establishing that he was a man of good character, but rather constituted a denial of the allegations made against him. Robinette further contended that it was an essential part of Simard's defence that his role as overseer of the Simard family investments involved his being a director of numerous public and other companies and that he was removed from the day-to-day operation of the various Simard companies. As for the Crown's cross-examination of Simard on the Marine Building transaction, Robinette argued that it could not be justified on the basis that it directly proved that Jean had lied in his examination-in-chief since he had not testified to this transaction in response to questions from his counsel.

The Court in its reason was inclined to accept the validity of the last argument that the cross-examination did not contradict what Simard said in chief. However, the Court accepted the Crown's more general argument that Simard had put his character in issue by testifying that he conducted his business in an ethical manner and the cross-examination on the Marine Building transaction was admissible as being directed to establish that this assertion was not true. The Crown's questioning thus went to his credibility as a witness and to his denial that he had any knowledge of bid rigging.

This, however, was not the end of the matter. The Crown was not content to rely on the Marine Building transaction solely for the purpose of testing Jean Simard's credibility as a witness. This unwillingness arose from the limiting instruction that inevitably goes with the admissibility of such evidence: it is not to be used to demonstrate a propensity to commit crimes. The Crown wanted the jury to be told that this evidence *was* admissible to show propensity on the basis that it was evidence of similar acts, that is, evidence that would tend to show a pattern or scheme of illegal business transactions by Simard. The Crown persuaded the trial judge that such an instruction was proper, and thus the trial judge told the jury that because Simard had left to trusted lieutenants the details of the illegal Marine Building transaction, it was open to them to find that he was also aware of the bid rigging and was content to leave the details of carrying out these illegal activities to Rindress.

The Crown overreached by insisting on this instruction. The Court of Appeal reversed the trial judge on this portion of his charge to the jury. It held that he misdirected the jury on the use that could be made of the Marine Building evidence. While the evidence had a bearing on the general credibility of Simard, it had no other probative value in its own right, and it could not be used to show that he was likely from his character to have committed the offence. As the Court explained, there was no underlying unity or striking similarity between the Marine Building transaction and the counts charged in the indictment so as to make this evidence admissible as similar fact evidence and therefore probative of guilt. Thus, while the trial judge properly directed the jury that the evidence was relevant to Jean Simard's credibility and to his denial of knowledge of bid rigging, he erred in directing the jury that it was also relevant to show how Simard and his family ran their businesses and whether or not Rindress had a mandate to run J.P. Porter as he did. The Building Company transaction was only probative of guilt in the sense that it rebutted the inference that J.P. Porter's books did not reflect bid rigging, and it also confirmed that Simard and his family left the running of the companies to trusted subordinates. However, this latter fact was not in issue and did not prove that the accused gave Rindress a mandate to rig bids other than by the forbidden reasoning that Jean Simard was likely from his character to have done so.

The Court further held that in view of the importance attached to this evidence during the trial and in the charge to the jury, it could not be said that no substantial wrong or miscarriage of justice resulted. While there was other evidence that was capable of being corroborative, this evidence was not so cogent or compelling as to inevitably require a finding of guilt. Moreover, with respect to some of this evidence, the trial judge did not adequately instruct the jury as to the inferences they would be required to draw for some of the items to be corroborative.

The Court then concluded that while the Marine Building evidence was admissible, in view of this misdirection and the serious misdirection in also leaving this evidence (and certain other evidence) as capable of corroborating the accomplice Rindress, Jean Simard's convictions must be set aside and a new trial ordered.

Robinette was not the only counsel to achieve success on this appeal. The appeals of Frank Hamata, Albert Gill, and Sceptre Dredging were allowed, their convictions were quashed, and a new trial was ordered. Marine Industries was successful with respect to one count, count seven. That conviction was quashed and a new trial was ordered.

Robinette had reason to be pleased with the result of this appeal. He had once again performed well in a difficult case. I asked Lloyd Houlden, the only survivor from the panel and now retired from the court, about Robinette's performance on the appeal. He told me that when he first got to his feet to speak he was a little uncertain as to the criminal law, which he had been away from for some time, but he became more assured as the argument developed and he was "brilliant" in reply. In fact, said Houlden, he won the case in reply.

In my interview with Scott, I reminded him of Robinette's age and asked him if this affected his presentation in any way. He said:

> He clearly wasn't a young man. I recall we'd be walking
> up to court, we'd walk back and forth from the court to

the gowning rooms, or we'd be at lunch, and he moved with a stateliness and a dignity. He was a big man. He was an imposing figure physically but he moved with grace. Through the eyes of a young lawyer and obviously a big fan, it seemed he carried that physical grace through to the way he dealt with the court and the way he dealt with other people. He wasn't a pussycat; he didn't allow people to get away with things, particularly people he thought were not dealing the way the case ought to be dealt with. He was capable of anger; he was capable of emotion; he was capable of being forceful, but it was always done with a grace and a style that kind of reflected the way that he carried himself.

Mindful of my own conversation with Robinette about his personal relations with the senior Crown, Rod McLeod, I asked Scott how Robinette got on with McLeod. Scott could not recall that he expressed any irritation with McLeod personally, but he was critical of the manner in which the case had been put in by the Crown. As Robinette's preparation of the appeal proceeded and his knowledge of it increased, he became more and more partisan. Scott said:

When we first went over and spoke to Mr. Robinette, we had come off a long trial. As you recall from the trial, there had been motions and conflicts, and there had been eighteen months of pretty hard, tough sledding. And, I think at the start, when we started to try to explain some of the atmosphere of the trial and what had gone on to Mr. Robinette, he didn't disbelieve it, but I think he took it all with a grain of salt and sort of took it in but didn't immediately buy into the theory we were trying to develop with him about how there had been too much gone on and too much in favour of the Crown in the case.

I'm not sure whether he invented the word or somebody else did, but he came to firmly believe that the case had been overburdened. And I think that he was quite disappointed in the way that the case had been led as to how much extraneous evidence there was, as to how much inadmissible evidence there was, how much of this evidence not only had been led in front of the jury but had been reinforced by the Crown and, indeed, by the trial judge as part of his charge to the jury and that this was not as good a trial as the province was able to provide. And I think he came to believe that this was a trial that ought to have been, in effect, the trial of the century. The defendants had lots of money; the Crown was well prepared; the Crown had spent a huge amount of money on it; there were fabulous lawyers involved; it had taken a long time. It wasn't just a pure advocacy point he was making on behalf of the client. He was disappointed at the way the system had operated, and he brought the force of his learning and his stature and his personality and his reputation to bear to try and make that point with the court. It was a very interesting thing to see develop in him, and it was a powerful, powerful weapon when he came to make the argument before the court.

Apparently his indignation continued to grow as the Crown asked the Supreme Court of Canada for leave to appeal to that court. By this time Robinette was fully in charge of the case and had reduced Simard's factum as a respondent in the leave application to ten pages. In addition to the Crown's request for leave, those appellants who had failed to obtain any relief in the Court of Appeal also asked for leave to appeal to the highest court.

The hearing of all the applications was by way of oral argument and started on April 5, 1981, before Chief Justice Bora Laskin and Justices Brian Dickson and Anthony Lamer. It ran into a second day before Robinette was reached. He was the last or at least second last to be heard. Scott described him as "a tower" at the Supreme Court of Canada. He had sat through the best part of a day listening to the Crown's arguments and had become "visibly upset with some of the submissions the

Crown was making and, by the time he stood up, he was, so far as John Robinette became, pretty darned angry about the whole thing, and he was very forceful." Scott shared his notes of the hearing:

> The court was Chief Justice Laskin, to-become Chief Justice Dickson and to-become Chief Justice Lamer, so he wasn't dealing with second-stringers up there, he was dealing with the first string, and he was very direct with them. At one point, he made the comment to them that some of the directions that the trial judge had made in respect of an issue of collaboration were so wrong as to be funny almost. He was that dismissive of some of the things that had gone on at the trial. Towards the end of his submissions, he said that some of the submissions the Crown had made just before him that he was responding to had been "an utter *red herring*," and his summary to the Supreme Court of Canada was that the Crown's application for leave was so devoid of merit that it raised "no serious point of law." It was as if he was, as I guess a lot of the good lawyers have seen him do, vouching personally for that proposition, and, coming from John Robinette, it carried enormous strength and enormous weight, and the Supreme Court of Canada dismissed the application for leave entirely. So it was a *tour de force*.

The Crown's application was indeed dismissed, but four of the corporate applicants were successful in persuading the Supreme Court to look at the issue of the criminal liability of a corporation when liability is based on the misconduct of a directing mind of the corporation. The successful corporations were Canadian Dredge and Dock, Marine Industries, J.P. Porter, and Richelieu Dredging Corporation.

Winning a new trial in the Court of Appeal is very much a mixed blessing for counsel, especially when he can look forward with considerable trepidation to another lengthy trial. However, the victory was to be complete. There was a change of government at Queen's Park and the new attorney general, Ian Scott, decided that the Crown had expended enough of its resources on this case and announced that in the exercise of his prosecutorial discretion, there would not be a new trial. Following this announcement, Edward Then, Q.C., now Justice Then of the Superior Court of Justice, who had assisted Rod McLeod during the trial and appeals, issued a number of documents as agent for the Attorney General of Ontario. On September 19, 1985, he directed the clerk of the court to stay the proceedings pursuant to the relevant provisions of the *Criminal Code* with respect to, *inter alia*, Jean Simard on counts three, four, and six. The prosecution thus ended in vindication for Jean Simard and for those others who had been awarded new trials. I am sure they received some sombre satisfaction in noting that when all the dust was cleared the Crown had not done very well in its prosecution of the alleged massive conspiracy.

I cannot leave this matter without commenting on Robinette's statement of account delivered shortly after the hearing in the Court of Appeal but before the decision was handed down. It described in foreshortened language his conferences with Simard and with Morphy and Scott, meetings with other counsel arguing the appeal, and a brief reference to reading authorities, revisions of the factum, and to preparation generally (which we know from Scott was extensive), followed by his attendance in the Court of Appeal for forty-two days (his figure). The total amount of the bill was $150,000, which works out to a little over $3,500 per appellate court day exclusive of all preparation and preappeal conferences. It was a substantial bill for the 1980s, but modest considering the seniority and stature of counsel and the importance of the matter to the client. It became more of a bargain when the degree of success achieved became known.

But what intrigued me with Robinette's accounts and covering letters were the little things. They were an art form unto themselves. Here he had been instructed by Morphy to send the account to the Simard corporate solicitors in Montreal. This he did, but he was careful to add a paragraph in his letter to the Tory firm where Morphy and Scott practised confirming these arrangements, and of course he sent a copy to Montreal. The letter included the paragraph, "Once again may I express my deep gratitude both to Mr. Morphy and Mr.

Scott for their invaluable assistance in connection with the presentation of Mr. Simard's appeal." This had the Robinette touch. He had been retained by Morphy but was being paid by the firm that represented the Simard family interests. Morphy and Scott were actively involved in the preparation of the appeal, and Morphy at least participated in the argument. They would have a substantial account themselves, if they had not already submitted one. This letter validated their contribution and kept the door open for future referrals.

By way of a postscript for this chapter, to show how far I had miscalculated Robinette's "best before date," in April 1983, when he was aged seventy-six, he appeared in a lengthy and complex jury case in Halifax. He acted as counsel for a Nova Scotia businessman, Charles MacFadden, who along with James Simpson and Senator Irvine Barrow was accused of conspiracy to present themselves as having or pretending to have influence with the Government of Nova Scotia. The trial took five weeks. Austin Cooper, Q.C., a friend and former classmate of mine who restricted his practice to criminal law from the outset of his long and spectacular career, acted for Senator Barrow. In a recent interview[178] he expressed surprise that Robinette was seventy-six at the time of that trial. He said he was the Robinette he had always known. He "hopped" on the plane from Toronto to Halifax every Sunday evening during the weeks of the trial and "hopped" back on the plane from Halifax to Toronto on the Friday of that week. Cooper noted that he always travelled economy class. "He didn't act like he was seventy-six. He appeared vigorous, with it, self-contained. An active, effective counsel." As Cooper pointed out, jury trials are an enervating experience. Counsel can never relax. Robinette did not appear to suffer from any particular strain during this experience. As to the result, Simpson pleaded guilty, and MacFadden and Barrow were convicted by the jury and fined by the trial judge. Barrow alone appealed to the Court of Appeal and again to the Supreme Court of Canada, where he was rewarded with a new trial. Barrow was acquitted by a jury at his second trial.

Chapter Fifteen
Counsel to Canada

A COUNSEL BECOMES RECOGNIZED BY his peers in a slow and uncertain way, but once his name consistently appears as representing the Government of Canada in constitutional cases, it is clear to all that he has arrived. The federal Department of Justice has its own lawyers who are highly skilled in the constitutional arena. They must be constantly vigilant in this area of the law to ensure that the provinces have not encroached on federal heads of power. These lawyers handle the majority of constitutional cases. However, when a matter of particular significance or political sensitivity arises, the department is not averse to retaining counsel from the private bar. During the period covered by this memoir, those counsel from Ontario were Norman Tilley, Cyril Carson, and John Robinette.

The introduction of the *Canadian Charter of Rights and Freedoms* in 1982 (and I will deal with this process in some detail later) has obscured the importance of the division of powers enumerated in the *British North America Act* of 1867. This statute of the Parliament of the United Kingdom created Canada as we now know it.[179] It is the basis of our federal system of government. The *BNA Act* controls all issues of the limits of sovereignty of the individual provinces and confers distinct powers on the Government of Canada.

The distribution of powers between the federal and provincial legislatures was always a matter of contention and often prompted litigation ultimately resolved by the Privy Council of the House of Lords until 1949 and thereafter by our own Supreme Court of Canada. The provincial governments, all of which were jealous of their individual rights, were careful to select the best counsel when these cases arose.

Robinette stressed that he did not have any political or sociological axe to grind in constitutional matters. He saw each problem under the distribution of powers created by sections 91 and 92 of the *BNA Act* as questions of statutory interpretation. He did not favour appearing for the Government of Canada as opposed to a provincial government and simply took the cases as they came along.[180]

In one of his first constitutional cases of some importance, *Brant Dairy Co. v. Ontario (Milk Commission)*,[181] he acted for the Ontario Milk Marketing Board in support of the constitutionality of the delegation of certain powers by the Milk Commission of Ontario to the Ontario Milk Marketing Board under the *Milk Act, 1965.* He lost the case in the Supreme Court, but his performance certainly impressed a young Department of Justice lawyer, T. Bradbrooke Smith (of whom we will hear more), who had intervened on behalf of the Attorney General of Canada.

Two other cases of Robinette's, which involved the same issue in different provinces, are worth noting because they decided an important point for those who seek to challenge legislation on the basis that it is unconstitutional. They are *Thorson v. Canada (Attorney General)*[182] and *Jones v. New Brunswick (Attorney General).*[183]

Joseph T. Thorson was the former president of the Exchequer Court of Canada (now the Federal Court of Canada). He decided to challenge the constitutionality of the *Official Languages Act*[184] personally. This act is the statute of Parliament that designates French and English as the official languages of Canada. Joe Thorson was very much a man with an independent streak. He had in common with a number of westerners (he came from Winnipeg and was of Icelandic stock) an opposition to governmental action that encouraged in Canada any language but English. As Robinette said of Thorson, "He was retired and he was opposed to the *Official Languages Act*. He did not favour, either politically or intellectually, making French an official language throughout Canada even so far as matters in relation to which the Federal Parliament would ordinarily have power."[185]

In impeaching the validity of a federal statute, Thorson was not deterred by the fact that he formerly held a senior judicial post in the

Government of Canada. Nor that he might embarrass his son, Donald Thorson, Q.C., who as deputy attorney general had drafted the impugned legislation.

Robinette was retained to act for the Attorney General of Canada, and Brad Smith of the Department of Justice was assigned to brief him and appear as his junior counsel. I interviewed Smith in Ottawa[186] where he now practises law in the private sector, and he turned up an interesting vignette. It appears that he was born and raised in Hamilton, and his home was located about a mile from where the torso of John Dick was found. His first knowledge of Robinette came from following his exploits in the trial of Mrs. Dick. More pertinent to his preparation to assist Robinette in a case, Smith graduated in 1956 from Dalhousie Law School and was called to the Bar of Nova Scotia in 1957. After studying overseas at the Graduate Institute of International Studies, he practised for a short time in Nova Scotia and then joined the Department of Justice in Ottawa. He was later called to the Bar of Ontario and again spent a short period in private practice before he came back to the employ of government. His career in government included working in the Advisory Section of the Department of Justice where he did some constitutional and international law work and later became director of the Constitutional and International Law Section for a period of time. He then became the assistant deputy attorney general for civil litigation, and after a short hiatus he served as chief general counsel for a year or so. He left the Department of Justice in 1988.

I bring out Smith's background in some detail because he and Robinette became good friends. As Robinette said about his experience working with Smith on the *Reference re: Anti-Inflation Act (Canada)* case:[187]

> Brad Smith was, and is, a very industrious and good lawyer. We worked together very closely, and as a result of that we became rather close friends. I have been out to his home, and I still see him when I am in Ottawa. I can recall working in his office, going through the material, considering the case. We jointly prepared the factum. I probably came back to Toronto to draft that, and we got together again and finally settled the form

of the oral argument. But it is the one case that I can
very definitely recall the close co-operation with a leading lawyer in the Department of Justice.[188]

What I take as typical of Robinette from this discussion about his
preparation of this most significant case is that he always arrived alone.
He never brought anyone with him to the table. He was content to use
whatever assistance the client or its staff made available to him. If the
assistance was excellent, as in the case of Smith, so much the better. But
if it was unsatisfactory, there was never any suggestion from Robinette
that he would like the help of someone else. I heard him complain on
occasion about how unhelpful the lawyer was who had retained him, or
how generally tiresome he could be, which was worse. However,
Robinette always ignored my obvious suggestion that he bring someone
along from McCarthy & McCarthy to act as his personal staff. This
response was characteristic whether he had been retained by the
Department of Justice or by a lawyer from a small town. The reality was
that he preferred to work alone. In later days when I was much too busy
and expensive for him to bring along for my company, as he had earlier, our only close working associations came when I acted as his junior,
as in the *Imperial Oil and Nova Scotia Power* case, or when we had com-
plementary briefs in the same case or I had been designated for some
reason to be the contact with the client.

Returning to the *Thorson* case, Robinette and Smith first moved
before Justice Lloyd Houlden, then of the High Court of Justice, to have
Thorson's action dismissed on the ground that Thorson, as a private citizen, had no status to challenge the validity of a public statute because
he was not specially affected or exceptionally prejudiced by it. The hearing was in Toronto, and Smith arrived from Ottawa on the appointed
day. He was to encounter a similar experience to mine in *Hood v. Hood*,
as I described earlier.

> I got off the train and went to the Royal York Hotel, and
> there was a note from Robinette. Something had come
> up. He couldn't appear; here were his notes. Go ahead!
> Well, of course, the notes were very good, and Thorson,

when I was riding back on the bus to the airport with him, said, "Oh, you did marvelous. You did just as well as Mr. Robinette," and I said, "Well, I had his notes!" Robinette never went off extemporaneously, yet it all seemed to flow so easily.

Smith's imitation of Robinette worked wonders before Justice Houlden, who granted the motion to dismiss. But Robinette in person could not uphold this judgment at a higher level. Ultimately, a majority of the Court, of which Fauteux was chief justice, held that a question of alleged excess of legislative power is a justiciable one, and it is open to the Court in the exercise of its discretionary power to allow a taxpayer to have such a question adjudicated in a class action. The majority ruled that Thorson's action for a declaration was in effect a class action by members of the public and should be permitted. Otherwise the *Official Languages Act* would be immune from judicial review because there was no person or class of persons particularly aggrieved by it, the Attorney General was unwilling to institute proceedings, and the Government did not direct a reference.

The *Thorson* case was to proceed on its merits, but in the meantime a lawyer named Leonard C. Jones commenced a companion action in New Brunswick. He maintained that the New Brunswick legislature had improperly implemented the *Official Languages Act* by permitting French to be an option as of right for witnesses and litigants in the New Brunswick courts. The province did this by amending its own *Evidence Act* to make the Canadian *Official Languages Act* operative in New Brunswick. A reference was directed by the New Brunswick cabinet to the Supreme Court of New Brunswick, Appeal Division, to consider five questions of law dealing with the validity and effect of official languages legislation enacted by the Parliament of Canada and by the provincial legislature. Jones was declared to be a person entitled to be heard on the reference and was joined as a party. This case came to Ottawa by way of appeal and cross-appeal from the judgment of the New Brunswick appellate court.

The reference was scheduled to proceed before the *Thorson* matter. Joe Thorson was up to the challenge of leading the attack on the legislation. He arranged to represent Jones and appeared as his counsel before the Supreme Court of Canada. I do not know how effective Thorson was as a counsel prior to his appointment to the bench, but his performance before the Supreme Court was additional proof, if more is required, that you can never go back home again. He proceeded as if he were the president of that court and not bound by any of the restrictions that apply to counsel. In short, he felt that he could go on interminably. He was entirely out of touch with the reactions of members of the Court. Where Robinette had a unique sensitivity to the body language and feedback of his audience, Thorson was oblivious even to the Court's presence. He certainly tried the patience of Chief Justice Laskin, who was doing his courteous best to move Thorson's argument along.

The kernel of the problem in the case arose out of the declaration in section 2 of the *Official Languages Act* that English and French are the official languages of Canada for all purposes of the Parliament and Government of Canada and possess and enjoy equality of status and equal rights and privileges as to their use in all the institutions of the Parliament and Government of Canada. As indicated earlier, constitutional questions before the Charter were almost invariably restricted to determining whether the power asserted by the government came within one of the enumerated heads of power in the *BNA Act*: section 91 for the Parliament of Canada, and section 92 for the legislatures of the provinces. Thorson argued that there was no enumerated head of section 91 that authorized Parliament to enact the *Official Languages Act*, and indeed it was foreclosed from doing so by other provisions of the *BNA Act*.

I am not concerned here with exploring the complex arguments advanced in the Supreme Court. Instead, I am content to refer only to that portion of Chief Justice Laskin's reasons on behalf of a unanimous Court dismissing Thorson's arguments and accepting Robinette's position that the "peace, order and good government" clause in section 91 of the *BNA Act* carried the day for Canada. The Chief Justice said:

> I am in no doubt that it was open to the Parliament of Canada to enact the *Official Languages Act* (limited as it is to the purposes of the Parliament and Government of Canada and to the institutions of that Parliament and Government) as being a law "for the peace, order and

good government of Canada in relation to [a matter] not coming within the classes of subjects … assigned exclusively to the Legislatures of the Provinces". The quoted words are in the opening paragraphs of s. 91 of the *British North America Act*; and, in relying on them as constitutional support for the *Official Languages Act*, I do so on the basis of the purely residuary character of the legislative power thereby conferred. No authority need be cited for the exclusive power of the Parliament of Canada to legislate in relation to the operation and administration of the institutions and agencies of the Parliament and Government of Canada. Those institutions and agencies are clearly beyond provincial reach.

The peace, order, and good government clause has always been a safety net for federal legislation, but a useful one. We will see its application later in the *Patriation Case*. In the *Official Languages Act* reference, once the constitutional validity of the legislative action of Parliament was established with respect to federal institutions, it was not much of a step to accept that since the intent and effect of the New Brunswick legislation was to make applicable the federal policy on language to its provincial institutions, it was clearly within its jurisdiction to do so.

Smith's undoubted rapport with Robinette uniquely qualifies him to give an opinion as to the reasons for Robinette's success before the Supreme Court of Canada. He appeared either with him or on a companion brief in at least six other cases in that court alone.[189] Agreeing that he had a great deal of exposure to Robinette as a counsel on both sides of issues involving the Government of Canada he went on to provide his view on what it was that made Robinette distinctive as a counsel:

I think that everybody acknowledged that he was able to reduce issues to their essence. There are some who would say he made it too simple, that he was perhaps too inclined to condense the issues from a case in order to simplify the appeal. I don't agree. He had that ability to look at something that was fairly challenging from both a legal and factual point of view and focus on what the essentials were. His other strength, I think, was his use of language, which was very simple and direct but very well chosen. Not only in written language, but in spoken language he was able to convey a simplicity and a directness that escapes most of us. I think, in a subsidiary way, that he was never long-winded; he got to the point and dealt with it and moved on. He also was very adept in looking at the court and judging what to do in a particular circumstance.

He had a reputation as well. In the *Agricultural Products Marketing* reference, we got the Court totally confused, and I forget who looked down at him – this was after the thing was pretty well over – and said, "Mr. Robinette, could you help us?" Mind you, I'm not sure that he was able to, but that was the kind of reputation that he had, that he was able to slice through things.

It is evident that Smith's description of working with Robinette in government factums is at odds with Robinette's description of the same event in his oral history as set out above. I have indicated that I do not always find Robinette's oral history reliable and this is another example. Smith was quite clear in his perception that Robinette regarded his function as delivering the oral argument. Robinette did not want to be concerned with the factum except to be sure that he agreed with the positions taken and that they were supportable in argument.

I think that Robinette did take a different view of government briefs: that he regarded himself as a spokesman, not an architect, for decisions made at the political and policy-making level. On the other hand, he may simply have been satisfied with the quality of the drafts submitted by persons such as Smith. Either position would be consistent with his attitude towards referred briefs. If they did not get in the way of what he wanted to say in argument, he would not insist on redrafting them. I can recall that when I was told that I had been appointed to the Court of Appeal, I asked Robinette to take over from me an appeal I had pending in that court. He agreed. I had spent a good deal of time preparing that factum because I considered a good first impression to be vital. When the matter was listed for hearing, I took a look at the appellant's factum to see what changes Robinette had made. I was flattered to see that apart from retyping the last page to substitute his name for mine, he had made no changes at all. He was successful on the appeal.[190]

In the first case I propose to deal with in some detail, *Reference re: Anti-Inflation Act (Canada)*, Robinette was retained by the Department of Justice on the recommendation of Minister of Finance Donald S. Macdonald, a former partner of mine at McCarthys. Mark Jewett, now general counsel and corporate secretary to the Bank of Canada, detailed the circumstances that led to this retainer in the interview I had with him along with Smith.

In 1975, with the creation of the Anti-Inflation Board, Jewett was asked to be the counsel to the board and eventually became its general counsel. He is familiar with the economic and political climate that gave rise to the passage of the *Anti-Inflation Act* in 1975. As he put it:

> The circumstances giving rise to the legislation were very worrisome inflation numbers and conditions. Inflation had been a serious issue in the General Election in 1974, and I recall that Prime Minister Trudeau and Mr. Stanfield sparred extensively over economic conditions and whether or not wage and price controls were required. Indeed, one of Mr. Trudeau's famous lines to Mr. Stanfield, as I recall during the campaign, was something like "Zap! you're frozen" and, of course, within a year of the election, Mr. Trudeau himself had brought in wage and price controls. He was careful not to call them price controls; he called them profit controls. But certainly, they were wage controls.
>
> Those were the circumstances. I think those same circumstances and the measures that were required also led to the resignation of John Turner as Finance Minister in the fall of 1975. He was replaced by Mr. Macdonald, and shortly thereafter, the anti-inflation program was announced. It was in mid-October of 1975, and it start-

ed very quickly with a relatively small group of people. Very shortly into the program, there was a challenge to the application of the law to the provincial government's public sector, and at that point, the government was faced with a relatively lengthy period of appeal, assuming that there would be an appeal, during the entire time of which the inclusion of the provincial public sector in the program would be in question.

The public sector referred to was the Ontario Public Service Employees Union (OPSEU), represented by Ian Scott, Q.C., Stephen T. Goudge (now of the Court of Appeal for Ontario), and Christopher G. Paliare.

Jewett was not involved in the initial drafting of the legislation to implement the anti-inflation program. This was done by a small group from Prime Minister Trudeau's office, headed up by Donald Thorson, who, in addition to being the deputy minister of justice, was a skilled legislative drafter. The *Anti-Inflation Act* was passed December 15, 1975,[191] to provide for the restraint of profit margins, prices, dividends, and compensation in Canada. In the Government's view, in the best interests of all Canadians it would contain and reduce the current level of inflation. The Act provided for the establishment by the Governor-in-Council of guidelines for the restraint of prices and profit margins, compensation of employees, and dividends. These guidelines applied to the Government of Canada and its agents and the territorial governments and their agents. The Act did not purport to apply to matters within the provincial public sector, but it did stipulate that the Minister of Finance might, with the approval of the Governor-in-Council, enter into an agreement with a provincial government to make the act binding in that province and its public sector.

The statute was of course controversial, but what threw the cat among the pigeons was Ontario's decision to take advantage of the provision for an agreement to introduce the guidelines into the provincial sector. It also created its own controversy by implementing the agreement by Order-in-Council, thus avoiding any debate in the provincial legislature. My colleague, Stephen Goudge, takes up the narrative:[192]

Back in 1975–76, this was a very, very hot political issue and a very significant one for OPSEU because the province of Ontario had purported to opt into the federal legislation through an Order-in-Council as opposed to passing an Act themselves. The constraints that were put on bargaining in the public sector by the legislation were very severe, and so the union took it very seriously.

In the spring of 1976, there were a number of occasions on which the union was able to raise the legality of what Ontario had done in arbitration contexts, that is, where there was interest arbitration designed to set wages for various parts of the public sector. There was one case in particular in front of a professor of law from University of Western Ontario, Gregory Brandt, where we had made the argument that Ontario was not properly bound by the federal legislation because they hadn't enacted a law, they'd simply done it by Order-in-Council. We had expanded that argument, and my recollection is that Brandt agreed with us and therefore refused to apply the constraints of the legislation to the interest arbitration he was conducting, much to the government's consternation. I have a sense and a memory that that was a significant part of the creation of the second question in the reference. That forced Ontario really to try to get a senior judicial determination of whether they'd done the proper thing. So I think Ontario was moved in part because of the role that OPSEU had played in these interest arbitrations and, in particular, the Brandt arbitration.

Jewett agrees that it was the Ontario government that requested the federal government to invoke the authority conferred by the *Supreme Court Act*[193] to refer for the opinion of the court the following questions: (1) Is the *Anti-Inflation Act ultra vires* of the Parliament and of Canada? (2) If the Act is *intra vires*, then is the agreement between Canada and

Ontario effective so as to make the Act and Guidelines binding on the Ontario public sector?

Ontario was very supportive of the Act and was anxious to have it introduced into Ontario and not be limited to federal institutions. Roy McMurtry, now the chief justice of Ontario, was the attorney general of Ontario at the time. He had this to say in an interview:[194]

> I can recall being part of the delegation that went to Ottawa to discuss the situation with Donald Macdonald, the then Minister of Finance for Canada. This may have been in the context of a possible reference to the Supreme Court of Canada. The economists advising the Government of Ontario regarded this double-digit inflation as a very serious problem for the economy and particularly for retired people and other people living on fixed incomes who were witnessing their savings being very negatively affected and, of course, the value of pensions was seriously reduced. In Ontario, we had no difficulty in regarding this as a very serious, urgent matter for the country.

After the reference was announced, Robinette was retained as counsel for the federal government and commenced his preparation. Jewett worked closely with Smith and Robinette in preparing the factum. This was the first time Jewett had met Robinette, and I was interested in his impression. He said:

> As I said to you earlier, Mr. Robinette, if I had one word to describe him, was "economical." We prepared the drafts of the questions and the draft arguments, Mr. Smith and I together, and would present them to him. He would look at them, make a couple of minor changes, and say, effectively, "I can work with that." I have no doubt that he could have written it better from scratch if he'd done it himself, but that was his style. My lasting impression of him was that he had his own idea

of how the case would go; if the basic materials that were prepared for him were adequate, he could take them and work with them and make whatever adaptations were necessary. It was, I found, a very efficient way to work, but it takes someone with a very agile mind to be able to do that. He was able to take other people's work, see that the essence of what he needed was there, and then work with it. He then would focus on the strategy and the tactics to be applied in the case.

It is noteworthy in this case that Robinette made use of a device that is employed routinely now, some say over-employed. I am referring to the filing of extrinsic evidence in support of an argument before the Court. As Robinette discussed in his oral history, the thrust of the argument by Canada was that this legislation was, in the last analysis, justified as a form of emergency legislation under the peace, order, and good government provision of section 91 of the *BNA Act*. The question then became: What represents an emergency? Robinette decided that the Attorney General of Canada would place before the Court a number of documents that supported the position that there was either a national problem of double-digit inflation and high unemployment or alternatively that the economic circumstances amounted to an emergency. Smith emphasized to me that the word "emergency," because of its subjective nature, "was the last arrow in our quiver." However, it proved in the end to be dispositive of the reference in Canada's favour.

The Attorney General of Canada included in its case book the federal Government's White Paper, entitled "Attack on Inflation," being the policy statement that the Minister of Finance tabled in the House of Commons on October 14, 1975, and the monthly bulletin of Statistics Canada for October 1975, which contained various consumer price indices showing the index positions for certain periods up to September 1975. This move led to a flood of material being introduced by other parties, and the Attorney General of Canada was then given permission to file a reply to some of the new material. Robinette took personal advantage of this latitude with extrinsic evidence to engage in a ploy of his own. Jewett explains:

We had several of the provinces intervening against the validity of the legislation, and we had voluminous agreements with these provinces by which they brought their public sectors under the scope of the *Anti-Inflation Act* to be governed by wage and price controls. Mr. Robinette asked me to put together a compendium of all these agreements. By the time you added them up, they were rather thick. When we appeared before the Court, he had me march in these thick documents and lay them down on the table. He used them very effectively in argument against the provinces' position, saying, "Here you are contesting the legislation, on the one hand, and here is this very thick agreement that you've entered into that brings your public sector under the *Act*. Aren't you trying to suck and whistle here?" It was very effective.

The decision in the *Anti-Inflation Act* reference is one of the leading authorities on the admissibility of extrinsic material and the use that a court can make of it. Robinette pointed out that he was able to persuade the Court that it should be accepted not to show that there was a crisis in Canada, but to demonstrate that Parliament was informed when it stated as a recital to the Act that there was a crisis or an apparent crisis that had to be dealt with.[195] The recital was:

WHEREAS the Parliament of Canada recognizes that inflation in Canada at current levels is contrary to the interests of all Canadians and that the containment and reduction of inflation has become a matter of serious national concern;

AND WHEREAS to accomplish such containment and reduction of inflation it is necessary to restrain profit margins, prices, dividends and compensation; ...

The ruling by Chief Justice Laskin, delivered on behalf of himself and Justices Judson, Spence, and Dickson to form the lead judgment of the Court, demonstrates the importance of Robinette's decision to include this material. Accepting Robinette's submissions, the Chief Justice ruled:

> The present case is likewise one in which federal legislation is challenged as involving unconstitutional regulation, and I am of the opinion that extrinsic material, bearing on the circumstances in which the legislation was passed, may be considered by the Court in determining whether the legislation rests on a valid constitutional base. There is no issue in this case as to the meaning of the terms of the legislation nor, in my opinion, is there any issue as to the object of the legislation. As will appear from what follows, the arguments of the proponents and the opponents of the *Anti-Inflation Act* turn substantially on whether the social and economic circumstances upon which Parliament can be said to have proceeded in passing the Act were such as to provide support for the Act in the power of Parliament to legislate for the peace, order and good government of Canada. The extrinsic material offered in this case was directed to this question and may, hence, be properly considered thereon.[196]

In the end, Robinette and those counsel who supported the legislation persuaded a majority of the Court that the *Anti-Inflation Act* was valid legislation for the peace, order, and good government of Canada and, considering the circumstances under which it was enacted and its temporary character, did not invade provincial legislative jurisdiction. Chief Justice Laskin was of the view that the Court would not be justified in concluding that Parliament lacked a rational basis for viewing the Act as temporarily necessary to address an economic crisis that imperiled the well-being of Canadians and required Parliament's intervention in the interests of the country as a whole. The preamble to the Act was sufficiently indicative that Parliament was introducing a far-reaching program prompted by what was in its view a serious national condition; the absence of the very word "emergency," he found, was not unduly significant. While the validity of the Act did not stand or fall on the preamble, the preamble provided a basis for assessing the gravity of the circumstances giving rise to the legislation. In considering the relevance and weight of the extrinsic evidence and the assistance to be derived from judicial notice, the Chief Justice concluded that the Court need not look at the material in terms of proving the exceptional circumstances as a matter of fact, but merely as being persuasive that there was a rational basis for the legislation.

Robinette felt the majority of the Court came to the correct decision. Asked whether, looking back on the inflation of the day, there really was an emergency, he said:

> You had to get the atmosphere at the time. It really was a critical economic situation involving the whole of Canada. I don't care whether you call it an emergency or not, I don't think the word is necessary. There may be different situations arising today when we are a little more familiar with inflation. Then the Court might say otherwise. Oh, let's cope with that. That is not too bad. But this was unique at the time, and you have to look at the situation as it was at the time.

Accordingly, the federal government was vindicated, and the *Anti-Inflation Act* was declared *intra vires*. However, the Province of Ontario and Roy McMurtry did not fare as well. McMurtry's appearance in the Supreme Court of Canada was the first by an attorney general from Ontario in more than thirty years. In explanation, McMurtry stated:[197]

> There had been a tradition of Attorneys General appearing in Ottawa in the Supreme Court of Canada, but it hadn't happened for a long time. And actually I was concerned enough about it to discuss it with my colleagues, in particular my legal advisers. I didn't want to look like I was grandstanding by being the first in three decades to

appear, but I was convinced that it was a tradition that had been respected for many years, and indeed, when I arrived in the Supreme Court of Canada, one or two members of the Court, probably the Chief Justice, indicated that they welcomed what they hoped would be the return of the tradition of provincial Attorneys General appearing in person.

Unfortunately for the Attorney General, while the Court welcomed his presence, it answered "No" by a vote of nine to zero to the question referred to the Court on the point peculiar to Ontario, namely, whether the Order-in-Council made the Act and guidelines binding on the provincial sector in Ontario as defined in the agreement with the Minister of Finance. Chief Justice Laskin, for the Court, held that there is no principle in Canada that the Crown may legislate by proclamation or Order-in-Council to bind citizens without the support of a statute or the legislature. Obtaining such a statute did not turn out to be a problem, because the legislature was fully under the control of the Progressive Conservative government of the day.

I cannot leave this case without referring to the impressions of a young lawyer, less than six years out of law school, to the drama that unfolded over a week in the highest court in Canada, where twenty-eight of the country's leading constitutional lawyers gathered to argue a matter vital to the economic and political health of this nation. I quote from my interview with Goudge:

> The government in Ottawa decided they were going to make this reference to the Supreme Court. It was front-page news at the time, and I remember all of us involved in the case taking it very seriously. We knew that the government had retained Mr. Robinette and others had retained senior litigators.
>
> We all had our hip pocket academics: one of the unions involved retained Peter Hogg; we [for OPSEU] retained a constitutional law professor, a young professor from Osgoode, Ed Belobaba, to help put our mate-

rial together, and we really sweated at putting together the best material we could. Belobaba had clerked for Laskin, and we thought that was an inside track for us. I remember going down to Ottawa with all our preparation in hand for what would be probably seven or eight days, five of them in court. It's amazing to think now that the Court actually devoted a full week to hearing that case. I have a strong mental image of walking in on the Monday morning to courtroom packed mostly with lawyers because of the number of parties that were participating in the case. I remember we were towards the back on the right, two or three rows back because the Attorneys General all got front-row seats. Mr. Robinette was at the front on the left-hand side like the major actor in the centre of the stage. We were all set to go, having spent a great deal of time working with both the people on our side of the case, other parties and ourselves and our academic, putting together our peace, order, and good government arguments and so on. I remember thinking when I walked in, "This is going to be the most complicated argument I've ever heard." There was Bora Laskin presiding, somebody who personified constitutional law, in my eyes. There were academics from across the country. Bill Lederman was there, Peter Hogg, who had written all the key articles on the subject, was there. I remember Mr. Robinette getting up and holding the courtroom spellbound for about no more than I suspect an hour-and-a-half. I think it was the first time I had heard him, and I remember being mesmerized by how simply he was able to put things. All of a sudden, a case that we had worked on for weeks and had made so unbelievably complicated became as simple as a four- or five-word sentence. I remember being stunned by how he was able to take these ideas and make them simple and understandable. The Court seemed to listen without a question, without a comment, as if they were being told what to do. The sense of command he was able to project, all in a low-key way, was really quite amazing. There was very little flamboyance about him. The overwhelming sense I had was of his ability to make simple and comprehensible what we'd succeeded in making an unbelievably complicated case. That's my very strong mental image of Mr. Robinette arguing the case and doing so everyone paying rapt attention and absolutely no challenge from the Court.

Goudge had a vivid recollection of another counsel's performance that was also remarked on by Smith and Jewett. As indicated, Professor William R. Lederman was present and apparently advising the teachers' unions that had intervened.[198] To the surprise of most, this eminent constitutional scholar also addressed the Court as counsel. Even more surprising, Chief Justice Laskin seemed to resent his participation and engaged in a spirited debate with him. Goudge remembers:

> Bill got to his feet himself to argue and as soon as he did, he and Laskin got into a very, very significant tiff that had a personal edge to it that seemed to me to say, "This goes back through years of academic debate that is now being replayed in this courtroom."

Later events support Goudge's supposition.

I imagine that Robinette, in his own mind, was reconciled to thinking that the *Anti-Inflation Act* reference would be his last appearance on a major matter in the Supreme Court of Canada, certainly his last major constitutional case, but the gods were still smiling on him. His last hurrah was to represent Canada in the constitutional case of the century: bringing home our founding instrument, the *British North America Act*.

Chapter Sixteen
The Mother of All Constitutional Cases

THE CENTENNIAL YEAR OF 1967 marked the passage in 1867 of the *British North America Act,* the principal document creating the Constitution of Canada. When passed by the Parliament of the United Kingdom, it was referred to as an Imperial Statute because it applied to what was then the British colonies of Canada. While some minor provisions in the *BNA Act* could be amended by the Parliament of Canada and the provincial legislatures, the central provisions, which set up our federal system of government, could be amended only on a request to Westminster. These are the so-called entrenched provisions, which set out the division of legislative powers between the Parliament of Canada and the provincial legislatures, and which also contain certain fundamental rights involving language and education.

To many Canadians, the centennial of the *BNA Act* seemed an appropriate occasion not only to celebrate one hundred years of nationhood, but also to reflect on our constitutional history and to consider appropriate changes. First and foremost was the desire on the part of many Canadians to throw off the last vestiges of colonialism by shedding our reliance on a British statute as the basis of our Constitution and eliminating the requirement that we attend at Westminster to request constitutional amendments. The goal of those who sought change was the patriation of the *BNA Act* to Canada and the inclusion in the Constitution of an amending formula.

One of the first and certainly more effective attempts to formulate a process for bringing about this result was the Confederation of

Tomorrow Conference, convened in Toronto in November 1967 by Ontario Premier John Robarts.[199] This was a meeting of the provincial premiers,[200] and while the Government of Canada was not formally present, it did send a small number of observers. Robarts set the tone of the meeting by recognizing the reality of Quebec as one of the founding cultures of Canada. He promoted the concept of "special status" for that province. This conference, while not expressly advocating constitutional change, generated a certain momentum that led to lively discussion and culminated in a constitutional conference hosted by Prime Minster Trudeau in Victoria in 1971. It was here that Trudeau presented an ambitious constitutional package that included a domestic amending formula for the Constitution along with what he described as a charter — a constitutional entrenchment of basic individual rights such as language rights — which, he thought, would have a special appeal to Quebec. He was to be disappointed, however, as Quebec showed no interest in his patriation package.

Nevertheless, the fires of nationalism had been lit, and a lively and informed discussion concerning the patriation and reconstruction of the Constitution ensued among academics, politicians, and the public, keeping the subject front and centre until the culmination of these efforts in the eventual passage of the *Canada Act, 1982* (U.K.) c. 11, proclaimed in force April 17, 1982. The issue even aroused the normally somnolent Canadian Bar Association to strike a national committee (of which I was honoured to be selected as the Ontario representative), which produced a comprehensive and instructive report in August of 1978 called *Towards a New Canada/Vers un Canada Nouveau.*

My experience with this most knowledgeable committee, which was under the chairmanship of Jacques Viau, Q.C., of Montréal and the scholarly guidance of its executive vice-chairman, Gerard V. La Forest, Q.C. (later Justice La Forest of the Supreme Court of Canada), whetted my appetite for constitutional review, and I was to follow all proceedings related to this issue with an informed interest.[201] However, I will let a man who was very close to the legal and political scene, R. Roy McMurtry, pick up the narrative from here. McMurtry had been appointed attorney general in the government of Premier William G. Davis following his election to the Ontario Legislature in September

1975. As we will see, McMurtry has been a student of political history, particularly of Ontario, and he will appear and reappear throughout this account of the patriation process as a knowledgeable and passionate advocate of Canadian nationalism. He gave the following account of what happened after the failed Victoria conference:[202]

> I think Trudeau lost his appetite for constitutional reform for a few years. I think he was somewhat disillusioned by what happened in Victoria. He became pretty skeptical. It wasn't until the election of the Parti Québécois in 1976 and when the separatists were getting stronger in Quebec that he started to think about this a little bit again.
>
> When the *Canadian Charter of Rights and Freedoms* was proposed, I think Trudeau knew that this would be popular in Quebec amongst the ordinary people, even if it wasn't popular amongst the politicians, particularly those on the government side of the House. I think he also saw it, quite frankly, as a way of strategically dealing with the ever-increasing demands of Quebec for additional legislative powers under our Constitution. I think he thought that while proposing a *Charter of Rights*, the Constitution would attract not only a great deal of support from Quebec but would be a bit of a distraction, if I might put it in those terms, for those who were only interested in greater legislative powers. In any event, a number of us, including Jean Chrétien [then Minister of Justice] and Roy Romanow [Deputy Premier and Attorney General of Saskatchewan], representing all the provinces, spent most of the summer of 1980 travelling the country and meeting people trying to work out something.
>
> I should back up a step and say that the Quebec referendum in the spring of 1980 [calling for the secession of Quebec from Canada] was an important event in relation to the evolution of the *Charter of Rights* and

the patriated Constitution, because during the debate on the referendum in 1980, Prime Minister Trudeau continually promised the people of Quebec that there would be constitutional reform, without being overly specific as to what that was going to be.

I recall that the day after the referendum and the successful 60% "no" vote, Trudeau had Jean Chrétien meet with Bill Davis and me the very next night, and we agreed that we would participate in the process in which we would try to arrive at serious constitutional reform. When we embarked on this process in the summer of 1980, the *Charter of Rights* was one of twelve topics that were going to be discussed. They included everything from the amending formula to financial resources, communications, and so on.

A key player on Prime Minister Trudeau's constitutional team was Barry L. Strayer, Q.C., now a justice of the Federal Court of Appeal and the chief justice of the Court Martial Appeal Court of Canada. Strayer was from Moose Jaw, Saskatchewan, and was educated at the University of Saskatchewan, Oxford, and Harvard. He was a law professor at the University of Saskatchewan and also served for a time as an assistant deputy minister in the Department of the Attorney General of Saskatchewan. From 1974 to 1983, he was in Ottawa as the assistant deputy minister of justice for public law. As such, he was responsible for the constitutional, administrative, and international areas of the Department of Justice. Even before coming to Ottawa, Strayer had been very heavily involved in constitutional reform as a member of the Saskatchewan delegation to some constitutional conferences in the late sixties and early seventies leading up to the Victoria conference and thereafter. Here are his own words on his participation in the patriation process:[203]

I was quite heavily involved personally, and I also had responsibility for a number of lawyers who were working on the project. I had more experience with the patriation issue than anybody else because I had been involved in meetings in London in 1971 when we thought we were going to patriate the Constitution and worked out some arrangements at that time. In any event, during that summer, in the midst of all of our travelling around the country – the summer of 1980 – at these federal-provincial meetings, we also were busy working on a paper for the government on whether it could proceed unilaterally if necessary.

We did most of the work internally in the Department of Justice, but part of the summer we had amongst our advisers Michel Robert from Montreal and Reynold Langlois, who had been involved on particular subjects. We were talking to them about this as we were developing our paper. We developed a cabinet document which had a lot of other things in it apart from legal advice, but basically our advice was that it was legal to do this, that the United Kingdom Parliament still had the authority to do it, and there was nothing to stop the Parliament of Canada from requesting these amendments as they had always done in the past.

There did not appear to be much of an issue that the proper way to amend the *BNA Act* was for the federal government to introduce a resolution in the Senate and the House of Commons in Ottawa proposing a Joint Address to Her Majesty the Queen of England to request that legislation be placed before the United Kingdom Parliament to patriate the Canadian Constitution and to provide for an amending formula to avoid the necessity of future requests. The problem was that there did not appear to be any practice that provided an effective role for the provinces in expressing the Canadian will for amendments. The single issue of whether there was a convention of consultation and agreement with the provinces by the federal government on constitutional change was to dominate the political and legal stages. Strayer had this to say about the role of convention in the constitutional amendment process:

We did flag the problem of the constitutional convention. We recognized that the Supreme Court had given a certain amount of importance to a constitutional convention a couple of years before in the Senate Reference taken to the Supreme Court[204] to see whether Parliament could abolish the Senate and replace it with something else. There was talk at that time of a House of Confederation. So, we had taken this paper to cabinet in which we indicated legally they could do it. The conventions were not something the court should enforce; the conventions were not at all clear and, if anything, probably supported unilateral action if necessary, given the history of efforts over the course of something like fifty years to get agreement on the patriation of the Constitution.

Strayer and his group were of the firm opinion that no convention existed, and even if one did, it was irrelevant. In their view, the Government of Canada could proceed to submit its amendments to Westminster and Parliament was bound to pass them. Because of the importance of the matter, however, the Minister of Justice of the day, Jean Chrétien, wanted another opinion on the matter, and Strayer was "dispatched" (his word) to see John Robinette. Strayer had never met Robinette, and so Donald H. Christie, Q.C., an associate deputy minister in the department at the time who normally worked with Robinette, arranged the meeting. On September 3, 1980, Strayer flew to Toronto and saw Robinette in his office at McCarthys. His description of the meeting follows:

> I had, I think, faxed or couriered or somehow sent to him a copy of our memorandum of what we had prepared internally, so we had that to discuss when I was there. Before I left, he said that he would send us an opinion in a couple of days, but that he basically was in agreement with the memorandum that he'd have thought that there was no doubt that, if we could get

the United Kingdom Parliament to pass the law incorporating our package, that law would be valid and wouldn't be assailable before the Canadian courts. On the question of the convention, he was doubtful that there was any convention, and he didn't see that as a big obstacle. He did advise from the outset that the smaller the package we sent, the better it would be, if it did go to court, if it was attacked in court. It would be better if we stuck to patriation and the amending formula, that would be the safest. And he said, "Don't put anything about the Supreme Court in there or you'll run into more trouble." [He was referring to suggested changes to the *BNA Act* that would constitutionally entrench the role of the Supreme Court of Canada.]

He also was fairly bullish on the pace with which we should do things. He felt that we should get the UK Parliament to act as soon as possible and not await the outcome of the [threatened] court cases, that it was much easier to defend our actions as a *fait accompli* rather than as a gleam in the eye of the Prime Minister. Anyway, that was his initial reaction, and he sent us an opinion after, which essentially followed the same pattern.

Asked for his reaction to Robinette, Strayer said:

I thought he had a very quick mind to grasp the subtleties of the issue. He had, I think, maybe seen our paper no more than twenty-four hours before I got there, maybe less than that, and he very quickly grasped the issues. I frankly thought I would have a more arduous task in explaining and justifying our conclusions to him, but he seemed disposed to agree with what we concluded, and as the weeks went on, we had no serious conflicts in terms of either the substance or the strategy of it that I can recall. His position for quite some time was that we should keep on with the legislation and the resolution in Parliament and as soon as it got through the Parliament of Canada, it should go to the UK.

On his return to Ottawa, Strayer prepared minutes of this meeting, which he addressed to Roger Tassé, Q.C., the Deputy Minister of Justice, and copied to Donald Christie and Michael Kirby, the Assistant Deputy Clerk of the Privy Council and later Senator Kirby:

> September 4, 1980
> Subject/Objet – Patriation – Legal Validity
> Of Unilateral Action
>
> I met with Mr. J.J. Robinette in Toronto on September 3. He will have a written opinion in our hands by Friday night, September 5. Briefly his views appear to be as follows:
>
> 1. There is no doubt that the U.K. patriation legislation would be legally valid.
> 2. He doubts that there is any relevant convention. Even if there is, it cannot affect the legal validity of such action.
> 3. In terms of legal strategy, to minimize the hazards if we do end up in court:
>   (a) a package confirmed by an amending formula would be the safest; the more additions, the greater the potential problems, in particular it would be unwise to include provisions concerning the Supreme Court;
>   (b) it would be much better to have the measure already enacted by the U.K. before the case is argued.

Michael Kirby was also the secretary to the cabinet for federal/provincial relations and answered to the prime minister. He addressed issues of strategy and politics with respect to the patriation problem. Upon receipt of Robinette's written opinion, he had Strayer's group put together a paper that was known as the Kirby Memorandum, which picked up on Robinette's strategy of proceeding unilaterally to get the matter introduced into the Parliament at Westminster. The paper not only dealt with the question of unilateral action, but also with the extent that such action should be taken if the government could not get agreement on a joint federal-provincial approach. Much of the paper analyzed the probable reactions and positions of the provinces on various subjects and suggested how federal government representatives could deal with them. It was clearly a document that was intended for a highly select group as an *aide-mémoire*. Unfortunately, the Kirby Memorandum was leaked to one of the provincial delegates the day before the First Ministers' Conference on the Constitution in September 1980.

According to McMurtry, there were a number of reasons for the tensions that erupted at the Conference. Premier Peter Lougheed of Alberta was still "stewing" about the National Oil Policy, the burden of which fell largely on his province. Premier Brian Peckford, "who could be pretty abrasive," wanted more control by Newfoundland of offshore fishing rights. Indeed, almost all of the provinces had their own shopping list of desired constitutional changes. The leaked Kirby Memorandum, however, seemed to light the fuse. It was even suggested by one of the provincial representatives that it would be inappropriate for Trudeau to chair the conference. In the end, the conference did not really get past the welcoming dinner at the official residence of Governor General Edward Schreyer. There was so much bickering during the dinner that Trudeau finally lost patience and said to the Governor General, "God damn it Ed, serve the dessert so I can get out of here!"

McMurtry remembers calling his wife Ria at home in Toronto that night and telling her that the First Ministers' Conference was pretty much over before it started. He felt frustrated, having spent most of the summer working with the first ministers and hoping that some consensus could be reached to permit patriation. He found the attitude of some of the ministers, particularly those from the west, to be less than helpful. So when it was apparent that the First Ministers' Conference was not going anywhere, and it seemed there was no possibility of a consensus, a number of the delegates, particularly Premier Davis, thought, in McMurtry's words, "My God, our Constitution remains an *Act* of the British Parliament after all these years. All that time we've been debating, the provinces and the federal government, for I think fifty-four years, and now we're going to see the end of it." McMurtry explained further:

> So we thought that strategically, it was in the national interest for us to support Trudeau when he announced that he was going ... to proceed unilaterally and go to Britain and ask Britain to pass the necessary legislation. This infuriated most of the provinces; only Ontario and New Brunswick were prepared to support Trudeau and the federal government. The other provinces became the Gang of Eight. Everything had become polarized, it was very confrontational, and the result was, of course, that Manitoba, Newfoundland, and Quebec launched these three provincial References to challenge what Trudeau was doing.

Strayer recounts that within a few days of the failure of the First Ministers' Conference, he and some of his group went to London with a draft of a package that was proposed as the unilateral approach to patriating the Constitution. Unexpectedly, they started getting some vibrations from their contacts in London that their request of Parliament without the concurrence of the provinces might not be as easy to satisfy as they thought. Notwithstanding this chilly reception, on October 2, 1980, the Government of Canada published the "Proposed Resolution for a Joint Address to Her Majesty the Queen respecting the Constitution of Canada," which called first for the Constitution to be brought home in a way that would lead to a new amending formula free from the straitjackets of unanimity, and second, that it would contain a charter of rights and freedoms.

Trudeau addressed the people of Canada that day.[205] In terse but eloquent language he explained the problem. After referring briefly to the history of the Constitution and the recent failures of the Government of Canada and the provinces to reach agreement on the manner in which the Constitution could be patriated, he said, in part:

That we first ministers failed is for me a matter of great personal regret, the same regret that has been felt by every prime minister and many of the premiers who have held office since the 1920's, when the first of many attempts to canadianize our constitution ended in failure. Why have we not succeeded? Why has every attempt in more than a half a century led to frustration and failure?

It is because we sought perfection in a real and very human world. We assumed that it was possible in a system of diverse governments for all to agree in all respects on everything. In accepting that the only agreement could be unanimous agreement, we took the ideal of unanimity and made it a tyrant.

Unanimity gave each first minister a veto: and that veto was increasingly used to seek the particular good of a particular region or province. So we achieved the good of none; least of all did we achieve the good of all, the common good.

We were led by the dictates of unanimity to bargain freedom against fish, fundamental rights against oil, the independence of our country against long distance telephone rates.

But we were led further still, towards a radically new concept of Canada, one in which the national good was merely the sum total of provincial demands, one where the division of powers upon which our federation traditionally rests, could be altered for no other reason than that the Provinces agreed among themselves that it should be altered.

Canadians cannot accept that kind of Canada. It would not be the Canada we know, much less the Canada we want. It would be ten countries each seeking advantage over the other, without any means to seek the good of all.

As Strayer recalls, there was a growing amount of criticism in Canada about this unilateral approach to patriation. But more significantly, from a practical point of view, there were misgivings in London, England. Trudeau did not help the situation by stating publicly, "If the British parliamentarians don't like it, why don't they just hold their noses and pass the God-damned thing." I vividly remember a cartoon in the *Toronto Star* by the incomparable Duncan McPherson in which he depicts a frowning Queen Elizabeth sitting on her throne dressed in Victorian regality and stating firmly, "We will not hold Our nose."

According to Strayer, some of the provinces had done a very effective job of lobbying in London, "wining and dining MPs and members of the House of Lords and journalists and so forth." The Aboriginal peoples were also involved. Chief Robert Manuel and 123 other Indian chiefs commenced an action in the Chancery Division against the Attorney General of England for a declaration that the Parliament of the UK had no authority to amend the Constitution of Canada so as to prejudice the Indian Nations of Canada without the consent of those nations.[206]

It appears that the British Parliament did not have enough to do. The Foreign Affairs Committee of the House of Commons under the chairmanship of Tory backbencher Sir Anthony Kershaw decided on November 5, 1980, to inquire into the role of the UK Parliament in relation to the *BNA Act* and proceeded to hear evidence and argument in November and December of that year about whether in fact there was a convention that governed constitutional amendments on behalf of Canada.

The committee's first report on January 21, 1981,[207] seemed to me simply to muddy the waters further. It made twelve findings, the first of which confirmed the exclusive power of the UK Parliament to amend fundamental parts of Canada's Constitution. The ninth finding postulated a circumstance where fundamental changes were sought by the Parliament of Canada against the express opposition "of Provincial governments." The tenth finding read:

> In those circumstances, it would be proper for the UK Parliament to decide that the request did not convey the clearly expressed wishes of Canada as a federally structured whole because it did not enjoy a sufficient

level and distribution of Provincial concurrence. But Parliament would be justified in regarding as sufficient a level and distribution of Provincial concurrence commensurate with that requested by the least demanding of the formulae which have been put forward by the Canadian authorities for a post-patriation amendment (similarly affecting that federal structure).

This report was a major problem for Robinette's position. If the UK Parliament were to insist that the request for patriation by the Canadian Houses of Parliament was not sufficient and that evidence of some level of provincial concurrence was required, this would render moot any legal argument that there was no convention of provincial concurrence, and even if there was one, such convention was of no legal effect. Apparently, the provinces had succeeded in making quite a case for themselves and had aroused a fair amount of public support in England. Rallying against unilateral constitutional change became a popular and risk-free campaign for do-gooders of all political stripes in the Commons and the House of Lords. To make matters worse, the Prime Minister of England, Margaret Thatcher, made it abundantly clear that she did not regard this as her fight and did not intend to waste any political capital on it. She would not use what is called in the British parliamentary system a three-line whip, which would have made the passage of Canada's bill a matter of confidence in the ruling party, essentially ensuring its passage in the House of Commons.

I will return to Strayer's narrative:

> It became more and more difficult to get this thing through quickly and, in the meantime, sometime in the fall, I think it was in October, three provinces announced that they were going to refer to their courts of appeal the questions concerning the validity of this unilateral move: they were Manitoba, Quebec, and Newfoundland. Manitoba was the first reference to be heard in early December, and we retained John Robinette for that. We put together a factum which was refined as we went

along and then was basically recycled in one form or another in the other two appeal courts.

In the *Manitoba Reference Case*,[208] Robinette appeared with John A. Scollin, Q.C., and R.D. Gibson for the Attorney General of Canada before a court composed of Chief Justice Freedman and Justices Hall, Matas, O'Sullivan, and Huband. Michel Robert, Q.C., of whom we will hear more, was present and gowned but did not address the Court.

The constitutional questions involved both the legality of the unilateral approach and the existence, if any, of the convention of obtaining provincial agreement before seeking a constitutional amendment. The first question was hypothetical in that it asked, If the amendments to the Constitution sought by the proposed resolution were enacted, would federal/provincial relationships or the powers, rights, or privileges granted or secured by the Constitution to the provinces, their legislatures, or their governments be affected, and if so, in what respect or respects? The Chief Justice and Justice Matas declined to answer the question because it was tentative and premature. Justice Hall declined because he believed that the question was not appropriate for judicial response and that, in any event, it was speculative and premature. The remaining two justices answered the question in the affirmative.

The second question was, Is it a constitutional convention that Canada will not request the Queen to lay before the Parliament of the UK a measure to amend the Constitution of Canada affecting federal/provincial relationships or the powers, rights, or privileges granted or secured by the Constitution of Canada to the provinces without first obtaining the agreement of the provinces? A four-person majority answered, "No." Justice Hall again declined to answer the question because he believed that it was not appropriate for judicial response.

The third question asked, in effect, whether provincial consent was constitutionally required where the amendments sought by Canada alter the powers, rights, or privileges of the provinces or their legislatures or governments. The Chief Justice and Justices Hall and Matas answered, "No," and Justices O'Sullivan and Huband answered, "Yes."

The Department of Justice regarded this decision as a victory. Strayer said that Robinette made most of the argument before the

Manitoba Court of Appeal. The other active counsel was Scollin, who later became a judge of the Court of Queen's Bench in Manitoba. I offer a commentary by another counsel who was present. Colin K. Irving was retained by the Province of Quebec to represent that province in all three references. He contributed this vignette on his reception in Manitoba as an adversary of Robinette:[209]

> In Manitoba I was forcefully reminded of the breadth of his reputation when I was arguing the Quebec case in front of a decidedly hostile five-man Court of Appeal bench (the Lévesque government was not popular in Manitoba). As I made my points as best I could, I noticed that quite frequently the judges' attention seemed to be elsewhere. I soon discovered that the notes they were taking related not so much to my argument but to JJR's reaction to it. A shake of his head (which he did whenever he disagreed) led the judges' pencils to move rapidly.

Another interesting commentary from the *Manitoba Reference* related to Justice O'Sullivan's attitude towards Robinette. According to Michel Robert, Robinette's audience, as usual, was intensely interested in what he was saying and respectful of him as a leading counsel. O'Sullivan, however, peppered him with hostile questions. Robinette had told me why. Justice O'Sullivan was a brilliant scholar and a prodigious worker who brought his devout and passionate Catholicism with him to the bench. (This was to be confirmed to me some years later when I attended an appellate judges' seminar in Victoria, B.C. O'Sullivan and I were part of a small breakout group discussing various themes and perceptions that we encountered during the course of our judicial duties. During a wide-ranging discussion about ridding ourselves of personal bias and stereotypical thinking, O'Sullivan stated categorically that he regarded himself as a Roman Catholic appointee to the bench, and that he was there to represent the Church and the adherents of that faith.)

Now, one of the concerns of the Court in the *Manitoba Reference* was that patriation, an amending formula, and particularly the *Charter of Rights and Freedoms* would jeopardize the special constitutional protection that Catholics had acquired under section 93 of the *BNA Act*.[210] This was very much on O'Sullivan's mind, and he was relieved to find that Robinette was the lead counsel for Canada. According to Robinette, O'Sullivan assumed from his French name that he was a Catholic and was looking forward to discussing his concerns with a kindred spirit. His anticipation turned to displeasure, however, when he found out before the hearing that Robinette was a Protestant of Huguenot heritage. Robinette had prior intelligence on O'Sullivan and was prepared to encounter him in a grouchy mood, which he did.

Strayer confirmed to me that O'Sullivan was grouchy at this session, but he did not know the reason. I asked Michel Robert if he knew anything about the background to the O'Sullivan anecdote. He answered:

> This was a bit awkward in a way, but Mr. Justice O'Sullivan was insisting very much that the *Charter of Rights* might affect the religious rights guaranteed to the religious minorities under s. 93 of the *BNA Act*. As a matter of fact, we did not want to argue this, and we had specific instructions from the government not to go into this. We had enough problems with other pro-visions of the *BNA Act*; we did not want to raise the question of religious rights. As a matter of fact, we all believed that the *Charter of Rights* did not affect reli-gious rights, even though freedom of religion and free-dom of conscience were guaranteed by the *Charter*. I don't think it had an impact on the rights of s. 93, but Mr. Justice O'Sullivan was constantly insisting that we argue this point, and he was asking Mr. Robinette, "Well, Mr. Robinette, don't you think that the *Charter* might have an impact on s. 93 and the rights of the reli-gious minorities?" and Mr. Robinette said, "No, no, no. We do not believe that, and we don't have any submis-sions to make on this point." But, despite that, Mr. Justice O'Sullivan, during the whole hearing, came

back at least two or three times on this point, and each time he got the same answer from Mr. Robinette.

I think Mr. Justice O'Sullivan was Irish and a strongly devout Catholic, and I think he was very interested by this point, but I don't think it was part, really, of the case that was being argued before the Court of Appeal of Manitoba.

Robert is now the chief justice of Quebec.[211] Before his elevation to the bench in 1995, he was an outstanding counsel with a reputation throughout Canada. He was admitted to the bar of Quebec in 1962 and in the years 1974–75 became le bâtonnier, a position similar to the treasurer in the other provinces. After that, he was president of the Canadian Federation of Law Societies, in 1976–77. He was appointed Queen's Counsel in 1982. Robert was involved in the patriation process for the Government of Canada during 1980 and 1981. He appeared in all three provincial references and before the Supreme Court of Canada. He is very knowledgeable about all aspects of the patriation process, both legal and political. As we know, there were eight provinces (the Gang of Eight) opposing the patriation process by Parliament and two supporting it (Ontario and New Brunswick). And, as part of their strategy, Robert says, the Gang of Eight decided to launch three references before three courts of appeal contesting the validity of the proposed resolution. The first reference to be argued was the one before the Manitoba Court of Appeal; the second reference was argued before the Newfoundland Court of Appeal;[212] and the third was before the Quebec Court of Appeal.[213] The appeals from these decisions were all heard together by the Supreme Court in April and May 1981.[214]

These court tactics, in combination with the provincial proselytizing of MPs in Britain, were successful in one important regard. They effectively stymied Robinette's strategy of pushing ahead with the patriation process. As Strayer put it:

> Once the date was fixed for the hearing of the Supreme Court appeal, the strategy which John had preferred and which, I must say, I was quite in favour of — trying to get the thing through expeditiously — was brought to a halt

because of the growing objections in Britain. It became pretty clear that unless we had a favourable decision from the Supreme Court, or failing that an agreement with the provinces, it was going to be very difficult to get the patriation package through over there.

Robinette was engaged in as difficult and important a brief as he had ever taken on, and he was to turn seventy-five in November 1981. He was involved in the three provincial appellate court references and was to lead the federal government team in the final appeals to the Supreme Court of Canada. Notwithstanding his age, Robinette was the lead counsel. In the words of Robert, "He was the one directing our group." He not only worked with Scollin in Manitoba and Robert in Quebec, he also was associated with Clyde K. Wells, Q.C., in Newfoundland. Wells, of course, later became the Liberal premier of Newfoundland and Labrador and played a fateful role in derailing the Meech Lake initiative of Prime Minister Brian Mulroney to bring Quebec into the constitutional fold.[215]

According to Strayer and Robert, all counsel worked well together as a team. There were about twenty-five of them, supplemented by others from the Department of Justice. Roger Tassé, the Deputy Minister of Justice who acted under the close scrutiny of his minister, Jean Chrétien, coordinated their efforts. Prime Minister Trudeau was very much involved, as well. Strayer gives an account of Trudeau's first meeting with Robinette:

> During these meetings and preparations here in Ottawa, we had word that the Prime Minister wanted to meet with Mr. Robinette, and so I ushered him into a car to the Justice Building. We got out and he said, "Where are we going?" and I said, "We're going to see your client." I don't think he still quite twigged to this. Anyway, we got over there and were ushered into the Prime Minister's office, and they had a little chat.
>
> Trudeau was quite interested in how John foresaw the argument unfolding and what his view of the strategy was and what he thought the Court would do with it. Trudeau, I don't think, had ever met him and

wanted to have the opportunity on an intellectual basis to talk about the issues in the case. Trudeau was exploring as much as he could what Robinette really thought would be the outcome. This was, of course, before the hearing. I guess we probably had a better idea as to the outcome after we observed what went on in the Court at that time.

Robert recalled a number of occasions when the litigation group, or part of it, met with the Prime Minister. It was apparent to Robert that the PM was personally overseeing the preparation of these reference cases. He recalls that sometimes they sent drafts of their briefs to the PMO. The Prime Minister would read them in the evening, make annotations on the drafts, and send them back to counsel through Tassé. Just prior to the hearing before the Supreme Court, Trudeau wanted to explain his strategy to his counsel. At this meeting, he demonstrated his total involvement in the patriation process, both emotionally and intellectually. His basic concept was that there had been ten attempts to secure the agreements of the province to amend the Constitution, beginning in 1927 and continuing up to 1980, each one a failure. As recounted by Robert:

> [Trudeau's opinion was] that the Court would not go into the constitutionality aspect or the convention aspect; he was of the view — and I think it was the good view in legal terms — that courts do not enforce constitutional conventions. It's not a matter for courts. It's a non-justiciable issue. This was the position that we had taken both before the Courts of Appeal and the Supreme Court of Canada.

I cannot leave this discussion of the briefing meetings of counsel without repeating McMurtry's account of a consultation at which Jean Chrétien was present. On the eve of the hearing in the Supreme Court of Canada, all government counsel and their advisers met in the Department of Justice boardroom in Ottawa to discuss strategy. McMurtry recalls going there with Robinette and a couple of his "old constitutional advisers." McMurtry was surprised to see the boardroom jammed with people, all of whom apparently had been working on some aspect of the reference for the federal government. He estimated that there were sixty people in the room. Chrétien, as minister of justice, decided he better come to the meeting. I will let McMurtry take over:

> I recall Robinette sitting right across the table from me and looking a little surprised, wondering, "What the hell are all these people doing in this room?" I don't think he had any idea how many people had been working from the Department of Justice on this matter. We talked about strategy a little and who might emphasize what and several of the lawyers, I suppose, including me, got off onto sort of a detached, almost academic-sounding discussion as to how each particular judge might respond to a particular argument and the possible response of the Court collectively. It was the type of theoretical argument that lawyers often are attracted to, particularly in the context of major litigation. And it may just have something to do with collegiality.
>
> But there was a lot of what I'm sure sounded to Chrétien like idle academic, theoretical musings. I knew him well, and I knew that, to him, this case was the most important ever to come before the Supreme Court Canada. It would be one of the most important events in the history of the country. I could see that he was getting very restless and obviously irritated with this academic discussion. He had not said a word until finally, all of a sudden, he just slammed his fist on the table. He looked right across the table at me and said, "I tell you this Roy. Jeeesuus Christ, if we don't win this God-damned case, it'll be Jonestown revisited around here!"[216]
>
> Looking around the room, I could see all these federal officials and advisers and lawyers waiting a little uncomfortably as he was saying, "You guys screw this up …" I thought it was a memorable intervention.

It was typical of Robinette that he was there alone. Robert noted that while all the other senior counsel, including him, were accompanied by younger lawyers and law students, Robinette was always by himself. Also, while they worked from summaries and précis of the facts and the case law, Robinette pursued his usual practice of doing his own preparation. He would read the cases himself. While too polite to reject memos that were handed to him, he put them aside unread. As Robert put it:

> I think Mr. Robinette was a more traditional litigator in the sense that he was more solitary in his approach. First, he was reading all the cases himself. In other words, he was not relying on any briefing notes. Many of the lawyers for the government were preparing all kinds of briefing notes on cases and so on, summaries of cases. Mr. Robinette, of course, would not discard them, but I know that he was reading all the cases himself and was making his own notes on the cases. He was not relying on notes prepared by others.

As Robert also observed, Robinette did not work with the big team that the government had put together. No one would have begrudged him a junior from McCarthy & McCarthy or anywhere else. It could not have been the lack of funding or the significance of the case that deterred him; it was simply not his style. A by-product of this practice was that the Ministry of Justice got a bargain when it hired him. I am reminded of Brad Smith's remark that Robinette's fees to the government were so modest that the Minister of Justice did not follow the usual government practice of setting an hourly rate and asking for detailed accounts. They appreciated that in Robinette's case, they were doing better letting Robinette set his own standard. Robinette told a number of lawyers that he deliberately kept his fees low when working for public agencies because he did not want to be embarrassed by later media coverage citing his "extravagant fees." I do not accept this explanation. That would be much too calculating for Robinette. In my opinion it was just habit that caused him to keep his fees low.

As Robert also observed, Robinette was "a very meticulous litigator," one who showed an economy of effort. In the meetings of counsel in preparation for the hearings, he would only occasionally offer his advice. If Tassé would ask, "Mr. Robinette, what do you think of this point?" he would give his advice and in Robert's words, "It was always short, concise and, I must say, to the point." Robert continued:

> The other thing which really impressed me and many others who were around him was the fact that he had a fantastic memory for cases and for arguments which had been made before the courts. He told us once that he had argued fifty constitutional cases before the Supreme Court of Canada. I never checked if the number was right, but I think he was involved in almost all of the main litigations concerning the Constitution of Canada before the Supreme Court, let's say in the first part of the twentieth century. He had a memory of all of these cases. He would say, "Well, when we argued this case before the Supreme Court, this argument was brought forward …" and so he would remember everything.
>
> He had a corporate memory of the constitutional history of Canada, which none of us had of course because we were too young. There were twenty-two amendments which had been made to the Canadian Constitution from 1870 to 1964, I believe, and part of our argument before the Supreme Court was to review all those amendments and to determine if the consent of the provinces was obtained or required or asked for in each one of those amendments. He was seventy-five in 1980, so he had been in practice for at least, I think, fifty years. So many of these amendments he had lived through, like the unemployment insurance amendment, the retirement age for Superior Court judges amendment, and the entrance of Newfoundland into Confederation in 1949. There were two amendments in 1949: the admission of Newfoundland and Labrador

and then the amendment conferring power on the Parliament of Canada to amend its own internal constitution. He remembered many of these, and I was very impressed with him.

In dealing with the provincial references, I have focused heavily on Manitoba because it set the tone for the other references. The same three questions were put in the *Newfoundland Reference* as well as a fourth question relating to the particular circumstances of Newfoundland joining Confederation in 1949. In the *Quebec Reference,* there was a different formulation of the questions, but they still followed the *Manitoba Reference* model in their effect.

The federal team split up its representation on behalf of the Attorney General of Canada for the hearing in the Supreme Court of Canada. Robinette appeared with Scollin and Robert in the *Manitoba Reference.* Wells, Strayer, and Barbara Reed (later Justice Reed of the Federal Court of Canada) appeared in the *Newfoundland Reference*, and Robert, Langlois, and Louis Reynolds in the *Quebec Reference.* Only one federal factum was filed for all three references.[217] The factum set out the four questions presented to the Court, three of which were common to all three references, and the fourth of which dealt with the unique Newfoundland question. Robinette argued the first two questions.

The first question and the Attorney General of Canada's position on it were as follows:

> If the amendments to the Constitution of Canada sought in the "Proposed Resolution for a Joint Address to her Majesty the Queen respecting the Constitution of Canada", or any of them, were enacted, would federal–provincial relationships or the powers, rights or privileges granted or secured by the Constitution of Canada to the provinces, their legislatures or governments be affected and if so, in what respect or respects?

In its factum, the Attorney General contended that this question was too broadly worded and too vague for a simple yes or no answer, but if the Court deemed it appropriate to answer the question, the answer should be as follows. First, that an amending formula that gives the provinces a *de jure* role in amendments to the Constitution does affect federal–provincial relations to the benefit of the provinces. Second, the division of legislative powers is changed to the benefit of the provinces by extending their jurisdiction in the areas of indirect taxation of resources and interprovincial trade in resources. Third, the *Charter of Rights and Freedoms* does not change the balance of federalism in Canada but limits both Parliament and the provincial legislatures in the exercise of their legislative authority in order to protect certain fundamental rights and freedoms of the individual. And fourth, patriation, the entrenching of the rights of native peoples, and the entrenching of the principle of equalization do not affect federal–provincial relationships or the division of legislative authority.

It is to be noted that the first position of Canada was that the request by our Parliament and Senate to the Queen of England to place the patriation package before the Parliament at Westminster had no legal status and thus was not an issue that was properly before the courts. This leads into a further observation by Colin Irving. He said of Robinette's appearance in the Supreme Court of Canada on this case:[218]

> He was fairly elderly at this time and when the case came to the Supreme Court of Canada his hand was not as steady as it had been. I remember helping him with his collar before we went in and watching his hand shake as he lit his pipe, which in fact he never seemed to actually smoke. His hand may have been shaky, but his mind was not. The issue was the joint resolution of the Senate and the House of Commons requesting the British Parliament to amend the Canadian Constitution over the objection of all of the provinces but two. One of the federal arguments, put with his usual succinctness by JJR, was that a resolution of the House of Commons and Senate had no binding legal effect, and that the issue of its appropriateness was not justiciable. Bud Estey [the son of Wilfred Estey referred to in *R. v. Suchan and Jackson*] put

the question: "Are you saying, Mr. Robinette, that this resolution is something like a resolution wishing the Queen a happy birthday?" to which J.J.R. immediately replied, "Yes, neither has any legal effect."

The lawyers acting for the federal government in the Quebec case were appalled by this, and I heard one of them saying at the break that the "old man" had lost it. The Quebec appeal came on after the federal appeal had finished, and so the counsel in question had the opportunity to repair what they saw as the damage done by Mr. Robinette's answer. In the course of argument, one of them said (I am not quoting exactly), "We acknowledge of course that this is a very important resolution not like, for example, a resolution wishing the Queen a happy birthday." Estey immediately intervened. "What's the difference?" "Well it's a very important resolution and it has serious political implications." Estey persisted. "We all know that, but is there any real difference in law?" This went on for some time, and within about ten minutes a somewhat battered counsel was forced to give the answer the "old man" had had the intelligence and courage to give immediately.

The second question that Robinette argued was as follows:

Is it a constitutional convention that the House of Commons and Senate of Canada will not request Her Majesty the Queen to lay before the Parliament of the United Kingdom of Great Britain and Northern Ireland a measure to amend the Constitution of Canada affecting federal–provincial relationships or the powers, rights or privileges granted or secured by the Constitution of Canada to the provinces, their legislatures or governments without first obtaining the agreement of the provinces?

The position of the Attorney General was that the question was really one of political science or parliamentary procedure, not law. If the Court nevertheless saw fit to answer the question, the answer should be in the negative. The federal government objected to the question because it asked the Court to adjudicate on a question of internal parliamentary procedure; the alleged convention is a question of political exigency, not law. Moreover, the definition of conventions is itself unclear and a matter for debate and the imprecise and flexible nature of conventions (as opposed to laws) makes conventions unsuitable for judicial determination.

The Supreme Court delivered its reasons on September 28, 1981. In a groundbreaking move, the Court announced that it intended to announce the decision on television. I can remember that at McCarthys, management was sufficiently impressed with the significance of the event that it rented a television set and placed it in a boardroom. I watched the event along with others and was flabbergasted when the full Court appeared on television and the Chief Justice read out the results. There was a swift recital of the appeal in matter so-and-so is allowed and the appeal in so-and-so is dismissed in part followed by a list of yeses and noes and not applicables to a series of questions. It was entirely incomprehensible. Then the television announcer turned to the station's constitutional expert and asked him who had won. It was then that we learned that advance copies of the judgment had not been distributed, not even to counsel for the parties. This did not keep the media from talking about the case throughout the day, but the stage for utter confusion about the result had already been set with representatives of the federal and provincial governments both claiming victory.

Robinette was in Toronto, and a copy of the judgment was couriered to him from Ottawa. Late in the day, I managed to get a copy of it and took it home to read. It was then that I realized that far from a Government of Canada victory, it was a total loss. Trudeau was right back to where he started. He needed a favourable consensus from the provinces to proceed. The claims of success were just a spin placed on the case by Chrétien. I learned of this from Robert. I asked him if he was one of the counsel present:

Yes, I was there. I was there the day the judgment was released. I was asked to come to Ottawa and to advise the Minister who was Mr. Chrétien on what should be his response. So after the judgment, I met Mr. Chrétien just outside the courtroom in the Supreme Court Building, and he asked in French, "Est-ce qu'on a gagné ou perdu?" [Have we won or lost?] I said: "Les deux." [Both.] And then he said, "Bien, je ne peux pas aller dire ça au média, tu dois me donner quelque chose d'autre!" [Well, I can't go and tell the press that, you must tell me something else!] I said, "Le mieux que je peux faire c'est de dire que du point de vue légal vous avez gagné; du point de vue conventionnel vous avez perdu" [The best I can do is tell you that you've won on the legal front; you've lost on the conventional front.] And then I remember he said, "Donc nous avons perdu." [Then we lost.]

Of course the press people were there waiting for him so he had to give some sort of an immediate reaction to the judgment. But in this case everybody came out winning. Chrétien said, "We won. The Court said that we're not legally bound to get the consent of the provinces," and he was right. And then the provinces said "We won because there is a constitutional convention requiring the consent of the provinces," and they were right also. So everybody won; there was no loser like the reference on the secession of Quebec. There was no loser, all winners.

The Supreme Court's decision is not easy to read, but the constitutional questions are answered in a straightforward way. The Court effectively resolved the issues by dividing the argument into the two basic essentials: Did the Canadian Parliament have the legal authority to make the request in issue, and was there a convention of provincial concurrence that was an impediment to the UK Parliament acting on the request? Chief Justice Laskin and Justices Dickson, Beetz, Estey, McIntyre,

Chouinard, and Lamer answered the first question in the affirmative. Justices Martland and Ritchie dissented. The majority of the Court was of the opinion that the proposed Resolution was within the legislative competence of the Houses of Parliament, notwithstanding that it affected provincial legislative powers. There were no legal principles of federalism that were offended by the House of Commons and the Senate proceeding without the concurrence of the provinces. If there was a requirement of provincial consent, it had not crystallized into law. In any event, any questions about the procedures adopted by the two Houses of Parliament in making a request of the Mother Parliament to amend the *BNA Act* had no relevance to its authority to act on the request.

On the issue of whether any convention of provincial consent existed that had the force of law, the majority reasons, which resonate with Chief Justice Laskin's powerful voice, take up the academic cudgels with Laskin's rival, Professor Lederman:

> A contrary view [to the opinion that the validity of conventions cannot be the subject of court proceedings] relied on by the provincial appellants is that expressed by Professor W.R. Lederman in two published articles, one entitled "The Process of Constitutional Amendment in Canada" (1966–67), 12 McGill L.J. 371 and the second entitled "Constitutional Amendment and Canadian Unity" (1978), Law Soc. U.C. Lectures 17. As a respected scholar, Professor Lederman's views deserve more than cursory consideration. He himself recognizes that there are contrary views, including those of an equally distinguished scholar, Professor F.R. Scott: see Scott, *Essays on the Constitution* (1977), at pp. 144, 169, 204–5, 245, 370–71, 402. There is also the contrary view of Professor Hogg, already cited.
>
> Professor Lederman relies in part on a line of cases that has already been considered, especially the reasons of Duff C.J. in the Labour Conventions case. The leap from convention to law is explained almost as if there was a common law of constitutional law, but originat-

ing in political practice. That is simply not so. What is desirable as a political limitation does not translate into a legal limitation, without expression in imperative constitutional text or statute. The position advocated is all the more unacceptable when substantial provincial compliance or consent is by him said to be sufficient. Although Professor Lederman would not give a veto to Prince Edward Island, he would to Ontario or Quebec or British Columbia or Alberta. This is an impossible position for a court to manage.

The provinces had relied heavily on the fact that in the overwhelming number of cases where the Government of Canada had sought amendments to the Constitution in the past, it had in fact had the consent of the affected provinces. In his oral history, Robinette conceded that this was Canada's weakest point, particularly when read along with a government white paper, to which reference will be made almost immediately. However, the majority of the Court adopted Robinette's argument, pointing out, once again, that what was politically desirable did not necessarily translate into law:

> It was urged before us that a host of cases have given legal force to conventions. This is an over-drawn proposition. One case in which direct recognition and enforcement of a convention was sought is *Madzimbamuto v. Lardner-Burke and George* [[1969] 1 A.C. 645]. There the Privy Council rejected the assertion that a convention formally recognized by the United Kingdom as established, namely, that it would not legislate for Southern Rhodesia on matters within the competence of the latter's legislature without its government's consent, could not be overridden by British legislation made applicable to Southern Rhodesia after the unilateral declaration of independence by the latter's government. Speaking for the Privy Council, Lord Reid pointed out that although the convention was a very important one, "it had no legal

effect in limiting the legal power of Parliament" (at p. 723). And, again (at the same page):

> It is often said that it would be unconstitution-
> al for the United Kingdom Parliament to do
> certain things, meaning that the moral, political
> and other reasons against doing them are so
> strong that most people would regard it as
> highly improper if Parliament did these things.
> But that does not mean that it is beyond the
> power of Parliament to do such things. If
> Parliament chose to do any of them the courts
> could not hold the Act of Parliament invalid. It
> may be that it would have been thought, before
> 1965, that it would be unconstitutional to dis-
> regard this convention. But it may also be that
> the unilateral Declaration of Independence
> released the United Kingdom from any obliga-
> tion to observe the convention. Their Lordships
> in declaring the law are not concerned with
> these matters. They are only concerned with the
> legal powers of Parliament.

And finally, on the issue of the validity of the procedure adopted by our Houses of Parliament, the majority stated:

> How Houses of Parliament proceed, how a provincial leg-
> islative assembly proceeds is in either case a matter of self-
> definition, subject to any overriding constitutional or self-
> imposed statutory or indoor prescription. It is unneces-
> sary here to embark on any historical review of the "court"
> aspect of Parliament and the immunity of its procedures
> from judicial review. Courts come into the picture when
> legislation is enacted and not before (unless references are
> made to them for their opinion on a bill or a proposed
> enactment). It would be incompatible with the self-regu-

lating —"inherent" is as apt a word — authority of Houses of Parliament to deny their capacity to pass any kind of resolution. Reference may appropriately be made to art. 9 of the Bill of Rights of 1689, undoubtedly in force as part of the law of Canada, which provides that "Proceedings in Parliament ought not to be impeached or questioned in any Court or Place out of Parliament".

The second question was another matter. Justices Martland, Ritchie, Dickson, Beetz, Chouinard, and Lamer held that a substantial degree of provincial consent, to be determined by the politicians and not the courts, was conventionally required for an amendment to the Constitution. In arriving at this conclusion, they relied heavily on a white paper published in 1965 by Minister of Justice Guy Favreau, entitled "The Amendment of the Constitution of Canada." The White Paper described accepted constitutional rules and principles, the following of which was used by the provinces as the club with which to beat the feds throughout the entire patriation process:

> The fourth general principle is that the Canadian Parliament will not request an amendment directly affecting federal–provincial relationships without prior consultation and agreement with the provinces. This principle did not emerge as early as others but since 1907, and particularly since 1930, has gained increasing recognition and acceptance. The nature and the degree of provincial participation in the amending process, however, have not lent themselves to easy definition.

The majority of the Court on the second issue took this statement very seriously. They said:

> This statement is not a casual utterance. It is contained in a carefully drafted document which had been circulated to all the provinces prior to its publication and had been found satisfactory by all of them (see Commons

Debates, 1965, at p. 11574, and Background Paper published by the Government of Canada, The Role of the United Kingdom in the Amendment of the Canadian Constitution (March 1981), at p. 30). It was published as a white paper, that is as an official statement of government policy, under the authority of the federal Minister of Justice as member of a government responsible to Parliament, neither House of which, so far as we know, has taken issue with it. This statement is a recognition by all the actors in the precedents that the requirement of provincial agreement is a constitutional rule.

Accordingly, we get the odd conclusion from the case as a whole that conventions have no legal effect but are a constitutional impediment to amending our founding statute. No authority was cited for such a conclusion.

McMurtry had appeared as lead counsel for Ontario in support of the position of the federal government. Like Chrétien, he took an all-smiles approach to the media after the decision was released. But once he had an opportunity to absorb the reasons of the Supreme Court, he realized that there would have to be another First Ministers' Conference. It was set for the first week of November 1981 in Ottawa.

Once again, McMurtry became active behind the scenes with his friends Chrétien and Roy Romanow, both of whom were anxious to renew the patriation process. Initially, McMurtry did not have much optimism that they could reach a consensus, but as he renewed acquaintances with those political leaders with whom he had worked in the summer of 1980, they reformed their old alliances as personal friends if not necessarily political allies. In the course of numerous discussions, he felt that they could come out of the conference with something, not with Quebec, but with the others. He told me in his interview that he flew to Ottawa the day before the conference and had breakfast or lunch with Chrétien. He recounted the following exchange with him:

> I said to Chrétien, "I've been talking to people in different provinces, and I think there is a good chance

there could be a breakthrough, but your job, Jean, is to keep the Prime Minister from losing his cool and prevent him from getting highly argumentative at least for the first two or three days because you know how he loves to argue and he ends up putting down people who just get irritated on a personal level."

I remember Chrétien saying to me, "You're right, Roy. Da boss, he sure like to argue." And he paused and said, "You know, he won a lot of arguments." But there was an interesting pause and then, "But, you see, he also lose da war."

In McMurtry's mind, Chrétien was shrewd enough to realize that Trudeau had to be persuaded to behave. Trudeau was not the sort of person like Lyndon Baines Johnson who believed in, "Let's sit down and reason together." Chrétien had to let Trudeau know that McMurtry and Romanow had been in close touch with the provinces, and if anything was to be accomplished, he had to avoid insulting some of the premiers. The message seemed to get through, but the conference was still very confrontational. Even on the first day, the organizers could not get everybody together for more than a part of the day because the Gang of Eight wanted to caucus by themselves. However, this gave McMurtry an opportunity to spend some time with Trudeau alone and to talk about the notwithstanding clause, a proposed provision that would permit Parliament or a provincial legislature to declare that a particular statute or a provision thereof would operate notwithstanding the provisions of the *Charter of Rights and Freedoms*.[219]

McMurtry had no love for this opting-out provision, but he recognized that it had some special appeal to Peter Lougheed and Alan Blakeney because of their deep-seated respect for Parliamentary supremacy. The Prime Minister did not like the idea at all. It ran counter to his view of entrenched Charter rights. According to McMurtry:

In any event, discussion went back and forth, and what broke the logjam really was the fact that since it appeared that we couldn't agree amongst the provinces, particularly with respect to the *Charter* rights and the amending formula, both these questions should be put to the public through a national referendum. Trudeau had been exchanging comments and needling Quebec about the fact that they lost the Quebec referendum in 1980 and that these referendums were good things. The premier of Quebec was obviously committed to this very special democratic process of going to the people, and when Trudeau said that since they weren't going to be able to agree on the patriation formula, "Let's have a national referendum on the amending formula and the *Charter of Rights*," Lévesque said yes he would certainly be happy to debate the Prime Minister again with respect to these referendum questions.

But I knew Lougheed and Blakeney quite well by that time, and I knew that referendums were an absolute anathema to them because they perceived quite accurately a referendum as an excuse for the federal government to go directly to the people of Alberta and Saskatchewan and ignore their governments. I knew that Lévesque had really created a great opportunity to break the logjam. We were all meeting in a private room, and I remember, within five minutes, getting Trudeau to have a coffee break because there were some important things to discuss. I still can remember running, I mean literally running, over to Lougheed and saying, "Look, I've been spending some time with Trudeau. He's absolutely serious about this business of a national referendum which your pal, Lévesque, is supporting him on. I can tell you, Peter, after all this work, for all these years, all we are going to come out of this is with a referendum, and you can thank your friend, Lévesque, for this."

Well, I knew that Peter, just by what he said and his body language, had decided that this was the time to part company with Lévesque. By this time, a pretty

close personal friendship had developed between
Lévesque and Lougheed, and Blakeney and Trudeau
had sort of provided the glue between these premiers
that created a fairly close relationship even though they
had obviously very different views of the future of the
country. But that kind of broke the logjam, and we
knew that we had something to consider and review.
Chrétien and Romanow and I prepared notes and we
wrote out little memorandums on what we thought
would sell. We then spent the next fifteen hours trying
to get everybody on side, as Lévesque later said, "while
he was peacefully sleeping across the hall during the
Night of the Long Knives."

The principal compromise was the notwithstanding clause, because this gave Lougheed and Blakeney,
who were really the leaders of the other premiers with
the exception of Quebec, an honourable compromise,
believing as strongly as they did in the traditions of
parliamentary supremacy. Also, we agreed to an
amending formula that would not give either Ontario
or Quebec an automatic veto because of our population. There was an amending formula that we called for
political reasons the "Alberta formula," although we
talked about it in Toronto the year before, where you
could amend the Constitution with the support of
seven provinces representing fifty percent of Canada.
So this would prevent Ontario and Quebec having an
automatic veto and this had some appeal, of course, to
the western provinces in particular.

Meanwhile, the indefatigable Kershaw Committee continued its
labours in London. It seemed to have assumed that its responsibility was
to critique the proceedings in Canada and report to the public at large
from time to time. Its Second Report[220] commented on the judgment of
our Supreme Court of Canada, and its Third Report[221] seemed to provide
a qualified imprimatur to our proceedings. After noting disapprovingly

that "for many months the U.K. Parliament seemed about to be faced with an urgent request that would have been truly unprecedented because it would have been made outside the conventional rules of the Canadian constitution," the committee concluded on a note of self-congratulation:[222]

> In the event, however, the situation has not arisen. The present request does not invite Members of the UK Parliament to participate in unconstitutional action. We therefore think that Members can properly welcome this opportunity finally to discharge the responsibilities of the UK Parliament to the federal community it established in Canada in 1867 and for whose convenience it retained anomalous legal powers for fifty years after its first attempt to transfer them. We trust that the contribution made by your Committee to the consideration of these matters on both sides of the Atlantic have been of assistance in maintaining good relations between our respective nations and peoples and for their extension into the future. While the legal ties are now to disappear, we shall continue to hold in common the principles, practices, power and potential of Parliamentary democracy.

Another impediment, Chief Robert Manuel's action on behalf of 123 Indian chiefs from Canada, also disappeared. The Attorney General of England moved before Sir Robert Megarry in April of 1982 and had the Statement of Claim struck out as revealing no cause of action.[223] An appeal to the Court of Appeal was unsuccessful, that court holding on July 30, 1982, that the fact that the preamble to the *Canada Act, 1982* declared that it was enacted with the request and consent of Canada confirmed the validity of the process.[224]

So the Constitution was finally patriated, and we had the *Charter of Rights and Freedoms* and an amending formula. But it was a messy business. In the strongly held opinion of one man, Pierre Elliott Trudeau, it need not have been that way if six judges of the Supreme Court of Canada had stuck to their judicial knitting. In a remarkable address on the occasion of the opening of the Bora Laskin Law Library at the University of Toronto,[225] Trudeau praised the late Chief Justice Laskin's great intelligence, which, combined with a concern for human beings and a desire to live in a society that permitted self-fulfillment to all, contributed mightily to the wisdom of the dissent he formulated along with Justices Estey and McIntyre in the *Patriation Reference*. To an audience packed with judges, senior lawyers, and academics, as well as the graduating student body, Trudeau launched into an attack on the majority reasons of the Supreme Court. In the audience was Chief Justice Brian Dickson, who was a member of the majority on the convention issue. It was the most remarkable criticism of a major judgment given before an academic gathering that has ever been brought to my attention. It was also brilliant. I will share a few of his comments:

> That dissent, I shall argue in this address, was not only the better law, but the better common sense, and consequently it was also wiser politically. Had it prevailed over the majority view, I believe that Canada's future would have been more assured.
>
> ...
>
> I have long ceased to be a student of Canadian constitutional law. But I have not quite forgotten all I learned during my political career. It is against that background that I propose to review with you some aspects of the fateful Supreme Court decision on the patriation of the Constitution, arguably the most important decision it ever rendered or ever will render. Indeed, the various judicial opinions that were handed down in the *Patriation Reference* went to the very roots of the Constitution, determining at a particular point in time the nature of the constituent power for Canada, and therefore defining – albeit indirectly – the essence of Canadian sovereignty. Because of that, the political consequences flowing from those opinions were of

great importance, and they will continue to reverber-
ate into the future, throughout whatever history may
yet lie ahead.

...

In such circumstances [of a surge in provincialism], the
first ministers could only fail to agree. They so failed in
1927, under Mackenzie King's Prime-ministership. And
since the issue was never put to rest, they failed again
under Bennett in 1931, as they would fail under St.
Laurent in 1950, under Diefenbaker in 1960, under
Pearson in 1964, and under Trudeau in 1971.

The first ministers failed because they could not
agree on the nature of Canadian sovereignty, that is to
say whether it ultimately rested with the provinces,
who – by coming together – made up a country called
Canada, or whether it resided in some undefined combination between the federal state and the provinces,
all existing in their own right and each exercising a
share of the overall sovereignty. And it seemed rather
obvious – given the unlikelihood at the time that a
prime minister of Canada would ever capitulate to the
compact theorists – that the first ministers would continue failing forever and Canada would never be a
truly sovereign country, unless the problem were
somehow resolved.

...

There were only two ways to solve the conundrum. The
government of Canada could accept the "compact theory," that is to say recognize that our country was nothing more than a community of communities wherein
fundamental powers — including the power to patriate
the Constitution — flowed from the provinces which

had freely united to form a loose confederation. Or the government of Canada, as the sole governing body empowered to act in the name of all Canadians, could reject the compact theory, hold that Canada was something more than and different from the sum of its parts, and proceed to patriate the Constitution unilaterally.

We chose the latter course...

What I find most remarkable about the majority judgment [on the question whether provincial consent was required by convention] is the number of times their Lordships chose to turn a deaf ear and a blind eye to the legal arguments which might have led them in another direction. [Trudeau then listed eight points that the majority overlooked.]

. . .

On the basis of all of the foregoing eight points, there seems to be little doubt that the majority judges had set their minds to delivering a judgment that would force the federal and the provincial governments to seek a political compromise. No doubt believing in good faith that a political agreement would be better for Canada than unilateral legal patriation, they blatantly manipulated the evidence before them so as to arrive at the desired result. They then wrote a judgment which tried to lend a fig-leaf of legality to their preconceived conclusion.

. . .

Some of you may remember that I always have been wary of conventional wisdom. After fifty-four years of failure to patriate the Constitution through compromise, it seemed to me that Canadians had a right to expect a legal decision from their Supreme Court, rather than some well-meaning admonitions about what was politically proper. And my purpose in returning to the *Patriation Reference* today is to point out — with the benefit of hindsight — that the minority judgment, couched in what Professor McWhinney has described as Chief Justice Laskin's "clearly identifiable drafting style," was not only the better law but also the wiser counsel.

McMurtry was one of those present. On leaving Convocation Hall, he caught up with Trudeau and said, "Don't you think you were pretty hard on Dickson? He looked pretty upset." Unrepentant, Trudeau replied, "He's upset? I'm the one who appointed him Chief Justice."

Robinette was of the same opinion as Trudeau about the quality of the judgment in issue, although he never to my knowledge went public with his opinion. He was even careful in his oral history[226] to describe the majority judgment on the status of conventions as "embarking on an act of judicial statesmanship." To me privately, he was much more direct. "It was politics, George, just politics. They decided to throw the problem back to the politicians." He was very disappointed, not just because he had failed to persuade the Court to reach a result that he was satisfied in law was the correct result, but because he recognized that by ducking the problem in the manner that they adopted, the majority of the Court had missed a great opportunity to bring the constitutional argument to an end. Instead of thinking like judges and deciding the law as it appeared from the legal precedents, they became concerned about the wisdom of forcing the provinces, particularly Quebec, into a constitutional marriage, or, more accurately, a renewal of their vows of marriage. Those who were concerned that the *Charter of Rights and Freedoms* would stimulate our judges into a rash of judicial activism could relax. It had happened already.

In my view, the members of the Court who were concerned about the political reactions of the provinces underestimated the power of the rule of law. Canadians may respect convention, but they obey the law. If Quebec had been continued as a member of Canada under the *Canada Act, 1982,* the Québécois would have griped but would have gone along with it, just as they are doing now while ostensibly outside of Confederation.

Epilogue

JOHN ROBINETTE DIED ON NOVEMBER 18, 1996, two days before what would have been his ninetieth birthday. The last five years of his life were neither memorable nor elevating. In fact they were very sad. Instead of a continual festival of fond farewells in the company of friends, John Robinette was isolated at the Central Park Lodge on Spadina Avenue — ironically, as he remarked to me, across from the home where he grew up — as he became progressively more dependent on professional caregivers to assist him with his most elementary needs. He had Alzheimer's disease, the incurable and irreversible organic mental disorder that increasingly deprived him of his self-control and caused his slow decline into dementia.

I am informed that Alzheimer's disease is difficult to diagnose in its early stages, and I would think that this was be very much the case with Robinette. When I severed my professional relationship with him on my appointment to the bench on December 4, 1984, I made a point of maintaining our social bond. I lunched with him regularly and kept in touch generally. He had become physically frail, but much of this was attributed to the aftermath of a fall he suffered on a trip to the Middle East in 1978. The Advocates Society had arranged for a trip to Israel, and Joan and I, along with John and his wife, Lois, joined with our fellow advocates for the trip. It was a memorable excursion, but an accident befell Robinette that seemed innocent enough at the time. In descending from a tour bus, he turned his ankle and fell. He suffered a very bad sprain to that ankle, and unfortunately, he did not go to a hospital about it. His ankle never fully recovered, and it became obvious that because of it Robinette lost some of his confidence in walking.

Another shield to an early diagnosis was Robinette's formidable reputation. You do not readily question statements made by a person whose pronouncements had become almost Delphic. If an observation of his appeared somewhat off-centre, the listener was more likely to question his own knowledge of the soundness of the utterance than Robinette's. The fact that he appeared reticent and withdrawn on occasions did not strike others at the firm as at all unusual because Robinette was never voluble in any case.

However, in the summer of 1991, at Southampton, Robinette had another bad fall and was admitted to the Owen Sound General Hospital.[227] There were no significant physical injuries, but the concussion that ensued from the fall caused him to become disoriented and delusional. This state continued for about six weeks. His doctors suspected that his condition had gone beyond brain trauma and that he was in the preliminary stages of cognitive degenerative dementia. He was transferred to Toronto, where the diagnosis of Alzheimer's was confirmed, and the family, after giving the matter agonizing consideration, made the decision to have him admitted to Central Park Lodge in September 1991.[228]

The news came as a surprise and a shock to me, and I hurried over to see him in his new quarters. He had recovered from the bout of dementia and spoke quietly and with composure about his condition. He said that at first he had resisted the suggestion that he be placed in a nursing home, but he was now satisfied that it was the correct decision. He was reconciled to remaining there indefinitely. He spoke with some enthusiasm about the spacious suite he was occupying and the standard of care he was receiving. I had not seen him since June 1991, shortly before he went on his usual two-month holiday, and in one sense he did not seem that much different to me. However, Dale Robinette had briefed me about his medical condition and, with that background, I realized that there was something radically wrong him. He spoke of himself as if he were a third person that he was representing and in this case apologizing for. Dale had been most upset when she told me about her father, and I could see why. It was bad enough for me to come to grips with the knowledge that the greatest counsel in Canada was losing control of the mental faculties that made him the wonder of the professional world. It must have been devastating to a daughter who worshipped the ground he walked on to see him committed to the care of persons with whom, save for now, he had nothing intellectually in common.

I visited him regularly every ten days or so until a few months before his death when it became obvious that he did not recognize me anymore and in fact regarded my presence as an intrusion. Visits in the early years were no chore at all. I had always enjoyed his company, and his pleasure at seeing me gave me a great lift. He was eager to talk, and we discussed my life on the court and recent judgments that had been delivered. His secretary, Muriel Reid, visited him regularly and brought mail, best wishes cards, and the recent Ontario Reports. He tried for a while to keep up with the profession and read the daily newspapers. However, as time evolved it was obvious that he was not reading much and was increasingly dependent on the television for what news he was interested in. However, while his areas of interest progressively narrowed, we still had sports to talk about. In those their halcyon days, the Blue Jays were "in flight," as Jerry Howarth, my favourite baseball announcer, likes to say.

These were difficult days for Lois, her three daughters, and their children. I kept up with John's medical developments through Dale and knew how deeply distressed they were about his deteriorating mental condition. They tried to see the humour in the situations that arose, and I did the same. As his memory failed, I retreated more and more into his deep memory to the point where he ended up remembering me as his student. On this road back, he became confused and asked me on a number of occasions just what it was that I was now doing. When I told him I was a member of the Court of Appeal, he looked surprised but unfailingly congratulated me on the appointment.

The death of this kindly man was a release. The manner of his passing left me deeply depressed, and it took some time for me to put out of my mind the confused and fearful old man I saw huddled in his bed on my last visit. I am pleased that I was given the opportunity to write this book. It has allowed me to relive that part of my professional life that I shared with his and to remember the bold, even brash, advocate who dominated every courtroom and rejoiced in hurling back every confrontation with a challenge of his own. "Does this man look like Jimmy Cagney?" Not if his lawyer is John J. Robinette, he doesn't.

Notes

1   Memorandum of December 1997, supplementing Oral History of John J. Robinette, Law Society of Upper Canada (recorded beginning June 18, 1987).
2   The following account is based on JJR, Oral History.
3   From a family memoir written by JJR in November 1970.
4   JJR, Oral History.
5   Curriculum Vitae, John Josiah Robinette, Archives, Law Society of Upper Canada (LSUC).
6   Jack Batten, *Robinette: The Dean of Canadian Lawyers* (Toronto: Macmillan of Canada, 1985), pp. 27–28.
7   JJR, Oral History.
8   JJR, Oral History.
9   Minutes of Convocation, Archives, LSUC.
10   JJR, Oral History.
11   [1945] O.R. 411 (H.C.J.), affirmed by [1946] O.R. 90 (C.A.), leave to appeal to Supreme Court of Canada refused [1946] S.C.R. 462.
12   Batten, *supra*.
13   See *Roncarelli v. Duplessis*, [1959] S.C.R. 12.
14   R.S.C. 1927, C. 206 and 1940 (Dom), c. 13 respectively.
15   Robinette also argued as a procedural matter that the application for a declaration against the Crown should be initiated in the Exchequer Court of Canada, not the Ontario High Court of Justice.
16   JJR, Oral History at p. 247.
17   [1948] 4 D.L.R. 123 (Ont. H.C.J.); affirmed by [1949] 4 D.L.R. 375 (Ont. C.A.); reversed by the Supreme Court of Canada [1951] S.C.R. 64, 1 D.L.R. 321.

18   I am restricting my analysis of this case pretty much to what appears in the reported case itself, but I would be remiss if I did not acknowledge my reliance on a chapter by James W. St. G. Walker in his informative book, *"Race" Rights and the Law in the Supreme Court of Canada* (Waterloo: Wilfrid Laurier University Press, 1997), Chapter 4, p.183 for his account of the political background to the fight against discrimination in Canada and the involvement of the Canadian Jewish Congress in supporting the *Noble and Wolf* litigation.

19   (1848), 2 Ph. 774, 41 E.R. 1143.

20   JJR, Oral History.

21   JJR, Oral History at p. 287

22   The evidence led by the Crown at Evelyn's trial is summarized from the transcript prepared for the appeal presided over by Chief Justice Robertson and appears in the report of the appeal in the Ontario Reports. I had available to me the original transcript, which I read, (Archives of Ontario, Series R.G. 22-523, Court of Appeal File 34125) but saw no point in duplicating the Chief Justice's effort and simply paraphrased some of his findings. I also made extensive use of the notes of the argument in the reported case by Alan B. Harvey, K.C., who succeeded Robinette as editor, which are particularly helpful. So far as I am aware they constitute the only official record of what was said by the various counsel and the members of the panel composed of Robertson C.J.O., Henderson, Laidlaw, Hogg, and Aylesworth JJ.A.

23   JJR, Oral History at p. 202.

24   [1945] O.W.N. 1, 1 D.L.R. 767, 83 C.C.C. 23.

25   Archibald, *Criminal Pleading, Evidence & Practice*, 31st ed. (1943), p. 371.

26   *Taylor on Evidence*, 12th ed. (1931), vol. 1, pp. 556-7.

27   *Journal of Criminal Law*, vol. 8 (1944), p. 148.

28   [1927] S.C.R. 436, 48 C.C.C. 97, [1927] 4 D.L.R. 245.

29   [1943] S.C.R. 250, 79 C.C.C. 221, [1943] 2 D.L.R. 417.

30   *Ibrahim v. The King*, [1914] A.C. 599.

31   [1945] 3 W.W.R. 280, [1946] 1 D.L.R. 521, 62 B.C.R. 16, 85 C.C.C. 158.

32   (1914), 20 B.C.R. 81, 24 C.C.C. 157.

33   *Wigmore on Evidence*, 3rd ed. (1940), vol. 3, pp. 345 et seq.

34   Patrick Boyer, *A Passion for Justice*, The Osgoode Society for Canadian Legal History, 1994, pp. 200-1.

35   *Ibid.*, pp. 183-84.

36   Transcript commencing p.882 at p. 877.

37   Transcript commencing at p. 882.

38   *Ibrahim v. The King*, [1914] A.C. 599.

39   Transcript at p. 199.

40   It must be remembered that this post-war era evidenced little concern about what we would now regard as inappropriate ethnic designations.

41   Transcript at p. 970.

42   JJR, Oral History at p. 290.

43   *R. v. Dick*, [1947] O.R. 695.

44   Boyer, *A Passion for Justice*, *supra* at p. 201.

45   Transcript of Trial, *Rex v. Evelyn Dick* for the murder of the infant Peter David White MacLean, Spring Assizes, 1947, Hamilton, Ontario.

46   *An Evening to Celebrate John J. Robinette*, Four Seasons Hotel, Toronto, October 23, 1989.

47   *Ibid.*

48   *McCarthy & McCarthy, A History*, 1978. This book was prepared under the direction of Beverley Matthews and was intended for private circulation only. I received my copy in 1978 when I was a partner in the firm. I have relied upon it extensively for the early history of the firm and for the period immediately after my arrival. A comparison of this text and that of the *History* will show that I accept the explanation given as to the spectacular expansion of McCarthys and other established law firms in the period following the Second World War. However, for the period following 1951, I have liberally inserted my own recollections and observations.

49   It is noteworthy that in selecting "The Ten Greatest Lawyers Ever" in its May 2000 publication, *Canadian Lawyer* chose as two of the ten Robinette as an advocate and Matthews as a law firm builder.

50   Duncan Finlayson enjoyed an enviable career as a civil trial and appellate counsel with what he claimed was the oldest law firm in Ontario, Kingsmill, Mills, later to be merged with the much larger firm, Miller Thomson. Because of a strong family resemblance, my brother and I were often mistaken for each other. To add to the confusion, we both shared our mother's maiden name, Duncan. My brother was to be called Kenneth, but thanks to our maternal grandfather, David Duncan, who persistently called him Duncan, this Christian name endured for my brother.

51 R.S.O. 1950, c.243 ss. 162, 174 and 179.
52 See reported case: *Regina ex rel. Revie v. Horovitz* [1953] 3 D.L.R. 403.
53 [1950] O.R. 137.
54 [1951] O.R. 205.
55 [1952] S.C.R. 94.
56 [1955] A.C. 627.
57 (1681) 3 Ch. Ca. 1.
58 [1891] A.C. 531 at 583.
59 [1951] O.R. 224.
60 [1951] O.R. 225.
61 *Minister of National Revenue v. Anaconda Brass.*
62 An Act to amend the Supreme Court Act, S.C. 1949, Chapter 37, s. 3.
63 JJR, Oral History.
64 Boyd's exploits and those of his fellow gang members are chronicled by Brian Valée in his highly readable book, *Edwin Alonzo Boyd: The Story of the Notorious Boyd Gang.* (Toronto: Doubleday Canada Ltd., 1997).
65 *Toronto Star*, March 24, 1952.
66 Batten, *supra.*
67 The following is taken from Perry's evidence at trial.
68 I have relied on Marilyn M. Litvak, *Edward James Lennox, "Builder of Toronto"* (Toronto: Dundurn Press, 1995) and a City of Toronto brochure commemorating the 100th anniversary of Old City Hall for the history and part of the description of the Old City Hall.
69 Transcript, Ontario Archives.
70 *R. v. Suchan* [1952] O.J. No. 292 in a court composed of Pickup C.J.O, Hope, Hogg, Aylesworth, and Gibson JJ.A.
71 The selection proceedings in this case are considered unique enough that when challenges for cause gained some popularity in the 1970s, the transcript of this challenge procedure was reported separately as *R. v. Lesso and Jackson* in volume 23 of the 1973 Criminal Reports at page 179.
72 Steven Suchan was referred to throughout the trial as Valente Lesso, but he is referred to in this writing as Steven Suchan.
73 [1948] S.C.R. 226.
74 *R. v. Lizette* [1951] S.C.R. 115 and *R. v. Noor Mohamed* [1949] A.C. 182.

75 JJR, Oral History.

76 Charles Pullen, *The Life and Times of Arthur Maloney,* The Last of the Tribunes, The Osgoode Society for Legal History, 1994.

77 Batten, *supra*, pp.117-18.

78 *R. v. Suchan and Jackson* (1952), 104 C.C.C. 193 (S.C.C.).

79 JJR, Oral History.

80 Batten, *supra*, p.121.

81 JJR, Oral History.

82 John Arnup, personal interview with the author. November 14, 2001.

83 This information was obtained from the Archives of the Law Society of Upper Canada (LSUC) and from the reported case *Re The Law Society of Upper Canada and Robinette*, [1954] O.R. 349.

84 Letter dated December 31, 1953 from Robinette to Smith, LSUC Archives.

85 Minutes of Convocation, LSUC Archives.

86 *R. v. McNamara (No.2)* (1981), 56 C.C.C. (2d) 516 (Ont. C.A.).

87 The original leaders of Upper and Lower Canada were entitled to be addressed as Prime Minister. This designation continued in Ontario until William G. Davis became Premier.

88 John Arnup, personal interview, *supra*.

89 I recall that Robinette did not start wearing a director's coat to Convocation until after his resignation as a judge. He had bought the formal wear upon being appointed and it was intended to be his judicial out-of-court attire, which was mandatory in those days.

90 Trial before McLennan J. and a jury, which rendered its verdict on September 27, 1954. First decision by Court of Appeal reported at [1955] O.R. 542; Decision of Supreme Court of Canada reported at [1956] S.C.R.366; Second jury trial held in Fall of 1956; Second decision by Court of Appeal reported at [1957] O.R. 402.

91 R.S.O. 1950, c. 243, s. 263.

92 The judgment of LeBel J., is reported as *Re Ross and Board of Commissioners of Police for the City of Toronto*, [1953] O.R. 556, [1953] 3 D.L.R. 597, 107 C.C.C. 134, and that of McRuer C.J.H.C. under the same style of cause, [1953] O.R. 947, [1954] 1 D.L.R. 706, 107 C.C.C. 147.

93 [1972] O.J. No. 656 (H.C.J.); [1974] O.J. 186 (C.A.); (1976) 66 D.L.R. (3d) 186 (S.C.C.).

94 *Globe & Mail*, September 24, 1954.

95   JJR, Oral History, p. 510.
96   George Archer-Shee was the teenaged boy who was expelled
       from a naval academy in England just before World War I after
       being falsely accused of stealing a postal note from a classmate.
       His battle for vindication and readmission became a *cause
       célèbre* and was fictionalized in the play and movie "The
       Winslow Boy."
97   [1955] O.R. 542 et seq.
98   Headnote in [1955] O.R. 542.
99   *Ibid.*
100   [1956] S.C.R. 366.
101   William Kaplan, *Bad Judgment: The Case of Mr. Justice Leo A.
       Landreville* (Toronto: University of Toronto Press, 1996).
102   The specific accounts of what transpired and the documents to
       which I refer are contained in a number of reports: Report of the
       Law Society of Upper Canada, *The Special Committee Re:
       Landreville J.* (April 26, 1965); Ontario Securities Commission
       papers, Ontario Archives; The Hon. I.C. Rand, Q.C., *Inquiry Re:
       The Honourable Mr. Justice Leo A. Landreville* (1966); Minutes of
       Proceedings of The Special Joint Committee of The Senate and
       of The House of Commons Respecting Mr. Justice Landreville,
       jointly chaired by The Hon. Senator Daniel A. Lang and Mr.
       Ovide Laflamme, M.P.
103   The *Municipal Franchises Act*, as amended in 1955, was the con-
       trolling statute at this time. It gave to the Ontario Fuel Board (later
       the Ontario Energy Board) authority to approve the terms and
       conditions of gas franchises and to dispense with the assent of the
       electors of the municipality to the granting of a gas franchise.
104   Unreported reasons, Magistrate Albert Marck at Sudbury, Ontario
       (October 8, 1964) and filed as Appendix "D" to the Minutes of
       Proceedings of The Special Joint Committee, *supra.*
105   *Ibid.* at p.198.
106   Rand Report, *supra*, at p. 7.
107   R.S.O. 1950, c. 351.
108   *The Queen v. NONG Ltd., R.K. Farris and C.S. Clark:* unreport-
       ed judgment of Magistrate Elmore; Ontario Securities
       Commission Papers, Ontario Archives.
109   Rand Report, *supra*, at pp. 21-24.
110   *Ibid.* at pp. 20-21.
111   Law Society's Report, *supra*, at paras. 8-14.

112   *Ibid.* at para. 8 (iv).

113   Kaplan, *Bad Judgment, supra*, at p. 198.

114   Rand Report, *supra*, at pp. 48-77.

115   Special Joint Committee Report, *supra*, at Appendix "D," p.198.

116   *Ibid.*

117   According to the press release, a Bill of Indictment before a grand jury would amount to a repetition of the proceedings before the magistrate. It was an extraordinary proceeding only to be used where there has been some defect or omission in the enquiry before the magistrate. See *Ibid.* at p. 199.

118   Oral History of John Arnup, Law Society of Upper Canada (November 4, 1982) at p. 302.

119   Rand Report, *supra*, Appendix "A" at pp.117-18.

120   Arnup's Oral History, *supra*, at pp. 304-05.

121   R.S.C. 1952, Chap.154.

122   Special Joint Committee Report, *supra*, Appendix "F."

123   Rand Report, *supra*, at p. 95.

124   David Humphrey, personal interview with the author. April 13, 2002.

125   Rand Report, *supra*, at p. 71.

126   *Ibid.* at p. 107.

127   *Ibid.* at p. 108.

128   David Humphrey, personal interview, *supra*.

129   See Minutes of Proceedings, *supra*, and particularly the "Second Report."

130   *Ibid.* at p. 266.

131   *Ibid.*

132   *Bad Judgment, supra*, Chapter 8 at pp. 157 et seq.

133   *Landreville v. The Queen (No.2)* (1977), 75 D.L.R. (3d) 380 (F.C. T.D.), Collier J.

134   *Landreville v. The Queen (No3)* (1980), 111 D.L.R. (3d) 36 (F.C. T.D.), Collier J.

135   JJR, Oral History.

136   [1938] S.C.R. 680.

137   [1988] 2 S.C.R. 680.

138   Ian Binnie's comments here and elsewhere in this chapter are from a letter to the author dated June 15, 2002.

139   See *Hamilton Harbour Commissioners v. City of Hamilton* (1978), 91 D.L.R. (3d) 353 (C.A.)

140   Reported as *R. v. Cooper* (1975), 22 C.C.C. (2d) 273.

141   Reported 34 C.C.C. (2d) 18.

142   David Doherty, in an audio cassette delivered to the author on June 28, 2002.

143   This and other material in this chapter I owe to Colin K. Irving's letter to the author dated May 24, 2001.

144   Now s. 649 of the *Criminal Code of Canada*, which was first enacted in 1972.

145   Appeal decision reported at [1949] O.R. 315-340.

146   See reference to the Ash Temple case, *ibid.*

147   John Honsberger, letter to the author dated April 29, 2001.

148   Reported at (1975), 62 D.L.R. (3d) 91.

149   (1976), 77 D.L.R. (3d) 1.

150   [1977] 2 S.C.R. 817.

151   John Arnup, personal interview, *supra.*

152   Oral History at pp.143-44.

153   John Arnup, personal interview, *supra.*

154   The Supreme Court of Canada's decision is reported at (1971), 19 D.L.R. (3d) 669 and [1972] S.C.R. 244.

155   The Court of Appeal's decision is reported at *Fowler v. London Life Insurance Co.* (1959), 20 D.L.R. (2d) 642.

156   *Regina ex rel Revie v. Horovitz, supra.*

157   (1958), 126 C.C.C. 175.

158   See *Ibid.* at p. 231.

159   Not reported, probably because from the anecdote, the motion to strike out the Statement of Claim was conceded.

160   David Brown, personal interview. April 15, 2002.

161   *McNamara Construction (Western) Ltd. et al v. The Queen* (1975), 66 D.L.R.(3d) 258; reversed by the Supreme Court of Canada, [1977] 2 S.C.R. 654.

162   This case and Brown's involvement with it will be developed in a subsequent chapter.

163   *Canadian Pacific Ltd. v. Quebec North Shore Paper Co.*, [1977] 2 S.C.R. 1054.

164   [1933] A.C. 508.

165   The case is reported as *Leitch Gold Mines Ltd. v. Texas Gulf* at [1969] 1 O.R. 469. The decision of Chief Justice Gale, which exceeds 100 pages, is the basis of all my references to the facts and the arguments, except where otherwise indicated.

166   Agreement between Leitch and Texas Gulf, dated February 1, 1963.

167 Gale was the chief justice of the High Court at the commencement of the trial but he was elevated to chief justice of Ontario while presiding over the case.

168 John Arnup, personal interview, *supra*.

169 David Brown, personal interview, *supra*.

170 John Arnup, personal interview, *supra*.

171 (1981), 56 C.C.C. (2d) 193.

172 When money was offered as compensation, the amount was recorded on documents known as "score sheets" which were kept by Quinlan, Schneider, and Rindress. The three would meet periodically to reconcile the commitments recorded in the score sheets and to settle accounts: see *ibid.* at pp. 250-1.

173 Charles F. Scott, personal interview. January 17, 2002.

174 (1981), 56 C.C.C. (2d) 193 at pp. 317-18.

175 *Ibid.* at p. 335.

176 A graduate of the University of Toronto Faculty of Law, he was called to the Bar after completing the Bar Admission Course.

177 Charles F. Scott, personal interview, *supra*.

178 Austin Cooper, personal interview. March 19, 2002.

179 30-31 Vict., c.3 (U.K.).

180 JJR, Oral History.

181 [1973] S.C.R. 131.

182 [1975] 1 S.C.R. 138.

183 [1975] 2 S.C.R. 182.

184 1968-69 (Can.), c. 54.

185 JJR, Oral History.

186 Brad Smith, personal interview. April 30, 2002.

187 [1976] 2 S.C.R. 373.

188 JJR, Oral History.

189 They are *Canadian Industrial Gas & Oil Ltd. v. Saskatchewan*, [1978] 2 S.C.R. 545 (whether oil and gas legislation was direct or indirect taxation); *Reference re: Agricultural Products Marketing Act, 1970 (Canada)*, [1978] 2 S.C.R. 1198 (validity of legislation dealing with egg marketing scheme); *R. v. Rhine*, [1980] 2 S.C.R. 442 (jurisdiction of the Federal Court to entertain a claim by the Crown to recover debts guaranteed by the Crown); *Reference re: Residential Tenancies Act, 1979 (Ontario)*, [1981] 1 S.C.R. 714 (constitutional validity of landlord and tenant legislation); *Reference: re Proposed Federal Tax On Exported Natural Gas*, [1982] 1 S.C.R. 1004 (validity of legislation imposing tax on

provincial drilling on Crown lands); and *Multiple Access Ltd. v. McCutcheon*, [1982] 2 S.C.R. 161 (paramountcy issue where Parliament and Ontario passed legislation containing identical insider trading provisions).

190   *Re Moog and Moog* (1985), 50 O.R. (2d) 113 (C.A.).
191   With some retroactive effect from October 14, 1975.
192   Stephen Goudge, personal interview with the author. May 21, 2002.
193   R.S.C. 1970, c. S-19.
194   Roy McMurtry, personal interview with the author. May 8, 2002.
195   JJR, Oral History.
196   *Anti-Inflation Act (Canada)* [1976] 2 S.C.R. 373 at p. 385.
197   Roy McMurtry, personal interview, *supra*.
198   Renfrew County Division, District 25 Ontario Secondary School Teacher' Federation and Ontario School Teachers' Federation.
199   The Hon. R. McMurtry, "The Search for a Constitutional Accord: A Personal Memoir" (1982/83) 8 Queen's L.J. 28.
200   Only the Premier of British Columbia, W.A.C. Bennett, did not attend.
201   The other members of the Committee were John A. Agrios, later Justice Agrios of Edmonton, Alberta; Douglas McK Brown, Q.C. of Vancouver, B.C.; L. Yves Fortier, Q.C. of Montreal, Quebec; Joseph A. Ghiz of Charlottetown, P.E.I.; William A. Hoyt, Q.C., later Justice Hoyt of Fredericton, New Brunswick; Robert Lesage, Q.C. of Quebec City, Quebec; David Matas of Winnipeg, Manitoba; D.E. (Tom) Gauley, Q.C. of Saskatoon, Saskatchewan; and Clyde K. Wells, Q.C., later Chief Justice Wells of Corner Brook, Newfoundland.
202   Roy McMurtry, personal interview, *supra*.
203   Barry L. Strayer, personal interview with the author. April 30, 2002.
204   *Reference re Legislative Authority of the Parliament of Canada in relation to the Upper House*, [1980] 1 S.C.R. 54.
205   A copy of this speech was appended as Annex iv, p.49 of the First Report of the Kershaw Committee, *infra*.
206   B.L. Strayer Q.C., *The Patriation and Legitimacy of the Canadian Constitution*, Dean Emeritus F.C. Cronkite Q.C., Memorial Lectures, 3rd Series, (October 1982).
207   U.K., H.C., "First Report from the Foreign Affairs Committee," vol. 1 & 2, Session 1980-81.
208   *Reference Re Amendment of the Constitution of Canada*

(1981),117 D.L.R. (3d) 1.

209 Colin K. Irving, letter to the author dated May 24, 2001.

210 Section 93 gives exclusive jurisdiction to the provinces to make laws in relation to education and specifically protects denominational and separate schools.

211 Michel Robert, personal interview with the author. June 12, 2002.

212 *Reference Re Amendment of the Constitution of Canada (No.2)* (1981), 118 D.L.R. (3d) 1.

213 *Reference Re Amendment of the Constitution of Canada (No.3)* (1981), 120 D.L.R. (3d) 385.

214 *Manitoba (Attorney General) v. Canada (Attorney General); Canada (Attorney General) v. Newfoundland (Attorney General); Quebec (Attorney General) v. Canada (Attorney-General)*, [1981] 1 S.C.R. 753.

215 Wells was Premier from 1989 to 1996. He was appointed chief justice of Newfoundland in 1999.

216 The reference is to a town established in Guyana, South America, by Jim Jones, a charismatic cult leader who was responsible for the ritual murder/suicide of 913 of his fanatical followers, including young children, by having them drink Kool-Aid laced with cyanide on November 18, 1978.

217 Factum of the Attorney General of Canada dated April 21, 1981.

218 Colin K. Irving, letter to author, *supra*.

219 This is now section 33 of the Charter.

220 April 15, 1981.

221 December 22, 1981.

222 pp. viii and ix.

223 Strayer, *Cronkite Lectures*.

224 *Manuel et al v. Attorney-General* [1982 3 All E.R. 822 (C.A.).

225 Convocation speech by the Right Honourable Pierre Elliott Trudeau upon the occasion of his receiving the degree of Doctor of Laws, *honoris causa* (LL.D., h.c.), Convocation Hall, University of Toronto, Thursday, March 21, 1991, at a convocation held in honour of the opening of the Bora Laskin Law Library, (1991) 41 U.T.L.J. 295.

226 JJR, Oral History, p.790.

227 This information came to me from an interview with Lois Robinette on January 30, 2001, at the Briar Crest Retirement Home.

228   I was to read later that former president Ronald Reagan suffered a similar fate. His diagnosis of Alzheimer's followed the trauma of a fall from a riding horse: see Edmund Morris, *Dutch: A Memoir of Ronald Reagan* (New York: Random House, 1999) p. 664.